Marvin P. Engelsdorfer

D1480053

9-21-51

THE FAITH
OF THE
CHRISTIAN CHURCH

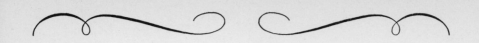

THE FAITH
OF THE
CHRISTIAN CHURCH

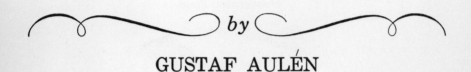 *by*

GUSTAF AULÉN

Translated
from the fourth Swedish edition
by
ERIC H. WAHLSTROM and G. EVERETT ARDEN

THE MUHLENBERG PRESS
PHILADELPHIA

COPYRIGHT, 1948, BY
MUHLENBERG PRESS

Third Printing

PRINTED IN U. S. A.
UB655

PREFACE

This book is a translation of the fourth revised edition of *Den allmänneliga kristna tron*. The Swedish word *allmännelig* is the word that is used in the Apostolic Creed: "We believe in one holy catholic (Christian) Church." Because the word "catholic" can easily be misunderstood, the title of the book has been translated: *The Faith of the Christian Church*. It is of course not my intention to assert that the statements of this book could be or ought to be accepted in all Christendom. The title does not imply a claim but indicates a most important direction which systematic theology cannot ignore without failing to fulfill its function.

Systematic theology has a special object—as does every science. The object of systematic theology is the Christian faith as a living reality. To explain the significance of this faith, to make clear what essentially belongs to it, and to bring to light, wholly and completely, its own characteristic viewpoints, is the task of systematic theology. Thus theology must reveal what the eyes of faith see. In other words, theology must conscientiously endeavor to set forth the meaning of Christian truth.

Therefore, theology must firmly adhere to the ecumenical perspective. Its endeavor must not become the private confession of a theologian. In that case theology would surrender its scientific-critical purpose in relation to its object. The same thing would happen if theology would confine itself to a narrow and self-satisfied confessionalism. That does not constitute a plea for indifference to confessional points of view. But it does mean that no doctrine can be accepted as truly Christian simply on the basis of its confessional relations; for instance, its relations to Luther, Calvin, or Thomas Aquinas. We do not refer to Luther as a final arbiter of truth, but only in so far as he helps us to see more clearly the soul of Christianity. In the measure that systematic theology is faithful to its aim, it must imply a self-examination. It must be thankful for the gifts received in our own confession and at the same time condemn every tendency toward being *incurvatus in se* as sinful.

In the nineteenth century as well as in the first decades of the twentieth century there has been a conflict between two main theological types, one known as the fundamentalist and the other as the modernist. The first has had a scholastic or a pietist character, and sometimes it has tried to combine both of these attitudes. The second type has reinterpreted Christianity according to the viewpoint of idealistic philosophy and a rather vague humanism. In reality both of these types have been equally incapable of accomplishing the theological task of understanding and explaining the Christian faith. In both cases the radical realism of Christianity has been obscured. The alternatives seemed to be either narrow-mindedness or a disintegrating misinterpretation.

Fortunately, it is not necessary to choose either of these alternatives. The theological outlook is in the process of changing. In that respect two factors have had a dominating influence: first, a new and deeper insight into the meaning and motif of the Reformation; second, and foremost, a new, fresh, and realistic approach to the biblical message. Above everything, the endeavors of theology must be to see Christianity as it actually is, according to its uniqueness. That is, one must liberate the Christian message from all that obscures its fresh colors and so let it appear in all its original power.

The Bishop's Residence,
Strängnäs, Sweden,
October, 1947

GUSTAF AULÉN

CONTENTS

Part I

FAITH AND THEOLOGY

Parts II, III, IV

THE CONTENT OF CHRISTIAN FAITH

INTRODUCTION

Part II

THE LIVING GOD

DIVISION A

THE CHRISTIAN CONCEPTION OF GOD

DIVISION B

THE GOD OF ACTION

Part 1

FAITH AND THEOLOGY

1. The Function of Systematic Theology

1. Systematic theology has as its object of study the Christian faith. The intention of the discipline is to clarify the significance and meaning of the Christian faith with all the means at its disposal. The task is neither demonstrative nor normative, but analytical and critical. Its purpose is neither to furnish proofs for faith nor to determine what "ought to be believed." Everything is concentrated on the attempt to *understand the faith* and to present the ideas and viewpoints of faith itself with the greatest possible clarity.

2. Since the Christian faith is by its nature completely theocentric, the presentation of its content must appear as one organic whole.

3. Systematic theology is differentiated from philosophy of religion, which aims to establish the specifically religious "category" and its place in the life of the human spirit. It is entirely foreign to that kind of "philosophy of religion" which appears as rational metaphysics.

4. Since faith relates itself exclusively to God, and its affirmations therefore concern the relationship between God and man, systematic theology is differentiated from psychology of religion which deals with the religious subject and is limited to an analysis of the religious consciousness.

5. Since the function of systematic theology is to clarify the meaning of *the Christian faith,* it cannot be bound by confessional limitations. It can be confessional only in so far as this is of assistance in the comprehension of that which is genuinely

Christian. It is thus differentiated from symbolics, which interprets the various confessions and their mutual relation.

6. The function of systematic theology is purely scientific in so far as its task is to clarify the significance of the Christian faith. It can serve the Christian life only by performing this scientific study without any secondary purposes.

1. The Project: to Understand the Faith.

In defining the function of systematic theology it is necessary first of all to emphasize that the object of study is the Christian faith as a given, objective reality. Systematic theology is therefore that discipline which has as its purpose the study and investigation of the Christian faith.

Faith is the only object of study that can be legitimately considered. God himself cannot be made the object of scientific investigation, so that theology in that sense should be a *study of God*. God is not a "thing" which can be scientifically investigated. As far as faith is concerned God is Alpha and Omega, but analytical theology can be concerned only with the elucidation of the nature of the Christian relationship between God and man and with that idea of God which is characteristic of Christian faith.

It must be emphatically stated that systematic theology is confronted with the same situation as are all other scientific disciplines, namely, that it is concerned with the study of a definite object. This insight is obscured if theology is presented as a kind of confession expressed in a "purified and scientific" form. Such an attempt would place theology in the same category as preaching. It would then be a confessional proclamation in a complete and logical form. One reason why such a conception of the function of theology has been presented from time to time is that theological expositions of the Christian faith have neglected essential elements in that faith and consequently have become misinterpretations. Such presentations are intended to protect

4

the faith by emphasizing the confessional viewpoint. But even though the intention is good, the result is a tragic confusion of the viewpoints of the religious life and scientific research. The theological function as a science is of an entirely different nature from the confessional function which belongs to the religious life. In view of this fact, we must insist that systematic theology is concerned simply with investigating and clarifying a certain area of research. This study must be characterized by the greatest possible objectivity since the purpose is to express the genuine significance of the faith. If theological interpretations of the Christian faith have sometimes become perversions and the real nature of faith has not been expressed, the remedy is not to be sought in a demand that theology should be given the character of a subjective confession, but rather the opposite, namely, in a purely scientific and objective approach. The guarantee that the interpretation will not become a misinterpretation and perversion lies in this scientific and objective attitude.

In maintaining this view of the function of systematic theology, the confusing discussion about the personal qualifications of the investigator disappears. Often in the history of theology an attempt has been made to transform the scientific discussion concerning the significance of faith into a discussion about the personal faith of the theological investigator. When the task is defined as indicated in the previous paragraphs, there can be no other requirement than the demand to understand the subject under investigation. This is likewise the situation in all scientific research.

The function of systematic theology is, therefore, to make clear the meaning and significance of the Christian faith by the use of all available resources. The purpose of the study must continually be directed toward this one central point. The task is to unveil and reveal everything that is essential, to brush aside all nonessential and foreign elements, to remove all unnecessary accretions, and to bring out clearly the very heart of the matter. It is self-evident that such an approach must assume a critical

5

character. The investigation cannot stop at the surface or with the most obvious formulations. By a critical analysis it must penetrate through shifting forms to the underlying and fundamental religious ideas[1] and at the same time be continually mindful of that which is uniquely and essentially Christian.

But systematic theology must be given neither a demonstrative nor a normative character. It does not seek to demonstrate "the truth" of faith, nor to provide rational grounds for faith, nor to furnish proofs of the reality of God. Such attempts are as scientifically impossible as they are foreign to faith since faith is not conscious of being founded on any rational proofs. They are therefore also foreign to that scientific discipline whose only purpose is to understand faith. Even if rational arguments could be presented, they would have no reference whatever to faith. The god whose "reality" could be thus demonstrated would be of an entirely different nature from the God of faith. Systematic theology can discuss the question of the certainty of the Christian faith only in so far as it investigates the nature of this certainty (cf. § 10).

Neither can the function of systematic theology be of a normative character. Theology does not write laws for faith, nor act as lord over faith. It does not determine faith, but analyzes the Christian faith as it actually exists. Just as little as ethics can undertake to tell men what they ought to do, so systematic theology, which is directed toward a study of faith, cannot presume to determine what ought to be believed. There is really no such "normative" science. Just as Christian ethics has to make clear the specifically Christian ethos, so theology must make clear and establish the unique character of Christian faith. But personal attitudes toward these factors are an entirely different matter, which must not be confused with critical research. Rather, systematic theology must focus its attention upon what is and what is not characteristically Christian. This critical examination is the prin-

---

[1] The approach of Lundensian theology has been characterized as *motivforskning*, i.e., the investigation of principal ideas or themes. The important word *motiv* has been translated as "fundamental idea" or "fundamental theme."

cipal concern of systematic theology because its task is to understand the *Christian* faith and to present the ideas and viewpoints of faith itself with the greatest possible clarity.

In this connection it must be strongly emphasized that the specific problem with which systematic theology deals is the *meaning* and *significance* of the Christian faith. The problem is not to set forth the origin and development of the Christian doctrines. This belongs to the history of dogma. The study of this history is of utmost importance as a prerequisite for systematic theology, but these two are distinct and separate disciplines. Systematic theology does not ask how faith in Christ originated and what elements may be regarded as having belonged to the confession of faith as it emerged in the primitive church. It asks rather whether a confession of Christ is essential to the Christian faith, and, if so, what is the import and meaning of such a confession.

Systematic theology has its own clearly defined function, but in performing this task it stands in close relationship to a number of scientific disciplines and must utilize all available resources. It has close contact with all departments of religion and theology since all these disciplines touch the religious and Christian life. But its associations extend far beyond the study of religion proper, especially toward the critical analysis of the concepts of philosophy. In the following paragraphs the relation of systematic theology to these disciplines will be further defined. It is not isolated but is closely connected with a number of scientific disciplines, but none of these undertakes to treat of that which is the specific function of systematic theology: to expound the meaning and significance of the Christian faith.

2. *"Systematic" Theology.*

When systematic theology seeks to investigate the significance of Christian faith, it does not deal merely with a multitude of disparate doctrines which, as in the so-called "loci theology," appear as unrelated statements. There is rather an inner, organic homogeneity in everything that constitutes the object of systematic theology. This unity is given in the completely theocentric character of faith. It is therefore a confusion of terms to speak of a "theocentric theology." This redundant expression is no doubt intended to enhance the theocentric character of faith, and this is indeed a point which cannot be overemphasized.

In the realm of Christian faith the question is always about God and man's relation to him. God is the only center of faith. Christian faith is a faith in God and in him alone. Nothing can be equated with God. Faith cannot be divided so that it is directed partly to God and partly to other "objects." When we speak about a faith in Christ, or in the Spirit, or faith in the forgiveness of sins, in the church and eternal life, and so on, it does not mean that a number of objects of faith have been introduced which might in a certain sense compete with God for attention. This mechanical and superficial viewpoint would completely obscure the living, simple, and immediate character of faith. To speak about different objects of faith has significance only if thereby different aspects of God's activity in behalf of man are clarified, and it thus becomes apparent that in everything it is a question of faith in God. If we speak about Christ as an object of faith, we are talking about God revealed; if we speak of forgiveness of sins, we are referring to that God who establishes communion with men; if we speak about eternal life, we are talking about the eternal and life-giving God. If other "objects of faith" are placed by the side of God and compete with him, God has already lost that sovereignty which belongs to him in the realm of faith. There is nothing more obvious and inescapable to faith than that "we should trust God above all things," nothing less than this. In this connection the word of the Bible is appropriate: "God is Alpha and Omega, the beginning and the end" (Rev. 21:6).

If the Christian faith possesses this unitary, theocentric character, the presentation of systematic theology must become, if it does justice to its subject, an organic whole. It cannot be a

"loci theology," which presents a series of more or less discon-
nected doctrines. The various pronouncements of faith stand in
an inner organic relation to one another, and this fact must be
reflected in the theological analysis. In reality there is only one
subject, but it must be seen from various points of view. The
analysis is concerned at all times with *the relationship between
God and man,* and the central point is that idea of God which
lies behind and illuminates the various affirmations of faith. Since
faith itself possesses this organic character and unitary direction,
nothing can find a place in the analysis of the content of faith
which is not connected with and does not express that idea of
God which gives this character to faith.

But this organic and systematic character of the theological
analysis would be completely misunderstood if it be concluded
that the theological presentation ought to appear as a rationally
completed system. The unity in question is not a closed system
of reasoning but rather a unity that is characterized by an inner
tension in which the various fundamental ideas struggle with
and balance one another. This fact will have to be noted time
and again in our presentation. This tension cannot be eliminated
by a rational compromise for in so doing faith is misinterpreted
and perverted. On the other hand, in spite of the tension, this
faith which is directed toward only one center has the character
of an organic whole. The object of systematic theology is a most
sensitive organism, in which one aspect stands in intimate relation to the other, and what happens on the periphery is reflected
at once at the very center.

3. *Systematic Theology and Philosophy of Religion.*

In view of the diverse interpretations of the function of philosophy of religion and the obscure conceptions of its relation
to systematic theology, it becomes necessary to define this function and clarify the relation between these two disciplines. If,
as we have seen, it is the intention of systematic theology to
permit the content and significance of the Christian faith to be

expressed fully and completely, this can be accomplished only by letting the unique and vital viewpoints of faith itself be brought to light. But this cannot be accomplished if faith is examined and judged in accordance with perspectives which are external and foreign to faith. The task is to unveil and expose that which is essential to Christian faith. Faith must be understood from its own center. If it is forced into conformity with a system foreign to itself, it is misinterpreted and perverted.

From this starting point we are now able to decide how the relation between systematic theology and philosophy of religion ought to be determined. It cannot be denied that there has often been a confusion between the functions of these two disciplines, and that philosophy of religion has often attempted to be a substitute for systematic theology. In doing so it has also claimed a certain superiority. It has been assumed that philosophy of religion should endeavor to create a common, primary delineation of the "essence of religion." Such a delineation would serve as a starting point and as a dependable, critical standard for the examination and evaluation of various historical religions, including Christianity. Philosophy of religion would then be able to deal with Christianity from a higher and more scientific point of view than "dogmatics," which is bound by confessional presuppositions and cannot assume as free and detached a position as can philosophy of religion.

This type of thinking nevertheless represents a warped view of the function of systematic theology, and it also misunderstands the function of philosophy of religion. It has become perfectly clear that this confusion of the functions of these two disciplines neither contributed anything to philosophy of religion nor furthered the study and clarification of the Christian faith.

Religion exists only in historical manifestations. When philosophy of religion in one way or another constructs a certain "common religion" and then makes this idea the basis of its judgment of Christianity, the result is inevitably that the Chris-

tian faith is investigated and judged from the outside, from a
point of view and by a methodology which is not its own. This
cannot lead to clarity about the nature and significance of Christian faith. The interpretation becomes a reinterpretation according to a previously arranged outline. In spite of all claims to
scientific objectivity, this method becomes highly subjective and
arbitrary. It generally happens that the investigator who makes
the greatest claims to have found an objective, scientific, and
safe basis of judgment turns out to be the most arbitrary and
helpless. In substantiating this claim we can point to the attempts
of the Enlightenment to reinterpret Christianity in accordance
with its "philosophical common religion," and also to the nineteenth-century idealism with its philosophy of religion and theology. Here Christianity has been forced into forms which are
foreign. The reinterpretations which inevitably appear cannot
hide the fact that Christianity has been subject to a transformation which has obscured its nature, and that its own characteristic ideas have been only partially understood, if at all. Even
Schleiermacher, who attacked the "philosophical" common religion and prepared the way for a better understanding of the
function of theology by presenting the Christian faith as the
proper object of the study of theology, was not able to liberate
himself from the baneful influence of idealistic philosophy of
religion. He was not able to develop the program which he outlined for himself. In his celebrated treatise on the Christian faith
he made theology dependent upon philosophy of religion because the criterion for determining the "essence of Christianity"
was found in a religious idea whose content was characterized
by the monistic philosophy of immanence. This idea exercised
a tremendous influence on the subsequent presentation of the
Christian faith and its content and rendered it impossible for
him to permit the characteristic ideas of faith to appear.

If ability to discern and clarify the objects of a scientific study
is evidence of scientific research, then the kind of philosophy of
religion which has here been described has little reason to look

11

condescendingly at that systematic theology whose function has been defined in these paragraphs. The scientific methodology claimed for the philosophy of religion that was influenced by idealism is an illusion; it is not able to understand Christianity. Evidently it is not sufficiently free from its own presuppositions. It judges—and reinterprets—on the basis of postulates whose contents it has not clearly examined. If it is at all possible to "understand" Christianity, to understand the meaning and significance of the Christian faith, such a possibility can be actualized only by a study which intends nothing else than to allow the ideas and viewpoints of faith itself to appear in their rightful place, and which desires nothing else than to understand faith from within.

If, therefore, it can be established that a philosophy of religion which has been influenced by idealism cannot serve the positive study of Christianity, it can also be affirmed that the purely religio-philosophical function has not been understood in a scientifically satisfactory way. It is clear that the idea of religion obtained by such means is not achieved through scientific analysis but is based rather on highly subjective principles. It is nothing but a subjective conception of faith on which an attempt is made to superimpose the marks of objectivity and philosophical scholarliness. It is a "confession" which lays claim to being philosophical. But such a combination as a "philosophical confession" is a *contradictio in adjecto*. A personal confession, no matter how much it attempts to clothe itself with the robe of philosophy, cannot claim a proper place among scientific studies.

If philosophy of religion is to assume a really scientific character, it must free itself resolutely from all tendencies to create philosophically a commonly accepted religion which would be primary in relation to all historical religions. It must become a *critical* philosophy of religion in the real meaning of the word. This implies that the research of philosophy of religion is an attempt to clarify the specifically religious "category" and to determine its position in man's spiritual life, i.e., to examine its relation to the theoretical, ethical, and esthetic categories: the true, the good, and the beautiful. Such a conception of the function of philosophy of religion means that it must renounce all pretensions of superiority to theology. Such renunciation ought not to be impossible in view of the fact that these pretensions can be maintained only by denying the scientific character of philosophy of religion. The specific function of this critical discipline is very important for all scientific study of religion. Philosophy of religion enters into a very close relation with systematic theology, but both disciplines have nevertheless their clearly defined areas of study. They co-operate, but at the same time they must be liberated from the confusion which in the past has led to such baneful results.

Although systematic theology is related to a critical philosophy of religion, it is completely differentiated from that "philosophy of religion" which appears as rational metaphysics. This is clear from what has already been said, but it deserves to be emphasized again, especially since such a rational metaphysics has again and again forced its way into theology. "Philosophical" metaphysics pretended to be able to offer a rationally motivated and outlined "doctrine of God and the supersensual world." Even in the primitive church rational metaphysics made its influence felt. Since that time all *scholastic* theology, both of the medieval and the post-Reformation periods, has attempted to build upon such a philosophical metaphysics in order to parade as a so-called "natural theology." A distinction was made between *articuli puri,* which were rooted in revelation and had the character of affirmations of faith, and *articuli mixti,* which were based partly on revelation and partly on rational metaphysics. It cannot be denied that from one point of view this broader basis represented a certain protection for theology against exclusiveness during those times in which the function of systematic theology was conceived of in a rather narrow confessional and doctrinaire form. But on the other hand, it must be said that this wider perspective was purchased at too great a price. Nothing could obscure the difference in nature between the Christian faith and metaphysics more than this idea that the "doctrine about God" should appear in the form of *articuli mixti*. The epistemological criticism of "philosophical" metaphysics, issuing from Kant, has really accomplished a liberation of systematic theology and has furthered a critical self-analysis. This has helped to prevent theology from building on an illusion and has also removed conceptions which threatened to unsettle and obscure the real purpose of theology.

The reason systematic theology does not want to have any part with rational metaphysics is not simply because such a metaphysic is suspected from a critical point of view, and that therefore a criticism of the metaphysics would also involve a theology containing this element. The reason is rather that faith has really nothing to do with metaphysics. As far as faith is concerned it is not a question of a metaphysic differing from that of the rational, but of something wholly other than metaphysics, since Christian faith in God is something else than a rational explanation of the universe. Theology has no other task than to inquire into that which is given in and characteristic of faith. From the very beginning and in those periods when it has been most conscious of its own nature, Christian faith has testified boldly that the God about whom it speaks reveals himself only to the eye of faith and is not apprehended by any human wisdom (cf. Matt. 5:8, 11:25, John 7:17, I Cor. 1:17 ff., 2:10, etc.).

4. *Systematic Theology and Psychology of Religion.*

Psychology of religion, understood as a purely empirical and descriptive investigation of the religious consciousness as such, has a secure place and an important function within the science of religion. Such researches can in various ways become a preparation for and an assistance to the work of systematic theology. But the two cannot be identified. Just as there has frequently been a commixture of philosophy of religion and systematic theology, so there has been a similar mixture of the latter with psychology of religion. This confusion can really be traced back to

Schleiermacher. We have already noted that he was not able to carry out his theological program because in his interpretation of the Christian faith he placed it under the pressure of religious concepts whose content was fixed and determined beforehand. And furthermore, he did not accomplish his purpose because he made faith practically identical with the religious consciousness as such, and in this way gave systematic theology a psychological direction. In view of the influence which Schleiermacher's method has had, it is important to point out that the task of systematic theology is in principle something else than that of psychology of religion, no matter how great an importance the latter may have for the former.

If the problem of systematic theology is to elucidate the content of the Christian faith, to *understand* the faith, then this elucidation must take into account the fact that faith always appears as an expression of a relation in which everything is concerned with God as the only object. Faith cannot be "understood" without the realization that *every* affirmation of faith is a statement about God and his activity. If a statement is made about the significance of the work of Christ, that here God "reconciled the world unto himself," then the question is not about an empirical history or a purely psychological affirmation, but rather a word about God and his activity. The same is true, if we take another example, in regard to what faith says about forgiveness of sins. It is a question here not simply about a variation in the religious consciousness, but a divine act through which a communion between God and man is established. The nature of faith is not revealed if we say with Schleiermacher that the Christian doctrines are *"Auffassungen der christlich frommen Gemuthszustände in der Rede dargestellt."* [2] Precisely because all the affirmations of faith are statements about God and his activity, systematic theology must differentiate itself from pure psychology of religion in its attempt to understand faith. In the

[2] Schleiermacher: *Der christliche Glaube*, p. 15, "Christian doctrines are accounts of the Christian religious affections set forth in speech."

elucidation of the significance of the Christian faith everything moves around that *idea of God* which in one way or another is reflected in the several affirmations of faith. It may be said that the chief concern of psychology of religion is with the religious "subject," while systematic theology, endeavoring to understand faith, is chiefly concerned with the clarification of the view which faith has of its object, namely the idea of God peculiar to faith. We must add here, however, that the word "object" in this connection is an inadequate expression, since, as far as faith is concerned, God is not an object, but rather the subject. If this qualification is taken into account, the relation between psychology of religion and systematic theology can be expressed in the manner here indicated.

5. The "Ecumenical" Christian Faith. Systematic Theology and Symbolics.

The purpose of systematic theology is to investigate and elucidate the meaning and significance of the *Christian* faith. This purpose would be distorted and limited if systematic theology were to start from and allow itself to be bound by a denominational or confessional conception of faith given once and for all. Systematic theology cannot assume as self-evident that a certain confession in every respect represents that which is perfect and genuinely Christian. In that case the task would be to reproduce, arrange, and define those doctrines which have been presented in a certain set of confessional writings. When Schleiermacher in his encyclopedia says that the function of dogmatics is to present the doctrine accepted in a certain communion,[3] he obscures the fact that systematic theology is concerned with the task of understanding *the genuinely Christian*. It should also be pointed out that this statement of Schleiermacher contradicts what he asserts elsewhere: that the object of theology is not a certain limited, individual and confessional "Christian consciousness," but rather "the Christian religious affections in general."

---

[3] Schleiermacher, *Zur Darstellung des theologischen Studiums,* § 195.

It is evident and quite understandable that an exclusive and doctrinaire confessionalism has given "dogmatics" a certain bad reputation. It cannot be denied that systematic theology would lose its scientific character if its investigation of the significance of the Christian faith were from the beginning bound to a specific and authoritative conception in which the result is already given. This would mean that the confessional writings are regarded as boundaries at which theological research is compelled to halt. The investigation of the Christian faith would then be governed by other purposes than the desire to understand, which is the truly scientific purpose. This closed and narrow conception of the function of systematic theology bears part of the blame for the supplanting of theology by the abortive "philosophy of religion" previously mentioned. Against the exclusive confessionalism this "philosophy" could successfully maintain that the Christian faith must be viewed from a wider and more comprehensive perspective. It could say that the study of Christianity by "dogmatics" was in advance bound to certain restrictive forms, which prevented a free outlook and had to be defended at all costs. It could also point to the confessional polemic which emerged as a result. These criticisms were no doubt well founded. The trouble was that a "philosophy of religion" which looked at Christian faith from the outside and judged it from foreign points of view could not present an adequate substitute. This could be done only by a systematic theology which is guided by no other purpose than to penetrate to the very nature and meaning of the Christian faith.

It is of course a legitimate theological study to describe the conception of faith accepted by a certain communion, being guided in such work by the existing, authoritative documents of that communion; and also to extend such a study to include the variety of conceptions which may arise within the church. This is a historical and statistical study, which belongs to symbolics or to the study of the church. But this can never be the legitimate function of systematic theology. It cannot, without proving false

17

to its calling, surrender its right to evaluate any confessional documents, to determine whether and to what extent these express that which is genuinely Christian and not simply that which is peculiar to a certain section of Christendom.

Systematic theology can be confessional only in so far as the confessional element is of assistance in understanding and perceiving that which is essentially Christian. It cannot be "Lutheran" in the sense that it rests on statements by Luther *solely* because he made them, but only in so far as Luther proves himself able to help theology to penetrate deeper into the meaning of the Christian faith. The work of systematic theology involves, therefore, with reference to confessionalism a continual self-examination, far removed from all naive confessional self-sufficiency. Theology is not looking for denominational expressions of Christianity but for genuine Christianity itself; and it does not recognize a denominational expression unless it can document itself as genuinely Christian. Its purpose is to present "the ecumenical Christian faith." "Ecumenical" is therefore a watchword against every kind of closed and self-sufficient confessionalism. This does not mean that theology should produce a kind of extract of doctrines which would be common to all Christians. Such an endeavor would be of very little value.[4] We are not dealing with a kind of common conception which would represent a Christianity stripped of all denominational expressions. Such a common Christianity has never existed, just as there has never been a "common religion." Christianity has from the very beginning appeared in different forms, each of which has its own peculiar character. But the central theological problem posed by these denominational forms must always be whether or not and to what extent they express that which is genuinely Christian. The genuinely Christian exists only within and

---

[4] Cf. Schleiermacher, *Zur Darstellung,* § 197, note: *Eine lediglich irenische Zusammenstellung wird grossenteils so dürftig und unbestimmt ausfallen, dass es nich nur um eine Bewährung hervorzubringen überall an Mitgliedern fehlen wird, sondern auch an der nötigen Schärfe der Begriffsbestimmung, um der Darstellung Vertrauen zu verschaffen.*

through these denominational expressions, but the decisive question in relation to these forms is the question about their genuinely Christian quality. When Luther and the Reformation are seen from *this* point of view, their contribution toward the understanding of Christianity can be justly assessed. The Christian universalism of Luther has often been very much obscured because this point of view has been ignored, and Luther has been isolated by being circumscribed within a narrow confessionalism.

That systematic theology which is conscious of its function and also critically oriented must adopt the program which is comprehended in the term, "the ecumenical Christian faith," and which has as its purpose the discovery of that which is genuinely Christian. If this is not the case, an "evangelical" theology would have to limit itself to describing a variant of a Christian conception of faith, which would then stand side by side with a number of other equally legitimate variants, as for instance the Roman. Systematic theology cannot be expected to be interested in anything else than the genuinely Christian. This is not something new within evangelical Christianity; the first evangelical "dogmatics" was rightly called *Loci communes*. This name was certainly proper, for the Reformation did not aim to present simply a variant of Christianity in addition to that which already existed, but rather to give expression as far as possible to the genuinely Christian. The evangelical principle of Scripture bears witness to this fact.

It is evident that the research project which according to this interpretation is given to systematic theology cannot be successfully and finally accomplished by any one single theologian. Every individual student and every period have their own limitations. The object of research is an ideal goal toward which theology can only strive in its endeavor to attain to the truth. But this does not mean that we should make this limitation into a principle which would circumscribe the work. Theology cannot under any circumstances deviate from its concentration on that which is essential and genuine in Christianity since this is the

19

whole purpose of its work and dare not be overlooked.

6. The Scientific Character of Systematic Theology.

It is clear from what we have already said that the function of systematic theology is of a purely scientific nature since its purpose is to investigate a definite object, the Christian faith, and to elucidate its significance in the clearest possible way. This theological discipline which we call systematic theology has often, especially during the nineteenth century, been regarded with suspicion both by those interested in scientific study and those interested in the spiritual life.

When such suspicion has manifested itself on behalf of scientific interest, the reason has generally been that certain conceptions of the function of "dogmatics" have been accepted as axiomatic. Four such conceptions may be distinguished: the exclusively confessional, the metaphysical apologetic, the churchly, and the purely subjective. In the first of these the scientific point of view is obscured because the genuinely Christian is identified with a specific confession. This is often combined with an apologetic purpose: the intention is to defend a particular confession contained in the tradition. In the second case the scientific character has disappeared because attempts have been made to present "scientific" proofs of the truth of faith and of the reality of its object. Such attempts cannot be scientifically realized. In the third case the scientific character is corrupted because theology is made to serve the practical ends of the church rather than being a purely scientific investigation. Even Schleiermacher can say that the work of theology is to be done as a service to the government of the church.[5] Even if this is not taken quite literally, it reveals a misunderstanding of the function of systematic theology which obscures its scientific character. And finally, it is quite clear that the scientific character cannot be maintained if the function of theology is transferred to the sphere of the confessions. In this way the purely scientific

---

[5] Schleiermacher, Zur Darstellung, § 5 ff.

task is confused with a function which belongs to the area of the Christian life. In view of these various conceptions it is not at all strange that this discipline has been suspected of being something less than scientific. On the other hand, it is not surprising that it has also been the object of suspicion by those interested in the religious life. This has been due sometimes to bigotry, but also to the fact that theology has not always been directed, consciously and clearly, toward *understanding* the faith, but has allowed this purpose to be obscured by subordinate interests and metaphysical speculations.

The situation becomes quite different when systematic theology is defined as has been done in this chapter. The problem is then to investigate and with all possible means clarify that Reality which is called the Christian faith, and to examine and analyze its significance and content. When the task is thus defined and limited, it is evident that this is a definite and necessary research, which cannot be challenged from the point of view of either scholarly study or the religious life. All presuppositions which limit the investigation beforehand are then removed. It is not a matter of setting up verifiable goals which cannot be scientifically attained. The study is carried on simply to understand and elucidate, which is the purpose of all scholarly research. Thus, systematic theology is not influenced by secondary aims which lie outside its purview and warp the scientific nature of the work. The lodestar here, as in all scientific research, is the same: objectivity, reality.

What we have said here must not be interpreted to mean that systematic theology cannot serve the Christian life and Christian society. But it can do this only on the condition that its scientific purpose remains unencumbered, and that theology therefore fulfills its one commanding and purely scientific function. When the function is defined in a purely scientific manner as has here been done, those interests which belong properly to the Christian life are always given consideration. The religious life cannot ask anything more of theology than that it try to

21

understand faith. In principle the opposition between faith and theology is removed by this definition. The problem is actually to understand faith; to elucidate it, not from any foreign points of view which reinterpret and pervert it, but from its own, purely religious, viewpoint. All investigations which do not from beginning to end see the matter from the religious point of view are bound to fail for want of being scientific. In principle the opposition between faith and theology is removed, as has already been pointed out, even though in practice it may still occur. When the antithesis remains, it is due to the fact that the accomplishment of the scientific task is imperfect, or that not everything which goes by the name of Christian faith is the genuine article.

2. Faith as the Expression of the Christian Relationship Between God and Man

1. Faith is the comprehensive expression of the Christian relationship between God and man. The Christian faith has a theocentric character. This implies that faith directs itself toward God alone and that in this relation God is the Sovereign. This relationship expressed by Christian faith is characterized both by fellowship and remoteness.

2. Faith conceived in terms of relationship may be perceived from two points of view. On the one hand, it implies that man is subdued and dominated by God; on the other, that man turns toward and commits himself to God. This paradox means that, in the first place, faith is grounded in "the divine revelation," and in the second place, that this revelation can be apprehended only by the eye of faith. The divine revelation and faith are therefore, correlative concepts. However, from the religious point of view the divine revelation is primary in relation to faith.

1. Preliminary Definition of the Concept of Faith.

According to the definition of the function of systematic theology previously given its task is the clarification of the Christian faith. At the very outset, therefore, the word faith appears as the principal word. If now the chief task of systematic theology is the exposition of the Christian faith, then it follows that the complete and definitive presentation of the subject can be given only by an investigation of the entire field. This does not preclude the necessity, however, of endeavoring to give a preliminary definition of the concept of faith at the beginning of our investigation. The following exposition in its entirety will bear witness to the accuracy of such a definition.

Needless to say, there are many difficulties involved in the designation of faith as the principal concept of Christianity. A survey of the history of dogma indicates that through the ages this word has been given various meanings and has ofttimes been employed to becloud rather than to clarify the essential nature of Christianity. Moreover, in popular usage it has often come to mean uncertain knowledge, which is an interpretation as foreign as possible to traditional Christian thought. Whatever else faith may say about itself, it does not say that it is some sort of subordinate knowledge, a kind of uncertain opinion about God and his work. Under these circumstances one might be tempted to search for a substitute for the word "faith." But however desirable it might be that the principal word of Christianity be more unequivocal, we are nevertheless obliged to use it, for there is no other expression which can more adequately serve our purpose. It is not accidental that, from the beginning, the word faith has forced its way to the forefront.

The famous words of Luther in the Large Catechism may well serve as a preliminary definition of the Christian connotation of faith: "These two, God and faith, belong together and must be conjoined." In other words, faith implies a relationship between God and man. We cannot speak of "faith" without simultaneously being conscious of man's relationship to God. Faith has reference to that situation wherein God is the center and in which life is dominated by God alone. The nature of

23

faith is therefore entirely theocentric.

As has already been indicated in the previous chapter (§ 1), the theocentric character of faith implies, from one point of view, that God is the sole object of faith. Faith does not concern itself with several objects but is directed toward God alone. Faith may be strong or weak, but whatever may be its quality in this respect, as faith it is entirely a faith in God and in him alone. But the theocentricity of faith has another aspect which must now be delineated. This aspect becomes apparent as God in relation to man appears as the absolute Sovereign. In the realm of faith God is the ruler. His will is supreme. From this viewpoint it is improper to speak of God as the "object" of faith, for as that Power which creates, determines, and controls faith he is rather its subject. This phase of theocentricity has a profound, almost conclusive meaning for the Christian conception of the God-relationship. It certifies that faith is not some sort of anthropocentric approach, more or less subtle, which makes man central and God the obedient servant of human needs, interests, security and self-esteem, and so on. In this relationship God is always Lord and man always the servant.

In connection with what has now been said, it can be stated as axiomatic that the significance of faith must be understood as a personal fellowship between God and man. Faith does not conceive of God as simply remote, but, above all, as the One who in and through faith unites man with himself. The vital element in faith is the conviction that the God who "dwells in light unapproachable" (I Tim. 6:16) is at the same time the God who is present with us and walks in direct fellowship with us, who, as Augustine declares, "is closer to us than we ourselves." From the viewpoint of faith God is immediately present, living and active. In a variety of expressions Christian faith speaks of God—Christ and the Spirit may be used as parallel expressions—as "dwelling in our hearts," "ruling us," and so on. Thus the significance of faith may be defined as an immediate fellowship with God. "We have fellowship with the

Father and with his Son, Jesus Christ" (I John 1:3).

But if the idea of fellowship is primary to the Christian conception of faith, then in order that its nature shall from the outset be clearly delineated, it must be added that this fellowship of faith does not abolish the distance separating the divine from the human. The Christian faith knows of no hazy commixture of the divine with the human. In the realm of faith God is always God and man is always man. The relationship does not pass over into identity. Instead, the proportion between nearness and remoteness, between fellowship and distance, is this: the closer man comes to God in faith and the more the relation with God is realized, the more clearly man becomes aware of that which separates him from God. In the presence of God man's consciousness of sin is intensified. But this peculiar dialectic of the faith-relationship does not nullify man's fellowship with God. The consciousness of remoteness, with which we are here concerned, is itself a manifestation of God's nearness and of the relationship with him, and in no way precludes the idea that the faith-relationship is essentially a fellowship of the most immediate nature. This relationship is therefore the fundamental principle of faith. It cannot be divorced from faith. Wherever it ceases to exist, there faith has also ceased to exist. All other affirmations concerning faith are further clarifications of that which is implied in this fellowship with God.

Accordingly, Christian faith is differentiated from all characteristic mysticism as well as from all idealistic theories of the relation between the divine and the human. It is distinctive of both of these that they confuse the divine and the human, and that therefore the idea of fellowship tends to become identity. The difference between Christian faith and mysticism does not lie in the fact that the God-relationship of mysticism represents a higher degree of immediacy, but rather that in mysticism the remoteness is obliterated in the same degree that the divine fellowship is realized, while in the case of faith the situation is exactly the opposite. On the other hand, the significance is misinterpreted if, in a legitimate emphasis upon remoteness, the idea of fellowship is weakened and actually dissolved and faith is thus reduced to merely an eschatologically determined hope. Similar tendencies in contemporary theology can be historically understood as a reaction against the appreciable influence which mysticism and idealism have exerted during a previous theological era. Even in this case, however, the paradoxical character of Christian faith has been obscured.

It has been pointed out that all definitions of faith are statements of that which is implied in the fellowship with God. Among the innumerable definitions which have appeared we desire in this connection to consider two of the most important: trust and assent. Especially during the latter part of the nineteenth century, when Ritschlian theology was dominant, it was customary, citing the Reformation as witness, to consider "trust"[1] as the fundamental element of faith. Actually, there can be no legitimate objection to the characterization of faith as trust as long as it is clearly borne in mind that it is a quesion of designating an essential aspect of the theocentric fellowship with God. The Reformation can be cited as witness only if the matter is thus understood. But as soon as this viewpoint is obscured, it becomes apparent that the projection of "trust" as the primary definition involves some real dangers, two in particular. The above-mentioned nineteenth century provides sufficient evidence of these two dangers. In the first place, the definition of faith as trust is said to involve a contradiction of faith as assent, with the result that the precise content characteristic of Christian faith is obscured. It would mean that the essential element is trust, as such, while actually the all-important consideration for faith is that qualitatively determined will of God to which trust and confidence are given. In the second place, there is the danger that the theocentric character will not receive sufficient emphasis. Faith interpreted as trust becomes a means and a guarantee

---

[1] The Swedish word *Förtröstan* here translated "trust" is to be understood in terms of *fiducia.*—Tr.

of the "personality development" of man, of man's *Selbstbehaup-tung,* as the Ritschlian expression has it. Nevertheless, we maintain that trust expresses an essential element of Christian faith, but that this definition has reference to the theocentric God-relationship. The definition of faith as assent is analogous to the above. In the measure that fellowship with God is understood as an unqualified assent to that revelation in which faith is rooted, this definition also gives expression to an essential element of faith. But when this definition is no longer considered as expressing simply an element of the theocentric fellowship, but is made primary, then faith becomes prescribed within an intellectual orbit and its significance thereby obscured.

2. *Faith and Divine Revelation.*

If faith is thus an expression of the relationship between God and man, it may be considered from two points of view. With reference to what has already been said, faith implies, on the one hand, being subdued and dominated by God. Faith is the result of our being subdued by God, and it continues to exist by reason of our being dominated by him. God's domination prevails unabridged as far as faith extends. The tyranny of egocentricity must yield to God's dominion. Thus, faith is founded in and exists by reason of God's activity. It is entirely a work of God, as faith itself certifies again and again. But faith may also be considered from the human point of view. Here it appears, on our part, as a turning and a commitment to God. It originates through our turning to God and continues as we commit ourselves to him. This aspect of faith has often been obscured within evangelical theology. It has been feared that, with the emphasis upon the human activity, faith would no longer be entirely a work of God. Actually, however, this aspect of faith cannot be concealed. All the great witnesses of faith have testified to the fact that faith involves a choice and a decision. It was not simply fortuitous that Luther spoke of faith's audacious "despite all," or Kierkegaard of the way faith casts itself upon the deep waters, or Paul of how we must work out our salvation with fear and trembling. In spite of timidity, faith is the soul's audacious *yes* to God. It makes, therefore, the greatest demands upon our activity. Here, if ever, it is a matter of being willing to relinquish all else in order to build upon God alone.

If God and faith "belong together" so that it is impossible to speak of faith without also speaking of God, it then follows that faith has its basis in what it calls "God's revelation." The God who subdues and dominates us is the God who reveals himself to us. It is this God to whom, in faith, we make commitment. In and through his revelation he confronts and subdues us. Accordingly, Christian faith has at all times referred to something which it has denominated as God's revelation. Faith indeed speaks also of God as the "hidden God." It is persuaded that under the conditions of this earthly life we are able to see only "in a glass darkly." God is unfathomable and inscrutable. And this mystery does not disappear by reason of his revelation. On the contrary, faith is confronted with this paradox: the more God reveals himself and the more we understand his will and heart, the more he appears as the unfathomable one. But the essential basis of faith is that the hidden God is at the same time he who has not left himself without witnesses. A God who was entirely hidden could have no connection with us; even less could there exist, under such circumstances, a vital fellowship between him and us. Therefore, just as faith and God belong together, so faith and revelation are conjoined and cannot be separated.

But this twofold aspect of faith which we have noted is connected with the fact that this revelation can be perceived by the eye of faith alone. The divine revelation cannot be indisputably demonstrated; it cannot be substantiated like a mathematical proposition. It cannot be so clearly unveiled and divulged as to be irresistibly seen and acknowledged by everyone. It is impossible, for example, to pick out a certain segment of history and declare: here is an inescapable evidence of God's revela-

tion. It is faith alone which perceives it. We can observe a
noble, pure, and spiritual life, but we cannot observe God. We
can see religiosity, but not a divine revelation. It is faith that
opens the eyes. Through faith we discover something more and
something entirely different from that which we previously saw.
It is as if we looked at a transparency. When it is properly
illuminated and the light falls where it should, then we see not
only what we previously beheld, but moreover, just that which
the transparency was intended to display. In the same way, the
eye of faith discovers not only human religiosity, but first and
foremost the living God and his acts.

Thus the divine revelation and faith are certified as being
two *corresponding concepts.* On the one hand, faith has its origin
and nourishment in revelation, and on the other, revelation is
discerned and recognized only by the eye of faith. The latter
could perhaps be interpreted to mean that faith is conceived as
being primary to revelation. Nothing, however, could be more
foreign to the viewpoint of faith than such a notion. If it is here
a matter of ascertaining the characteristic viewpoint of faith and
of permitting this viewpoint to speak without reservation, it
must be affirmed that nothing is more essential to the peculiar
outlook of faith than its awareness of the fact that the basis of
faith is the divine revelation which dominates and subdues. All
eudaemonistic thoughts concerning the basis of faith are, from
the beginning excluded from its characteristic outlook. We *believe,* not on account of the advantages which faith is supposed
to deliver, but because we have been confronted by the revelation of a God from whom we cannot flee. That choice and that
decision, mentioned above, has nothing of subjective discretion
about it. The real reason for our *yes* is, from the viewpoint of
faith, nothing but that the hand of God has overwhelmed us.

Thus the paradoxical nature of faith is illuminated. On the
one hand, God subdues the human soul, and on the other, man
turns and commits himself to God. But when reference is made
to man's activity, it does not imply a denial that the origin and

29

existence of faith are altogether God's work. The most profound viewpoint of faith itself concerning that which occurs is that our own seeking is nothing else than that which the Bible calls "the Father's drawing" us. It implies that our timid but at the same time audacious *yes* is nothing but God subduing us so that we simply are unable to flee. Faith and revelation are corresponding concepts; nevertheless in principle revelation is primary in relation to faith.

3. The Revelation of God

1. Christian faith discovers a revelation of God both in nature and in history, but it does not identify this revelation with either nature or history in their entirety.

2. The context of revelation which is decisive for Christian faith is that in which Christ appears as the one in whom the divine will becomes incarnate and victorious.

3. Christian faith does not circumscribe the divine revelation; but neither does it recognize any other God than him who has revealed himself in Christ.

4. The relation of Christian faith to Judaism is different from its relation to other non-Christian religions, because, on the one hand, God's revelation of himself in Christ implies the completion of Judaism. On the other hand, the relation is the same, since the revelation in Christ supplants Judaism.

5. The divine revelation is God's self-impartation. Its nature may be defined in the following paradoxical statements: 1) It expresses itself in a struggle against that which opposes the divine will, and is at the same time a revelation of the God who transcends all strife. 2) It is completed in Christ, but is at the same time continually in progress. 3) It utilizes historical means, and

is at the same time the form of God's immediate fellowship with men. 4) It is an unveiling of God's "essence," and at the same time confronts faith with the Unfathomable.

1. The Relation of the Divine Revelation to Nature and History.

The problem is first of all the locus of the divine revelation. If we start with the fact that man participates in the realms of both nature and history, we may say provisionally that the Christian faith finds traces of a divine revelation in both of these "realms." But it must be immediately added that neither nature nor history in its entirety appears in itself to faith as a "revelation" or a reflection of the divine will.

The idea of a divine revelation connected with the world of *nature* is of long standing and finds support even in the Old Testament. "The heavens declare the glory of God and the firmament showeth his handiwork." (Ps. 19:2; also, Ps. 104.) Such a union of faith in God with the majesty and beauty of nature has time and again appeared also within Christianity. We need only to remind ourselves of St. Francis' celebrated "Hymn to the Sun," or to refer to any of the hymnals of the Christian church.[1] It makes little difference that the world view has changed completely during the last centuries; it might rather be said that the larger conception of the universe makes it easier to connect the idea of the majesty of God with the world of nature.

But this does not mean that the Christian faith conceives of nature as a whole in terms of an explicit and unambiguous revelation of the divine will. It is not a matter of identifying God and nature according to the pattern of Spinoza (*deus sive natura*), or deducing the divine will in a rational fashion from the course of nature, as has sometimes been attempted in the so-called cosmological and teleological arguments for the existence of God. If the cosmological argument concludes on the basis of

---

[1] The author makes reference especially to hymn 174:4 in the Swedish Psalmbook. "Thy magnitude, thy majesty, thy mysterious purpose I saw in the path of the sun and in the smallest blade of grass."

cause and effect that there must be a first cause, and then calls this cause God, Christian faith must answer, from its point of view, that this pseudonomous "first cause" has nothing in common with the God of faith. Nor can the teleological argument which attempts to find a wise providence on the basis of the purposeful adaptability of the world prepare a way to the God of faith. The God who in this way is demonstrated has only the name in common with the God of faith. But it is also true that this purposefulness is not so conspicuous that it can furnish a self-evident starting point. There is in the world of nature an abundance of phenomena which impress upon us the meaninglessness and the cold insensitivity of existence. These imply a testing rather than a support of faith. It is quite significant that certain natural catastrophes have deeply shaken that faith in God which has rested on the evidence of purpose in the world of nature. The most conspicuous example is the revolutionary impact of the great earthquake in Lisbon in 1755 on the contemporary world which lived in the naive and optimistic faith that the whole universe was governed in all its details by a consistent and benevolent purpose.

Nature does not under any circumstances give a compelling and unambiguous testimony about the God of faith. Even that revelation of God in nature which Christian faith recognizes is very much incomplete and fragmentary. If faith were dependent on this alone, it would be limited to certain indefinite and uncertain conjectures; it could not appear as a strong, living, and significant faith in God.[2]

History, however, appears to the Christian faith as the bearer of a divine revelation in quite a different way than that discernible in nature. In the sphere of history the Christian faith finds that revelation which is decisive. Faith meets here the divine "heart" of which Wallin spoke in the hymn. But it is important

---

[2] The author again quotes from Swedish hymn 174 by Wallin to illustrate this point. "And yet Thy nature was obscured, I did not find Thy heart; and in the dark and endless space as a speck of dust I disappeared."

to notice that, although history is in a very special sense the locus of the revelation, history as a whole does not appear to faith as a reflection of the divine will. If nature contains much that is mysterious and meaningless, this is true in a still greater measure of history. All attempts to find a reflection of the divine will in the course of history as a whole must necessarily fail, because there is so much in the human world that is hostile to this will. These factors do not reveal God, but rather a power separated from and opposed to him. If everything that happens in the sphere of history were to be regarded without further consideration as an expression of God's will, and the judgments of history were thus simply identified with his judgments, faith would become completely uncertain as to the real character of the divine will (cf. § 22 ff.).

2. *The Decisive Revelation of God.*

If the Christian faith finds the revelation of God first of all in history, but at the same time does not regard history in its entirety as the bearer of that revelation, the question arises where in history the divine will is revealed, or what in history is of decisive importance to faith. The answer to this question may be formulated in this way: it is found in that context of revelation in which Christ appears as the one in whom the divine will becomes incarnate and victorious.

This formulation contains especially two fundamental points of view. In the first place, faith has its absolute center in Christ. In the second place, Christ is never isolated but stands in a large "context of revelation," which extends from him both back into ancient history and forward into the future. The Christian faith does not conceive of the revelation of God as a point in time, nor as an isolated act of God, but rather as a continuous series of divine acts. God has not only spoken and acted once in the world's history; the record of God's dealings with men is rather a constant and continuous activity, which is characterized by the fact that the divine will is continually realizing itself.

But Christ stands in this context of divine acts of revelation as the decisive and final act. He is the "Lord and King" of this context, to use the expression by which Luther intended to illustrate the relation of Christ to the Scriptures, but which can also be used in reference to the continuity of the revelation. That Christ is the one in whom the divine will became incarnate and victorious will be more fully discussed later in this work. In this connection, however, it should be pointed out that the idea of incarnation implies the fullness and expressiveness of the divine revelation, and that the divine will has entered effectively into human life in this world of sin and death. This character of effectiveness and realization in action, which is hereby given to the idea of revelation, is further emphasized by the word victorious. The work of Christ is here understood as the struggle and victory of the divine will; it is that act in which the divine will achieves in principle the decisive victory over the opposing powers.

3. The Universalism and Exclusiveness of the Divine Revelation.

It is rather surprising, when we examine the way in which Christian faith speaks about the extent of revelation, to find side by side strongly universal and strongly exclusive pronouncements. This has been the case during the whole history of Christianity. Thus Paul declares that God has not let himself be without witnesses among the Gentiles. But at the same time no one has more strongly emphasized the exclusive character of the divine revelation in Christ which is "to the Jews a stumblingblock and to the Greeks foolishness" (I Cor. 1:23). In almost a similar way the theology of the ancient church, as it made its impact upon the Greek world, has declared that the rays of the divine *Logos* have appeared also outside of the Christian tradition. But this theology at the same time makes the idea of incarnation a safeguard of the exclusiveness of the Christian revelation. This paradox relative to the extent of the divine revelation which has characterized Christianity since its beginning

34

has repeatedly appeared in various forms. But at the same time it may be noted that this union of presumably opposite perspectives, this both–and, has at times been changed into an either–or. It has happened that the inclusiveness and absolute freedom of the divine revelation have been maintained in such a way as to erase the boundary around that which is characteristically Christian; and it has also happened that some have denied almost every possibility of a revelation outside of that given in Christ.

The problem has naturally become very serious when Christianity has encountered the non-Christian religions on the mission fields. It is possible to find here a vacillation between the two extremes. On the one hand, there has been a tendency to paint everything black or white and to eliminate all intermediary shades. The judgment on the non-Christian religions has been wholly negative, and all points of contact between them and the Gospel have been denied. On the other hand, both in ancient and modern times, mission work has been carried on in a spirit of syncretism, and it has been assumed that nothing more is needed than to supplement and correct the non-Christian religions with a few Christian additions.

In contrast to this vacillation between two extremes it must be maintained that it is not characteristic of Christianity to assert either universalism against exclusiveness, or vice versa. On the contrary, both the universal and exclusive points of view express the peculiar genius of the Christian faith. On the one hand, it does not establish any limits around the divine revelation, but, on the other hand, it refuses to recognize any other God than him who reveals himself in Christ. In fact, every attempt to regulate and determine the boundaries within which the divine revelation might express itself appears to faith as extreme presumption. In that case man would act as judge in regard to the divine possibilities, which would be both an unreasonable pretension to the ability of penetrating the mystery of the divine government of the world and a claim to divine authority. Rightly understood, the Christian faith has not the slightest interest in limiting and restricting the extent of the divine revelation. On the contrary it must be said that faith's encounter with the divine revelation in Christ empowers the eye of faith to discover what men in the ancient church called the broken rays of the divine *Logos*. The clearer that light is which the eye of faith beholds, the more it is strengthened to recognize every other light which is a part of God's light.

But on the other hand, this does not in any way imply a tendency in the direction of syncretism, so that the genuinely Christian is blotted out and the exclusiveness of the Christian revelation is weakened. This feature of exclusiveness is expressed in the fact that the Christian faith knows of no other God than him who actively reveals himself in Christ. The words of Luther in the great hymn of the Reformation are here in place: *"und ist kein andrer Gott."* These words are unconditionally valid in reference to that act of God which was decisive for human life, and therefore also in apprehending the real character of the divine will. The expressive words of Luther emphasize an idea which lies strongly embedded in Christianity and which in various forms meets us in the New Testament. We need only point to the well-known statement in Matt. 11:27: "Neither doth any know the Father, save the Son, and he to whomsoever the Son willeth to reveal him."

It is not an accident, therefore, that a certain evident tension between the universal and the exclusive points of view appears in the Christian conception of the divine revelation. The Christian faith is broad in so far as it does not set any limits to the possibilities of revelation; but at the same time it does not tolerate the obscuring of the uniqueness of the Christian revelation. This tension belongs in reality to the very nature of the Christian faith. It cannot be eliminated by compromise, as has been tried again and again in scholasticism and in the theology influenced by idealism. The divine revelation of the Christian faith must not be conceived as a complement to something already given or as an addition to a knowledge of God which already existed.

What separates the revelation of God comprehended in Christ and his work from everything which might be called divine revelation is not something quantitative, but qualitative. The question here is about an absolutely unique action of God. Furthermore, this action of God in a very peculiar way reveals that which in the language of faith is called "the heart of God." This corresponds to a unique conception of God which not only complements and surpasses, but actually eliminates all others. In this connection the words *"und ist kein andrer Gott"* are valid.

4. *Christianity and Judaism.*

In the discussion of the relation of the Christian faith to the non-Christian religions the problem of its connection with Judaism must be specifically dealt with, since Christianity stands in a peculiar relation to this religion and to the Old Testament. A review of the history of dogma indicates that the studies dealing with this subject have often been obscure and uncertain. There is a vacillation between one conception in which the difference in nature between Christianity and the Old Testament religion is so emphasized that the continuity is obscured, and another in which the continuity is presented in such a way that the unique nature of Christianity is overshadowed.

Since it is important for our study that both the actual continuity and the actual difference be presented with equal emphasis, the problem may be stated as was done in the beginning of this chapter: the relation of the Christian faith to Judaism is different from its relation to other non-Christian religions, because, on the one hand, God's revelation of himself in Christ implies the completion of Judaism; and on the other hand, the relation is the same, since the revelation in Christ supplants Judaism.

This statement has a certain formal resemblance to that made by Schleiermacher on p. 12 of his *Der christliche Glaube*, but it is meant also as a positive correction to his thesis, which is stated in the following words: *"Das Christentum steht zwar in einem*

*besonderen geschichtlichen Zusammenhange mit dem Judentum:
was aber sein geschichtliches Dasein und seine Abzweckung be-
trifft, so verhält er sich zum Judentum und Heidentum gleich"*
("Christianity stands to be sure in a special historical relation to
Judaism; but in regard to its historical existence and its separation, its relation to Judaism and heathendom is the same"). In
Schleiermacher's exposition of the relation between Judaism and
Christianity the actual continuity has not been properly expressed. He simply makes a general statement that there exists
a certain historical continuity. That Schleiermacher emphasizes
the difference at the expense of the continuity is easily explained
as a valid reaction to an earlier attempt to place the Old Testament on par with the classical document of Christianity, the
New Testament. In accordance with orthodox theology and on
the basis of its theory of verbal inspiration, the statements of
the Old Testament were regarded, without any further consideration, as having the same validity for Christian faith as those of
the New Testament. The suggestion of Schleiermacher has at
a later time been followed by Harnack, who in his book on Marcion emphatically denied the right of the Old Testament to be
included as a part of the "canonical" documents of Christianity.
It is surprising, however, that Harnack's harsh rejection of the
Old Testament is not connected with any clear insight into the
peculiar nature of the Christian faith in relation to Judaism.
Jesus' conception of God, on which Harnack places the chief
emphasis, appears to him simply as a reformation of the earlier
prophetic conception, in accordance with a line of thinking popular in nineteenth-century theology. The relation between Christianity and Judaism is therefore only partially understood.

In contrast to all tendencies to weaken the continuity between Judaism and Christianity it must be insisted that Christianity really stands in a very intimate relation to the Old Testament religion, so intimate that it may be regarded as its fulfillment. But it must also be added that since it is a question of a
new creation, this completion at the same time implies a radical

supplanting of Judaism. This twofold relationship can be further illustrated by giving attention to three principal conceptions which here come to the front: *the law, the promise, and the sacrifice.*

The Old Testament religion was pre-eminently the religion of *law.* The relationship between God and man is conceived of as a relation regulated by law. This fact is in no way canceled or even weakened by the frequent references in the Old Testament to that covenant which God in his grace has established with Israel, or because it often speaks emphatically, especially in the Psalms and the prophets, about God's grace and forgiving mercy. The covenant which God established with Israel is in itself an expression of his love, but it is definitely characterized by the emergence of the law as the irrevocable expression of the divine will and as the power which sets its stamp upon the God-relationship. The relation to God within the covenant is a legal relationship. The mercy which God shows is comprehended under a legalistic viewpoint. The words in Ps. 103:17 ff. are typical: "But the lovingkindness of Jehovah is from everlasting to everlasting upon them that fear him, and his righteousness unto children's children; to such as keep his covenant, and to those that remember his precepts to do them." Even if occasionally an exemption might be granted from the demands of the law, as we find much later in Thomas Aquinas, this in no way eliminates the fact that, in principle, grace moves within the boundaries of the law. The relationship is legalistic.

Within the New Testament the law is at the same time fulfilled and canceled. In the Sermon on the Mount we read: "Think not that I came to destroy the law or the prophets: I came not to destroy, but to fulfill." It is of utmost importance here to determine in what sense the law is fulfilled and not destroyed; for there is a sense in which the law really is destroyed, as the New Testament abundantly indicates. The teaching of the New Testament would be completely misunderstood if it were interpreted as implying a reduction or a weakening of the divine demand. In this sense there is no "cancellation." Here it is rather true that the law is *fulfilled*. All "commandments" are now gathered into the commandment of love as the one in which all commandments are included. And the love which is now required is a free and spontaneous love. In this sense it is said: "Ye therefore shall be perfect, as your heavenly Father is perfect" (Matt. 5:48).

But it is exactly this unprecedented and unparalleled sharpening of the demand of the law that leads to its destruction. Luther, as Paul before him, has fully developed the consequences of the New Testament position. The law as an expression of the divine will demands that man shall act spontaneously, voluntarily, and not under coercion. But on the other hand, because it appears as statutes, the law creates a legalistic relationship which is characterized by commandments enacted to be obeyed. The way of the law is therefore such that it cannot lead to the goal. The law cannot be "fulfilled" except by being set aside and dethroned. The viewpoint characteristic of Christianity is, in other words, that the heightening of the significance of the law to the demand of a purely spontaneous love destroys the whole legalistic system. The new "ethics" cannot be contained within the boundaries of the law.

The cancellation of the law as the expression of the relation between God and man appears most clearly, however, in what the New Testament *positively* says about the nature of the divine love. This divine love cannot be contained within the framework of the law or a legal system. This fact appears clearly in the evangelists' descriptions of Jesus' preaching and his work, because in him the divine love turns to and seeks fellowship, not with the righteous, but with *sinners*. According to the Gospels, nothing aroused the ire of contemporary Judaism more than this attitude of Jesus. The legal system ceased to be the highest authority in questions dealing with the relation between God and men. This new conception of the God-relationship, and likewise also of the nature of God, which so clearly shines through the evangelical narratives, appears again in still clearer form in the apostolic proclamation of *theologia crucis*. The cross *is* the event which pre-eminently reveals the nature of the activity of divine love, and manifests its character as a love directed toward sinners and as giving itself for them. Among the many passages which could be mentioned we cite the powerful words of Paul in Rom. 5:6-10, where the apostle again and again reiterates the fundamental thesis of Christianity and persistently inculcates this new conception of the relation to God and the conception of God. *"While we were yet weak,* in due season Christ died for the *ungodly.* For scarcely for a righteous man will one die: for peradventure for the good man some one would even dare to die. But God *commendeth his own love* toward us, in that, *while we were yet sinners,* Christ died for us. . . . For if, while we *were enemies,* we were reconciled to God through the death of his Son, much more, being reconciled, shall we be saved by his life." We meet the same viewpoint also in the Johannine writings. "Hereby know we love, because he laid down his life for us" (I John 3:16). It is through the cross that we really learn to know what it means that "God is love" (I John 4:16). After we have heard such words, it does not surprise us when the apostle Paul says bluntly, "for Christ is the end of the law."

From one point of view, therefore, the law is fulfilled in Christianity, but from another it is canceled. The relation to God is no longer in principle based on justice. The religion of justice has been supplanted by a fellowship based on spontaneous and unmerited love.

That which is true about the law is true also in regard to the promise and the sacrifice. These two are likewise both fulfilled and canceled. Since this in reality is contained already in that change which has taken place in regard to the law, these two need to be only briefly discussed.

It is indubitable that the New Testament regards God's action in Christ as a "fulfillment" of the Old Testament promise

41

and prophecy. The continuity with the Old Testament hope is expressed frequently and in various ways. Christ is incorporated into the succession of the prophets. But Christ and his work signified at the same time a radical transformation of the prophecy. The men of faith in the Old Testament, according to the Letter to the Hebrews, "did not receive the promise," but God has "provided some better thing concerning us" (Heb. 11:39 f.), and the fulfillment is connected with this "better thing." The transformation of the promise as it is fulfilled does not consist simply in being separated from Jewish particularism, nor in the radical eschatological conception which dominates the New Testament and finds expression in the view that the kingdom here considered does not belong to this "age" and is not "of this world." The new and transforming element is found in that qualitative transformation of the relation to God and the conception of God to which we have called attention in our examination of the significance of the law.

At the same time it must be stated that the sacrifice is also fulfilled and canceled. This is the well-known theme of the Letter to the Hebrews. That sacrifice which has been made in and through Christ is the final one which cancels all other sacrifices. But the radical element in this transformation appears not only in this, however, that sacrifices are no longer offered to God, but the act of sacrifice is vitally connected with the divine love itself. The idea of sacrifice *to* God was common both within Judaism and the other religions in the world.

But in the New Testament God is not only the exalted majesty who receives sacrifices, he is the divine majesty who himself brings the sacrifices. He offers of his own, yea, even himself as a sacrifice. This is the peculiar and revolutionary element which Christianity brings into the conception of sacrifice. But it is clear that this new element is intimately connected with the new conception of the God-relationship and the God-idea. Here all the varied elements find their center. In Christianity Judaism is at the same time fulfilled and canceled.

5. *The Nature of the Divine Revelation.*

The divine revelation is a divine self-impartation. It is, as stated in the old confession about Christ, "life of life, light of light." That God reveals himself means not only that he gives certain gifts to men, but, as the reformers used to say, that he gives nothing less than *himself*. Any definition of revelation which ignores this fact minimizes and misinterprets the significance of the Christian revelation either by intellectualizing or psychologizing the concept. Christian faith sees in revelation first and foremost the self-impartation of God. We shall elucidate this view further by four paradoxical statements.

1. The divine revelation expresses itself in a struggle against that which opposes the divine will; but it is at the same time a revelation of that God who transcends all strife.

That God reveals himself means that the divine will actualizes itself. The divine will realizes itself as a contending will, engaged in conflict against that which is hostile to it. The divine will overcomes all obstacles, and reveals and establishes its dominion. Revelation is altogether *active*, it is divine activity. Whether it manifests itself in word or deed, the divine will realizes itself in its triumph over that which is hostile. Christian faith sees God's revealing activity against a *dualistic background.* The self-disclosing divine will is revealed just herein—that it is ever in process of subduing and overcoming opposition. In Christ as the bearer of the revelation the divine will becomes victorious and triumphant.

Christian faith perceives the divine revelation as an intense drama; but not as an inevitable or automatic process. It cannot be incorporated into a pantheistic, monistic, and evolutionary world view. Such ideas are quite foreign to Christian faith, even though they have appeared frequently in nineteenth-century theology from Schleiermacher onward. In whatever form these ideas appear, they tend to obscure both the evil against which the divine will contends and the active and striving character of the divine revelation. In contrast to these evolutionary misinterpretations of revelation, the Christian faith perceives it as dualistic and dramatic.

But Christian faith finds it just as vital and important that the divine will reveals itself as the *sovereign* will, which, because it is sovereign, transcends all strife which belongs to life on earth. It can therefore not be numbered among the many contending wills as one competing with others. To this we shall return later. But here it must be made clear that this tension which characterizes the Christian conception of revelation cannot be removed by minimizing either the sovereignty or the struggle of the divine will within history.

2. Revelation is fulfilled in Christ, but at the same time is continually in progress.

Christian faith conceives of the divine revelation as something given once and for all, but at the same time as a continuous, active, and living revelation. Neither of these viewpoints must be minimized at the expense of the other. Faith accepts the word, "It is finished," unconditionally. It is not looking for a new divine revelation which should render obsolete the one given in Christ once and for all. The act of reconciliation and victory through which the new fellowship with God has been established cannot be superseded. Nor can the conception of God, given in and with this new fellowship, be improved. Christian faith has expressed this in the words of the confession of the ancient church, that Christ is "of the same substance with the Father." It is God's "nature," the real and divine essence, which meets us in Christ. Christian faith cannot conceive of anything beyond this divine essence.

But at the same time the divine revelation is not confined to any certain period of time. Christian faith sees clearly that the divine revelation is constantly in progress and that God is always active in the world. The divine act in Christ is finished, but at the same time continually going on as the divine victory is realized anew in every generation. Christian faith sees Christ as one who does not only belong to the past, but who as the living

Lord is present with his own until the end (Matt. 28:20). The fact that the Christian faith in God is also a faith in the Spirit preserves this dynamic character of revelation. It cannot be localized, but appears rather as a continuity extending to the end of time. Revelation always has the character of something present; it meets man in the present as a living and overwhelming power.

This conception of divine revelation is the opposite of that which is static and which limits it to certain isolated events, or localizes it in a portion of past history. Faith does not use such conceptions. Nothing is more essential to faith than that God continually manifests and reveals himself. Faith cannot tolerate the idea that God has withdrawn and ceased to be active. The living and continuous revelation is inseparably connected with the living God. When revelation is understood as finished at a certain point in time, a deistic conception is introduced which is foreign to faith. It may be granted, however, that God was present and active up to a certain point in history. When that point was reached, the revelation was finished and God thereupon withdrew. His subsequent relation to the world would then be exactly that envisaged in Deism. But in that case God would really cease to be the living God. This line of thought obscures both the conception of God and the significance of faith. If revelation were localized in some past history, faith would mean simply an intellectual assent to a past event and an acceptance of that which once happened. In that case it would not be manifested that faith means that God in the present overwhelms and dominates man.

3. Since the revelation is a revelation in history, it makes use of historical means, persons, words, acts, and the like. But the divine revelation implies also God's immediate fellowship with the soul. Wherever faith speaks of revelation it implies that God directly confronts and addresses man. "The Word" does not become a divine revelation to man unless God, as Luther says, "speaks it in the heart." God's revelation is therefore a manifes-

tation of his active and powerful *presence*.

There are good reasons for emphasizing that revelation is the direct word of God to man. There may otherwise be a temptation to regard revelation as a mediating agency between God and man. In discussing revelation and mysticism theology has tended to put the problem thus: Does God work immediately or through means? It has been argued that mysticism denotes an immediate God-fellowship, while revelation would mean that God works through mediators whose presence detracts from the immediacy of the fellowship. This conception rests on a complete misinterpretation of the nature of revelation. It is conceived as static and historical, and therefore mechanical. The revelation then becomes something independent of God, something that enters in between God and the soul. But this alternative disappears when faith's own view is maintained. The question is not whether God works immediately *or* through means; but rather whether he works or does not work. If God works at all, he always works immediately, no matter how many "means" he may employ.

4. The divine revelation is a revelation of God's "essence," but at the same time it confronts faith with the Unfathomable.

The revelation is a revelation of the divine will. "Hereby know we love, because he laid down his life for us" (I John 3:16). "Seeing it is God that said, Light shall shine out of darkness, who shined in our hearts, to give the light of the knowledge of the glory of God in the face of Jesus Christ" (II Cor. 4:6). Revelation means, therefore, that God is not simply the great Unknown, or that about which nothing can be stated, because faith has some very definite things to say about him. The Christian conception of God is clearly and qualitatively defined. What faith says about him is not something unessential, but rather, according to its own conviction, the most essential affirmation which can be made. It concerns nothing less than the disposition of his heart. God is exactly such as he is manifested in the act of Christ. There is no other God. All other "conceptions" of God are eliminated. As far as the Christian faith is concerned they are nothing but caricatures.

What has now been said would be highly misleading unless it be added that faith at the same time beholds God as the Unfathomable. In the presence of the revelation of the divine will faith is compelled to confess: "How unsearchable are his judgments, and his ways past tracing out" (Rom. 11:33). The God who reveals himself is at the same time "the hidden God," who dwells "in light unapproachable, whom no man hath seen, nor can see" (I Tim. 6:16). *Deus revelatus* is also *Deus absconditus*. What faith says about God is therefore radically differentiated from any rational metaphysics.

It is important to note in what manner God appears as the Unfathomable. It does not mean simply that there are certain limits to revelation, and that beyond these limits there exists a hidden territory which would grow less and less in the measure that revelation increases. Nor does it mean merely that under these earthly circumstances there always will remain questions which cannot be answered and riddles which cannot be solved; or that the Christian faith cannot become a rational world view to which the divine government of the world would be transparently clear. It means rather that the nature of divine revelation appears to faith as an impenetrable mystery. Since the very center of this revelation is the divine love which gives itself in order to establish fellowship with sinners, that love itself appears inscrutable and impenetrable. Faith beholds the revealed God as the Unfathomable, the "hidden" God. In fact, we may even agree to this proposition: the more God reveals himself and the deeper faith looks into the mystery of his divine heart, the more he appears as the Unfathomable. Thus the apostle writes: "Let a man so account of us . . . as stewards of the mysteries of God" (I Cor. 4:1).

4. Divine Revelation and History

1. The relation of faith to history is characterized by two antitheses. In the first place faith opposes every endeavor to separate divine revelation from history. This holds true whether it be by a speculative replacing of divine revelation with rational ideas, or by mystically dissolving the historical revelation, or finally by substituting "the spiritual Christ" for the Christ of history.

2. In the second place faith opposes every endeavor to identify divine revelation with something historical and human. This is true whether the identification is built upon a general theory of immanence or has reference to the "historical Jesus" as such.

3. Thus, for Christian faith divine revelation is indissolubly connected with history, but without being confused with the human element of history.

1. Divine Revelation Cannot Be Detached from History.
The problem of the relation of divine revelation to history now demands a more exact analysis. In principle, this relation is established in two negative propositions. Faith opposes alike all efforts to detach divine revelation from history and to identify it with something historical and human. When Christian faith speaks of a divine revelation *in* history, it has reference to *God's* revelation of himself. Christian faith discovers in history the God who acts and speaks. But faith has no concern with history as such. That which is historical has meaning only in the measure that it is a transparent medium of the *divine* revelation. Faith is concerned solely with a God-relationship, and in such a relationship man is exalted beyond all merely earthly and historical connections.

Through the ages various attempts have been made to separate divine revelation from history. Three such attempts are typical: the speculative endeavor to replace divine revelation in history with rational ideas; the effort of mysticism to make divine revelation in history ultimately superfluous; and the theological attempt to eliminate the historical Christ by directing attention to the "spiritual Christ." An examination of these types reveals the attitude of each toward that which is central to Christian faith, viz., the incarnation of the divine will in Christ.

The *speculative* and *rationalistic* line of thought has been given classic expression in the famous words of Lessing, "Eternal truths cannot be based upon incidental historical facts." Two things are here characteristic; in the first place, the attempt to effect a liberation from history, and in the second, the endeavor to interpret the content of "revelation" as "inescapable rational truth." The fortuitous "facts" of history cannot constitute a firm foundation for the "eternal truths." These do not depend upon that which occurs in the realm of history. If Christian faith pretends to give expression to these eternal truths, it must cease to seek support in history.

When this approach is applied to the problem of the meaning of Christ, it often results in an effort to separate the historically transient from the eternal verities. It is not the historical figure of Jesus but those eternal verities of reason to which he was able to give expression that are meaningful for faith. The essential element is the teaching which he gave concerning "God, virtue, and immortality." The significance of Jesus depends, therefore, upon the value of his teaching, and the value of his teaching depends entirely upon its agreement with that which human reason conceives to be eternal truth. Christianity is the true religion just because it does not need to depend upon the historical and in so far as it can be separated from the incidental and transient in human affairs which has accompanied the "teaching."

If the older rationalism of the later stages of the Enlightenment was inclined to separate itself as much as possible from history, later speculative theology, especially that which follows Hegel's philosophy, makes an even greater effort to unite revelation and history. It maintains that the basic and central principle of religion—the principle of a Divine Humanity—is realized in history. It is well known that from this starting point Christology became the center of theology and thus, ostensibly, the divine revelation in Christ was strongly emphasized. This approach is differentiated from the rationalism of the Enlightenment because history is no longer considered simply "incidental"; the Idea is realized in history. There is nevertheless an obvious affinity inasmuch as the historical person of Jesus is separated from the eternal principle of a Divine Humanity of which he is the bearer and which is realized in him. This type of thought is also characterized by a tendency to dismiss entirely every thought of a supernatural revelation, because the metaphysical-cosmological viewpoint becomes anthropological, and humanity as such is understood as "the incarnation of God" (Strauss).

It is obvious that the speculative approach has been unable to express the conception of the relation of revelation to history which is characteristic of faith. From the viewpoint of faith it is decisive that whenever history has been ignored the dynamic revelation has been lost. Speculation confuses the divine revelation of faith with rationalistic metaphysics. Faith is not concerned with eternal truths of reason or an eternal idea, but only with the living God who speaks and acts in history. But instead of this living God there now appears only an abstract idea conceived by the older rationalism deistically and by speculative idealism pantheistically. In the measure that the idea of God is in this way weakened, faith no longer implies being subdued and dominated by God, but involves rather an acceptance of certain religious ideas. When history ceases to be the bearer of revelation, the danger is that the meaningful and definite concept of God fades, and faith itself withers away.

In many respects *mysticism* is very unlike the tendencies of rationalistic speculation which we have noted. Nevertheless there does exist a certain obvious affinity between mysticism and rational metaphysics. A review of the history of Christian thought proves that these two magnitudes have often been drawn together and have in certain respects complemented each other. There has been a manifest agreement between them especially with reference to the question with which we are here concerned, the relation of the religious life to history. Both mysticism and rational metaphysics tend to separate the religious life from any connection with history.

This is of course the case wherever mysticism appears in its purest and most characteristic form as "the mysticism of infinity," as Söderblom expressed it.[1] In all such mysticism history plays no part. When it affirms an immediacy in the God-relationship apart from any connection with history, it of course ignores history. That infinity which absorbs personality has nothing to do with history. The consequence of this approach is first of all that the content and quality of the idea of God are lost. God can only be described in static terms; God is the great Infinity, the Absolute, the Exalted One, and so forth. Secondly, the relationship with God is lost. In the final analysis there can be no real relationship with a God who lacks quality. In other words, the mysticism of infinity, in spite of its talk about the extinction of the ego, never really gets beyond the magic sphere of egocentricity. It never reaches the living God who dominates and subdues. The dissolution of the idea of God involves the dissolution of the very God-relationship. Thus, the mysticism of infinity which separates itself from history demonstrates, no less than does speculative rationalism, how important it is for Christian faith to direct attention to a divine revelation in history. What may be observed from the foregoing is how the very content and dynamic character of the idea of God are indissolubly connected with that divine revelation which is located in history.

It must now be added that such a pure mysticism of infinity does not belong to the history of Christian thought. Within this area mysticism has been leavened by that conception of revela-

---

[1] Translated by Samuel McComb in *Prayer*, by Friedrich Heiler, p. 135, as "personality-denying mysticism."—Tr.

tion peculiar to Christian faith. Thus mysticism is here oriented to history and particularly to the figure of Christ. A characteristic example of this type of mysticism is that of the Middle Ages. Here the influence of the Christian conception of revelation was at times feeble, as with Eckhart, and at other times more pronounced, as with the Passion mysticism of Bernard of Clairvaux. But even in this later case where the Passion of Christ and the commitment to his path of suffering are central ideas, the characteristic approach of pure mysticism is apparent. The mystic's relation to Christ and his Passion is regarded as a stage upon the upward way toward the realization of the vision of and absorption in God. It is regarded as an aid which becomes unnecessary once its task is accomplished. This means, furthermore, that the concept of God is not delineated and determined by Christ and his work. This approach passes from a definite conception of God to a mystically indefinite concept which eventuates finally in negative statements. With this transformation of the concept of God, the approach of medieval mysticism to the God-relationship presents a singular vacillation between the most emphatic denial of the self and a vast self-assurance of being received into the divine.[2]

A third type of endeavor seeking to separate divine revelation from history has emerged in the recent theological attempts to detach the exalted "spiritual Christ" from the historical Jesus. Thus Paul's assertion that he no longer knew Christ "after the flesh" has received an interpretation never contemplated by the apostle. It has been vitally important ever since the days of the

---

[2] When reference is made in recent literature to a "Christ-mysticism" in the writings of Paul or Luther, such terminology is apt to confuse rather than clarify, inasmuch as this so-called mysticism is devoid of all the elements which characterize a genuine mysticism. In recent times the term mysticism has been so generally misused that it can be employed only with the greatest care. It would be well if the term were reserved to designate only the so-called mysticism of infinity. To speak of a mysticism of faith serves only to obscure the issue. The desire to "complement" faith with a so-called mysticism is simply an evidence of the fact that the nature of Christian faith has not been rightly understood. A "faith" which would require such a "complement" is beforehand in one way or another an ethically, or intellectually, or otherwise impoverished faith.

primitive church for Christian faith to direct attention to Christ
as Lord. It has been equally essential for Christian faith to insist
that the exalted Christ is identical with him who was crucified
outside the walls of Jerusalem. When tendencies to isolate the
"spiritual" Christ have emerged in recent theologies, among them
the dialectical, this may be explained by a number of conspiring
circumstances. It is partly due to a legitimate reaction against
previous one-sided and mistaken theological emphases upon the
"historical Jesus." And doubtless the exegetical uncertainty concerning that which can definitely be traced back to the historical
Jesus has also been partially responsible for the emergence of
these tendencies. Meanwhile, it is evident that the interpretation of revelation given by faith becomes a metaphysically
oriented viewpoint when the isolation of the spiritual Christ is
carried to its logical conclusions. In this situation there emerges
a phenomenon which is related to that which we have found in
the previous paragraphs, namely, that the concept of God tends
to lose that distinctive quality given to it by the work of Christ.
As a matter of fact, in whatever form it may appear, every effort
to separate divine revelation from history has the same result,
viz., the obscuring of both the God-relationship and the God-
concept which are characteristically Christian.

2. Divine Revelation Cannot be Identified
with Something Historical.

Just as Christian faith will not permit divine revelation to be
separated from history, so neither can it be comprehended in or
be identified with anything historical as such. The identification
of revelation with history was especially prevalent in the theology of the nineteenth century. Two principal types may be
discerned: that which is based on the theory of divine immanence in humanity and that which possesses the structure of
"historicism."

The first type emerges in the idealism of the nineteenth century and the theology which it influenced. Inasmuch as there is

here no clear distinction between "humanity at its highest" and the divine, the result is a confusion of revelation with history. As a consequence humanity at its best is regarded as identical with the divine.

From this point of view Christ is regarded as the incarnation of the religious ideal. He is the religious archetype (Schleiermacher) or the "ideal man." This latter designation enjoyed a wide popularity during the nineteenth century. The underlying thought is that here humanity at its best becomes and reflects the divine. This point of view gives to the figure of Christ an abstract quality. The "ideal man" is actually a hybrid being, partly divine and partly human, a fantasy to which various "ideals" may be imputed. Critically, the most important consideration, however, is that this line of thought involves a dissolution of the concept of *divine* revelation. That which is revealed is something which claims to be ideally human. As far as revelation is concerned, it is not a question of God's approach to man but rather the exaltation of the human to the divine sphere. Thus under the influence of idealism there occurs a dissolution of the fundamental theme which is characteristically Christian.

The Ritschlian theology, which was dominant during the latter decades of the nineteenth century, endeavored chiefly to concentrate divine revelation around the "historical Jesus." The purpose was to oppose both the metaphysical formulas of ancient Christology and the idealistic and speculative Christology of the first half of the nineteenth century. It implied a return to the "purely historical" figure of Jesus and to his teaching according to the Gospel.

A closer examination of this line of thought makes it clear, however, that this supposedly historical picture is in reality an invention. When, for example, Ritschl makes the teaching of Jesus concerning the Kingdom of God central, the conception of the Kingdom which he defines is certainly not a mere return to Jesus' strongly eschatological teaching according to the Gospel. On the contrary, Ritschl's concept of the Kingdom with its decidedly this-worldly, ethico-cultural orientation is obviously dependent upon idealistic theories and especially the thought forms of Kant. It is analogous to Harnack's presentation of "the essence of Christianity." In his famous book[3] which appeared at the turn of the century, he locates the essence of Christianity in Jesus' teaching of the Fatherhood of God, the brotherhood of man, and the eternal value of the human soul. It is clear that the definition of the content of revelation here given is strangely similar to the old theology of the Enlightenment; its "God, virtue, and immortality" reappear in modern dress. The decisive element does not lie in the historical as such, nor in the purely historical fact, if it can be shown to be a fact, that the propositions in question were once uttered by Jesus. On the contrary there occurs with Ritschl and Harnack a careful selection as well as a reinterpretation of the historical. They begin factually with something other than the purely historical. There is a certain standard by which the historical is judged, even though it is not clear just what this standard is. When finally Herrmann refers to Jesus' "inner life" rather than to certain aspects of his teaching, it does not mean that he is concerned with the "historical Jesus" as such. An investigation of Herrmann's line of thought reveals a return to that Christology which was typical of idealism. Jesus represents for both Herrmann and Idealism a certain "ideal." Herrmann's chief concern is the "moral ideal," as if the idea of moral goodness became incarnate in Jesus' "inner life."

From the viewpoint of Christian faith there are essentially two defects in the thought of historicism. In the first place, revelation is understood as dated and static. When revelation is located at an isolated point in the past, an imaginary chasm is created between faith and revelation. Because of its one-sided emphasis upon the "historical Jesus," the interpretation which historicism gives to revelation overlooks the fact that revelation for Christian faith emerges in a continuing context which is dis-

[3] A. Harnack, *What Is Christianity?*

tinguished by the fact that the Crucified is also the Exalted One, and that Christian faith in God is also faith in the Spirit. Historicism thus separates faith from revelation. From the point of view of faith, such a construction is unrealistic. In the second place, and of greater importance from the religious point of view, the fundamental defect of historicism lies in the fact that, like the idealistic theory of immanence, the character of revelation as being a revelation of God is obscured. It directs the attention of faith to a human life of the highest moral and religious quality and to high and pure human thoughts about God and his Kingdom. But that which is essential for faith does not have reference to human thoughts, however high and noble, nor to human personality, however completely religious. Faith does not practice a hero cult. It does not confuse humanity even at its best with the divine. Faith is related to nothing but God alone. When it speaks of revelation it has reference only and entirely to God's revelation, to God's approach from above to mankind; to this and nothing else.

3. *The Dialectic of Faith.*

The conception which Christian faith has of the relation of divine revelation to history may be said to be dialectic. The conclusions of the foregoing critical reflections may be summarized in the following formula: for Christian faith divine revelation is inseparably connected with history but without being confused with that which is human. This is a formula well known to the ancient church. The merit of this formula is precisely that which has often been considered its shortcoming, namely its negatively delimiting character. The conception which faith has of the relation between divine revelation and history can actually be described and defined only in the measure that it can be differentiated from two opposing misinterpretations.

Divine revelation cannot, on the one hand, be separated from history. Every attempt in this direction invariably eventuates, as we have seen, in a dissolution of both the relation to God and the concept of God characteristic of Christian faith. That God is present in the historical process and that he is active in history is the chief viewpoint of faith. Divine revelation is therefore something wholly other than general, abstract, and unhistorical ideas. Revelation is the activity of the divine will in history. But at the same time divine revelation cannot be identified or confused with anything historical and human. Divine revelation is not identical with some unique aspect of man's inner life, even though it be of the very highest religious quality. Such thoughts, by idealizing the human, destroy that distance between the divine and the human which is fundamental for faith. Divine revelation does not imply that something human has been exalted to the divine realm, but that the divine will from above condescends to and is active in the human. Luther has given this situation a meaningful expression when he says that God is "hidden in the despised person of Christ." In this connection one may employ the ancient Lutheran and Reformed watchwords, *finitum capax infiniti, finitum non capax infiniti.* It can be said that the Lutheran formula certainly seeks to express the factual character of divine revelation but in doing so lays itself open to certain misinterpretations. The Reformed formula emphasizes, to be sure, the distance between the divine and the human, but in such a way as to endanger the factual character of divine revelation. Sooner than abiding by any of these formulas, one would prefer to transcend both of them with the formula *infinitum capax finiti.* Such a formula would then affirm that God through his revelation in history creates fellowship with man.

Excursus.   Faith in Christ and Historical Criticism.

It has been stated in the previous discussion that Christian faith in God regards Christ as the center of divine revelation. Since our knowledge of Jesus Christ comes to us through the New Testament, and this historical document is an object of investigation by historical criticism, the problem of the relation between faith and this historical criticism becomes very real and important.

This problem was hardly known as long as the theory of verbal inspiration held sway, and it was therefore assumed that the content of the Bible was a homogeneous and uniform word of God. This situation changed when the classical documents of Christianity were subjected to the same examination by historical criticism as any other historical documents. The problem assumed a twofold aspect. On the one hand, historical criticism by its very nature must take into account probabilities and relative judgments. It was difficult, for instance, and sometimes impossible to state with certainty what parts in the Gospels came from Jesus himself and what may have originated with his disciples and others. On the other hand, it seemed that the older conception of the Bible as a unity without diversity would be changed into a conception of diversity without unity.

It was, of course, of greatest importance that the multiplicity and diversity of conceptions which are found within the Bible as a whole and within the New Testament were realistically appraised. But it seemed at times that the result would be, not only diversity, but the most acute contradictions. The most obvious was the contradiction believed to exist between Jesus' own "teaching" and the apostolic preaching, which divided the Christian message and rendered it uncertain. This was a critical situation, which by this time has been practically overcome through a continued and more decisive application of historical criticism. The theory of contradictions within the New Testament has been shown to be an invention which arose because the critics read their own "modern" ideas into the Gospel accounts of Jesus' preaching. The picture which historical criticism presents is not one of diversity without unity, but of unity in diversity. The diversity is obvious. The Synoptic Gospels, John, Paul, Hebrews, and so on, represent complementary types of New Testament teaching. But in the midst of this diversity the fundamental unity stands secure. The New Testament message is an indivisible unity and has a definite content throughout. Its center is Christ as *Kyrios* and the new age, the new aeon, which has come through him and his work. There is no contradiction here between Jesus and his disciples, but rather a clear and indisputable continuity. The apostles did not invent a new religion with Christ as the center. As far as we can go back to Jesus' own preaching, we find that his message is inseparable from his own person.

Even though it is extremely important that the mutual suspicions of faith and criticism have been removed, it is quite natural that there remains a tension between Christian faith and the investigations carried on by historical criticism. It is obvious that when historical criticism tries to determine what in a purely historical sense was Jesus' own contribution, it has to be satisfied with a lesser or greater degree of probability. It is likewise obvious that these investigations of areas which to faith are holy ground must vitally affect the interests of faith itself. But in spite of this tension faith preserves its complete fearlessness. The changes in our conception of the primitive history of Christianity which may be occasioned through this research cannot prevent faith from drawing fully and freely on the accumulated riches of the whole New Testament. This research cannot take away from faith anything which it regards as the revelation of God. It cannot challenge, and least of all destroy, that fundamental conception of faith which perceives and interprets the work of Christ in the light of the continuous context of revelation, and which in his life and work beholds the self-realization of the divine love in human life and the new age which comes in *Kyrios-Christus*.

5. Faith in God and in Christ

1. All Christian faith is faith in God. All typically Christian faith is at the same time centered in Christ. This raises the prob-

lem of the relation between the theocentricity and Christocentricity of faith.

2. Faith in Christ is the safeguard of Christian faith. It is not a faith in something besides God, but a faith in that God who was incarnate in Christ and in him reveals his essence and realizes his will. Faith in Christ defines the Christian relation to God and the nature of God, positively and qualitatively. The antithesis between theocentricity and Christocentricity is thereby dissolved. Christian faith is Christocentric just because it is theocentric.

3. A misleading conception of the relation between theocentricity and Christocentricity arises in three instances: 1) when Christ is separated from God and conceived of as an intermediary being; 2) when Christ is identified with God and takes his place; 3) when the divine Being is, so to speak, divided between God and Christ.

1. *The Problem.*

When we here take up the problem of the relation between faith in God and faith in Christ, we do not intend to anticipate the discussion of the Christological problem which has its own place in this exposition (§§ 25-29). Since Christian faith is both faith in God and in Christ, it is necessary to guard against misunderstandings and accusations of obscuring the monotheistic character of faith. In Part I, § 2, it has been stated emphatically that Christian faith has only one object, and that it is concerned with God alone. At the same time it is a well-known fact that Christian faith began as faith in Christ, and that this is its distinctive feature. It could be argued that this Christocentricity is opposed to, or at least obscures, the theocentricity of faith. It cannot be denied that this has often been the case in the history of Christian thought. Under these circumstances a preliminary explanation of the relation between faith in God and faith in

Christ cannot be omitted. We must then hold to the principle that, if Christocentricity should be in conflict with theocentricity, the former must be discarded. As has already been stated, faith cannot orient itself toward any other object than God.

2. *The Meaning of Christocentricity.*

The significance of faith in Christ is entirely misunderstood if it is assumed that because of its concern for Christ the Christian faith finds a center other than God. The attitude of faith in this matter can be illustrated by the words of Jesus in John 12:44: "He that believeth on me, believeth *not* on me, but on him that sent me." The Christian faith in Christ is a faith in God, who appears actively in the work of Christ, realizes his will, removes that which conceals his face, and triumphs over that which separates us from him. A complete analysis of this Christ-deed and God's activity can be given only as an exposition of the whole content of Christian faith. At this stage we can give only a preliminary suggestion of the fundamental idea of this faith in Christ and elucidate its relation to faith in God. It will then become clear that Christocentricity is not opposed to, but rather serves to emphasize, theocentricity. The confession of faith in Christ is really nothing else than a statement about *God*, his "essence," his presence, and his power to triumph over that which is opposed to him. The real point of view is simply this: where Christ is, there is God; and where Christ works, there God realizes his will. The work of Christ is God's own work, not something separated from him. Faith in Christ does not draw our attention away from God, but rather focuses the attention on that conception of him which is possible under the conditions to which human life is subject.

Faith in Christ is therefore the secure safeguard of Christian faith in God. Faith is certain that it has found in Christ the "essence," will, and inner disposition of the heart of God. When faith has found God in Christ, it does not seek him elsewhere. The character and quality of the Christian conception of God are given in and through Christ. Christian faith rejects every conception of God which differs from this thesis. *"Und ist kein andrer Gott."* The real purpose of Christology is, therefore, to guard the purity and completeness of the Christian faith in God. If the chief statement of the confession of the ancient church, "of the same substance as the Father," has any meaning at all, it must be that we learn to know the essence of "the Father" in "the Son." If the confession of faith in Christ is not permitted to perform this function, it loses its real significance and becomes merely empty words.

If this analysis is correct, the Christological problem must not be stated in such a way as to imply that the divinity of Christ can be measured by a previously determined conception of God. Faith regards such a proposition as unreal and incompatible with its situation and nature. It is true that revelation is not limited to Christ. But this does not mean that revelation apart from Christ can serve as a standard whereby the degree of revelation found in him can be measured. We cannot, for instance, measure the revelation in Christ according to the standard of the Old Testament; we must rather measure the nature of revelation in the Old Testament according to the standard of the work of Christ. From the point of view of faith the endeavor to measure the "divinity" of Christ under the tacit assumption that it is possible to achieve a clear and authentic idea of God apart from the work of Christ is inevitably misleading. This supposed possibility does not exist. God is not a previously definable magnitude, with which we can start and proceed without further reference. In reality these attempts to measure the "divinity" of Christ imply a denial of him as the revealer of God. It is not God who is the known magnitude, and Christ, the riddle; it is rather the opposite. The first and foremost question is: What is the nature of the hidden God? What is the nature of his will, and how does he act? The work of Christ supplies the answer to these questions.

Faith in Christ, therefore, does not obscure the consistent

faith in God, but rather provides it with power and decisive content. Exactly because Christian faith is altogether theocentric, it must at the same time be Christocentric. The whole history of Christianity illustrates and confirms this intimate connection between faith in God and faith in Christ. This history shows conclusively that faith in God has been strong, living, and dynamic in the measure in which Christ has been its focus and center. All great revivals have been intimately connected with a Christocentric emphasis. On the contrary, when the bond between faith in God and faith in Christ has been dissolved or weakened, faith in God has languished and the concept of God has become vague. The conception of God has lost its living features, God has been removed into the distance, and has been conceived in terms of an abstract idea rather than the living, present, and active God. The rationalism of the Enlightenment constitutes a classic example.

3. Misleading Interpretations of the Relation Between Faith in God and Faith in Christ.

We cannot conclude this chapter without observing that misleading interpretations of the relation of faith in Christ to faith in God have often appeared in the history of Christian thought. The fear that Christocentricity should prove to be a danger to theocentricity, and to the purity and unity of faith in God, arises from such misinterpretations. A study of these, therefore, will throw further light on the real significance of Christocentricity.

In the first place a misinterpretation of the significance of faith in Christ emerges when Christ himself is thought of as an intermediary being. This type of Christology has appeared in various forms within the ancient church and has found its most characteristic expression in Arianism. This line of thought both obscured the position of Christ as the revealer of God and threatened to destroy the unity and theocentric character of faith. The ancient church opposed this antithesis between theo-

63

centricity and Christocentricity with its formula, "of the same substance as the Father." The church thereby affirmed that when its faith was directed toward Christ, it was directed toward none other than God. Certain related conceptions have also appeared in later times, especially when Christ is spoken of as the religious "prototype" of humanity, or "the ideal man," and so on. This unrealistic Christology, influenced by idealistic philosophy, also makes of Christ an intermediary being. It obscures the most vital center of Christian faith, viz., that it is God himself who is incarnate in Christ and acts through him. It tends to deny that God's approach to man is through Christ and his work.

In the second place, the significance of Christocentricity is misinterpreted when God and Christ are identified, as occurred in Modalism. (See § 25.) This has often been done more or less naively in much popular preaching, in which the teachings about Christ practically supersede the broader teachings about God. It is undeniable that in this case Christocentricity tends to hide and impair the theocentricity of faith. Christ becomes synonymous with the entire concept of God. What is legitimate in this line of thought is its understanding that in the realm of faith nothing else matters but God alone. However, it fails to see that the real question is about a *revelation* of God in the real meaning of the word, and that this revelation takes place *in* history, in "the despised man, Christ," as Luther expressed it. As soon as this is realized, it becomes impossible to identify Christ with God, or to conceive of the divine "essence" as synonymous with the man Christ.

In the third place, this relation is misinterpreted if an attempt is made to divide the Supreme Being and to apportion certain aspects to God and others to Christ. Certain divine "attributes" are then given to Christ which do not in the same degree belong to God. Such ideas lie behind the theory of the atonement developed in Latin scholasticism, which has greatly influenced the history of Christian doctrine. In this line of thought Christ represents pre-eminently the divine love, while the idea of retributive justice dominates the conception of God as such. The result has been that Christ is placed, so to speak, over against God. Men are to trust in him as the one who offers protection from the God of judgment. It is quite evident why the divine love has in this way been connected especially with Christ. The fullness of divine love meets us in the person and work of Christ. Nevertheless, this conception of the relation between God and Christ is diametrically opposed to the fundamental idea of the confession of faith in Christ. It is misleading because the act of Christ is not in this case understood as God's own act. But when the work of Christ is conceived of as the work of God, it becomes impossible to ascribe a greater degree of divine love to Christ than to God, or to introduce a division into the divine Being. The act of Christ is altogether an act of God's own love, and an act through which this love realizes itself.

6. Historical Christianity and the Essence of Christianity

1. The relation between historical Christianity and the essence of Christianity cannot be approached either from a static, evolutionary, or metaphysical-eschatological point of view. The static conception would identify the essence of Christianity with a period of past history, and every differentiation from this past would imply apostasy. According to the evolutionary conception Christian history would appear as a continually progressing development toward perfection. In a metaphysically oriented eschatology, history would stand in a purely negative relation to the essence of Christianity.

2. A clear insight into the relation between the essential and the historical in Christianity can be obtained only on the basis of a dramatic point of view; that is, by a realization that under historical conditions the divine revelation stands in a continual conflict with opposing forces. This is true whether Christianity

65

is seen from the point of view of Christian life or Christian thought.

3. The essence of Christianity is characterized by the fact that everything in Christianity is related to and determined by the act of God in Christ.

1. Three Misinterpretations.

The history of Christianity and the multitudinous forms in which it has appeared pose the problem of "the essence of Christianity." It is self-evident that not everything that has been called Christianity has been worthy of the name, and likewise that within the Christian life different levels of attainment have existed and continue to exist. What then is the essential core of Christianity? How is this related to the historical development of Christianity? Three different interpretations must first be discussed. They are of such a nature that they must be critically examined.

The first of these interpretations may be called the *static*. The central thought is that the essence of Christianity is identified with a certain historical form of Christianity, and that the rest of its history must be appraised by its agreement with or departure from the form once and for all given and defined. The categories used are reproduction and apostasy. This interpretation follows a rigid scheme. The historical form which is supposed to represent the essence of Christianity is found in the primitive period, then follows the apostasy, and finally comes the call to return to the primitive and decisive form. The variations which may occur within this scheme are caused mostly by the differences in the fixation of the terminal points. Both the period of apostasy and the period representing the essence of Christianity may be lengthened or abbreviated.

Such ideas have often been presented, especially in post-Reformation theology. Doctrine, cultus, and organization have all been subjected to this process. It is well known that the

Reformation has often been interpreted as a pure restoration, either of primitive Christianity in its Pauline form or of the Christianity of the first centuries. The intermediate history would then be regarded as a period of apostasy from pristine Christianity. But Luther does not simply reproduce an earlier form of Christianity; neither that of the ancient church, although he stands in closer contact with it than has generally been recognized, nor even the Pauline, although Luther was more strongly influenced by Paul than by anyone else. It is absurd to regard the Reformation as simply a reproduction of an earlier Christian period, even though this point of view might in a certain sense be justified. Luther does not simply imitate. This whole point of view is impossible. History never repeats itself.

Pietism presents another variation of this static conception. It regards the primitive, biblical organization and cultus as the ideal and urges a return to these forms. But to maintain that any particular organization or cult is a reproduction of original Christianity is an illusion.

A third variation is found in a conception which originated in the Enlightenment, but has also had some influence in later periods, viz., that "the essence of Christianity" is identified with "the teaching of Jesus," and consequently a return to this teaching is demanded. But in that case the whole history of Christianity would appear to be an apostasy. That apostasy actually began on the first day of Christianity. It would already be present in the proclamation of the apostles and in their faith in Christ, since they substituted a doctrine about Christ for the teaching of Jesus and thus thoroughly changed and perverted that which was given once and for all. This theme is well known and has been pursued *ad nauseam* especially during the eighteenth and nineteenth centuries. It is, however, perfectly clear that this interpretation of history is doctrinaire and unrealistic. "The teaching of Jesus" cannot in this way be isolated from the apostolic testimony. Furthermore, this conception of the teaching of Jesus is a thorough reinterpretation of that given in the

Gospels. This reinterpretation is in perfect accord with the idealistic and humanistic background of the theology in question. For these reasons, not to mention others, such a systematization of the origin and essence of Christianity is impossible.

The *evolutionary* conception stands in sharp contrast to this static point of view. The theory of evolution determines the interpretation of history. The essence of Christianity expresses itself in a continuous "development." The beginning of Christianity is like a small seed that gradually grows and becomes a large tree. The static conception with its theory of apostasy and restoration takes a pessimistic view of the history of Christianity, but the evolutionary theory is thoroughly optimistic.

This conception appears also in several variations. In general it has closer affinity with Roman than with evangelical Christianity. The official Roman thought is at least related to the idea of evolution. Even if the thought is not directly evolutionistic, the Roman church recognizes a legitimate growth, which is, to be sure, evaluated and controlled by the official hierarchy. The common view is that the accepted system of doctrine has gradually developed and has found its perfection in what has been approved by the highest authority. This evolutionary perspective has found enthusiastic defenders also among the modernists in the Roman church, especially among those who have followed the lead of Cardinal Newman. Roman modernism delights in pointing to this evolutionary view of the history of Christianity as an expression of Catholic wealth in contrast to the narrowness and poverty of Protestantism. As an example, one may consider Loisy's book, *L'Evangile et l'église,* which was directed against Harnack's *What is Christianity?* From this standpoint the Roman apologetic found it possible to defend and explain almost all doctrines, cultic ceremonies, and ordinances originating within the Roman church, as being in complete harmony with the essence of Christianity. It therefore becomes apparent that the evolutionary view is not an adequate standard whereby the genuine core of Christianity can be defined.

But the evolutionary view has representatives also within evangelical theology, especially Schleiermacher and Hegel during the nineteenth century. They have interpreted Christianity in terms of a monistic-evolutionary world view. This evolutionary system is certainly more critically oriented than that described in the previous paragraph. The evolution is at the same time a process of purification. The optimistic feature is decisive. This has found a classic expression in Schleiermacher's formula: *"immer vollständiger durchdringt der Heilige Geist das Ganze"* ("the Holy Spirit permeates the whole more and more perfectly"). This formula has reference to the Christian life as well as to Christian thought. "The whole" appears as a continuous progress, an unceasing crescendo.

The *metaphysical-eschatological* conception can best be understood as a radical negation of the theory of evolution and its optimism. Schleiermacher maintained that the Holy Spirit more and more perfectly permeates the whole, but the exclusively eschatological viewpoint perceives the Spirit as fundamentally in complete separation from the world of history. Nothing else, therefore, can be said about human life as a whole, including Christian life, than that it stands under judgment, which in itself is a perfectly correct statement. Not only does the consummation of the Kingdom of God lie beyond the conditions of human life in this world, but in reality this Kingdom has nothing to do with the world of history. In this conception the optimistic evolutionary view of history has been replaced by a radical pessimism. It should be stated that this criticism is not directed against the eschatological perspective as such. The outlook of Christian faith is always eschatological. The criticism is directed only against that kind of eschatology which has been given a metaphysical direction, has lost the dramatic perspective, and consequently has lost contact with history.

If we now look back over these three conceptions, it must be admitted that each one expresses a relative truth, but also that in each one there are elements of fatal weakness. The strength of the static conception lies in its emphasis upon Christianity as being something given once and for all, something completed, secure, and abiding. Its weakness is that it conceives of the given in a stereotype and mechanical fashion, so that the divine revelation loses its living character. This living character is to some extent expressed in the evolutionary line of thought. But this conception suffers from a twofold weakness. In the first place there is in the evolutionary theory an evident tendency to obscure and dissolve that which is characteristically Christian. In the second place it idealizes historical Christianity in an unrealistic manner. The optimism which perceives the whole as an unbroken progress toward perfection is surely without foundation and does not correspond to the actual situation and conditions of the Christian life. The eschatological conception is a healthy reaction against this approach. But when this viewpoint becomes metaphysical and is unable to speak clearly concerning the meaning of history, the idea of revelation is in danger of losing its most essential content.

2. *The Dramatic View of Revelation.*

The reason all the interpretations of the history of Christianity discussed in the previous section prove unsatisfactory and doctrinaire is that they fail to consider how the Christian faith understands the divine revelation in history. The first ignores the active and living character of the revelation. The second disregards those difficulties which confront revelation because it takes place in a context of oppostion and conflict. The third emphasizes the separation between revelation and history in such a way that the revelation loses any positive contact with history.

Since Christian faith, always eschatologically conditioned, must hold fast to the reality of the divine revelation and at the same time emphasize the opposition encountered in history, the result is that its outlook assumes a dramatic character (cf. § 3. 5). Under the conditions imposed upon it by history, the divine revelation wages a continuous struggle against the opposing forces. This means, therefore, that the Christian life, both individually and collectively, is characterized as an emergent Reality and a struggle. Nothing in history is ever finally and conclusively accomplished. The divine presence and fellowship reveals more sharply that which separates the forces and thus intensifies the struggle. This wrestling between the divine will and the hostile powers takes place in every individual and every generation. History is the battlefield of the contending divine will. It has both a negative and a positive relation to the divine will, but it cannot be understood from the point of view of evolution as implying a continuous progress toward perfection. It cannot be said that a later period stands closer to the realization of the Kingdom of God than an earlier one. That there are times in history when victories are won over the hostile powers implies merely a change of front. The struggle remains essentially the same. The perfected Kingdom of God does not belong to history. It is equally near to and far from every generation. If the Christian faith is nevertheless confident of victory, the reason is that it beholds the decisive victory gained once for all in the person and work of Christ. Its outlook is therefore neither idealized nor resigned. It is uncompromisingly realistic in its awareness of the dark side of life, and yet full of confidence. This has been expressed in the classic words of Luther's psalm: "Though devils all the world should fill, All watching to devour us, We tremble not, we fear no ill, They cannot overpower us."

The fundamental view of the Christian life presented here applies also to some extent to the history of Christian thought. The dramatic point of view has its place in this field also. The history of Christian thought cannot be conceived of in a stereotyped fashion as a fluctuation between apostasy and reformation, nor from the viewpoint of evolution as a continuous progress toward greater clarity and purity. Both of these conceptions are false. Even in this field there is a constant struggle bringing both victories and defeats. The fundamental Christian theme,

71

the genuinely Christian view of divine revelation and its significance, must maintain itself under continually changing conditions against all rival powers which threaten to obscure and supplant it. The history of Christian thought appears therefore as an exciting drama with alternating superficial and profound elements, in which even the apparent or real defeats, by calling forth a healthy reaction, prove to have a positive significance for new victories.

3. *Preliminary Definition of the Essence of Christianity.*

The definition of the essence of Christianity in which the act of God in Christ comprises and determines everything is of a formal and therefore preliminary character. So far nothing has been said about the significance of "the act of God in Christ." This formula will be elaborated in the following exposition. The whole purpose is to illustrate the essence of Christianity from various points of view and to clarify the nature of that faith which has been created through the act of God in Christ.

The reasons for this formula have really been stated in the previous discussion. It is necessary to add only a few remarks about the qualifying phrase "in Christ." The formula is intended to emphasize that the divine revelation about which the Christian faith speaks is concentrated in Christ, that it has an active character, that the work of Christ is seen exclusively as God's work, and that as a result all conflict between theocentricity and Christocentricity, between faith in God and faith in Christ, is foreign to Christian faith. It should be particularly emphasized that the Christian life exists as a communion, as a church. This removes all individualistic and unrealistic conceptions. That life of faith which is created by the continuous act of God in Christ is a continuity and a progressive context into which the individual is incorporated and of which he partakes. The Christian fellowship with God is realized in and through the church. Christian faith is concerned with nothing else than God and man's relationship to him. God is for faith the completely decisive power. In this sense faith implies a fellowship with God. It is not a question of an identification, but of a relationship in which God remains God and man remains man. This has been sufficiently emphasized, especially in the statement that fellowship does not remove but rather enhances the consciousness of distance (cf. § 2. 2).

7. The Content of Faith

1. The divine revelation from which faith derives its existence gives it a definite quality and a fixed content. This content is in principle given in and with the God-relationship as such. The content of faith is therefore neither primary in relation to faith (intellectualism) nor secondary (subjectivism, psychologism).

2. That which is decisive for the content of faith does not lie in the forms of presentation as such. It is to be found in the fundamental underlying ideas for which the forms are the expression.

1. *Faith and the Content of Faith.*

The content of Christian faith is, in principle, something fixed and definite. It is not a question of just any vague and indefinite "faith" whatever, for God is not the great Unknown about whom nothing really positive can be affirmed. God is not only hidden, but is at the same time the God who has disclosed himself in the past and continues to make himself known. It is that divine will given in revelation and qualitatively determined by the work of Christ which faith embraces, or rather which embraces and subdues man and thereby creates faith and establishes the relationship to God. Faith is thus from man's viewpoint a *yes* to the self-disclosure of the divine will, and is determined by the divine revelation which both creates it and gives it a unique content. Faith cannot be isolated from this revelation so that it would have its own existence apart from divine revelation. Faith is nothing in itself. It is what it is by reason of that divine revelation which subdues man.

From what has now been said it follows that the content of faith in principle is given in and by the relationship to God. The implication of this statement becomes clear if we observe how this conception of the content of faith differentiates itself from two mutually opposing interpretations, the intellectual and the subjective or psychological. The first type belongs chiefly to the older period of scholasticism and rationalism. The second has repeatedly asserted itself especially during the last century. However, these two types can hardly be consigned to different periods. To a certain extent there has been a continual struggle between these two rival interpretations.

The *intellectual* interpretation considers the content of faith primary. It attempts to demonstrate rationally those ideas of God which are the objects of faith. This line of thought has from the beginning characterized scholastic theology, which attempts to "complement" rational demonstration by "revelation." Within fully developed rationalism, however, the rational demonstration becomes entirely dominant. Relative to all such demonstrations it is enough to say that as long as one is limited to this sphere there has been no real contact with the realm of faith. But the intellectual tendency within scholastic theology is not limited to such attempts to co-ordinate faith with rational metaphysics. It appears also in connection with the very concept of faith by making "assent" primary in relation to the other aspects of faith. In such a manner medieval theology distinguished between faith as "thinking with approbation" (*cum assensione cogitare*) and faith as *fides caritate formata* (Thomas). The post-Reformation scholastics of the seventeenth century distinguished similarly between faith as *assensus* and faith as *fiducia*. Under such circumstances faith was interpreted as man's submissive acceptance of certain authoritative and doctrinal theological propositions. This would mean that faith subsequently becomes *fides caritate formata* or *fiducia*. It is self-evident that this intellectual approach exercised a severe constraint upon the Christian life. In the measure that the acceptance of a certain

74

given system of doctrine became the chief concern, the Christian life was confronted by fictitious difficulties, while the real difficulties, which the Gospel describes as it points to life's pathway through "the narrow gate," were obscured. It gradually became necessary for theology to try in some way to ease the constraint originating in the intellectual conception of faith. This occurred within medieval scholasticism through the doctrine of *fides implicita,* that is to say, through the assertion that it was sufficient to possess a rather simple faith, so long as one lived in the certain conviction that the teachings of the church were true. Within the post-Reformation scholasticism there developed gradually an attempt to differentiate between "fundamental articles," which demanded acceptance, and teachings of lesser importance. It is clear that such adjustments, while bringing a certain amount of relief to the circumstances at hand, could not, however, produce any real clarity or give any promise of overcoming intellectualism.

The weakness in the intellectual approach to faith is not that the content of Christian faith is here presented as something definite and determined. This is rather its strength. The weakness is due partly to the confusion of divine revelation with some given, authoritative theological system of doctrine, and partly, to use the terminology of post-Reformation scholasticism, to the fact that *assensus* was considered primary in relation to *fiducia.* If one is, therefore, to be emancipated from the intellectual approach without losing the truth which is there affirmed, it is necessary to maintain that, as far as faith is concerned, it is a question of only one thing, namely, the will of God which is revealed in the work of Christ, and further that *assensus* is at the same time *fiducia.* In this way Luther can speak of faith as implying nothing else than an *assensus,* a *yes* to "God's work and promise," but this *yes* is at the same time an expression of the very highest trust, which is to say, an expression of man's having been subdued by the will of God.

The *subjective* or *psychological* conception of faith has often appeared as a reaction against intellectualism. This viewpoint is characterized by the notion that the content of faith is something secondary in relation to faith "itself." "Faith" is understood as identical with certain religious feelings or with a "pious state of mind." It is thought of as something given in the spiritual life of man, as a self-contained, independent magnitude. The pious feelings or state of mind are primary. The content of faith, however, is secondary and originates through reflection upon these pious feelings or state of mind. It is natural that from this point of view the significance of the content of faith will be sharply reduced. A distinction was made between *fides qua creditur* and *fides quae creditur,* and the latter was made subordinate to the former. This approach to the relation between faith and its content has received classic expression in the pregnant words of Schleiermacher in the fifteenth paragraph of *Der Christliche Glaube, "Christliche Glaubenssätze sind Auffassungen der christlich frommen Gemutszustande, in der Rede dargestellt."* Fundamentally, the question here is not about the affirmations of faith in God, but of affirmations concerning the religious subject. This approach which has its roots in pietism and romanticism exerted a great influence throughout the nineteenth century. It was responsible for the emergence of the so-called "experiential theology" for which the "religious experience," whether individual or collective, appears as the subject for theological analysis (cf. § 1. 4). It was claimed that this theory could be projected so that, beginning with the subjective experience and working from effect to cause, one could be led back to the "objective realities of revelation" (cf. von Frank). But the illusory element in this line of thought could not be long concealed.

The weakness in the psychological approach to the relation between faith and its content does not lie in its refusal to construct a supposedly objective doctrine of God. On the contrary, this is the very strength of this viewpoint in contradistinction to all rational metaphysics. But the weakness lies in that faith is no longer clearly understood as faith, but as a pious, spiritual state independent of divine revelation. In intellectualism faith tended to lose its character of a direct relationship between God and man by becoming chiefly a matter of adhering to a system of doctrine about God. Similarly the psychological interpretation obscures the character of faith as being a God-relationship. It does not become clear that faith is what it is only in and through the divine revelation, that the affirmations of faith are by their very nature affirmations about the God who reveals himself, and that therefore the content of faith is not secondary but essential to faith and its unique character. The content of faith is in reality nothing else than the God who reveals himself.

2. Ideas and Forms of Expression.

As theology investigates the content of Christian faith, it is important to make a distinction between the fundamental ideas and the forms of expression. If it is a matter of clarifying the content of Christian faith, then theology must not stop with a consideration of the various forms of expression which we meet at the first appearance of Christianity and which during the ages since that time have appeared in various new forms. It is necessary to push beyond these forms and formulas, and to reach the dynamic religious ideas, the religious themes, which are here active. The essential element is not the forms as such, but that which underlies the whole, that which these forms seek to express.

The distinction here proposed may be substituted for the usual nineteenth-century differentiation between "life" and "teaching." The intention which lay behind this latter distinction was indeed noteworthy, inasmuch as it recognized that theology could not, without becoming intellectually doctrinaire, stop simply with the "teaching" and its forms of expressions. But this differentiation exposes its subjective and psychological background when it places "the teaching" in contrast to "life," "experience," and the like. If the starting point is taken from this distinction, the consequence, on the one hand, is to make the content of faith something secondary or of minor importance in comparison with the so-called *fides qua creditur;* but, on the other hand, the position becomes obscure by reason of the ambiguity of the word "life." However, when a distinction is made between the religious idea and the form of expression, the purpose is both to escape the restraint imposed by the various forms and to assert freely the primary meaning of the content of Christian faith. From the viewpoint of the content of faith, that which is essentially Christian lies in the religious ideas which are inseparably connected with Christian faith.

A theological investigation which is not impelled by the effort to push beyond the forms and formulas to the underlying driving powers, to the decisive religious themes, will inevitably stop at the periphery in its effort to clarify the content of Christian faith. The inner quality of questions relating to faith would then be concealed. This has been exemplified by numerous theological debaters during the ages, who, just because they have become entangled in forms and formulas, have never pushed on through to the essential core of the matter. Such an approach to fundamental ideas is necessary because it may happen that the forms change while the religious theme remains the same. Furthermore, the same forms and expressions may have a completely different content, depending upon whether they express one religious theme or another. The former alternative may be exemplified in the dualistic approach, the struggle between the will of God and the demonic forces. This theme has often been given a very extreme form, but the idea is not inevitably connected with such an expression. The idea *can* be separated from the form and nevertheless continue to exist with unabridged power. It may be added that when a theology becomes entangled in the forms of expression, it is apt to lose sight of the significance of the dualistic theme for Christian faith. It may be natural to consider the extreme forms as a sure sign of a clearer and deeper conception of Christianity. Such a point of view has very often obtained in theology during the past several centuries. This fact has given rise to viewpoints which are very superficial. The fact has been overlooked that the process of exaggeration may imply a fundamental weakening of the central Christian ideas. The other alternative may be illustrated by the concept of sacrifice. This example makes it clear how forms can be transferred from one idea to another and thereby receive an entirely different content. The same expression may be employed even though it has reference to absolutely opposite ideas. For example, the concept of sacrifice can be used to serve the Christian "agape" theme, as an expression of the nature of divine love, but it can also be employed in the exact opposite context as an expression of the human will to influence and persuade God.

If it is a matter, with reference to all questions of Christian faith, of investigating the fundamental religious idea, then it is necessary to add that such an investigation must center in a single theme which is basic and fundamental. The theme which is here in question can be none other than that which is basic to the Christian relationship between God and man and which establishes this Christian relationship. It is the theme which is comprehended in the act of God in Christ and which is definitive for that Christian concept of God which is normative for faith. If God is the Alpha and Omega in the realm of faith, the central and decisive question regarding faith is the nature of the divine revelation in Christ. The character of this revelation and this divine will determines and defines all Christian ideas of faith.

8. The Validation of the Content of the Christian Faith

1. In its endeavor to present the significance of Christian faith, theology encounters the multifarious conceptions of faith within the Christian tradition. Its work must therefore assume a critical character. The question of the validation of the concepts of faith is thereby raised.

2. The problem of validation cannot be solved through a static and legalistic Biblicism, whether this rests on a theory of verbal inspiration or on the selection of certain portions of Scripture.

3. The solution cannot be found in traditionalism, in either its legalistic or evolutionary form.

4. The validation can be obtained only by showing that the content of faith is intimately and organically connected with the central fact of Christianity, namely, the act of God in Christ. The content of faith must be the expression of the relation to God created by this fact, and must be in harmony with the nature of God there revealed. From this point of view both Scripture and tradition are given their legitimate place, but Scripture is nevertheless primary.

5. The purpose of the critical examination made by theology is the delineation of a "sound doctrine." From one point of view this sound doctrine is something given in principle once and for all; but from another point of view it is an ideal goal toward which theology is constantly striving in its pursuit of truth. In this endeavor it must also pay attention to the gains obtained from the dramatic history of Christian thought.

1. The Problem.

It is evident that theology will encounter numerous difficulties when it attempts to present the significance of the Christian faith, since it must always take into account the collective testimony of all Christendom. This testimony is extremely multifarious, and so are also the many theological attempts to define the content of the Christian faith. The problem could be stated in this way: What conceptions really set forth the nature of faith according to its own intentions and its view of the divine revelation? It is obvious that, if this statement is definitive for the problem, the task of systematic theology must be of a critical character. But this "criticism" must be from within. A criticism which judges the affirmations of faith from external and foreign points of view is worthless. Criticism means rather that theology is able to hear the voice of faith itself and to recognize the note of authenticity and truth. The criticism must be from a purely religious point of view. But this does not imply that the criticism is less serious or decisive. In fact, a criticism "from within" demands the greatest measure of critical acumen and sensitivity.

What then are the standards of such a critical analysis? How can it be avoided that such an analysis becomes arbitrary, and that theology consequently becomes a "science" in which everyone may affirm whatever comes to his mind? How can the Christian affirmations of faith be *validated as Christian?* If there is no possibility of such a validation, the work of systematic theology is obviously futile. To say, as W. Herrmann does, that the function of systematic theology consists in letting each theologian express his own tenets of faith is to declare theological bankruptcy. This situation is not improved by expressing the hope that the result of a theologian's work will be of help to other Christians in working out their own ideas of faith. Theology remains, in spite of such "hope," within a subjective and arbitrary framework. If it is to produce anything scientific, it must establish fundamental principles according to which the Christian character of the various conceptions of faith can be examined. It must in some way validate as Christian those "conceptions of faith" which it presents and show that their Christian character rests on an inner objective necessity.

2. The Validation Cannot be Achieved on the Basis of a Mechanical Biblicism.

When attempts have been made to validate the Christian conceptions of faith on the basis of Biblicism, either the whole Bible has been used in reliance upon the theory of verbal inspiration, or, when this theory has been weakened or abandoned, certain portions have been selected as authoritative. If every syllable in the Bible is inspired, all statements have the same binding authority, since there can be no different degrees of divine authority. The Christian "teachings" can therefore be validated by a reference to any passage whatsoever. This is a very easy method. But the whole argument is nullified by the simple fact that the Bible does not possess this supposed uniformity. This fact is really very obvious, and historical criticism has made it inescapable. In reality the theory of verbal inspiration has never been consistently applied in practice even by those who are its most earnest exponents. A consistent application of the principle would mean that the same divine authority must be ascribed to the "prayers" of hate and vengeance in the Old Testament as to the most profound words in the New Testament. The entire content of the Bible cannot with impunity be declared as an equally normative word of God. It is obvious that no Christian theology can agree with such a doctrine without at the same time ceasing to be Christian. That theology which depended on the theory of verbal inspiration was compelled to adopt various means in order to escape the most serious consequences of the theory. It made use of the allegorical method and found "Christ in the Pentateuch." It used especially the tradition of the evangelical Reformation as a standard whereby the content of Scripture could be sifted and evaluated. In this sense it can be said that the scholasticism of the post-Reformation period placed tradition above Scripture. When the theory of verbal inspiration breaks down and proves itself useless for the validation of the Christian affirmations of faith, the reason is that, consistently applied, it does not lead to a verification, but rather to a dissolution, of the Christian character of that theology which builds on this foundation. If the theory of verbal inspiration were taken seriously, it would obviously imply that the divine revelation in Christ is equated with every other "biblical revelation." But this would also mean that the revelation in Christ ceases to be what Christian faith affirms that it is, namely, that standard by which all divine revelation is measured and judged.

If the validation cannot be based on the theory of verbal inspiration, neither is it possible to select certain portions of the Bible as infallible authority. Even such an abbreviated Biblicism is impossible in whatever form it appears: whether certain definite books or certain portions are accepted, or an appeal is made to "the teaching of Jesus." The attempt to determine beforehand by means of certain mechanical rules what passages are infallibly inspired leads to arbitrariness and absurdity. The attempt to set forth the teaching of Jesus as absolutely binding encounters the difficulty of determining in any particular case the extent of his teaching. It is further obvious that those who have attempted to use this approach as a basis have been forced to make a selection of various elements of Jesus' message. They have been compelled to speak about the "essential," and the like. This indicates that the decisive fact is not that something was spoken by the historical Jesus, but that other reasons are present, even though no one is willing to state clearly what these are (cf. § 4. 2).

We must here add two remarks which apply to all attempts to validate the Christian affirmations on the basis of Biblicism. If the validation consists only in proving that certain conceptions of faith are found in the Bible or in certain portions of it, this means, on the one hand, that the argument for the Christian character of these conceptions is of an external and *legalistic* nature. This legalism is the same whether the appeal is to the theory of verbal inspiration or to the teaching of Jesus. If this line of thought is consistently followed, the decisive element is the fact that something has been stated in a document invested with external authority. No consideration is given to that which is really decisive: the character of these affirmations in themselves. The authority is only formal. The legalistic line of thought has its ostensible strength in the supposed certainty with which it speaks about the content of Christian faith. But this confidence and assurance are in reality an illusion, because the judgments are not based on internal and positive facts. The decision is dictated by something other than the convicting and compelling character of the religious content itself.

In the second place, the approach which relies on a biblical validation becomes purely *static*. The task given theology, according to this point of view, could be only to reproduce the biblical conceptions and to combine them in the best possible manner. It would be extremely important that none of the concepts of faith, once given, be lost or changed in any degree. The greatest danger in this approach is that it become concerned simply with the letter. Actually the interpretation of the content of the Christian faith has never in recent times consisted in a simple reproduction of the concepts given in the Bible, not even by those who have *intended* that their exposition should be nothing more than a slavish following of the letter of Scripture. A process of change in regard to the way in which Christian truths are presented can be discerned even within the New Testament. The eschatological conceptions are one example of this. In this connection the distinction between the idea and the form of expression may be used (§ 7. 2).

It is obvious that certain dangers are connected with the changes which through the centuries have taken place in regard to the presentation of the New Testament ideas. It may happen that the disuse or change of the New Testament ideas has involved a transformation of central and essential biblical ideas and the introduction of foreign themes. In that case the interpretation of Christianity has been a misinterpretation. But it can also happen that a change in the presentation has become necessary in order to make the central Christian truths available and active in a new situation. In that case the change has served to clarify the real significance of the Christian faith. The most serious objection to the static conception, which is concerned almost exclusively with the external manner of presentation, is that it has no center around which the whole is gathered, and that it does not have a clear view of the central theme of Christianity and of its fundamental meaning. Under these circumstances, even though the interpreter is anxious to reproduce the New Testament ideas, he has no trustworthy standard and is in danger of confusing the essential with the unessential.

3. *The Validation Cannot be Made on the Basis of Tradition.*

Traditionalism may appear in two chief forms, the legalistic and the evolutionary. Neither of these is able to say the last word in answer to the question of validation.

A legalistic traditionalism may appear in various forms. The tradition may become incorporated in an ecclesiastical authority, as has happened in Rome in regard to the authority of the pope in questions involving doctrines. There is of course no possible guarantee that any such authority possesses the necessary qualification. The Spirit cannot be coerced. As an illustration of the impossibility of this line of thought, it may be pointed out that Rome prefers to give a mysterious character to its doctrine of papal infallibility. On the one hand the papal decrees are given a certain infallible sanctity, and on the other hand there is room for the possibility of changing the unchangeable. The idea of an ecclesiastical and legal authority as the court of highest appeal within the church is found also outside of the Roman church. Many who call themselves evangelicals would welcome an ecclesiastical tribunal for decisions on points of doctrine. The will to arrive at decisions in this way is strong enough, even though the power may be weak.

Another untenable form of validation by tradition is to reckon with the number of people who adhere to a certain conception of faith. Points of difference cannot be decided by counting the votes. *Vox populi* is not always *vox dei*. This line of thought is just as external and legalistic as the other. A concept of faith is not validated as Christian because it has been held by a greater or smaller number of people during longer or shorter periods. Nor can a decision be reached by pointing out that a certain point of view has been held by the majority of the historical churches. This line of thought has appeared at times within the Anglo-Catholic section of the Church of England. But this is also too external a method of deciding questions of faith, and it ignores the fact that "spiritual things must be spiritually discerned."

The same is true of that traditionalism which accepts certain confessional formulas as being invested with "the authority of the church," and therefore able to speak the decisive word in the questions of faith with which they deal. Both the ancient confessions from the time of the "undivided" church and the confessions of the Reformation have been so used. This does not imply a lack of appreciation for the positive significance of such documents. What is criticized is only the legalistic point of view which appeals to that authority with which these documents have been invested rather than to the positive significance they may have on the basis of their own inherent character. It is also most questionable and misleading to assume that in the confessions of the ancient church a certain number of problems of faith have been solved once and for all. These would then constitute a basis for Christian unity, and each denomination would find it possible and proper to add its own special affirmations of faith to this common core. Such a conception has sometimes appeared in modern ecumenical discussions, but it ignores entirely the organic character of Christian faith. The Reformation did not imply that a certain number of new affirmations were added to the old faith, but rather a deeper insight into that which is essentially Christian. This new insight transformed the whole content of Christian faith.

On the whole, the purpose of theology must be to examine the Christian quality of both the confessions and other Christian documents. The confessions do not have a preferred standing by virtue of that authority with which they have been invested. The goal of theology can be nothing else than to discover the genuine core of Christianity. As far as the Reformation is concerned, it would be a fatal mistake and an abridgment of the task of theology if, without further consideration, the Augsburg Confession or the Formula of Concord were placed in the center. It is more important for that theological study which desires to penetrate into and clarify the significance of the Christian faith to delve into Luther's own writings than to stop with an analysis of the formulas given in the confessions, no matter how important these may be.

The evolutionary traditionalism contains a modicum of truth in so far as Christian ideas have developed through the centuries, and the significance and power of these ideas have appeared more clearly. When the over-all viewpoint of the history of Christian doctrine becomes purely evolutionistic, the conclusions derived therefrom are misleading (cf. § 6. 1). Furthermore, regarding the problem of validation, the content of Christian faith is not considered as having in principle been given once and for all, and therefore it becomes at the same time impossible to find a norm by which the results of the development can be judged.

4. The Nature of the Validation.

It is clear from what has already been said that a successful validation of the content of the Christian faith can be attained only by focusing the attention on that which is of decisive importance. This can be nothing else than the *fundamental fact* which is given to faith in and through the act of God in Christ. This is of such fundamental importance for faith that, if it is lost, faith also ceases to exist. The Christian God-relationship is absolutely determined by this fundamental fact. The unique character of faith is given in and through this fundamental fact. The Christian God-relationship is what it is through the act of God in Christ. When we say that the Christian relationship between God and man is thus determined, it implies that the uniqueness lies in that relation of *God* to men which is realized in Christ. It is this attitude of God which creates and characterizes the Christian faith. But this implies also that in this connection we are concerned with a unique idea of God. The unique God-relationship and the unique idea of God are inseparably connected. The phrase "idea of God" in this connection does not mean a completely defined conception of God. The aim is rather to designate that manner of action which in and through the act of God in Christ characterizes God's relation to men, and which therefore determines every phase of the Christian relationship between God and man.

On the basis of this principle it is obvious that the validation of the content of the Christian faith can be accomplished only by showing how the separate affirmations stand in an inner organic relation to this fundamental fact of Christian faith, the act of God in Christ. This principle may also be formulated thus: every Christian affirmation must in some way express the God-relationship which is fully defined as uniquely Christian. It may also be formulated in this way: the content of faith must thoroughly reflect that idea of God which is given in and through the act of God in Christ. There is no positive difference between these two formulations of the principle of validation.

The examination of the Christian character of the affirmations of faith must be qualitative. No merely formal points of view and no historical analysis of the origin of a certain tenet can by themselves decide the question of its Christian character. A doctrine is not validated as Christian by having excellent references, nor by the fact that it has been accepted by a large number of Christians. Everything depends on the inner, organic, and living connection with the fundamental fact of Christianity. If an affirmation of faith does not evidence an inner vital connection with this fundamental fact, it has no legitimate place in Christian faith, even though it may be widely held. If the denial of a certain affirmation of faith negates or obscures the fundamental fact of Christianity, the validity of this affirmation as Christian is thereby firmly established.

It is obvious that under these circumstances theology must

direct its attention with all its energy toward the inner connection of the various tenets of faith and to the inner unity of the whole content of faith. If every Christian affirmation of faith must evidence its immediate connection with the center, the act of God in Christ, there must also be an apparent inner connection between the several tenets of faith. If this connection is missing, it is a sure sign that something is lacking in the Christian character of this particular affirmation. The Christian affirmations do exhibit certain inescapable tensions (cf. § 9), but this does not militate against the inner connection between the affirmations of faith. One affirmation cannot be made to contest or deny what is expressed in another. When scholastic theology, both before and after the Reformation, in its Christology strongly affirmed the effective presence of God in Christ, but in its doctrine of the atonement put the decisive emphasis on the work of the man Christ Jesus, and did not present the work of reconciliation as a uniform and unbroken act of God, it created a great chasm between Christology and the atonement. This apparent incongruity is a sure sign that the fundamental Christian principle has not been fully expressed.

By this kind of validation theology, as it analyzes faith, is freed from a legalistic dependence upon external authority and also from subjective arbitrariness. When the decisive element lies in the inner connection of the affirmations of faith with the fundamental fact of Christianity, it no longer depends on subjective caprice as to which affirmations are to be given a place in the total of the Christian content of faith. It is not a question either of furnishing a description of the content of faith of a particular person, or of describing a normal or average Christian consciousness within a certain denomination. In neither case could the theological study overcome its arbitrary character. The *possibility* of going beyond arbitrariness obtains only if theology validates the Christian affirmations on the basis of their connection with the fundamental fact of Christianity. In this way theology will have a method for the solution of its problems. It is a different question relative to the measure in which theological study has actually been able to solve these problems. It is clear that a validation of this nature is more difficult than that which imagines that the solution can be found by an appeal to some formalistic and legalistic authority. Even if the goal is never reached so as to make further study and evaluation unnecessary, this does not nullify the scientific character and function of systematic theology.

From this point of view both the "principle of Scripture" and the "principle of tradition" are given recognition. The work of systematic theology is not purposeless. Its function is not to create but to understand. Its subject is the Christian faith as this has been expressed through the centuries. It must therefore be positively but not legalistically dependent upon the continuous testimony of faith given through the ages, or, in other words, on the tradition. But within this tradition the writings of the New Testament occupy a special place. They belong to the tradition since they constitute that part of the primitive tradition which has come down to us. It is abundantly clear that the New Testament has not created Christianity, but is really a product of the faith-life of the early Christians. Nevertheless, these writings occupy a peculiar position, because they are the first and decisive testimony to that deed of Christ which is the fundamental fact of Christianity. Nothing can take the place of this testimony. The character of the Christian relationship to God and the nature of the Christian conception of God are given in and through this original testimony to the deed of God in Christ. This gives to the New Testament its unique significance.

The exposition of the content of the Christian faith by theology is forever determined by the testimony of the New Testament. But this does not mean that no other conceptions of faith are permitted except those produced within this most ancient testimony, nor that every one of the conceptions of faith found within the New Testament should without further consideration be accepted as legitimate parts of the Christian faith. A review of the history of doctrine proves conclusively that from the very beginning some conceptions of faith have disappeared, although they were a part of the biblical testimony; and that others have undergone more or less radical changes. This change is already evident within the New Testament. It is also obvious that the tremendous change in our conception of the universe has brought a change in the *formulation* of the affirmations of faith. But though all this must be granted, the inner quality of the Christian faith has been established once and for all by the fundamental testimony of the early witnesses. If the real constitution of Christianity is changed, Christianity ceases to exist. About this foundation in the deed of Christ it must be said, "other foundation can no man lay." In this respect the evangelical principle of Scripture as the "only infallible rule of faith and life" is forever valid.

But the theological investigation of Christian faith must be concerned also with the continuous testimony of faith throughout the centuries. Faith knows that the Spirit of God did not cease from his work at the completion of the New Testament. It speaks of the guidance of the Spirit into all the truth and of a continuous exploration of those riches which have been given us in Christ. The attention is drawn especially to those heroes of faith who have appeared in Christendom from time to time, and who have given powerful and original expression in sermons, prayers, and hymns to their own insight and experience. The theological investigation cannot pass these by, since it is focused on the Christian faith as a living whole.

In the relation between the primary and the continuous testimony of faith the fundamental testimony of the New Testament takes its place as a regulative principle. That which appears within Christianity in the later development must be in inner harmony with that conception of God and that fundamental principle of the relationship to God which is given in the work of Christ and proclaimed in the New Testament. In this sense Scripture is the *norma normans*, as evangelical Christianity has vigorously maintained. In the history of Christianity the Roman church has exalted the "tradition" as the central principle. But this has developed more and more into a caricature, because tradition has become dependent upon an external and legalistic ecclesiastical authority. The remedy for this situation is not the rejection of the living tradition and the substitution of Scripture as another legalistic authority, but rather the assertion that the living and continuous tradition must be evaluated according to the degree in which that Spirit is herein effectively working, which is qualitatively determined through that act of Christ to which the first and fundamental affirmations of faith bear witness.

5. *"The Sound Doctrine."*

The expression "sound doctrine" has sometimes been used in a disparaging sense. The reason for this has been twofold. On the one hand, the theology which most energetically emphasized the sound doctrine revealed in itself many shortcomings in regard to purity of teaching. On the other hand, the obscure and misleading distinction between *fides qua creditur* and *fides quae creditur,* common in the theology of a later period, created the impression that the content of faith was something relatively unimportant. It was not without good reason that our fathers placed such great emphasis on "the sound doctrine." The content of faith cannot be separated from faith itself. From one point of view faith depends entirely on what it believes about that God who is the object of faith. It is not unimportant for faith that the Christian relationship to God and the conception of God be "clearly and purely" conceived.

Christian history testifies to the fact that clarity in this matter is of immense importance for the life of faith. All the great revivals in the history of Christianity have been connected with a clearer insight into the nature of divine revelation. It soon becomes apparent that the neglect or contempt of the efforts to secure clarity in regard to the significance and content of faith leads to a weakening of faith itself. It can be stated that the uncertainty which has recently characterized the religious situation has been intimately connected with uncertainty in regard to the most central problems of Christian faith.

When it is stated that the purpose of theological work is to produce "sound doctrine," the function is exactly that which was stated in the first chapter. The function of theology is to state what Christianity really is and what is genuinely Christian. This is something given once and for all in that relationship to God and that conception of God which is founded on the deed of God in Christ. In this sense "the pure doctrine" is something in principle given once and for all. But it is at the same time an ideal goal toward which theology must always strive. The "teaching" of any one period in the history of the church cannot lay claim to have spoken the last word. The theological task is never finished. This is due to the fact that the object of theological study is so enormously rich that every new generation finds new treasures in it. It is true, however, that it is not a question of taking over certain concepts and formulas, but rather of fundamental ideas which must be expressed in terms of the new situation if they are to be understood at all. Each generation is confronted with the problem of interpreting the content of the Christian faith anew. The continuity lies in the fact that the fundamental principle and theme are the same in all ages. The Bible expresses this in the words: "Jesus Christ is the same yesterday, today, and even for ever" (Heb. 13:8). The changing aspects appear because the expressions change, and also because the fundamental Christian principle is engaged in a continuous struggle with rival powers. This struggle at times threatens to obscure the significance of faith, but it may also serve to reveal new aspects of its rich treasures. Theology must take this into serious consideration.

If theology therefore must continually work toward its ultimate and ideal goal, its attention must at the same time be fixed on that which has been given once and for all, and likewise on that work which has been accomplished in the interest of clarifying the content of faith. The continuous theological research must be in intimate contact with this work. The history of Christian thought is not only a history of apostasy from an originally pure and genuine Christianity (cf. § 6. 1). There is much in this history which appears both temporary and imperfect, but there are also gains which cannot, indeed, *must* not, be ignored. Theology may also gain a certain negative insight even from that which is imperfect. The history of Christian thought does not present simply a blurred confusion. There is in reality a deep, inner coherence, which is such that the vital viewpoints of faith itself break through wherever they have been suppressed. Each such experience brings new gains. But if theology consequently has something to learn from the whole history of Christian thought, it must be understood that it does not stop with the external formulas but penetrates to the ideas and purposes which these formulas are intended to express.

9. The Nature of the Affirmations of Faith

1. The affirmations of faith are *faith's* affirmation about God. They are therefore radically different from all rational metaphysics and cannot be connected with metaphysical propositions.

2. The affirmations of faith are, without exception, of a symbolic character.

3. The affirmations of faith are characterized by the fact that God is for faith both *Deus revelatus* and *Deus absconditus*. The consequence of this is not only that faith understands in part, but even that which faith grasps has an unfathomable character.

4. The affirmations of faith have, without exception, a certain paradoxical character. The paradoxical element is of a *religious*, not logical or metaphysical, nature. As soon as this is given a

logical or metaphysical character, there arises an irrationalism which is foreign to faith.

5. If theology really wants to understand faith, it must cease from all attempts to remove the paradoxical element. This applies both to the attempts of scholasticism to create a rationally consistent system and to the endeavor of idealistic theology to remove the cause of the paradox. The collection of affirmations of faith which theology presents must be made to appear as a tension-filled unity.

1. The Affirmations of Faith Are Not Metaphysical Statements.

When the nature of the affirmations of faith is to be determined, it must first of all be stated that these affirmations are affirmations of *faith*. This statement is tautological and may seem quite unnecessary. But in the history of theology it has frequently happened that this simple fact has been ignored. It is of utmost importance that a clear distinction be made between the affirmations of faith and rational metaphysics. Faith and its affirmation are one thing, metaphysics is something entirely different. That the differences are kept clearly in mind implies that the affirmations of faith are of a different nature than metaphysical theses, and that no combination of the theses of faith and metaphysics can be allowed.

Since Christian faith is a faith in God who has revealed himself in Christ, it has something very definite to say about this God. The affirmations of faith, therefore, have their foundation in the divine revelation and in nothing else. They do not rest on a rational demonstration, nor on a theoretical and logical argumentation. They are not in the nature of conclusions drawn from that which can be theoretically demonstrated about the world and humanity. Faith does not become certain on the basis of logical proofs. In contrast to theoretical knowledge the position taken by faith is "existential," to use Kierkegaard's terminology. From the point of view of man's activity, faith appears always as an audacious and daring decision. Faith's affirmations about God, therefore, do not represent a segment of theoretical knowledge which might complement and correct the rest of our knowledge. It is not a question about some metaphysical knowledge of "God and the supernatural" which might complete and perfect the empirical knowledge of "the sensual world."

In the pure rationalism of the last period of the Enlightenment the affirmations of faith were simply identified with rational metaphysics. Apart from this the history of theology shows two ways in which the affirmations of faith have been united with metaphysics. One of these received its classic formulation in scholasticism, in which the affirmations of faith were regarded as complements to a knowledge of God received in a purely rational manner. A distinction was made between *articuli mixti* and *articuli puri* (cf. § 1. 3). Among the "mixed articles" derived partly from *ratio* and partly from *revelatio* were especially the theses about God. Metaphysics therefore found a place in the very center of the conception of faith. The result was that faith was confused with a supposed theoretical knowledge, and that the nature of the Christian conception of God was seriously obscured. The other way is that of the more recent idealistically influenced theology which places the Christian faith into an already given rational conception of the world. Schleiermacher may stand as the best example of this tendency. When the Christian faith is incorporated into a monistic and evolutionary world view, the natural result is that the pressure of this view is felt at all points and that it produces a perversion of the central content of faith. If the purpose of theology is to understand faith, it has every reason to be careful lest the affirmations of faith are mixed with metaphysics. This confusion has done more than anything else to prevent theology from performing its proper function.

2. *The Symbolic Character of the Affirmations of Faith.*

Since God is the whole content of Christian faith, and since the expressions which must be used in faith's affirmations about this God belong to this finite world, the affirmations necessarily are of a figurative or symbolic character. God is to faith the Eternal who cannot be contained within the limits of time and space. But all the categories which may be used belong within these limits. Under such circumstances no words can be found which are adequate to the subject. If theology pretends to speak of God in adequate terms, it is a sure sign that the interpretation of faith has become metaphysical and that the God of faith has been changed into an "object" among other objects. A theology which adheres to its function of understanding and interpreting faith must realize fully that all its expressions are of symbolic nature.

All the words used by faith to designate the attributes of God are figures taken from personal life. God's love, his wrath, God as Father or as Judge, are all human figures of speech. Faith itself is quite conscious that these words are imperfect tools, that it can speak only in a groping way about that which belongs to God, and that the reality is something much more than the words suggest. But this does not imply that faith should regard these symbolic expressions as unnecessary, or less essential, or not serviceable, or that they do not reveal that which is essential to faith. Quite the contrary. The symbols are filled with the richest content. When faith speaks of God's love, forgiveness, wrath, and judgment, these expressions are concerned with that which is most real and essential to faith.

This fact that the affirmations of faith are of a symbolic character presents a twofold temptation. On the one hand, theology is tempted to seek to become independent of the figures and to remove from its exposition of the content of faith everything of anthropomorphic character. This tendency appears both in scholastic theology and especially in that theology which has been influenced by idealistic philosophy. The desire is to elevate faith into a more rarefied and intellectual atmosphere. The actual result, however, is that faith is reinterpreted along metaphysical lines, the vital content of the conception of God is lost, and theology finally becomes nothing but unrealistic abstractions. The attempt to remove these allegedly offensive anthropomorphisms does not serve the best interest of theology.

On the other hand, it is important that theology is conscious of the limitations and dangers which are presented by the symbolic character of the affirmations of faith. Theology must not succumb to the temptation to regard the symbolic expressions as adequate definitions. There is always a danger that these human figures of speech may bring the conception of God down into the temporal sphere of human measurements and judgments. This is absolutely contrary to the intention of Christian faith, since the idea of the distance between the divine and the human is its most fundamental axiom. It may be added that the history of theology records many a discussion which has been more confusing than clarifying just because the symbolic character of the affirmations of faith has not been adequately recognized. Thus, for example, it has been frequently debated whether it is legitimate to speak of God's "wrath," and the debate has been conducted on the assumption that this is a really adequate expression. When it has then been concluded that the use of this term is not proper, the result has been that some essential features of the Christian conception of God are in danger of being lost. The inescapable conclusion is, therefore, that these figures of speech are necessary, but they must not be accepted as adequate concepts.

3. The Comprehensible and the Incomprehensible.
The affirmations of faith are statements about the significance of God's revelation or self-disclosure. Faith declares what it has comprehended of this revelation. But God is to faith not only *Deus revelatus* but also *Deus absconditus* (cf. § 3. 5). God does not cease to be *absconditus* because he appears as *revelatus*. The problem is to find what this means and what the consequences are in regard to the nature of the affirmations of faith.

It is obvious that the idea of the hidden God tends to limit the scope of the affirmations. This means, in the first place, that faith does not perceive the whole, it does not look at it with the eyes of God. When speculative theology used to say that man with the help of divine revelation thinks God's own thoughts, such an assertion is understandable from the point of view of rational metaphysics, but it is completely foreign to faith. Faith does not, like the philosophy of immanence, remove the boundary between the divine and the human. Faith understands, but it understands *in part*. The claim cannot be made that faith is able to perceive the whole world development from the point of view of the divine government, or that it can survey the whole from God's point of view, or claim to be informed about the significance and purpose of everything that occurs. Faith does not have a ready answer to all the questions of the human spirit, nor can it solve all the riddles of human existence. The revelation of God means a revelation of God's inmost character, which provides a sure foundation for life; but it does not mean that all the obscurity which surrounds human life and history is removed. The desire to remove this obscurity would be a transgression of the limits which have been established as the conditions of the life of faith. Faith cannot be transformed into a rational world view. It is pertinent to mention the constant warnings of Luther against rationalistic speculations about "the hidden divine Majesty." Such speculations would be arrogance. This is the tempter's voice: "Ye shall be like God." To fall for this temptation is to commit *crimen laesae majestatis,* and implies that man brings the divine activity before the judgment seat of human reason and judicial concepts. *Deus absconditus* stands guard lest the limits of faith be transgressed, and emphasizes that under the conditions of this life faith only "understands in part."

But the idea of "the hidden God" does not mean merely that the understanding of faith has its insurmountable limitations. As has already been indicated (cf. § 3. 5), this idea is significant also in regard to the nature of these affirmations of faith. That which faith comprehends is likewise unfathomable, and the revelation itself is inscrutable. The New Testament often declares that the revelation is a revelation of a mystery (cf. Matt. 13:11; I Cor. 4:1; Eph. 1:9). But the decisive element is that revelation does not remove the mysteriousness. Two things must be emphasized in this connection. In the first place, every pregnant affirmation of faith bears the mark of incomprehensibility. When faith declares that God is love, it is an expression of something that faith "comprehends." But at the same time it is perfectly clear that the divine love just here appears as incomprehensible. The divine love is not of a rational character, and cannot be demonstrated in a rational fashion. It comes as a miracle. It cannot be measured according to human standards. It is perfectly obvious to faith that the love of God exceeds all human measurements, that human "love" can be so called only if it is an overflow of divine love, and that even then it is only a weak reflection of this divine love. When divine love reveals itself and meets man in action, it "passeth knowledge" (Eph. 3:19), and the peace it gives "passeth all understanding" (Phil. 4:7). In the second place we must note the relation which exists in the realm of faith between the comprehensible and the incomprehensible. On the basis of what has already been said it is clear that this relation cannot mean that the incomprehensible grows less and disappears in the measure that faith perceives the revelation. In reality the very opposite is true. The more faith penetrates into the realm of divine revelation, the more it is confronted with the unsearchable. When R. Otto in his book, *The Idea of the Holy,* seems to understand the "rational" and the "irrational" in faith as two magnitudes which counterbalance each other, the characteristic viewpoint of faith is not thereby very clearly expressed. The unfathomable is not something which lies by the side of the comprehensible, but that which faith perceives is by its nature incomprehensible even to faith. The deeper Luther penetrated into God's act of forgiveness whereby he enters into

100

communion with sinful man, and the more this divine activity appeared as something *contra rationem et legem,* the more clearly he perceived that here he confronted an inscrutable mystery, a miracle which defied all description. The "miracle" in a religious sense is not identical with that which one does not understand, but with that which faith perceives. The miraculous is inseparably connected with the perception of something of God's activity. Consequently it is not something which is to be abolished as soon as theology has accomplished its work of clarification, but rather something which appears more clearly in the measure that the viewpoint of faith becomes clearer.

4. The Paradoxical Character of the Affirmations of Faith.

"Every real revival in the history of the church has been connected with a consciousness of the paradoxical content of faith."[1] These paradoxes have found expression already in the New Testament. Paul saw clearly that the most central content of his preaching was "to the Jews a stumblingblock and to the Gentiles foolishness" (I Cor. 1:23).

It must be clearly realized that this paradoxical element does not belong simply to a few affirmations of faith, but that it pervades and characterizes the whole content. Nor is it a question of a temporary character of these affirmations which might be removed by the theological analysis; it belongs rather to their very nature. If theology succeeded in removing this characteristic it would constitute a reinterpretation of faith of such a nature that its declarations would no longer be affirmations of faith.

If, therefore, all the affirmations of faith have a paradoxical character, the reason is that directly or indirectly they are statements about God. Faith cannot avoid the use of paradox in speaking about God. It appears already in the very idea of revelation in so far as this retains its active character and as long as it is a question of that God who works in history. Faith per-

---

[1] G. Ljunggren, "The Paradox as a Theological Expression," *Swedish Theological Quarterly Review,* 1928, p. 333.

ceives God as the Eternal, exalted above all temporal change; but also as the One who is active in the changing phases of history and present in contemporary life. The resultant tension cannot be removed by an application of the philosophical concepts of transcendence and immanence without at the same time removing the living God of faith. A very important aspect of this tension appears in the fact that the God of faith is the Sovereign who at the same time is engaged in a struggle against hostile forces in history. A solution cannot be found by taking the edge off either point of view. The peculiar viewpoint of faith would be obscured, whether the attempt is made to incorporate the dualistic element into a monistic system, or to find a rational world view on the basis of a thoroughgoing dualism. The same tension is apparent in regard to the central content of the conception of God, the divine love. It may be illustrated by faith's understanding of divine forgiveness. God stands as judge in a radical opposition to sin, but at the same time he enters into communion with sinful man, who then, as Luther says, becomes at the same time just and a sinner (*simul iustus et peccator*). On the basis of this inner tension in the conception of God (cf. § 13) all the affirmations of faith might be examined. The same conditions would prevail everywhere. Two examples may be added. Sin is something given in the very condition of human life, and at the same time something completely voluntary. Faith is altogether a work of God, but it is at the same time man's choice and decision. Every attempt to harmonize these leads to a "synergism" which is foreign to faith.

It is obvious that the paradoxical character of the affirmations of faith places the most drastic demands on the theological analysis of the content of Christian faith. A review of the history of Christian thought indicates that two dangers lie particularly near. On the one hand theology is tempted to adjust or eliminate the tension in one way or another. On the other hand the danger is that the paradoxical character is misinterpreted, so that paradoxes are constructed for their own sake. This is just as foreign to faith as rationalistic reinterpretations.

The paradoxical character of the affirmations of faith is purely *religious*. It is misinterpreted and perverted when it becomes logical or metaphysical. The paradoxes then become an end in themselves, and the result is an irrationalism that is foreign to faith. It becomes necessary to hold together contradictory theoretical and metaphysical propositions. *Credo quia absurdum* becomes the watchword. The background of these ideas has generally been a scholasticism or idealism which has attempted to adjust or to eliminate the paradoxical character of the Christian affirmations of faith. But this "irrational" reaction is dependent on the methodology of the opposition. This was the case with the nominalistic theology prior to the Reformation, and the same is true, at least partly, of the dialectic theology of the present. A metaphysically oriented rationalism is opposed by a metaphysically oriented irrationalism. But this is something entirely different from the paradoxical character of the affirmations of faith. It is not a question here of holding fast to contradictory propositions of a logical and metaphysical nature. When, for example, God in forgiveness receives the sinner into communion with himself, this is a paradoxical act, but it is not at all a logically contradictory proposition (cf. § 33. 2). Here the paradoxical element is not found in theories but in the active revelation and in the tension-filled event itself. It is this event which is reflected in the conceptions of faith. There is nothing of absurdity in this tension. It is rather a question of a content which cannot be rationally motivated and which is so abundant that it cannot be contained within rational categories.

5. The Tension-filled Unity of the Content of Faith.

It was stated in the previous paragraph that theology is tempted to remove the inner tension which characterizes the Christian affirmations of faith. In the history of theology the principal attempts have been made by scholasticism and the theology influenced by idealism.

The essential mark of all scholastic theology is that it seeks to polish off those ideas of faith which stand in a relation of mutual tension in order to arrive at a rational adjustment. The most obvious examples of this process are found in Thomas Aquinas and in the scholasticism of the seventeenth century. In both of these the atonement is conceived of as an adjustment between God's love and his severe justice. The compensation given to God through Christ is the logical middle way between the exaction and remission of punishment (cf. § 26. 4). This means that both the divine love and the divine justice have been so adjusted that they can be logically held together. The divine love has lost its unmediated and spontaneous character, and has lost that paradoxical depth which transcends the judicial system as it enters into communion with the sinner. But divine justice has also lost its full power. If its demand is satisfied by a compensation, its barb has been removed and its radicalism broken. Scholasticism treats all the other affirmations of faith in the same way. The process of rational adjustment is everywhere in evidence. As an additional example its understanding of the idea of faith is a case in point. In one way or another the offensive tension between faith as altogether God's work and faith as man's choice and decision is lessened. The result is invariably a "synergism" in which neither point of view is properly recognized.

Idealistic theology has attempted to remove this tension by suppressing its causative factors. The tension between divine love and divine justice or wrath is here removed by suppressing the latter. The idea of God is humanized. Everything is concentrated around the divine "Fatherhood," and divine love is given a rational character, even though it is still derived from the "revelation."

It is obvious that the viewpoint characteristic of faith cannot be expressed either in scholasticism's adjustments or in idealism's removal of the cause of the tension. If theology is to understand and clarify the content of faith, it must obviously pay strict attention to this element of tension which belongs to the life of faith and expresses itself in the affirmations. Otherwise the interpretation of theology becomes a reinterpretation. But the presence of this tension does not at all mean that the content of faith lacks unity. Unity exists in spite of tension. Even if this unity cannot be expressed in a harmonious system of thought, faith nevertheless has a unified point of view which includes all tensions. The reason for this is that it is not concerned with metaphysical propositions which are logically contradictory and mutually incompatible. Faith's conception of God is in the last analysis not broken, and the divine activity is not divided but unified. The unity is the tension-filled unity of the active revelation. Faith is not rationalistic. Its nature is not metaphysical irrationalism. But its affirmations have a paradoxical character, since the wealth of the divine activity of revelation is so vast that it cannot be comprehended within the categories of human thought.

10. The Certainty of Faith

1. The certainty of faith is a certainty about that revelation of God whereby faith lives. The problem of the certainty of faith can be dealt with by theology only in so far as it analyzes and defines the nature of this certainty.

2. Certainty of faith does not possess a demonstrable character. The idea that it can be based on rational proofs is contrary to the nature of both science and faith.

3. Neither does the certainty of faith possess a *pragmatic* character. It cannot be certified by citing the significance of faith for other areas of life, or by showing that faith satisfies a human "need." A pragmatism of this kind is contrary to the theocentric character of faith and is apt to destroy rather than to establish certainty.

105

4. Nor is the certainty of faith *experiential* in the sense that the certainty of the God-relationship should be based on an inference drawn from past "experiences" and events. The individual experiences do not undergird faith, it is rather faith that undergirds and makes possible these experiences.

5. In the analysis of the nature of certainty of faith it must be noted that from one point of view faith is audacious; but, on the other hand, it must be emphasized that its audacious *yes* is an inescapable necessity, the subjugation of man by the revelation of God through which he "is led away from himself." In this sense the *testimonium spiritus sancti internum* determines the nature of this certainty.

1. Theology and the Problem of Certainty of Faith.

The problem of Christian certainty must receive notice in this part which deals with faith and theology. There are few problems that have received a more questionable treatment from the point of view of both faith itself and scientific study. The history of theology is full of so-called apologetic attempts which display as much ignorance of the nature and conditions of faith as they are questionable from a theological and scientific point of view. Under these circumstances the manner in which this problem can be treated by theology must be defined.

The same principle must govern here as in all theological research, which is that the only purpose is to understand and clarify the nature of Christian faith. The problem of Christian certainty must be treated from the same point of view. The intention must not be to present some kind of "apology" for faith or in a general way to demonstrate its "truth." The problem is rather to analyze and clarify the nature of that certainty which can be observed in faith itself.

It has already been shown that faith and divine revelation are correlative concepts (cf. § 2. 2). The certainty of faith cannot have reference to anything other than to that revelation of

God which manifests itself to faith and by which faith lives. An investigation into the problem of the certainty of faith must under the circumstances have no other purpose than to define the nature of the relationship of faith to this revelation and to indicate how this relation appears to faith itself. The theological investigation cannot go beyond this point. To do so would be at the same time to transgress the boundaries of theology.

2. The Certainty of Faith is Not Demonstrable.

The certainty of Christian faith is not dependent upon the demonstrable character of divine revelation. The idea that scientific studies and investigations should provide a solid foundation for faith and give it certainty is contrary to the nature of both science and faith. If this were indeed possible, it would mean that science, within the empirical reality which is the object of its study, could discover something of that revelation of which faith speaks. The discoveries of science would in that case verify faith. But this would obviously be to ask something of science which it cannot give without ceasing to be scientific. Whether it be a question of a scientific investigation of nature or history, such a study cannot penetrate to that which is decisive for faith—the revelation of God. What has been said in section 4 about historical research is just as true in regard to the study of nature. God is not found by telescopes and chemical experiments any more than through a methodical analysis of humanity's historical documents. By its very nature science must reject such ideas.

But faith must do the same thing from its own point of view. Faith is not conscious of having originated in or of resting upon any argumentation of a theoretic and demonstrative character. It is, however, fully conscious of its character as an audacious personal decision and a bold *yes*. This may be expressed by saying that for faith revelation is always an unveiling of Reality in secret. Every attempt to demonstrate theoretically the reality and universality of revelation is absolutely foreign to faith and contrary to its fundamental point of view. Even if some results could be obtained in this way, these could produce only a metaphysically defined idea of God, which is something entirely different from that living and active revelation of which faith speaks. Consequently the affirmations of faith about God and his revelation do not contain any theoretical knowledge which could be added as a correction and complement to that gained through investigation (cf. § 9). From its own point of view faith must decline the gifts of science in so far as it presumes to impart something of the revelation of God, since such a revelation would be entirely different from that whereby faith lives.

3. *Certainty of Faith is Not Pragmatic.*

If then scientific study cannot give a decisive testimony for the certainty of faith, it might easily be suggested that the defense of the Christian faith must be made on the basis of the significance which this faith has in the various areas of life. Such pragmatic arguments have been widely used in Christian apologetics. It can hardly be denied that Christian faith has demonstrated its value both in the general cultural life and especially in the sphere of ethics. As a matter of fact it is also important that these values be studied and clarified. But it is quite a different matter to base Christian certainty on the consideration of the significance of faith for the various areas of life. It is impossible to complete such a demonstration. On the one hand, it is obvious that by this method one arrives only at a postulated certainty. The achievements of faith are noted and the conclusion is drawn that the power which has produced these must be inviolate. It goes without saying, however, that such a reference to human achievements of faith hardly affords the desired security; but, on the contrary, the continuous search for external results must lead finally to a constant insecurity. On the other hand, it must be said that the evidence here adduced is not congruous with faith itself. It implies that the Christian faith should be evaluated and verified according to other criteria than those which are essential to faith itself. The dominant principle of faith is communion with God, and faith must unconditionally decline to be judged in a court in which this principle is not recognized as supreme. It does not recognize civilization, culture, or any other human values as the court of last appeal. Through its communion with God it is lifted up above everything that belongs to the world, and in it there is always something other-worldly and supramundane. Under such conditions it would be impossible to accept the judgment of the court of civilization and human values as decisive. A judgment from this court would be decisive only if faith were nothing more than a world-affirming optimism. It generally becomes apparent that the attempt to maintain Christian faith by emphasizing its universally cultural significance is easily combined with a reinterpretation of faith along this line. But then it happens, strangely and characteristically enough, that this reinterpretation of faith undermines and finally destroys even that significance which faith actually has in reference to human values. This significance is inseparably connected with the fact that faith is *not* merely a world-affirming optimism, and that it does *not* establish in the world a new immanent goal in addition to others. The real significance of faith depends entirely on the fact that it lives in "a kingdom which is not of this world."

In this connection the attempts to verify the certainty of faith through its ethical effects must be noted. It is especially important to note this "ethical proof," because in the recent period of theological study it has been frequently regarded as being in the last analysis decisive. The claim is thus made, as for instance by O. Kirn,[1] that the verification of Christian faith is to be found in that the moral demand of Christianity is the consummation of the moral testimony of conscience, and the Christian faith is the necessary condition for the realization of the moral task. The moral ideal which is contained in the Christian idea of the Kingdom of God is the *absolute* moral ideal, and

[1] O. Kirn, *Grundriss der evangelischen Dogmatik*, 5th ed., I. 31.

Christian faith appears as that power which actualizes this ideal and guarantees its realization within ourselves and others. This is the validation of the Christian faith. It cannot, of course, be said that a reference to the moral power of Christianity is unwarranted and unessential. It must rather be acknowledged that the emphasis on the ethical character and effects of Christianity throws light on one of its very important phases. Whatever value may be given to the argumentation here recorded, it cannot be denied that Christianity implies a heightening of the moral demand, and that it has proved to be the mightiest ethical power. But the question is whether this constitutes a decisive argument in regard to the certainty of faith. It must rather be maintained that this argumentation, if it claims to be decisive, does not lead to certainty, but to continuous uncertainty. The certainty of faith cannot be based on the ethical effects of faith. What would this ultimately imply? Evidently that our certainty of faith would be entirely dependent upon our ability to fulfill the ethical demand which Christianity presents. A real certainty of faith would then be possible only when it has been definitely established that the ethical demand for perfection has been fully met. It is clear that this can lead to nothing else than a constant uncertainty. It is just as evident that this argumentation does not agree with the testimony of faith itself, and that it leads straight to moralism and to that "work-righteousness" against which the deeper testimony of faith reacts most vigorously. Even in this case faith has been judged and evaluated from without, not according to the points of view which are determinative for faith itself. The ethical "proof" could after all claim to give the decisive verdict only if Christianity becomes pure ethics. It is consequently very typical that this "proof" has been regarded as so important in the most recent period of theological study. This indicates how real the danger has been that Christianity may be completely transformed and become purely ethical.

Faith itself must reject all attempts to save faith by transforming it into something other than what it really is. It might be in the interest of faith to see and ponder its significance for the various areas of life, and especially for the moral life. But faith cannot buy its right to exist by selling its birthright for a mess of pottage. It is such a transaction which faith perceives in the attempt to make its significance for the various areas of life central, in utter disregard of that which faith itself conceives of as the beginning and the end, the Alpha and Omega, namely, communion with God.

4. Certainty of Faith—Certainty by Experience.

When in the interest of apologetics enthusiastic references have been made to "experience," the idea has generally been that these experiences should become a surety for faith and a guarantee of its security. In this sense the expression, "experiential proofs of faith," has been used. It is obvious that in so far as certainty belongs to the Christian life, it must be connected with experience. It is after all a part of human life. It is, however, indubitable that the nature of Christian certainty is completely misinterpreted if it is made to find its support and basis in the religious experiences and in the religious feelings as such. This would obscure the fact that faith knows no other basis than the divine revelation. If the strength and intensity of the religious feelings were made the basis of certainty, it would rest on something human, just as much as is the case when certainty is predicated on man's moral transformation and his ethical qualifications. In reference to certainty Luther has spoken a classic word: *haec est ratio, cur nostra theologia certa sit: quia rapit nos a nobis et ponit nos extra nos, ut non nitamur viribus, conscientia, sensu, persona, operibus nostris* . . . ("This is the reason why our theology is certain: because it snatches us away from ourselves and places us outside of ourselves, lest we rest upon men, conscience, feelings, character, our own work . . .").[2] The certainty of faith does not depend upon anything human; rather, faith "snatches us away from ourselves and places us outside of our-

---

[2] W. A., 40, 1, p. 589.

selves." It is just as impossible to depend on experiences (*sensu, persona*) as it is to build on our own works or on "work-right-eousness." In contrast to any such argumentation Luther points to the divine revelation, to "the word and promise of God."

The testimony of experience cannot therefore be accepted in such a way that the experience is separated from divine revelation as something given in and by itself. The certainty of faith about the revelation is not founded on personal experiences, nor is it a conclusion based on these experiences. Faith does not find God at the end of a logical syllogism. All experiences have their foundation in the divine revelation as far as faith is concerned. Faith is a faith in the divine revelation, not in personal experiences. This is fully attested by an analysis of the testimony of Christian life. Such an analysis indicates that the certainty of faith does not simply come and go, depending upon the changing religious experiences, and that faith does not rely on these changing experiences, but only on God. Consequently faith *can* persist in the midst of tribulation and distress—yes, even when the experiences of life speak a language directly opposite to that of faith. Faith is not confuted by this. Even under those circumstances faith finds expression in a "nevertheless." The living and striving faith finds that even these experiences which endanger its existence serve as an incentive to hold fast still more securely to that God from whom no temporal distress can separate the believer. Thus Christian certainty finds classic expression in the Johannine word: "Said I not unto thee, that, if thou believedst, thou shouldst see the glory of God?" (John 11:40). There is a faith that does not see, and yet believes. Because faith is not a faith in experiences, but altogether a faith in God alone, it can live even under those circumstances when God seems most remote, and can carry on to new experiences and a new vision of "the glory of God."

5. *The Nature of Christian Certainty.*

The examination of the various attempts to prove and substantiate faith which has been made in the previous paragraphs may appear as a process of undressing, until faith stands naked and in want of all protective covering. In reality it is self-evident that faith cannot in the last analysis rely on any such line of argumentation. Faith is communion with God. When faith is true to its own nature, it is clear that no certainty of faith can arise and continue except as an inner conviction of being overwhelmed by God, or as an encounter with something which validates itself as a "revelation" of God. All other argumentation is merely a substitute. If this foundation is wanting, all other supports are in vain; if it is there, all other supports are superfluous. The foundation of faith is the divine revelation; and the certainty of faith is characterized by an inner conviction that this revelation really is a *divine* revelation, or, in other words, by that which faith calls "the testimony of the Holy Spirit," *testimonium spiritus sancti internum.* Christian faith has from the beginning again and again pointed to this testimony of the Spirit. The decisive element is, according to Paul, that "the Spirit himself beareth witness with our spirit" (Rom. 8:16), because "the things of God none knoweth, save the Spirit of God. But we received not the spirit of the world, but the spirit which is from God; that we might know the things that were freely given to us of God" (I Cor. 2:11 ff.). In a similar way the Johannine writings speak at length of that testimony which "the Spirit of truth" gives (cf. I John 4:13; 5:10). "Consequently," says Luther, "God must tell you in your heart: this is God's word." It is true that sometimes in the history of Christian thought this testimony has been co-ordinated with other foundations of certainty by reference to a multitude of reasons supporting the divine authority of the Scriptures, but this cannot be justified. The proof of which we are here speaking cannot be either replaced or complemented by attempts to verify the divine revelation in any other way.

The nature of Christian certainty can be defined only by delineating those features of faith which are relevant and important in this connection. We have already called attention to the twofold aspects of faith. On the one hand it is a daring decision, and on the other hand it is man's subjection by God.

Faith, as decision, as a daring and audacious *yes*, stands guard against all attempts to make certainty of faith secure by means of external proofs. The decision in question lies beyond all such argumentation. The revelation of God cannot be certified by any rational arguments. It is, as stated before, a revelation in secret, a revelation which appears in the guise of history. The revealed God is also the hidden God. This is true of everything that is called a revelation of God, and consequently also of the revelation in Christ. In him, too, the revelation of God appears in a humble form and in the guise of history. This character of the revelation cannot be reasoned away by constructing a humanly idealized Christ. This would lead only to a fatal confusion between the divine and "the highest human." There is always something of audacity and bold discovery when faith perceives in the guise of history the direct voice of God.

But the interpretation of the nature of faith could not be more thoroughly perverted than if, on the basis of what has now been said, it is concluded that faith's *yes* to the voice of God should have a subjective and arbitrary character. This is completely contrary to the testimony of faith about itself. We must listen very carefully to this testimony if we are to be able to understand and define the nature of Christian certainty. It is not within the realm of possibility to suggest that man should place the alleged voice of God before his own bar of judgment and decide whether or not it is a real voice of God. This voice meets man rather with an authority which he cannot escape and from which there is no appeal. It overwhelms and subdues him with an inner compulsion which he cannot escape. That which is decisive for faith is that man is vanquished and, in Luther's words, snatched out from himself. In this inner, inescapable compulsion the certainty of faith is hidden. This is *testimonium spiritus sancti internum.*

Parts II, III, IV

THE CONTENT OF CHRISTIAN FAITH

INTRODUCTION

11. The Outline

The following exposition of the content of Christian faith will be divided into three chief parts: The Living God, The Act of God in Christ, and the Church of God.

It has already been stated (§ 6. 3) that the essence of Christianity is characterized by the fact that its entire content is referred to and defined by the act of God in Christ. The task now at hand is to clarify what is essential to Christian faith: its conception of that God who is the sovereign ruler in the realm of faith; its view of the act of God in Christ; the realization of the God-relationship; and the position of that relationship in the communion within which faith lives and is nourished. Part II begins with a presentation of the essential features of the Christian conception of God centered in the divine Agape, and then proceeds to define faith's conception of the divine activity in its three parts: salvation, creation, and judgment. On the basis of this exposition Part III considers in more detail how the divine Agape establishes the God-relationship. The subject of the first division of this part is the divine Agape's act of reconciliation in Christ; of the second, that divine act of forgiveness which establishes the Christian relationship to God. Finally, Part IV presents the continuous activity of God which creates the communion of saints, and then proceeds to examine the constitutive factors of this communion and the relation of the individual Christian to it.

It may be necessary to indicate briefly why this particular order has been adopted, and especially why the Christian conception of God has been placed first. Since we have already declared in previous chapters that the foundation of Christian faith has been laid in the context of revelation dominated by the act of Christ, it might be assumed that this act of Christ which is definitive for the conception of God ought to be placed first. But from a systematic point of view this is not necessary. It is absolutely necessary, however, that the revelation in Christ be allowed to give the decisive character to the conception of God here presented.

From another point of view it might be suggested that the presentation ought to begin with the communion which has been created by the act of God. It could be pointed out that this communion has a fundamental significance for the individual's faith and life, just as Luther says, that the church is the mother who bears and fosters each individual Christian. Such an outline would no doubt be the most logical, if the task of theology were to give a psychological and genetic description of the origin of Christian faith. But its purpose is quite different, viz., to clarify the meaning and significance of Christian faith. Since this is the purpose, we begin with a presentation of the conception of God, so that even the order of subjects indicates that God is sovereign in the realm of faith, that Christian faith is thoroughly theocentric, and that all its affirmations are affirmations about God. The character of the conception of God is decisive for the whole content of Christian faith.

In other respects the outline of the subject speaks for itself. The main purpose has been that the method of presentation might to some extent indicate the inner, organic connection between the various phases of Christian faith.

A remark may be added relative to the treatment of the eschatological problems. It was formerly common to treat these questions in a final chapter. This method could be interpreted to mean that eschatology constitutes the highest and final point in the content of faith. But in reality the result was that the subject came to be regarded as an appendix to the main discussion. In recent expositions of the Christian faith the eschatological point of view has, as a rule, been sadly neglected. Even though these problems are not directly discussed in any special section of this work, the intention is not to obscure their significance for Christian faith. Since they are here treated in various places in all parts of this work, it becomes clear that the eschatological viewpoints must not be regarded as an appendage, but rather represent an essential aspect which belongs to the whole content of Christian faith, and that Christian faith and life as a whole are eschatologically determined.

Part II

THE LIVING GOD

DIVISION A

THE CHRISTIAN CONCEPTION OF GOD

12. Holiness as the Background of the Conception of God

1. The expression, the Holy One, is synonymous with God. Holiness does not express the content of the Christian concept of God, but is that background without which the idea of God cannot be projected. Everything which belongs to God and his realm bears the imprint of holiness, and appears, therefore, in relation to everything human as separate and wholly other.

2. As such, holiness has a fourfold significance. It asserts the purely religious character of the idea of God (in contrast to moralism and ethicism), the majesty of God (in contrast to eudaemonism), and his unfathomableness (in contrast to rationalism), and it repudiates all attempts to identify the divine and the human (in contrast to mysticism).

1. The Background of the Concept of God.

The word "holy" is such a fundamental word in religion that "the Holy One" is accepted as synonymous with God. In the religious language it denotes fundamentally that which is separate.[1] Its central position in the religious vocabulary depends on how faithfully this original and basic significance is preserved. "The holy" appears as the opposite of the profane, and as something wholly other than that which is this-worldly and relative.

That God is called the Holy One implies primarily that there

[1] Cf. N. Söderblom, *Gudstrons uppkomst*, pp. 181 ff.

is a definite line of demarcation between the divine and the merely human, and that God is God and man is man. The holiness of God stands as a guardian against all attempts to weaken and obliterate this line. The divine is something other than the human, and must not be confused with "humanity at its highest."

When the word "holy" is used in connection with God, it is important that it retain its original religious significance. It is well known that the idea of the holy has often been reinterpreted in the direction of ethics, in an attempt to identify it with moral perfection. It is indeed unquestionable that the idea of the holy in reference to the conception of God strongly emphasizes also moral perfection. But as holiness is reinterpreted in the direction of morality, sin is likewise interpreted moralistically and loses its religious orientation. It is therefore, as stated, very important that holiness retain its original and purely religious meaning. Only when the separation between the divine and the human implied in holiness is given due consideration, and the divine is allowed to appear as unconditioned majesty in relation to the human, can holiness be of fundamental significance for the Christian conception of God.

Even if the Holy One is accepted as synonymous with God, it does not mean that we have thereby obtained a living and significant conception of the God of faith. We may not even say that this holiness constitutes a divine "attribute" which could be compared with other divine attributes. It is not accidental that holiness is more easily defined in negative than in positive terms. If holiness were understood as a divine attribute among others, as has often been done, this definition would be both too ample and too limited. Too ample, inasmuch as the idea of holiness is not significant simply because it is intended to give a certain concrete content to the conception of God; and too limited, for holiness is not confined to any one phase or feature, but belongs to the idea of God as a whole.

Holiness is the background and the atmosphere of the conception of God. This word background may seem to minimize its significance, but this is certainly not the case, for this background is first of all absolutely necessary. Without it there would in reality be no conception of God. The perspective would lack the depth which is absolutely necessary if the idea of God is to be properly projected. Holiness is the foundation on which the whole conception of God rests. In addition it gives a specific tone to each of the various elements in the idea of God and makes them parts of a fuller conception of *God*. Every statement about God, whether in reference to his love, power, righteousness, and so on, ceases to be an affirmation about God when it is not projected against the background of his holiness. Only when holiness colors the concept of love do we understand that we are dealing with divine love (cf. § 14).

The God of Christian faith is, therefore, not less holy than the God of the Old Testament, even though the word itself may not appear as frequently in the New Testament. The relation between the Old and the New Testaments could hardly be more grossly misinterpreted than by setting the Fatherhood of God in opposition to the idea of God as the Holy One. Holiness is the obvious presupposition of the testimony of primitive Christianity concerning God. It is significant that the first petition of the Lord's Prayer reads: "Hallowed be thy name." It is also significant that the word holy, or its cognates, almost automatically enters the Christian vocabulary when we talk about something which belongs to the sphere of God: Christ, the Holy One of God; the Holy Spirit; the Holy Christian Church; Holy Writ; holy sacraments, and so on. Neither is it an accident that the Swedish Mass begins with the *Trisagion,* which constitutes an important background for the whole subsequent worship service.

2. Holiness as a Sentinel.

When holiness constitutes the background of the idea of God, it guarantees that every affirmation about God retains its *purely religious* character. It has been customary to divide the attributes of God into metaphysical and ethical categories, but this division, although it may be serviceable for a rationally constructed idea, is entirely inappropriate to a Christian conception of God. Metaphysical scholastic theology, both before and after the Reformation, had no inner contact with faith itself, and consequently lost itself in abstract and unrealistic speculations about the essence of God. It can readily be understood that as a reaction to this approach "the ethical attributes" should be made central, as in the theology of the nineteenth century, but the result was a moralism which left out of religion much that was essential. When A. Ritschl found that holiness could not be contained within the ethical categories and consequently eliminated it from his conception of religion, it indicates how strong this moralistic tendency really was. This moralistic limitation of religion cannot be overcome by adding the metaphysical attributes to the ethical. This is not a guarantee that the religious character of the conception of God will be adequately expressed. The only method whereby this can be accomplished is that holiness really be allowed to appear as the background of every statement that is made about God. Then, and only then, is there a guarantee that abstract and irrelevant speculations will be eliminated, and that religion will not be transformed into ethics.

Holiness stands as a sentinel against all eudaemonistic and anthropocentric interpretations of religion. Holiness meets us as unconditional majesty. Every attempt to transform Christianity into a religion of satisfaction and enjoyment is thereby doomed to failure. Egocentricity masquerading in the robes of religion is excluded. Faith in God cannot be measured and evaluated from the point of view of human happiness and needs, even if these concepts be ever so refined and spiritualized. God is not someone whom faith employs with an eye to the higher or lower advantages which he may be able to furnish; nor is he someone we can call upon in order that our needs and desires may be met. Even if anthropocentricity should disguise itself in the most clever costume, it will inevitably be unmasked by the Holy One. Every tendency to make God serve human interests is irrevocably doomed. When Ritschl found the value of religion in its ability to give man "dominion over the world" and spiritual *Selbsbehauptung*, he misinterpreted Christian faith in an anthropocentric direction. To meet God as the Holy One is to be placed under a supreme compulsion, and to be confronted by a power advancing in sovereign majesty. If God is the Holy One, he is also the One on whom we are absolutely dependent. We are in his power, not he in ours. He is the undisputed ruler in the realm of faith.

Finally, the idea of holiness emphasizes the separation between the divine and the human in opposition to both rationalistic and mystical interpretations of religion. Rationalistic speculation and mysticism are, to be sure, very different. They have, however, more in common than is at first apparent, and it is not accidental that mysticism very often runs parallel to rationalistic speculation. Each in its own way tends to eliminate the distinction between the divine and the human. When rationalistic speculation with profane familiarity attempts to capture the divine in human thought forms and to make the spirit of man think the thoughts of God, the idea of holiness resists such presumption, because it will not let us forget that the revealed God is at the same time the hidden God (cf. § 9. 3). But it is likewise opposed to the elimination of the separation between the divine and the human by that mysticism whose goal is identity and the absorption of the human into the divine. To stand before the Holy One is something entirely different from being absorbed into the infinite where all differences are obliterated and disappear.

The idea of holiness is well expressed in the hymn by Reginald Heber:

> Holy, Holy, Holy! though the darkness hide Thee,
> Though the eye of sinful man Thy glory may not see,
> Only Thou art holy: there is none beside Thee
> Perfect in power, in love, and purity.

13. Tension and Unity in the Conception of God

1. The tension between different phases which characterizes the conception of God cannot be resolved by a rational compromise between the fundamental religious ideas, nor can it be eliminated by a humanizing of the idea of God.

2. If the Christian idea of God nevertheless appears as a unity, it is a unity of opposites. Only in such a tension-filled synthesis can Love appear as the last word of faith about God, and consequently as the governing center of the Christian conception of God.

1. The Tension.

When, by way of introduction to our discussion of the content of faith, the subject of tension and unity in the conception of God is here introduced, we may be permitted to refer to what has already been stated in principle about the paradoxical character of the affirmations of faith (cf. § 9. 4, 5). The fundamental principles there enunciated must now be applied as we sketch the Christian conception of God. The word in I John, "God is Love," tells us what is the center and focus of this conception. This is the most essential and important statement that can be made about God. But it is one thing that love is maintained as the center of the Christian conception of God, it is quite a different thing *how* it is maintained. It can never be sufficiently emphasized that this latter, *how divine love is treated,* is the most important question of all. That Christian faith centers in divine love as the essential element in the Christian conception of God is of utmost and decisive importance. The history of theology makes it very evident that this divine love has easily been interpreted in such a way that its depth has been lost and its distinctive features obscured. This is inevitably the case when, on the basis of love, the attempt is made to construct a uniform, homogeneous and rational idea of God; or, in other words, as soon as the inner tension which characterizes the Christian conception of God is resolved or eliminated. The peculiar viewpoint of the Christian faith cannot be consistently maintained unless this tension is seriously taken into consideration. It then becomes impossible to arrive at a rationally constructed concept of God. But in its stead appears a living figure whose features change and clash one with the other, but whose character nevertheless, as far as faith is concerned, bears the mark of unity, the living God.

In regard to the Christian affirmations about God three thematic ideas may be distinguished: the idea of *power*, to which a number of expressions belong, such as omnipotence, sovereignty, eternity, omnipresence, omniscience, etc.; the idea of *judgment*, which deals with God's avenging and condemning justice, his wrath, etc.; the idea of *love*, which contains a number of varying expressions such as goodness, mercy, grace, etc. The relation between these three ideas has always been a source of difficulty to theology, because, humanly speaking, there seems to be a tension between them. This tension can be illustrated most readily by asking the following questions. How can God's love for men co-exist with his radical condemnation of sin? How can God be Power and Love at the same time? If all power belongs to him, then this power does not seem to possess the character of love. But if God is love, then this love does not seem to be the sovereign power in the world. When theology has had to take account of this tension within the relationship between God and man, it has (cf. § 9) sometimes adopted an irrationalism which is satisfied to place contradictory, theoretical propositions side by side (metaphysical irrationalism), and at other times has tried to readjust or to eliminate the tension by a process of rationalization.

We have stated in previous chapters that all scholastic theology is characterized by the attempt to adjust the tension rationally, and that the theology influenced by idealistic philosophy has always tried to eliminate it. These attempts must now be more closely analyzed. The attempt of *scholastic* theology to effect a rational adjustment has always been characterized by *compromise*. The scholasticism of both the Middle Ages and the post-Reformation era abounds in such compromises. One example of this has already been given (§ 9. 5), namely, the rational adjustment of the tension between divine love and retributive justice in the Latin theory of the atonement. The result is that both love and justice lose their radical opposition to evil. But it may also be added that, although the sharp point of "justice" is broken, it nevertheless appears as primary in relation to love. Divine love is incorporated into a system of retributive justice; it is governed by *iustitia*. Love is not free until justice has been given due compensation. In the same way scholastic theology attempts by compromise to adjust the tension between power and love. Thomistic theology furnishes abundant illustrations. In his interpretation of the divine power Thomas makes use of the category of cause. The "omnipotence" of God means that God is *causa prima,* and consequently he is the cause of everything that occurs. When divine love is incorporated into this scheme of cause and effect, it becomes, so to speak, naturalistic. From this point of view it is not strange that divine "grace" is obscurely defined as substantial "powers," and that thus love is demoted. But it may also happen that the theology of compromise leads to an infringement on the divine power. Thus man's salvation and "justification" are not completely the work of divine love. Human "merits" must also be given a place. Then, no matter how closely these merits are circumscribed, the divine sovereignty is limited. The post-Reformation scholasticism, which at least *desired* to maintain the *sola gratia* of the Reformation, was naturally strongly opposed to the medieval idea of merits. But its very scholasticism forced it into making compromises. This can be seen in the idea, popular in orthodox circles, that God justifies man *ex praevisa fide*. Finally, it is characteristic of all scholasticism that it attempts to give an explanation of how the evil in the world can co-exist with the divine will. This is connected with the desire to extend faith into a rational explanation of the universe. It is self-evident that this must lead to a minimizing of the radical opposition of the divine will to evil.

The theology which began with the Enlightenment and flourished during the eighteenth and nineteenth centuries attempted to remove the tension by humanizing the idea of God. In contrast to scholasticism it accepted divine love as the central content of "the Christian conception of God." The program of this whole theological approach was expressed in the title of a book published in the eighteenth century: "The Doctrine of God's Fatherly Love is the Fundamental Doctrine of the Christian Religion." Thus Schleiermacher also summed up his theory of the reflection of the divine "attributes" in "the pious state of the soul" in this statement: God is love (*Gott ist die Liebe*). From a purely formal point of view there can be no objection to this. Schleiermacher's statement is formally identical with the Johannine word: God is Agape, which includes everything that is essential to the New Testament as a whole. But here we must use the criterion that the most important question in relation to the conception of God is *how* the divine love is brought in. It cannot be denied that the dominant theology during the eighteenth and nineteenth centuries often described divine love in such a way that its sovereign majesty, its radical opposition to evil, and its unfathomable depth were obscured. The idea of God became superficial by being humanized. There has been an abundant proclamation of the love of God which has lacked power and firmness. There have been two reasons for this superficiality. In the first place, the radical opposition of divine love to evil has been obscured and broken—which, from another point of view, means that the conception of sin has been weakened or lost. In the second place, the attempt has been made, on the basis of idealistic philosophy, to incorporate Christian faith into a monistic and evolutionistic world view. If it is assumed, on the basis of such a monistic metaphysic, that divine love is reflected everywhere, the danger is that it loses its character, and

128

also that the supposed everywhere becomes nowhere. Under these circumstances men were unable to comprehend the difficult conditions under which divine love operates in human life, and became insensible to the deepest perceptions of Christian faith, which sees divine love as a cross-bearing love engaged in a bitter struggle and winning its victory by a self-giving sacrifice. We may summarize, therefore, the result of our investigation in this statement: In the measure that the tension is removed, divine love loses its most significant content.

2. *The Unity of the Conception of God.*

If theology really desires to understand and interpret faith, it cannot either rationally adjust or eliminate the tension between the various ideas in the conception of God. Such an interpretation would be reinterpretation. But neither can theology be satisfied with presenting discordant metaphysical propositions. This would not express the peculiar nature of faith, and its active point of view would be transformed into a foreign metaphysic. The idea of God which is revealed through the activity of revelation contains an inevitable tension, but this does not destroy its unity. Faith's conception of God is not divided or disparate —it has a center, or, as faith itself expresses it, a heart. Its final and most exalted affirmation about that God who is active in Christ is the word of God's Agape. The "nature" of God is, as Luther says, *eitel Liebe.* But theology cannot properly analyze the significance of this love without taking seriously into account the tension in which this love appears to faith. The divine love cannot be incorporated into either a legalistic or a monistic and rationalistic system. It acts *contra legem.* But this does not mean that the radical opposition of the divine will toward evil disappears; it is rather expressed more emphatically. The divine love disrupts the system of monistic rationalism: God's Agape under historical conditions strives against opposing forces. And yet, the divine sovereignty does not disappear, it stands forth in unconditional majesty. In the last analysis all the affirmations

129

of Christian faith about God are concentrated around the central idea of God's Agape. This Agape destroys all legalistic and rational systems. But at the same time the condemning God who judges is the God of love, and the sovereign power is the power of love. Faith cannot penetrate deeper than to this divine Agape. The more clearly faith perceives its activity, the more it sees itself confronted by the unfathomable and the paradoxical. Every theology which dissolves the tension of this divine Agape obscures its unfathomableness and misinterprets faith. But the same is true also of the theology which replaces the religious paradox with a metaphysical irrationalism.

14. God is Love

1. The inmost character of the Christian conception of God is determined by Christ and his work. This implies that here faith finds the God who seeks and enters into communion with sinful man; or, in other words, a love which destroys that system in which legalism and rationalism would incorporate the relationship between God and man. This explosive power of love is a fundamental Christian theme.

2. When love therefore appears as the dominant center of the Christian conception of God, the peculiar nature of this love is revealed in its spontaneity and its self-giving. The divine love is not called forth by anything outside itself. Its character is defined by the Cross.

3. Although the divine love is most easily perceived in the Cross, it appears there at the same time as most incomprehensible.

1. The Love of God as a Fundamental Christian Theme.

The Christian idea of God is not a vague and undefined conception. On the contrary, Christian faith has something very definite to say about God's relation to men, and therefore also about the character of the divine will and the divine person.

The character of God is decisively defined by Christ and his work. When faith looks at Christ, it beholds in him the God who imparts himself to men. When faith speaks about Christ as the One in whom the divine will is incarnate and that he is "of the same substance" with the Father, the "substance" or nature of God must then be defined by what faith finds in Christ. If this is not so, then all "Christology" is merely empty formulas (cf. § 3. 3; § 5. 1).

The essential element in the fellowship created by the work of Christ is that God here seeks sinful man and enters into communion with him. This is the most important characteristic of the Christian fellowship between God and man. If that were removed, the fellowship would lose its character and would cease to exist. Consequently it must be accepted as a fundamental Christian idea.

This implies that the inmost character of the conception of God is love. Consequently, every affirmation about God becomes an affirmation about divine love. Nothing can be said about God, his power, his opposition to evil, or anything else, which is not in the last analysis a statement about his love. The Johannine statement, "God is agape," summarizes not only that which is essential for the New Testament, but also everything that can be said about the character of the Christian idea of God. No other divine "attributes" can be co-ordinated with love, nor can these express something that would cancel love. Nothing more decisive can be stated about the Christian conception of God than the affirmation: "God is agape." Paul agrees with John. His whole Christian faith is expressed in this word: "Nothing shall separate us from the love of God in Christ Jesus." In the same way the great evangelicals in Christianity, for example Augustine and Luther, have been able to proclaim in a fresh and living way that God is love. "The law," says Luther, is God's foreign work (*opus alienum*), "the gospel" is his own work (*opus proprium*). Even though Luther spoke emphatically and realistically about the "wrath" of God, love was nevertheless to him the very "nature" of God. "In God's great hall and castle dwells only love." "Christ is the mirror of God's fatherly heart." *"Und ist kein andrer Gott."*

But the most important element in this connection is not the mere statement that God is love, but the manner in which this love appears as characteristic for the Christian faith. The divine love active in Christ is that love which seeks sinful man and enters into communion with him. The distinctive mark of this love is that it creates a fellowship between God and man which is different from that which is based on reason and law. Divine love is not a rationally motivated idea obtained by reflection on the nature of the world and human life, and it is not a goal which human thought reaches by sublimating the highest human qualities. A divine love which descends to and enters into communion with sinful man is a paradox to reason. But in the same way that it is foolishness to the Greeks it is also a stumblingblock to the Jews. It cannot be contained within an order of legal justice. It is not legalism, not the law, that has the final word about God's relation to men. Fellowship with God cannot be attained on the basis of law. It can be attained only when divine love breaks the legal ordinances and, in a way that is offensive to all exclusive legalism, receives sinful man into communion with itself (cf. § 3. 4). The fellowship with God thus created rests exclusively on the foundation of divine love.

When we seek to define the character of divine love according to Christian faith, it is important to note the antitheses in which this fellowship with God, created by divine love, stands to rationalism and to legalism. This is a fundamental Christian idea. It is perfectly proper to speak of this as a fundamental idea, since it is a question of something constitutive for the Christian relationship between God and man, and not about something which may be removed without impairing this relationship itself. The whole history of Christian thought from one essential point of view is the history of this idea, the history of its struggle against rationalism and legalism, and the history of its triumphant emergence with new and irresistible power in spite of all opposition.

2. *The Nature of Divine Love.*

The nature of divine love, which we have touched upon in previous chapters, must now be more fully investigated. But it is possible to deal with only the main features of this subject. The whole exposition of the content of Christian faith is in reality the only adequate presentation of this fundamental theme. Christian faith cannot make a statement which does not in one way or another throw light on the nature of divine love. In this preliminary presentation there are especially two features which must be emphasized: the spontaneity and the self-giving of divine love.

In the first place, divine love is *spontaneous.* This implies that its cause is contained within itself, not in anything else. It is not called forth by external causes, but breaks forth by itself. Another expression for the same idea is the old formula: "the prevenient grace of God." God's love is *always* prevenient. Its cause is not something outside of God, but in God himself and in his nature. "To the question, Why does God love? there is only one right answer: Because it is His nature to love." [1]

It is important to emphasize this point of view, especially since it has often been obscured by attempts to supply a motivation for the divine love. But this very fact that the love of God in Christ appears as a love which seeks sinners and enters into fellowship with them proves conclusively that the cause of the divine work of love is not to be found in anything human, nor in a certain value which the object of this love possesses and which should make it desirable, nor in the fact that man has in some way made himself worthy of the divine love. "Herein is love, not that we loved God, but that he loved us" (I John 4:10). Every attempt to demonstrate something in man, some incor-

---

[1] A. Nygren, *Den kristna kärlekstanken* (Stockholm, 1930). Eng. tr. by A. G. Hebert, *Agape and Eros* (London, 1932), p. 52.

ruptible essence or some quality pleasing to God, which would explain rationally why God meets man in love, is in principle foreign to Christian faith. Such attempts prove only that divine love is again being incarcerated within the walls of rationalism and legalism. "When God's attitude to men is held to be determined by legal righteousness, His love must be conditioned by the worthiness of its object. But in Christ there is manifested a Divine love which floods over all dykes, and depends, not on men's deserts, but on its own inherent nature. Natural affection is a love that is 'caused'; Divine love is spontaneous and 'uncaused.'" [2]

The spontaneous, divine love appears to faith as self-giving. Different aspects of this characteristic may be noted according as the emphasis falls on the first or the second part of this word. Divine love means that God gives himself. The reformers used to say that God not only gives certain gifts to men, but first and foremost he gives himself. The same idea may be expressed by saying that divine love opens the way to fellowship with God. A fellowship between God and men can be established only if God descends and gives himself to men. There is for man no way to God except the way of God's self-giving love. If we then try to analyze how this divine way to man is constituted, the emphasis is shifted to the second part of the word. This tells us that divine love "seeketh not its own," and does not spare itself, but rather empties and sacrifices itself. Faith perceives that the way of divine love is the way of the Cross. The nature of this love is determined by the fact that it is marked by the Cross. It is not an accident that the eye of faith has always been attracted to the Cross. There is nothing that better reveals the nature, depth, and sovereignty of divine love. When the Christian conception of God is characterized and defined by the act of Christ, the spontaneous self-giving of divine love appears most clearly, both in the fact that this love has descended into the human world and accepted its conditions, and also that it

---

[2] *Op. cit.*, p. 53.

has thus given the supreme sacrifice. The conception which faith has of the divine majesty is not that of a God who in exalted eminence receives sacrifices from below, which are meant to coerce him; it is rather the picture of a love which sacrifices of its own and in extreme humility sacrifices itself. This is the way the majesty of love appears to the eye of faith. In this experience faith learns to know what divine love is. "God commendeth his own love toward us, in that, while we were yet sinners, Christ died for us" (Rom. 5:8). "Hereby know we love, because he laid down his life for us" (I John 3:16).

3. The Unfathomableness of Love.

The essential content of the revelation of God is given in the self-giving of divine love. Through this self-giving, faith learns to know God. But this highest and most unmistakable revelation of love is at the same time entirely inscrutable. Here faith can speak only with groping and tentative words. Even the word "love" comes from the area of human experience. But this does not imply that faith conceives the love of God in terms of human love, nor that it measures his love by the standard of human love. The very opposite is true. "Love . . . that ye may be sons of your Father who is in heaven" (Matt. 5:44 ff.); "Ye therefore shall be perfect, as your heavenly Father is perfect" (Matt. 5:48). We can speak of human love in the Christian sense of this word only if divine love has become active in human life and has created this love, which even then becomes nothing more than a pale reflection of God's love. If divine love is conceived as a sublimation of human love, the result would be something radically different; it would be the very opposite of divine love, it would be "eros" instead of "agape."

What has been said about love applies also to the word Father when it is used about God. The "fatherhood" of God cannot be measured by the standard of human fatherhood. When faith speaks of God as Father and thereby intends to express something of fundamental importance to the idea of

135

God, it is very conscious that this "Father" is "the Father from whom every family in heaven and on earth is named" (Eph. 3:15).[3] God is "The Father in heaven." This expression serves to bring out the unfathomableness of the divine "fatherly love." To share in this love means to be filled with "that peace which passeth all understanding" (Phil. 4:7). In pure mysticism God is simply the inscrutable, and in rationalism he is contained within human reason. But in Christian faith, although God is love, he is both the revealed and hidden God (cf. § 3. 5; § 9). The hidden and unfathomable element in God's being is not a surplus remaining after we have understood a part of his essence. Nor, as in mysticism, is the unfathomable the undifferentiated and undefinable, but rather that which is definite and definable. The mystery of divine love increases in the measure that faith perceives more of its essence.

By way of transition to the next paragraph we may add that the intimate fellowship with the man of faith which divine love creates is at the same time a relation of remoteness. The distance between the divine and the human is not obliterated by this fellowship, it is rather brought more sharply into focus. The position of Christian faith is therefore quite different from the relation of identity common in mysticism. The reason for this remoteness lies in the fact that divine love is characterized by a continuous and implacable opposition to evil.

15. The Opposition of Love to Evil

1. God's will stands in radical opposition to evil. The reason that the tension between divine love and divine wrath against sin does not destroy the unity of the conception of God is that "divine wrath" appears to faith as merged with love. Consequently God's opposition to evil is in reality the opposition of love whereby love maintains its purity.

2. From a negative point of view God's opposition to evil is

Swedish tr., "From whom everything that is called Father derives its name."

expressed in a number of figures of speech, such as severity, hate, wrath, condemning and retributive justice, and so on. All such figures are legitimate and inseparably connected with the Christian conception of God, since and in so far as they express love's radical opposition to evil.

3. But faith finds the deepest expression of the opposition of divine love to evil in the fact that in its struggle against evil this love does everything to overcome it, even going so far as to carry its burden and to sacrifice itself. The Cross stands, therefore, as the synthesis of love's radical opposition to evil and of its sovereignty over it.

1. The Purity of Love.

The will of God stands in unbroken opposition to everything which is not in harmony with, or hostile and indifferent to it. Nothing could be more false than to assume that, because the New Testament speaks differently and in a more powerful manner about the love of God than the Old Testament, therefore God's opposition to evil should have been weakened. In reality the very opposite is true. This appears clearly in the fact that the demand placed upon man is infinitely greater: "perfect, even as God is perfect" (cf. § 3. 4). The New Testament picture of God as Father is not a humanized and enfeebled idea of God. The Father is at the same time the uncompromising judge. Christian faith has from the very beginning expressed this opposition of God in the strongest terms. It has well understood that, if this feature is missing or even slightly obscured, love loses its essence and is reduced to a caricature of real divine love. The idea that divine love is complacent and indulgent, that God overlooks sin and does not take it seriously, and that he will obviously forgive since it is his business to do so, is foreign to Christian faith.

A review of the history of the Christian conception of God indicates that theology has encountered two temptations in its endeavor to define the nature of the opposition of divine will to evil. One of these is the tendency to discount this opposition and thereby present an enfeebled idea of divine love. Examples of this can be found, not only in that "humanized" theology which has flourished during the later centuries since the Enlightenment, but also in ancient times. It appears in Marcion, who refused to combine the idea of active judgment with the God of love. It is present also in the hyper-evangelical wing of Pietism, since here also the idea of judgment is not given its proper place in the conception of God. The other danger has been that theology has isolated God's opposition to evil from his love, and then has sought to solve the problem of their relation by a rational adjustment (§ 13). The tension which is unquestionably present has been changed into a dualism within God's own nature, and the unity of the conception of God has thus become divided. For the Christian faith the existing tension does not result in a dualism, nor does it destroy the unity of the conception of God, because the divine activity in judgment does not appear as something separated from divine love, but rather as something inseparably connected with it. No one in the history of Christianity has more seriously struggled with this problem than Luther. It was far from his intention to weaken the idea of divine "wrath." He boasts, and not without justification, that he has spoken more powerfully about this than had been done under the papacy. The judgment of wrath, says Luther, is not only something in the future; sinful man stands here and now under the wrath of God. But the eye of faith discovers that in the last analysis love and wrath stand in intimate relation. Wrath, says Luther, is God's *opus alienum*, love is his *opus proprium*. Wrath is the mask behind which God hides himself, the means he uses to attain his purpose.[1] Without this connection with wrath, love would no longer be love, it would lose its purity. Love shines behind the dark cloud of wrath; yea,

---

[1] Cf. Karl Holl, *Gesammelte Aufsätze zur Kirchengeschichte*, I, "Luther," 2nd ed., p. 42.

even more, it is active even in wrath. Luther speaks of *die zornige Liebe*, "the angry love," and declares that it does not destroy anything, as hate and envy do, but simply wants to separate the evil from the good, in order that love and the good may remain. It is not only wrath which is defined and purified by its dependence upon love, but love itself is affected by its relation to wrath. When wrath is, as it were, merged with love, every possibility to enfeeble its meaning is removed; love remains strong and firm, and retains its purity under all circumstances. The radical opposition of the divine will to evil becomes then in the last analysis the opposition of divine love itself. This is the reason the opposition is radical and unconditional. No opposition to evil can be more decisive and critical than the opposition of love. It lies in the very nature of love that it must react against that which is incompatible with itself. If it is not to lose its own character, it *must* preserve its purity.

2. *The Wrath of Love.*

Within the Christian testimony of faith there occur a number of more or less anthropomorphic expressions which are intended to set forth plainly the incongruity between the divine will and that which is opposed to it. Thus sin is spoken of as an abomination in the sight of God, and mention is made of God's hate, enmity, wrath, and the like. In regard to these and other similar expressions it is important to remember that they are symbolic and that in the last analysis they tell us something about divine love. Only in so far as these two points of view are strictly maintained can such qualifications of God's relation to evil be validated as Christian. When such a word as God's "wrath" has been rejected sometimes in the history of Christian thought, or relegated to "the final judgment" (Ritschl), the reason has been either that the figurative meaning of the word has not been considered, or that the radical opposition of the divine will to evil has been weakened. Many a time, when theology has prided itself on having secured "a philosophically purified conception of God," it has become evident that this process of refining was only an expression of the lack of religious depth and the inability to comprehend the characteristic viewpoint of faith. Christian vocabulary cannot dispense with those figures of speech which belong to the sphere of human experience. These strongly volitional words serve to set forth in a picturesque, concrete, and active manner the constant, radical, and spontaneous opposition of the divine will to everything that is opposed to it. There is no reason to limit God's "wrath" to a final judgment. God is always and under all circumstances hostile to sin. His wrath expresses "the spontaneous intensity of his repudiation of sin." The God of faith is a God who wills, and his will in reference to evil is a radical indignation and unmitigated severity. The Christian church has a legitimate reason to sing, "Turn now away thy wrath." But wrath brings an element of strong-willed and healthy firmness into the divine love. Love does not hesitate to wound and break down. God's love does not appear at all to Christian faith as sentimental and effeminate. It was an expression of the deepest insight of faith when Luther was able to see the activity of God's love in the tempest of divine wrath.

When it has sometimes been said that God "hates sin but loves the sinner," we might approve the intention of such a distinction, provided it is meant to maintain the divine love in the midst of "wrath." But the distinction is of questionable value. It presupposes that sin can be distinguished from the sinner in a way that really obscures the nature of sin as a perversion of the will. It is very easy on this basis to relegate sin to some external part of man (§ 30). The very thing which this symbolic figure of speech is intended to express is thereby obscured, viz., the continuous and unconditional opposition of God to sin and therefore also to man as sinner. It is more correct to insist that God both hates and loves the sinner, and that his wrath is connected with and depends on his love.

As a comprehensive expression of God's opposition to evil,

theology has frequently used the term "God's righteousness." This word can unquestionably be used for this purpose. *If* righteousness is understood as a comprehensive expression of God's opposition to evil, this reaction also must be understood as the reaction of love, which then implies nothing else than the judgment and separation which occur of necessity when divine love appears in its purity. It is not, therefore, a question of a dualism between God's love and his righteousness. The theories of atonement which have been built on such a dualism obscure the nature of the Christian conception of God because they incorporate the atonement into a legalistic system. God's righteousness is not a righteousness which stands over against his love, but rather, it is, to use an expressive phrase by Nietzsche, "love with its eyes open." Righteousness watches over the purity of love and guards it against sentimental reinterpretations. But love also watches over the peculiar nature of righteousness. A righteousness without love is only hardness and a perversion of divine righteousness. It is significant that in the biblical language, in both the Old and New Testaments, the righteousness of God expresses not only his opposition to evil from a negative point of view, but is very often synonymous with his "grace," "help," "salvation," and "kindness." This indicates, on the one hand, that Christian faith can never under any circumstances separate righteousness from love or co-ordinate the two, but must always regard righteousness as an element defining love; and, on the other hand, that God's opposition to evil is never purely negative, but in reality always intends to conquer that which stands in opposition to his love.

3. *The Struggle of Love.*

The highest form of the self-assertion of divine love is its self-giving whereby it overcomes evil. Consequently the negative terms used to describe God's antagonism to evil are not adequate to express this relationship. It is understood in a much deeper and more conclusive sense through those affirmations about God which present the self-giving of divine love. When the negative terms are separated from these positive affirmations, they become really misleading. The nature of the antagonism of divine love is characterized as far as faith is concerned by the fact that the Cross stands in the center of the history of God's dealings with men. An interpretation of divine love which ignores this cannot claim to be Christian in the fullest sense. From this point of view the purpose of God's antagonism to evil is to overcome it; and even the negative aspects of the antithesis contribute toward this end. But the deepest expressions of the reaction of God's love are those which indicate how much it really costs God to overcome evil, how he has entered into this struggle rather than stand indifferently at a distance, how he takes the burden upon himself and pours himself out in the sacrifice of love. This activity of God will be discussed more fully in the following chapters (§§ 18, 25, 26). Here we are concerned simply to emphasize that divine love from this point of view is a self-giving and self-sacrificing love. Consequently, the nature of this love cannot be understood simply as passive, but rather as the most intense activity and as the basis of that activity which reveals God as a "saving," "forgiving," "merciful," and "gracious" God, who in giving himself triumphs over that which is antagonistic to love. This very fact, which so unmistakably reveals God's antagonism to evil, manifests at the same time the sovereignty of divine love. This cannot be more clearly revealed than in his triumph and transformation of that which is opposed to his love. It is quite appropriate that we read in one of our collects: God "declares his almighty power chiefly in showing mercy and pity."[2]

16. The Sovereignty of Love

1. The tension between God's love and his sovereignty, which has sometimes threatened to destroy the unity of the conception of God, cannot be rationally adjusted or resolved. But Christian

[2] Augustana Hymnal, Collect for the 10th Sunday after Trinity.

faith finds the solution in the paradoxical assertion that divine love itself is the sovereign power in creation. Every approach which separates power from love, and understands the former as a more or less undefinable, capricious, and despotic power, leads to a conception of God which is foreign to faith and below the Christian level. The same is true of every approach which limits the sovereignty of divine love.

2. From this point of view God's "omnipotence" is not the causality of the divine will in relation to everything that happens, but the sovereignty of love. The "eternity" of God is not an abstract timelessness, but the sovereignty of love in relation to time. God's "unchangeableness" is not an abstract passivity, but an expression of love's sovereign steadfastness. God's "omnipresence" is not deistic transcendence or pantheistic immanence, but the sovereignty of love in relation to space. God's "omniscience" is not abstract foreknowledge, but love's sovereign and penetrating eye to which everything is crystal clear.

3. Just as God's sovereignty is characterized by love, so also the divine love is characterized by sovereignty. Thus the competition between God's love and his sovereignty, which has sometimes occurred, especially in the relation between Lutheran and Reformed theology, is eliminated.

1. God's Sovereignty is the Sovereignty of Love.

We have already touched upon the tension which undeniably reveals itself in Christian faith between divine power and divine love (§ 13). The reason for this is that to Christian faith God appears both as the sovereign God exalted above all strife and change, and as the loving and divine will which in history is engaged in a struggle against opposing forces. The reality of this tension is abundantly evidenced in the history of Christian thought. Here we find again and again how these two principal ideas struggle against each other, and how men have repeatedly attempted to remove this clash by rational adjustments. History also indicates that this tension may eventuate in a division in which one of the ideas is maintained in opposition to the other. A typical example of how the idea of power suppresses the idea of love is seen in the nominalistic theology of the late Middle Ages. The suppression of divine love which had appeared even during early scholasticism (Thomas) had proceeded so far that God's *potentia absoluta* had now become a pure, capricious, and indefinable will to power. The Christian conception of God had thereby lost its characteristic nature. An example of the opposite type we find in Marcion. Here the idea of sovereignty is in reality suppressed by the idea of love. Marcion wants to maintain that the highest and "unknown" God is a God of love, and of nothing but love. But this is accomplished in such a way that the God of creation becomes another and lower god than the God of love. The significance of this is that the God of love is not sovereign in relation to "creation." Such ideas have been advanced also in more recent times, when it has been suggested that God is a "finite" God, or a "growing" God who emerges in history.[1]

In contradistinction to such a division between power and love, Christian faith maintains that the divine power is nothing else than the power of love. The power of God is not some obscure and inert *fatum* (fate or destiny) or a capricious and indefinable will to power, but only and exclusively the power of love. The Christian faith, therefore, makes this paradoxical affirmation that the sovereign power in the universe possesses the character of divine love. The tension in this affirmation cannot be removed by rationalization, since it is obvious to faith both that the divine power *is* sovereign, and that it is engaged in a continuous struggle under historical conditions against that which is opposed to it. That which prevents a rational solution of the

[1] Cf. H. G. Wells, "God the Invisible King," and H. R. Mackintosh, "The Conception of a Finite God," in *Some Aspects of Christian Belief.*

tension is, therefore, the reality of that evil which struggles against the sovereign will of God.

The viewpoint of faith cannot under such circumstances be transformed into a rational world view, either monistic or dualistic. A monistic world view can be constructed only by weakening or destroying the radical hostility of evil to the divine will. Only in that case can everything that happens be referred to the divine will and accepted as an expression of the same. This line of thought is completely at variance with that which is axiomatic and clear to faith, namely, that what faith calls sin cannot be the result of the divine will, but stands rather in open antagonism to this will. If in some way it could be shown that sin has its matrix in and is an expression of the divine will, then this will would no longer bear the marks of love and it would cease to be a divine will. Neither can the viewpoint of faith be transformed into a dualistic world view. Such a view would presuppose that the opposing evil is considered from a metaphysical point of view. When Marcion attributed the origin of this world, where the evil powers are active, to "a lower creator-god," his theory in reality represented a rational explanation of evil and of the universe along metaphysical and dualistic lines. Christian faith had good reasons to repudiate this dissolution of the divine sovereignty.

As far as faith is concerned it cannot accept *either* a monistic *or* a dualistic world view. The affirmation of faith that the divine love which struggles against evil is at the same time the sovereign power contains a paradox which cannot be dismissed.

When faith nevertheless maintains that the divine sovereignty bears the mark of love, and that there is no other divine power except love, it does so because the divine love which reveals itself in the act of Christ appears to faith as unconditionally supreme and as the only sovereign power. Every attempt to maintain God's sovereignty by discounting divine love implies not only a weakening of love but in reality also an impairment of divine sovereignty. If God's power were despotic, coercive, and violent, it would not be for faith the power beyond all power. Whatever the might of pure, external power may be able to accomplish, it cannot subdue human wills and set them free from the tyranny of egocentricity. Love cannot be induced by force. The hearts of men can be won only by the power of love.[2] If the might of God were simply an external power, it would be ineffective against evil; God would not be able to win that which, according to the certainty of faith, he has demonstrated himself able to win. Consequently, that point of view which regards God's power as despotic and capricious does not exalt but rather depreciates the divine power, and accords less to God than the Christian faith must give. The despotic power is a caricature of divine sovereignty. It is significant that Luther's emphasis on love as the "nature" of God is connected with a new and powerful view of the significance of God's "omnipotence." In medieval theology there had been room for a division between God's activity and human merit. But this division disappears when Luther discovers that God's power is the power of his love. Then all mention of human "merit" must cease. Then it must be said: "We do not act; we are acted upon" (*Wir handeln nich, sonderen wir werden gehandelt*).

As soon as God's sovereignty is separated from his love and is understood as something co-ordinate with it, the conception of God becomes unrealistic, i.e., it does not correspond to what faith beholds when the conception derives its essential content from the work of Christ. When the conception of God then is made the object of thoughtful analysis, it becomes *inert*. When the primitive, despotic feature is removed, there emerges a deistic or pantheistic reinterpretation of God's sovereignty. But in this way the conception of God becomes not only unrealistic, but also lifeless. The god of pantheism who penetrates all things is just as inactive as the god of deism who is exalted and removed from the world (§17). We cannot speak of a living God except in so

---

[2] Cf. W. Temple, *The Faith and Modern Thought*, pp. 124 ff.

far as his sovereignty is understood as identical with the sovereignty of divine love.

2. *The Various Aspects of God's Sovereignty.*

We touch here the whole array of conceptions of faith which in the history of theology have been brought together under such captions as God's "formal" or "metaphysical" or "absolute" attributes. It is not too much to say that theology here has used speculative concepts which are foreign to faith and has assumed that these belong among the so-called *articuli mixti*. There is hardly any indication that these belong to the study of *faith*. If we are to remain within the area of faith, it is necessary to maintain firmly the idea that God's sovereignty is entirely the sovereignty of love.

If God's sovereignty has this character, what is then implied in the *omnipotence* of God? It is clear at once that we need not be concerned with a number of meaningless questions about God's omnipotence which have appeared even within theology. Can God do everything? Can he transform a stone into an animal? All such questions are beside the point and completely meaningless. They have nothing to do with faith. They are based on a conception of the will of God as entirely capricious, which fails to understand that it is here a question about the power of love and nothing else. The question of God's possibilities is a question of the possibilities of divine love. God does and wills nothing else than that wherein divine love realizes itself.

In regard to the relation of the divine sovereignty to the course of history, two things are absolutely certain as far as faith is concerned. In the first place it is clear that not everything that happens is an expression of the divine will in the sense that everything that happens reflects the will of God. Such a point of view could be maintained only by identifying sin with the divine will. Faith cannot, therefore, incorporate the divine will under the aspect of a universal cause. It is completely misleading when Schleiermacher says that "the religious self-consciousness, by means of which we place all that affects or influences us in absolute dependence on God, coincides entirely with the view that all things are conditioned and determined by the interdependence of nature."[3] This thought is completely foreign to faith. The God of faith is not identified with "the interdependence of nature," which is nothing else than the attempt to trace the relation between the individual events. Such an identification is impossible and completely opposed to the viewpoint of faith. The reason for this is not simply that the God of faith is not an abstract idea, but a living and continually active God. The reason is rather that this point of view leads to the result that every event must be accepted as an expression of God's will. But this is obviously contrary to faith's viewpoint. Faith knows that in this universe there is much that stands in direct opposition to the will of God.

In the second place, it is evident to faith that the activity of divine love cannot be judged or verified according to human standards. It is not man who from the point of view of his own power decides what is and what is not the work of divine love. Faith knows very well that divine love can hide itself in wrath, which seems the very opposite of love. It does not presume to interpret the ways of divine love on the basis of the historical development. It does not forget that God is not only the revealed God, but also the God who under the conditions of this earthly life is hidden from us. The tenacity of faith in holding fast to divine love in spite of the testimony of earthly events always has the character of a "nevertheless."

Faith's view of the sovereignty of divine love implies that everything is unconditionally dependent upon the will and love of God. Nothing is outside the sphere of God's power; no situation can arise in which his power would not be able to assert itself. In relation to evil, therefore, the divine power appears under a double aspect: as *grace* and *judgment*. In grace the

---

[3] Schleiermacher, *op. cit.*, p. 170.

evil is overcome and compelled to serve the purpose of the divine will. In the judgment of condemnation the unconquered evil encounters the divine sovereignty. Understood in this way the divine will is not simply a power superior to all other powers, but, in the deepest sense of the word, is the sovereign power of the universe (cf. § 22). Everything else that is called power, or has a semblance of power, contains the seeds of its own dissolution, desolation, and destruction. It is subject to judgment. The power of divine love is the only power of life. To be separated from this power is destruction, to be united with it is "life eternal."

It should not be overlooked in this connection that God also realizes his will through the compulsion of law, as this is expressed in the ordinances of human society. The law is the bearer of God's benevolent will, which turns the stubborn will of men and thus limits and breaks the power of evil.

In accordance with the point of view here presented, the "eternity" of God does not imply any speculation about his being outside of time, or that time has no significance for God. It is, on the contrary, essential to faith to conceive of God as being present *in* time and effectively active in whatever happens here; although he nevertheless is "above" time. Eternal rest and blessedness belong to the Christian conception of God, but at the same time it can be said of him, in the words of Luther, that he "never rests" (*nimmer ruhet*). The "eternal" does not suggest something "before" time, or something that is to come "after" time. Eternity is not quantitatively different from time. As soon as we follow out the consequences of such a thought, we come to the conception of an unending extent of time; but even such a time is not eternity. The eternity of God is the *sovereignty of divine love in relation to time*. God's love is not transient and changing as is everything which belongs to time. The apostolic word is here perfectly applicable: "Love never faileth." God cannot be contained within any limits, spatial or temporal. Faith expresses this by saying that God is "he who was, and who is,

149

and who is to come." He is "Alpha and Omega, the beginning and the end," and "a thousand years are to him as one day." Eternal life, whether we think of the present or of the future, partakes of this sovereign love. Eternal life is to faith not *only* an object of hope. "This is life eternal, that they should know thee, the only true God" (John 17:3). Eternal life is a qualitative expression for a life which is lived in communion with the living God.

This independence of all temporal limits which characterizes the divine life expresses itself also with reference to divine revelation. There is a continuous reciprocal action between what has been done and what is being done. Faith knows of no past revelation of God which is not a living and active power in the present. The revelation of God, even though it took place some time in the past, always belongs to the present. It is an apt illustration of the viewpoint of faith when Luther says about Christ's complete victory over the evil powers that this "takes place daily in a spiritual sense in the life of every Christian."

In connection with what we have said about eternity we may add that God's *unchangeableness*, from the point of view of the sovereignty of divine love, cannot be understood as stereotyped inertia. This word has often been interpreted along that line under the influence of Greek philosophy, which tended to emphasize the so-called *apatheia* of God. In that case God is placed outside of history in a way that does not at all correspond to the viewpoint of Christian faith. Faith understands the unchangeableness of God as an expression of the unswerving direction of God's will and an affirmation that this will under all circumstances and in all its activity is characterized by love.

God's *omnipresence* must also be understood from the point of view of the sovereignty of divine love. It is not a question here of some abstract and deistic space-beyond-space, which in reality becomes simply another space; nor of a pantheistic conception of the presence of God in all that exists. All questions whether God is in the flower or in the stone, and the like, are immaterial to faith. The "omnipresence" which Christian faith affirms is entirely different. It implies nothing less than the ability of divine love to maintain itself everywhere unhindered by limitations of space. There is no place closed to the sovereign power of divine love. God can reach us wherever we are, and it is useless for a man to attempt to flee from his power. "If I ascend up into heaven, thou art there: If I make my bed in Sheol, behold, thou art there" (Ps. 139:8). But God *is present* only where his love realizes itself in grace and judgment. Wherever the love of God is active, there is God, even if human lips do not dare to speak the name of the Highest. But where his love is not active, there he is not, even though his praises may be sung in the most beautiful hymns. God's omnipresence is entirely the active presence of divine love.

Finally, God's *omniscience* becomes from this point of view something entirely different than the abstract idea of his "foreknowledge." This latter term is connected with a deistically conceived idea of God which is not compatible with faith's conception of the living God who is active in history. This idea of God's abstract foreknowledge has given rise to a number of speculations which are foreign to faith; as for instance, the question whether God saves man because he foreknows his faith. In reality God's "omniscience" expresses the unerring certainty of God's judgment, and denotes the all-seeing eye of love which sees everything in a crystal clear light. He knows what is in man (John 2:25). This omniscience is verified by faith again and again. It knows that nothing is hidden from God; yea, even "darkness itself is not dark in his presence," as the psalmist expresses this paradox. Every attempt to hide something from this all-seeing eye is doomed to failure. In this connection the word is entirely appropriate that there is nothing hidden which shall not be revealed.

3. *Love and Sovereignty.*

There is no divine power which is not the power of love.

151

Sovereignty is a necessary qualification of divine love. Love is always a sovereign, almighty, eternal, active, and all-seeing love. This sovereignty characterizes divine love and reveals its majesty. Divine love is not a power alongside of others, it is the sovereign power of all the universe.

It is not, however, always clear and unmistakable to faith that God's sovereignty is the sovereignty of love. Love can be hidden under the aspect of wrath. God's sovereign love cannot be measured and evaluated according to human standards. Luther's words in regard to God's righteousness apply equally well to love. "If the righteousness of God were such that human reason could declare it to be righteousness, it would not be divine and would not be different from human righteousness. Since, however, he is the only true God, who is unfathomable and inscrutable for human reason, it is proper, no, really necessary, that his righteousness also is inscrutable, as Paul says. . . . His ways would not be past tracing out if we could at all times perceive why they are righteous."[4] But even when God's love is hidden and his actions do not seem to bear the marks of love, faith holds fast its inmost and unshakable conviction that the sovereignty of God is nothing else than the sovereignty of love.

If God's sovereignty therefore implies a qualification of his love, the rivalry between love and power is in principle excluded. The question whether power or love shall be emphasized is meaningless. This question rests on the false assumption that these are two co-ordinate "attributes" of God, and that power should be understood as pure and unqualified might. The difference between the older Lutheran and Reformed theologies was sometimes expressed in this manner: that the Reformed emphasized power, the Lutheran love, as the primary attribute of God. The danger in such an analysis, from the point of view of faith, was that the former failed to perceive the character of power as the power of *love,* and the latter, departing from Luther's own fundamental insight, obscured the *sovereignty* of love. Even though

---

[4] Luther, *The Bondage of the Will,* pp. 385 f.

Lutheran theology in its emphasis on love may be said to be closer to reality, there occurred, nevertheless, a separation between power and love in the nature of God, which is contrary to faith's perception of divine love as the sovereign power in the universe. The inner tension which results from this point of view has been clearly indicated in previous chapters. We have not tried to hide the fact that divine love cannot be measured by human standards, nor that the attitude of faith always tends to have the character of a "nevertheless." But against this tension as a background Christian faith projects its unified conception of God, concentrated and comprehended in the idea of *sovereign love.*

17. The Living God

1. The God of the Christian faith is the living and active God. Every affirmation of faith is therefore at the same time a statement of his nearness and his remoteness.

2. The conception of God in Christian faith is distinguished both from a transcendental and deistic and from an immanent and pantheistic approach. At first sight it might appear that the former accentuates God's remoteness and the latter his nearness. In reality the remoteness is transformed into unapproachableness and impassivity, and the weakness into an identity between the divine and the human. At the same time the twofold aspect of nearness and remoteness which characterizes the Christian conception of God is disrupted. This twofold aspect depends on the fact that this conception is clearly and qualitatively defined.

3. When Christian faith speaks of God as a "person," it maintains both the activity of God as an expression of his will and the personal and spiritual nature of the Christian relationship between God and men. The term "person," which naturally is a figure of speech, stands guard against the transformation of the conception of God into an abstract idea, and against its being understood as a force of nature.

1. The God of Faith is the Living God.

In the previous chapters the essential characteristics of the Christian conception of God have been delineated. The next section will deal more in detail with the divine activity as faith perceives it. As a transition to this section we insert here a chapter on "the living God." The purpose is also to mark the essential difference between the Christian conception and the deistic and pantheistic ideas of God.

That the God of the Christian faith is the living and active God has already become evident in our earlier discussion of the nature of divine love and in the definition of the concept of revelation. The revelation of God is the divine self-impartation in the form of activity. There is nothing more essential to faith than the living character of this idea of God. God's revelation is from one point of view finished in the work of Christ, which to faith means the entrance of divine love into human life and the finished work of salvation and reconciliation on the basis of divine self-giving. This is the highest possible form of the divine presence. But the revelation of God is at the same time something which is continually going on, something that happens *quotidie spiritualiter in quolibet christiano.* This phase of a continuous and immediate activity is expressed in the fact that Christian faith is a faith "in the Holy Spirit." Fellowship with God rests completely on the divine activity. There is no other way to God than God's way to man.

Christian faith, therefore, speaks about God's nearness, an effective divine presence in the human world. But this does not imply that the divine can be contained within or confused with the human. It is perfectly clear to faith that the divine presence at the same time accentuates the separation between the divine and the human. The more faith perceives the presence of God and experiences the fellowship, the more definitely appears also the distance between God and man. The divine act of love which establishes the fellowship between God and man at the same time makes more vividly known to the man of faith his

154

separation and unworthiness in the presence of divine love. The twofold aspect of nearness and remoteness, fellowship and separation, which is inseparably connected with the Christian conception of God, depends on the clearly defined character of this conception. Its quality of sovereign love demands both distance and fellowship.

The living, clearly defined conception of God held by Christian faith is sharply differentiated from all conceptions of God which are "philosophically" or metaphysically oriented. Such speculations have always influenced theology in the direction of weakening the living content of the Christian conception of God.

2. *Deistic and Pantheistic Ideas of God.*

The metaphysical conceptions of God which have appeared in history may be divided into two representative groups: the deistic, which emphasizes the transcendental, and the pantheistic, which emphasizes the immanent conception of God. Even though these two types seem to be very different, history indicates that the one has often without difficulty passed over into the other. It must be emphasized, however, that from a religious point of view both are in conflict with the Christian faith. There is no overwhelming difference between conceiving of God as "the first cause," as deism does, or as pantheism's reasonable principle in the universe. In either case man is simply confronted with the idea of causality, and faith's living conception of God is lost.

Since we have stated that the twofold aspect of distance and nearness is inseparably connected with the Christian conception of God, it might seem quite natural to assume that these two metaphysical types represent these two aspects: the transcendental representing distance; and the immanent, nearness. In reality, however, the idea of nearness and distance is here quite different from that which is characteristic of Christian faith. In the transcendental type "distance" becomes unapproachableness, isolation, and impassivity. God is an "extra-mundane" being who is enthroned in abstract space, too highly exalted to have any concern for what happens in the human world. In the theology of the ancient church there was a constant conflict with this conception of God derived from Greek philosophy. The Christology of the ancient church represents from one point of view the attempt of theology to preserve the living and active revelation of God against the encroachments of transcendentalism. In the measure that this latter tendency influenced Christology, the Logos-Christ became an intermediary being between the distant God and the world. Arianism is a typical example of this. When the ancient confession of faith in Christ asserts that "the Son is of the same substance with the Father," this is in reality a decisive victory over the influence of metaphysical transcendentalism. In spite of this fact it has exercised considerable influence in theology, especially in scholasticism. The nature of this influence may be indicated in the following examples. The divine love was interpreted in medieval scholasticism primarily as self-love, and therefore became Eros rather than Agape. In regard to the work of Christ it was difficult, in spite of Christology, to take this seriously as the work of God. This is evident in the Latin theory of the atonement. Finally, the "grace" of God was not identical with God's love, but was understood as more or less mysterious powers emanating from the distant God. It is clear, therefore, that the metaphysical transcendental idea which was fully developed in the eighteenth-century Deism had deep roots in scholastic theology. Deism combined the idea of exclusive transcendentalism with the idea of order in the universe which the new world view had placed in the foreground. The ideal of the pure deist was a God who had constructed the machine so accurately that he did not need to pay any attention to the controls. But there was nothing in this conception of God as the ultimate cause of the universe that would hinder the divine Being from exercising a certain amount of control, or at least that the whole would proceed toward a final assize when judgment would be pronounced over the whole course of events with a dispensing of rewards and punishments. But the more exclusively transcendent the conception of God becomes, the more abstract, unrealistic, and insignificant the idea appears. What religious significance can there be in an idea of God as the first cause? Suppose this so-called first cause is removed, what then? The only result would be a slight revision in the theory of the origin of the universe.[1] This proves conclusively that the deistic conception of God has no religious significance. Only that idea of God has religious significance in which God is understood as the living, present, and active God.

The immanent pantheistic idea of God's nearness is also different from that of Christian faith. In this view it is not a question of God's entrance into and activity in history, but of a certain divine indwelling in the world. The idea of immanence blurs the distinction between the divine and the human, and results finally in an apotheosis of the human. The metaphysic of immanence has exercised a great influence on theology from the time of the ancient church down to the present. A characteristic example is found in mysticism's attempt to find God in the "depth" of the soul, and in its talk about "the divine spark" in man, etc. When this line of thought became influential in the nineteenth-century idealistic theology, it did not come as something completely new, even though it did not play as prominent a part in the theology of the ancient church as transcendentalism. The more this idea of immanence penetrated theology, the clearer became the difference between its conception of God and the living God of faith. In the measure that the conception of God, on the basis of speculative idealism, especially in Hegel, became metaphysically immanent and pantheistic, it was transformed into an abstract idea and lost its religious character. The God of speculative idealism was no more living and active than the God of transcendentalism, and did not permit a personal

---

[1] Cf. Sorley, *Moral Values and the Idea of God*, "Surely a God who does not interfere will hardly be missed," p. 146.

relationship such as Christian faith demands.[2] The religious character of the conception of God was lost because the fully developed pantheistic idea removed the distance, the qualitative difference between the divine and the human, and made God into a comprehensive symbol of all existence. It is not an accident that the speculative theology was followed by Strauss, who, on the basis of the conception that the divine spirit realizes himself in the human through the process of divine immanence, declared that humanity as such is the incarnate God.

If, therefore, the conception of God in Christian faith differs from the idea of both transcendence and immanence, we cannot arrive at a substitute by a combination of the two. That such attempts do not come very close to the Christian conception depends on the fact that the concepts of nearness and distance are entirely different. A combination of transcendence and immanence would result only in a metaphysical irrationalism (§ 9). But in this way one does not arrive at that tension-filled synthesis in which Christian faith combines God's nearness and distance. The clearly defined quality of faith's conception of God prevents the unity from being destroyed by this tension and at the same time differentiates this conception from all metaphysical concepts of God. It is this quality which is the basis of the fellowship between God and man, but it also delineates more sharply the distance between the human and God's sovereign love.

3. God's "Personality."

The designation "person" is not applied to God in primitive Christianity. God is spoken of rather as "Spirit" (John 4:24). Nevertheless, many personal terms, such as "Father," "Lord," and so on, indicate that the conception of God was personal. The ancient confessional formulas do not speak of God as a person, but about three "persons" in the Godhead. But the word person

---

[2] E. Troeltsch, "Protestantisches Christentum und Kirche in der Neu-Zeit," in Die Kultur der Gegenwart, I, IV: 1, 2nd ed., p. 706.

did not then have the sharply defined meaning that it has today. The use of the word person as applied to God did not come into theology until relatively late. To begin with, it seems that certain unitarian interests were served by the use of the word. That is true in the case of Socinus. Gradually, however, it appeared self-evident that the word should be used about God. In later theology, however, the question about God's personality has been the object of discussion. Schleiermacher regarded the word as a "one-sidedness," a *Bewusstseinsvergötterung* which represented one extreme, while *Naturvergötterung* represented another. The Hegelian theologian Biedermann refused to use the concept of personality with reference to "the absolute spirit," since the word belongs to the temporal sphere: "personality is the definition of a temporal spirit." The hesitation to use the concept of personality rests on the suspicion that the idea of God would thereby become too thoroughly human. Those defending its use have usually answered that the concept of personality does not imply any such restriction, and affirmed that in the personality is found "positively and intensively the power of a being over himself."[3]

Before we make a decision in this matter, we must note carefully, whether we attack or defend its use, that the term "person," with reference to God, is a figure of speech. If personality is not an adequate expression for God, it is not difficult to find points of attack. But even if the use of the word is connected with certain dangers, this does not necessarily destroy its usefulness. The question about the "personality" of God is not a question whether God *is* a person or not, but how and to what extent this word is able to express something that is essential to faith. *If* faith were compelled to understand God's "personality" as identical with human personality, it could certainly not use the word. One might then seek for a substitute, such as "super-personality," but this concept would be void of content and

[3] O. Kirn, *Grundriss der evangelischen Dogmatik*, II, 6.

unsuitable for the purpose.[4] As a figure of speech "personality" serves to guard the conception of God in important respects. It brings out vividly the voluntary and active character of the idea of God, and thus guards it from two directions: against the tendency to transform the conception of God into an abstract idea, and against the identification of God with some force of nature, thus obscuring the fact that God's power is nothing else than the power of love. In addition the concept of personality guards the spiritual and personal character of fellowship with God, and repudiates both the idea of the dissolution of personality into the infinite as conceived in the "mysticism of infinity," and all tendencies to understand God's "grace" in a more or less material sense; an example is the designation of grace as "medicine," to use the terminology of Melanchthon, rather than as the love of God which saves and restores man. A negative proof of the importance of the concept of personality is the fact that attacks on God's "personality" frequently are associated with the obscuring of the active volitional character of the conception of God and the spiritual and personal character of the relationship between God and man.

DIVISION B

THE GOD OF ACTION

18. God as Saviour

1. The living God realizes his love and will in continuous activity. Christian faith beholds this divine activity from three points of view: as an act of salvation, an act of judgment, and an act of creation.

2. When God's activity is seen as an act of salvation which establishes communion and fellowship with man, it implies the assertion both of the radical opposition of sin to the will of God and the power of this divine will to overcome the evil of sin.

[4] Cf. A. S. Pringle-Pattison, *The Idea of God,* p. 390.

The possibility of salvation rests entirely in the will of God and cannot be rationally explained. When evil which opposes the divine will is attributed to the finite as such, there emerge two different doctrines of salvation which are fundamentally at variance with the Christian conception. *Either* salvation is rationally motivated, as in idealism which suggests that human nature as such encompasses something divine, *or* when man is wholly consigned to the finite world, the religious paradox of the doctrine of salvation is replaced by a metaphysical irrationalism which attempts to combine the metaphysical antithesis, the finite and the infinite.

3. From the viewpoint of Christian faith history appears as the arena where the divine will struggles against the power of opposing evil. Here, indeed, as far as faith is concerned, the decisive victory is won. Nevertheless, though the struggle is indissolubly connected with the circumstances of history, the perfect dominion of God—the Kingdom of God—does not lie within the realm of history.

1. *Various Aspects of the Activity of God.*

It has been the purpose of the previous section to sketch the main outlines of that conception of God which is decisive for Christian faith. That sketch concluded with a paragraph about the living God. The purpose of this section will be to attempt to see this conception of God from the viewpoint of activity. Christian faith perceives in divine revelation a continuing activity on God's part. In this respect the words of Luther concerning God are applicable, *"er ruhet nimmer."* When, therefore, the attempt is made to apprehend the idea of God from the viewpoint of activity, it does not imply that the idea of God previously indicated is to be supplemented with any new features, but instead that the conception of God we have indicated may be more directly seen in action. It should be emphasized that only in this way do we obtain that perspective of the idea of God which is decisive for Christian faith, inasmuch as the relation of faith to God is entirely a relation to the active divine will.

Just as the content of the Christian conception of God is focused in divine love, so to the eye of faith all of God's activity is concentrated upon the realization of his purpose. Faith knows of no divine activity which can be separated from God's love, and which is not in some way or other an expression of his will. Every act of God signifies in the final analysis a realization of his love, even if the act at first sight would seem to have an entirely different significance. The activity of God has no other "goal" than that of realizing his loving will. Furthermore, it has no other basis than divine love itself. All attempts to advance other bases will eventuate in a conflict with the character of divine love as spontaneous love (cf. § 14. 2).

Just as we have spoken of a threefold conflux of fundamental ideas in regard to the conception of God, so with reference to the divine activity we may distinguish three cardinal points of view, and designate the work of God as an act of salvation, an act of judgment, and an act of creation. If the act of salvation is an immediate result of the spontaneous love of God, then the act of judgment accentuates especially the radical opposition of this divine will to evil, while the act of creation emphasizes the sovereignty of divine love. It must be expressly stated that this does not imply an isolation of the various principal ideas; all three are apprehensible in the three divine acts. Thus, for example, the act of salvation is indeed an act in which both the radical opposition of the divine will to evil and its creative sovereignty find expression. In conclusion it may be remarked that this section dealing with the activity of God intends to present simply an outline and that both of the following sections dealing with the act of God in Christ and the Church of God will seek to develop further the significance of the whole activity of God's love and will, and to make clear the ways in which this will is realized. When in the following exposition the act of creation is placed after the acts of salvation and judgment it must not be interpreted as a subordination of creation and its significance, which in reality is basic for Christian faith. The purpose is rather to guard the purely religious character of the idea of creation and to exclude every possibility of transforming the concept of creation into a rational explanation of the universe.

2. *Divine Activity as an Act of Salvation.*

To conceive of divine activity as an act of salvation is to emphasize that which faith has primarily to say about the action of divine love. In this context the word salvation has been chosen as the most comprehensive among the many expressions which are relevant to this subject and which include the ideas of reconciliation, forgiveness, sanctification, etc. The act of salvation is that act in and through which God establishes a communion and fellowship between himself and a humanity which is sinful and lost. In the word salvation there is this twofold implication: on the one hand that man is, by reason of sin, separated from God; and on the other that God overcomes that which separates him from man. If the relation of fellowship between God and man cannot be established by any other means than by an act of salvation on God's part, then both the character of sin as being a radical and devastating evil and the continuous opposition of the divine will to this evil become inescapably apparent. Sin is then revealed not merely as something imperfect, nor does it imply simply that divine love has not yet attained complete dominion. Sin is seen rather as a militant power diametrically opposed to the divine will and its purposes. Christian faith is uncompromisingly realistic and radically unreserved in its criticism of the evil in life. It considers as naive optimism the notion that evil is only the necessary shadows in the picture, or that there is a "growth toward perfection" which is a part of an inner necessarily progressive development in the direction of ultimate perfection. According to the realistic viewpoint of faith there is no basis in fact for such dreams; it tears them unmercifully apart like cobwebs. On the contrary, the divine will realizes itself only in bitter struggle against everything which opposes it. The victories of this divine will in the sphere of the human soul, as indicated by the word "salvation," are in the nature of a rescue, a radical transformation, a giving of new life, all of which is at the same time the infliction of death. It is definitely not a matter of the development of something given or of a salvation of self by self, but salvation actually implies, from one point of view, as Luther trenchantly expresses it, that we are "snatched away from ourselves and are placed outside ourselves," or, in other words, that the domination of egocentricity is broken and replaced by the dominion of God.

As far as Christian faith is concerned, the possibility of salvation lies entirely in the divine will and not in any human quality. Therefore, from the viewpoint of faith, it is idle to attempt to explain by rational means how salvation occurs. For faith there is no other explanation than that which refers to God's spontaneously active, unfathomable, and loving will. Salvation cannot be explained by asserting that man possesses such intrinsic worth as thereby to evoke the divine act of love. On the contrary, when man is confronted with the divine act of salvation, it becomes apparent to him that he does not possess such an intrinsic worth, that he is not gifted with any quality which would, in itself, move the divine will to activity. If for this reason the conclusion is drawn that the possibility of salvation must be excluded, inasmuch as there is apparently nothing in man which can motivate and thereby make salvation possible, then it must be emphasized that from the viewpoint of faith the possibility of salvation is clearly evident in and with its actual existence. In general, faith can say nothing more about the possibility of salvation than is given in the Bible passage, "With man this is impossible, but with God all things are possible" (Matt. 19:26). The divine will to save appears to faith as absolutely unmerited love, and salvation by faith as entirely a work of God. When it was asserted in a previous section that faith also, as seen from one point of view, has the character of a decision, an audacious choice on man's part, it does not mean in any sense whatsoever that the character of faith as entirely a work of God is encroached upon in any way. Every "synergistic" approach is excluded. Even when man assumes an affirmative position relative to God, this is nothing else to the eye of faith than the work of God, his conquest of man (cf. § 35).

The Christian conception of salvation is distinguished from both the idealistic and the metaphysical-dualistic doctrines. Both of these otherwise mutually hostile doctrines emanate from a metaphysical tension between the infinite and the finite, and both regard evil as synonymous with the finite as such. The difference between the two is that while metaphysical dualism regards man as entirely a finite creature, the idealistic type considers him as a citizen of both the finite and infinite worlds. Behind the idealistic thought lie the ancient conceptions emanating from Greek mystery religion and philosophy which divide man into two parts, a higher, spiritual self issuing from the world of divine infinity, and a lower, sensual, and finite self. Man's present misfortune is that his higher, spiritual ego has been confined in the prison of finite and material existence. Salvation consists in the release of the higher self from this prison. These ideas have during the ages exercised an influence upon Christianity in many ways. This influence has been primarily characterized by two tendencies; in the first place, with idealism as a starting point, there has been an inclination to regard salvation as an ascending movement of the soul. In the second place, by reference to the divine element existing in man, the attempt has been made to bring about a rational motivation for the possibility of salvation by claiming that man possesses an "untainted core" or something similar, in any event a value, which God must take into consideration and which is calculated to move him to an appreciation of man. Both of these tendencies stand in sharp contrast to the Christian conception of salvation. The former substitutes man's ascension to God for God's condescension to man, while the latter abolishes the religious "paradox" in the

Christian conception of salvation by permitting salvation to be at least partially rooted in something other than in God's unsearchable, spontaneous love.

When a *metaphysical-dualistic* approach has pushed its way into theology and influenced the interpretation of Christianity, it has, as a rule, been in the form of a reaction against the idealistically oriented doctrine of salvation. But even such a reaction has actually been negatively dependent upon the very idealistic viewpoint which it opposed. A similar phenomenon has in a more recent period been apparent in the reaction of dialectic theology. Against the blurring of the demarcation line between the divine and the human by the idealistic theory, metaphysical dualism seeks to guard this boundary line with utmost energy by conceiving the contrast between the divine and human as a contrast between the infinite and the finite. The purpose is to give the strongest possible expression to the contrast between God and that which is separated from him. Actually, however, the contrast is not clearly apprehended, for it is undefined and does not possess, as does Christian faith, a clear and qualitatively determined character. The consequence of the metaphysical-dualistic line of thought is that the religious "paradox" of the Christian conception of salvation is replaced by a metaphysical paradox: Salvation is found in the inconceivable union of the infinite and the finite. Since such a union is out of the question in the circumstances of life on earth, salvation must be conceived in terms of a metaphysical eschatology. Here also the opposition to the idealistic metaphysical doctrine of salvation appears. When this approach argues its case from the viewpoint of immanence and is inclined to permit the human to become absorbed in the divine, the emphasis is shifted from the eschatological to the present. The dominion of God becomes essentially something which by a process of evolution actualizes itself in life here on earth.

3. *The Twofold Perspective of Christian Faith.*

From the viewpoint of idealism, salvation is essentially a process of evolution belonging to life here on earth which, because of the inner necessity of its own nature, gradually advances toward perfection. For metaphysical dualism, salvation is located beyond this life, that is to say, it is eschatologically conceived. In contrast to these viewpoints, Christian faith regards salvation as something which both occurs in the present and is at the same time a part of the "good things to come" (Heb. 9:11).

To Christian faith history appears as an arena where the conflict between the will of God and that which is inimical to it takes place. Two things are therefore essential for faith; in the first place, that the decisive encounter between the mutually hostile forces has taken place, and that the work of Christ has resulted in a victory of God's will over that of the demonic powers (cf. § 26). In the second place, this does not mean that the battle between these forces has been concluded; it continues unabated, but because of the victorious work of Christ it is a battle under changed circumstances.

With reference to salvation, this implies on the one hand that already in the circumstances of life on earth salvation exists as a divine act of reconciliation and forgiveness through which fellowship between God and man has been established; on the other hand, this fellowship as existing under circumstances of this life is found to be a perpetually ongoing struggle. Therefore Christian faith conceives of salvation as something present as well as something eschatological. And the proportion between these two viewpoints is by no means such that an emphasis upon fellowship with God here and now leads to a suppression of the eschatological perspective or vice versa. The situation is rather this—that the more clearly salvation is seen to be a fellowship with God here and now, the more clearly does it receive the character of a hope of "good things to come" (cf. § 36). The reason Christian faith is characterized by such a two-sidedness is that for faith the fellowship with God *eo ipso* implies a keener appreciation of the distance between man and the divine will. The nearer God's saving love comes to man, the clearer he comprehends that which separates him from God. The Christian conception of salvation is radically different from all perfectionist doctrines. Indeed, it is the "justified" person, the one who has been incorporated into the divine fellowship, who understands with increasing clarity that he is still a sinner (Luther: *simul iustus et peccator*).

Therefore, as far as Christian faith is concerned, the perfect dominion of God, the "Kingdom of God," lies entirely outside the bounds of history. The Kingdom of God is, therefore, in principle an eschatological concept. The idea that the Kingdom of God is realized through an evolutionary and inner world-process is entirely foreign to Christian faith. The Kingdom of God does not belong to this world (John 18:36), nor does it have anything to do with earthly ideals of blessedness. From this point of view the eschatological character of the Kingdom of God *cannot* be emphasized strongly enough. But this does not imply, however, that the Kingdom of God has nothing to do with the world of history. On the contrary, history is the arena where the Kingdom of God struggles and wins its victories. If the evil spirits are driven out by the hand of God (Luke 11:20), then the Kingdom of God is indeed not perfected (this is not the meaning of the Gospel), but it is in action. It has not become, but is becoming. When new victories are won, it does not mean that in the circumstances of history the Kingdom of God ascends in a rising crescendo toward perfection. It implies only that the Kingdom is in constant activity; that after every new victory there comes a new struggle, though perhaps on another front. The battle lines may change, but fundamentally it is always the same battle. The Kingdom of God is just as near and just as remote for every new generation. The chief thing about the Kingdom of God in its relation to history is its active character. Luther speaks clearly hereof when, in the explanation

of the third petition, he answers the question, "When is the will
of God done?" by saying,

"When God frustrates and brings to naught every evil counsel and
purpose, which would hinder us from hallowing the name of God, and
prevent His kingdom from coming to us, such as the will of the devil, of
the world, and of our own flesh . . ."

This is the extremely realistic approach of Christian faith; no
evolutionary idealism, but neither a fatalistic resignation. In
spite of everything, the voice of victory sounds forth, "Though
devils all the world should fill, all watching to devour us, we
tremble not ——"

19. God as Judge

1. The viewpoint which conceives of the work of God as an
act of judgment expresses the radical opposition of divine love
to sin. The judgment of God either restores or rejects. It becomes a rejection and condemnation when the opposition to the
divine will continues unconquered. Judgment may therefore
be understood as being in part a judgment in the present and
in part a "final judgment." The significance of the judgment of
rejection consists in separation from God.

2. When the divine and loving will is not dominant, the conse-
quent desolation and suffering may be characterized as divine
judgment, with the qualification that: a) this viewpoint must
not be used to establish a rational explanation of the universe,
and b) the punitive activity of God is designated as his *opus
alienum* and not his *opus proprium*.

Excursus. The boundary line of faith. The result of God's final
judgment cannot be made the object of any definite statement
of faith. On this subject the groping thoughts of faith must emanate from and be determined by the following fundamental
rules: the possibilities of God's love must not be abridged and
his radical opposition to sin must not be obscured. Under such
circumstances faith will reject both a rationally motivated and

unconditionally maintained universal restoration (*apokatastasis*) and a rationally motivated and unconditionally maintained so-called twofold destiny. Thus, the viewpoint of faith must be distinguished from both idealistic and scholastic theories.

1. The Active Judgment of God.

The God of salvation is also the God of judgment. The interpretation of the divine act of judgment is exposed to two mutually opposed fundamental dangers: first, the possibility of separating God's act of judgment from his loving will; and second, the possibility of weakening the significance of the idea of judgment. The first possibility is characteristic of scholastic theology, and the second is typical of that humanized theology which has been influenced by idealistic metaphysics. If the characteristic viewpoint of faith shall receive due consideration it is necessary to preserve the connection both between the loving will and the judgment of God, and the unbroken radicalism of divine judgment against sin. Between these two points of view there ensues a relationship full of tension. But actually the latter viewpoint can be effectively maintained only under the assumption that the judgment of God is understood in the final analysis as an expression of his love. For the only really radical judgment of sin is that of pure love. Christian faith has frequently spoken of Christ as the one who exercises God's power of judgment, as judge of "the quick and the dead." This in itself is the strongest possible expression of the fact that Christian faith cannot conceive of God's judgment in any other terms than as a judgment of love itself, and that no assertion about God's judgment can be identified as Christian which cannot also be ascribed to and affirmed of Christ and the Holy Spirit.

It can hardly be denied that various notions have crept into the thought of the divine act of judgment which cannot in the least be reconciled with the idea that the work of God, from whatever viewpoint it may be considered, is always an act of love. Thus it has been possible for primitive ideas to appear which have attributed something capricious, unreliable, and envious to the nature of God. When such ideas have been connected especially with thoughts about God as "the avenger," it has been due to the fact that the anthropomorphic and symbolical character of this expression has not been sufficiently considered. The attempt has thus been made to find in "vengeance" a divine characteristic opposed to love, instead of understanding it simply as an imperfect figure of speech which may be used to illustrate the spontaneous power in God's opposition to evil. The act of judgment has, however, most often been given a judaizing interpretation according to the principle of pure retribution: like for like, an eye for an eye, a tooth for a tooth. Indeed, the idea of retribution has a relative legitimacy, inasmuch as it gives elementary expression to punitive justice, to that fundamental principle which says that evil must be condemned and punished in conformity with that law of life which requires that of necessity evil begets evil. Thus the idea of retribution may be said to be related to God's act of judgment, since his judgment occurs because of an inner necessity and on account of sin. However, the idea of retribution is dangerous whenever retributive justice is separated from divine love and is made the highest principle in the relationship between God and man. The consequence of such an isolation of the idea of retribution is that God's relationship to man is again imprisoned within the confines of the legal system which was burst asunder through the divine revelation in Christ. Furthermore, the idea of reward and punishment becomes, in the final analysis, decisive, and thus the purely religious conception of Christian faith concerning man's relation to God is replaced by a eudaemonistic moralism. Consequently, Christian faith accepts as relatively legitimate the idea of retribution, but this idea forfeits its rights when it is made the decisive principle between God and man.

If, therefore, the judgment of God cannot be separated from his love, but is, finally, simply an expression of his benevolence, then it is of fundamental importance for Christian faith that

171

the seriousness and severity of this judgment is not obscured or suppressed. It should be emphasized that, as far as Christian faith is concerned, the judgment of God has an active, and not only a passive, character. Judgment does not *merely* imply, as Marcion declared, that man separates himself from divine love. To be sure, that is, indeed, an aspect of judgment, as indicated in the words of the Gospel of John: "And this is the condemnation, that light is come into the world, and men loved darkness rather than light" (John 3:19). Nevertheless, judgment is at the same time a positive act toward men in such circumstances. When Marcion was unwilling to acknowledge such an active judgment of God, it was not because he was overemphasizing divine love, but rather that he had not penetrated deeply enough into the nature of this love.

To be confronted by divine love involves always and everywhere a judgment. To stand before God is to be judged. But this judgment may be of various kinds; it is inevitably a judgment either of restoration or of rejection. In the presence of divine love there are, fundamentally, only two possibilities: either it subdues man, or it does not. In the former case the judgment of God restores and saves; in the latter case it rejects and separates. In this connection we are primarily concerned with the latter alternative, inasmuch as the restoring judgment coincides exactly with God's act of salvation. With reference to this act it is sufficient to emphasize that God's act of salvation must also be understood as an act of judgment; it is a "justifying" judgment, which, while it restores and unites man with God, at the same time reveals man's estrangement from pure love and his unworthiness before God.

But since God's judgment of rejection or separation must also be understood as a judgment of love, it follows that this judgment is fundamentally nothing less than a *separation from God.* This occurs by reason both of the inner necessity occasioned by the purity of love itself and by man's unconquered hostility to God. The sole purpose of God's loving will is to realize the

172

dominion of love. This is also the sole purpose of divine revelation, as the words of John so well express it, "God sent not his Son into the world to condemn the world" (John 3:17). The purpose was entirely other than that of simply passing judgment upon the world. Nevertheless, all revelation of divine love implies a judgment; indeed, the purer and clearer the revelation, the higher must be the degree of judgment. Although love has nothing to do with external coercion, the very nature of love is such as to produce either attraction or repulsion.[1]

Therefore it may be rightfully said of the Lord of revelation, "He is set for the fall and the rising again of many" (Luke 2:34). In the same vein we sing of the Holy Spirit, "With him who unbelieving spurns Thy love, Thou canst ne'er abide" (Swedish Psalmbook, number 136, verse 6). Such an expression reveals that which is fundamental in God's judgment: love cannot abide with that individual who in unbelief has refused to be subdued by it. From another point of view, the same principle is apparent in the well-known scene before the judgment seat (Matt. 25:31-46). Here the revelation of divine love (the Son of Man) makes known those who have and those who have not permitted themselves to be subdued and ruled by divine love. That the judgment of God is a judgment of love means that no one will be rejected and separated except those who have refused to tolerate the presence of love. According to Christian faith, the judgment of God in history is a preliminary judgment. In addition to this constantly ongoing act of judgment, and in connection with it, faith speaks of a definitive judgment, which it identifies with the expression "final judgment."

2. Judgment and Punishment.

The idea of judgment is closely connected with the thought

---

[1] The expression "Whom he will he hardeneth" may also be interpreted from this viewpoint (cf. Paul in *Romans* and Luther in *De Servo Arbitrio*). The significance of the expression cannot be that of God's desire to "harden" man in sin. "Hardening" consists rather in the hardening reaction of sin itself when it is confronted by that which is good, by the revelation of pure love.

173

of punishment. Judgment implies punishment. As we have previously noted, the punishment of the judgment of rejection consists primarily in separation from God. But the conception of divine punishment has also at the same time been made to refer to "temporal" punishments of various kinds. It is, of course, indubitable that sin, that is to say, the absence of the dominion of divine love, is connected with and leads to the most extensive desolation and the deepest suffering; this is verified again and again in every new generation. To Christian faith the inner connection between sin and desolation appears as a divine law. It may then be asked in what measure this desolation and suffering shall be considered as a divine "punishment," and what is meant by the punishment of God. If we are to use this symbolical expression as a legitimate Christian designation of God's relation to that which opposes him, and at the same time do justice to the divine nature as pure love, such use must be limited to certain specific circumstances, namely the two following: this viewpoint cannot be used to establish a rational explanation of the universe; and the punitive act of God must be distinguished as his "alien activity" (*opus alienum*), in contrast to his "proper activity" (*opus proprium*).

In the first place, the conception of divine punishment cannot be employed as a rational explanation of the world's desolation and suffering. This tribulation cannot be thought of as a proportionate punishment in relation to the sin which has been committed. Such reasoning, which gives evidence of a relapse into the doctrine of pure retribution, stands most emphatically opposed to the fundamental viewpoint of the Gospel. Thus Jesus, according to Luke 13, dismissed the suggestion that those Galileans whose blood Pilate had mingled with their sacrifices were sinners above all others because they had suffered such things (Luke 13:1 ff.; cf. John 9:2 f.). And this Gospel viewpoint is abundantly verified by the mysterious contaminating and infectious nature of sin: the consequences of sin do not fall only upon the guilty; the innocent must suffer with the guilty, indeed, often in greater measure. Thus, the idea, which Jesus, according to the Gospel, repudiated, is clearly connected with a Pharisaic self-righteousness which judges without love and therefore unrighteously. Such judgments, which are in harmony with the predilections of "natural" man, are more concerned to establish the degrees of guilt than to conquer evil (cf. § 23).

In the second place, since faith includes a certain type of suffering in its conception of divine judgment, it must be assumed that such punishment is, as Luther termed it, an "alien work" of God, which ultimately serves his "proper work," that is to say, the work of divine love. Faith is certainly aware of the fact that the divine will can employ severe methods, but it sees the wrath of God as "fused" with love and the harsh strokes as the instruments whose purpose it is to prepare the way for God's "proper" work. There can be no question therefore of God's desire to inflict punishment simply to bring upon the sinner a certain amount of suffering. As far as faith is concerned, it is meaningless to speak of divine punishment in historical circumstances which does not in some way serve the divine purpose, viz., the establishment of the dominion of God's love. It is evident to faith, however, that desolation and suffering actually *can* serve this purpose. This is true in a negative sense, for these tribulations reveal the consequences of being separated from that power which is supreme in the life and growth of all creation. But this is true in even greater measure because divine love, as faith clearly testifies, is able to use desolation and suffering as a means to accomplish its positive purposes. From the viewpoint of faith, the concept of divine punishment is, therefore, indissolubly connected with the idea of warning, discipline, testing, cleansing, quickening, deepening, and so on, or, in other words, with positive purposes. However, when the thought of divine punishment is separated from these purposes, it loses its meaning and significance. A marginal note must be inserted at this point to the effect that faith cannot conceive of any suffering which emanates from sin, as a result of the divine will.

Faith, indeed, refers to *this type of suffering* as being related to God and points out that the inner connection between sin and desolation is an expression of divine law, and that God can even employ it as a means to accomplish his purpose. But this does not mean that this evil can be traced to the divine will and that therefore it is a direct realization of the will of God. Whenever these viewpoints are blurred the result is disastrous and the conception of God which is characteristic of Christian faith is consequently entirely obscured. When that evil which has its roots in sin is said to be an expression of God's will, it implies that sin, or in other words, that which opposes the will of God, is synonymous with that will (cf. § 22). Under no circumstances can Christian faith ascribe to God anything which stands in opposition to that which the work of Christ has revealed as divine, and which faith is unable to ascribe to God the Holy Spirit. The God of Christian faith desires no evil; his sole concern is to overcome it.

Excursus. The Boundary Line of Faith.

The judgment of God continues constantly. Divine love unceasingly carries on its activity of restoration and separation. But faith must simultaneously consider the divine act of judgment from an eschatological viewpoint, just as it does the acts of salvation and creation (cf. § 18. 3; § 20. 3). The judgment of God is not fully completed within a certain specified time. It cannot be assigned to some "final period" within history. From the viewpoint of faith, the identification of world-history with world-judgment is only a half-truth. Any attempt to discern the judgment of God, according to the pure laws of retribution, in the course of history would result in something less than a half-truth (cf. § 19. 2). Therefore, Christian faith looks forward to a *"final judgment"* for the full consummation of divine judgment.

The idea of this final judgment is an essential, inalienable, and fundamental aspect of the outlook of faith. But this does not mean that faith is able to answer all the questions which can be asked in this connection. Here we find ourselves at the boundary line of faith. Faith is unable to express itself relative to these matters in the same way that it can witness to the divine act of revelation in the present. It must relinquish all supposedly certain knowledge about that which lies beyond its grasp. In this connection it is well to recall Luther's reference to the three kingdoms in his *De Servo Arbitrio,* viz., the kingdoms of nature, grace, and glory. In the kingdom of grace, says Luther, much is revealed of that which is hidden in the kingdom of nature. Likewise, in the kingdom of glory much will be revealed which is now hidden in the kingdom of grace. Therefore, faith, which exists in the kingdom of grace, would be presumptuous if it endeavored to express itself about the kingdom of glory, as if all its secrets had already been revealed.

But if faith, in spite of everything, attempts, in groping thoughts, to feel its way across the boundary, it does so only on the condition that these thoughts must harmonize with that which faith has already seen of God's loving will and its activity in judgment. This is doubly important, for in these matters a number of viewpoints, which are foreign to Christian faith, have appeared from many directions. The ideas of faith concerning the final judgment and its consequences can contain no element which opposes those verities which have reference to the Christian concept of the nature of God and the relationship between God and man. If faith is convinced that the divine will never operates through external coercion but through the power of an inner compulsion, then this fundamental point of view cannot be set aside when it is a question of God's "final judgment." Divine love does not change its approach; it is "unchangeable." If faith has been confronted by God's love as the supreme power in all creation and knows something of those limitless possibilities which are at its disposal, it is not tempted to ignore or diminish these possibilities when the question of God's final judgment is being considered. If faith has also seen that to be united with this power involves "eternal" and indestructible life, but to be separated therefrom results in desolation and defeat, then this fundamental idea must also be applied to the question of the "final goal" set by the will of God. And finally, if faith has become aware of God's inexorable, unabridged opposition to evil, it cannot readily succumb to notions which attempt to blunt this unbroken opposition when it is a question of the consummation of the act of judgment. This discussion may be summarized in two principles, viz., the possibilities of the sovereign love of God cannot be abbreviated or diminished; and his radical, condemning opposition to sin must not be obscured.

With its starting point rooted in these principles, Christian faith overrules the theories of both scholastic and idealistic theologians. The characteristic viewpoint of scholasticism is a rationally motivated and unconditionally maintained twofold destiny; idealism is characterized by a rationally motivated and unconditionally maintained *apokatastasis*. As far as the scholastic type is concerned, we can ignore the question which it presents relative to the "eternal anguish" of the damned. It is clear, however, that this divine retributive justice triumphs both over evil and over the divine Agape when it is asserted, for example, that in the torments of the damned, the redeemed hosts behold and admire the justice of God. The chief objection of Christian faith to scholasticism is the assumption of this theory that its conclusions alone are acceptable, and that it can therefore arrogantly limit the possibilities of divine love. In contrast, Christian faith must reckon with the unlimited possibilities of divine love. But at the same time, faith is unable to assert, as does the idealistic and evolutionary theory, that everything is progressing toward a so-called *apokatastasis* because of an inner, positive urge. When this theory makes reference to the sovereignty of divine love as proof of its assertion, it forgets that this divine love never operates as a coercive force. It would be possible to construct an *apokatastasis* as a self-evident final goal only if divine love were found to operate as an irresistible force of coercion. When Christian faith gives due consideration to the manner in which divine love accomplishes its work—by means of an inner compulsion, without which it would not be love—and also takes into account the actual fact of opposition to this love, it must also reckon with the possibility of a hardening of the heart which definitely separates itself from fellowship with divine love.

Christian faith must therefore reject both a rationally conceived dualistic starting point and a rationally constructed doctrine of an *apokatastasis*. In general, it cannot establish any definite propositions in this matter. Instead, faith must reckon with the twofold possibility which is based upon the Christian conception of God's relation to man and the character of the Christian idea of God. Faith's view of that which lies beyond the boundary is therefore characterized by a tension-filled dialectic. Least of all can the idea of the continuing possibilities of divine love be used in the interests of a lax quietism without thereby losing its Christian legitimacy. Everyone who has been confronted by the divine love must thence live as if the present possibilities were the only ones, under the constraint that "the acceptable time" is now and that every day is the "last day." The idea of a continued possibility of decision beyond death is accessible *to faith,* and then only as a thought inspired by love and hope for the benefit of others. It emerges in the presence of the sovereignty of divine love and implies that this love, even less than our own, cannot be halted by death.

It should be added that a presentation of "the final consummation" must take into account not only the two possibilities already mentioned, but also a third, viz., the so-called theory of annihilation. A closer examination of this idea reveals, however, that this is but a variation of the theory of the twofold destiny.

When the argument relating to condemnation and annihilation is examined, it is evident at the outset that the discussion all too often rests upon postulates which are foreign to Christian faith, especially upon the theory which maintains that the "immortality of the soul" is something axiomatically given. This line of thought, which has emanated from a philosophical and ideal-istic matrix, stands in sharp contrast to the characteristic view-point of Christian faith. For Christian faith "eternal life" is not a self-evident prerogative of man, but is rather a gift which is given in and with man's fellowship with God and is realized in and through the "resurrection."[2] When the conflux of ideas that have emerged in connection with the concept of eternal con-demnation is further investigated, it becomes clear that a host of unworthy notions have made their appearance, since it has been possible to regard "torment" as an end in itself, or in any event, as having the purpose of celebrating the *iustitia distribu-tiva et vindicativa* which is separated from divine love. When these unworthy notions are eliminated, the legitimately Chris-tian element in the conception of condemnation appears, viz., the idea that the judgment of God confronts sinful man as an unconditional judgment of rejection. If the results of both of these investigations are now finally applied to the debatable question of eternal punishment and annihilation, the conse-quence is a certain obvious solution of their mutual opposition. That which remains is the twofold idea that the judgment of God reaches sinful man as an unconditional judgment of rejec-tion, and that this final judgment involves separation from God. When Christian faith employs the contradictory expression "the eternal death" to designate this separation from God, this very expression itself makes it plain that it is outside the realm of possibility for faith to affirm anything about the result of the judgment of rejection except that it involves a separation from God.

---

[2] Carl Stange has in several works made especially valuable investigations for the clarification of the essential difference between the Christian conception of resurrection and the philosophical and idealistic idea of immortality. We refer especially to the following works: *Die Unsterblichkeit der Seele; Luther und das fünfte Laterankonzil; Das Ende aller Dinge.* Cf. also the Dutch theologian J. de Zwaan: *"Paulinsche Weltanschauung"* (in *Zeitschrift für Syst. Theol.*, 1930). This author says, p. 576, *"Die Lehre der naturhaft unsterblichen Seele is nicht paulinisch. In seiner Weltanschauung hat sie keinen Platz."*

20. God as Creator

1. When the work of God is viewed as creative activity it expresses in a special way the sovereignty of divine love. Faith in God as Creator is not a theory about the origin of the world through a "first cause," etc. It has in reality nothing in common with a rational explanation of the universe. It arises out of the confrontation with the life-giving, sovereign God, and the relationship between God and man is determined by this encounter.

2. Christian faith as faith in the Creator differentiates itself, on the one hand, from metaphysical idealism which blurs the distinction between the divine and "the highest human"; and, on the other hand, from metaphysical dualism which regards this finite life as evil. On the contrary, faith in God as Creator affirms that all existence is entirely dependent on God, that this life is good since it is given by him who is "the giver of all good gifts," and that this gift therefore imposes an unconditional obligation on the creature.

3. If creation, therefore, is primarily the life-giving work of sovereign divine love, it implies that its origin as well as its perdurance depends on this loving will, which also gives it its meaning. The ultimate goal of creation does not lie within the course of this world. It is attained through the continuous creation, which at the same time appears as a new creation, "new heavens and a new earth."

1. The Religious Character of Faith in God as Creator.

Strictly speaking, it *ought* to be superfluous to emphasize the religious character of faith in God as Creator. But in reality nothing is more imperative, since it is at this point in particular that foreign metaphysical points of view have appeared. It has been very common to confuse the affirmations of faith about creation with cosmological theories, or to interpret these affirmations as a theory of the origin of the universe coincident with or perhaps in conflict with other more or less scientific theories of its origin and development. The old scholastic theology with its predilection for rational argumentation explained creation by reference to God as "the first cause." Even after this kind of argumentation had lost favor, the metaphysical points of view stubbornly remained. Faith in God as Creator was accepted as a theoretical proposition about that which had happened "in the beginning of time." Even if such a theory of origins could be theoretically demonstrated, which is impossible, this whole conception is completely meaningless to faith, since it has no religious character. The various theories about the origin and development of the universe which might be suggested by natural science cannot encroach upon or exercise any influence on the convictions of faith regarding creation. When the old geocentric world view was long ago abandoned and we now reckon with incomprehensible space, this serves simply to accentuate that which has always been a commonplace to faith: human lowliness in the presence of the divine majesty. But this cannot in any way change the Christian faith in God as Creator, nor affect its religious character.

It is, therefore, of fundamental importance to emphasize that faith's affirmations about creation do not imply a theoretical proposition about the origin of the universe, but rather a religious statement about the nature of the relation between God and man. Faith in God as Creator arises out of the confrontation of faith with the saving and condemning love of God. The divine act of salvation appears to faith in reality as an act of creation. It is significant that the psalmist prays: "Create in me a clean heart, O God" (Ps. 51:10), and that Paul says: "If any man is in Christ, he is a new creature" (II Cor. 5:17). The reason that the point of view of creation appears so insistently in this connection is that faith attributes the origin of the new life to the power of divine love. *Wir handeln nich, sonderen wir werden gehandelt* (Luther). This power appears, therefore, as a power which destroys and brings to nought all opposition. It appears not as a power coincident with other powers and perhaps stronger than they, but as the sovereign power of the universe which sustains and rules over all existence. To be separated from this power means desolation and destruction, but to be united with it and subject to it is to partake of eternal and indestructible life.

When creation is thus anchored to God's act of salvation, two aspects of creation are thereby immediately suggested: creation is a continuous process, and the creative activity is throughout an expression of God's love. If God's act of creation is the establishment of the dominion of his love, creation can no longer be conceived of as an isolated act, or as an act accomplished and finished by God at a certain point in time, "in the beginning." God's establishment of his dominion is a continuous activity, and his creation is therefore continually in process. It would be possible to speak of creation as confined to a certain period of time only by declaring that God no longer reveals himself. If he reveals himself continually, he also creates continually, for God's revelation is always a recreation. Nothing could be more contrary to the viewpoint of Christian faith than to speak of God's creative activity simply in the perfect tense. Furthermore, in creation we are concerned with the activity of divine love. It would be useless to speak about God's creation unless the reference is to the life-giving activity of divine love. The love of God must be understood as a creative love. The nature of divine love is to impart itself, to give itself; and this self-impartation implies creation. The creative activity of God is not something incidental, or something that could be separated from him. If God is love, then by inner necessity he is the creating God.[1] Faith cannot think of God as existing in lonely sep-

---

[1] K. Holl, "*Was verstand Luther unter Religion,*" *Gesammelte Aufsätze zur Kirchengeschichte,* I, 2nd & 3rd ed., p. 44. Holl points out that Luther's concentration on love as the "nature" of God gave him a different view of creation than that common in scholastic theology. God is "*der Brunnquell der sich ewig mit Gute ubergiesst. Deshalb will er kraft seines Wesen—nicht nur 'zufällig,' wie die Scholastik sagte—eine Welt, will er den Menschen, um seine Liebe in ihm auszuschütten.*"

aration "before the world," before creation; it cannot, if God really is love, think of him except as creating.

The significance of faith in God as Creator with reference to the nature of the relationship between God and man will be discussed in the following paragraphs. Here we are simply concerned to emphasize that this faith asserts that God in his relation to men and the world is the *sovereign* God. In this relationship God is God, and man is man and belongs among the *creatura*. As far as faith is concerned, every attempt to transgress this boundary line is prevented by the idea of creation.

2. The Demarcation of Faith in God as Creator.

The religious significance of faith in God as Creator is clarified when we note how this faith is differentiated from two opposing and foreign theories of creation.

In the first place, faith in God as Creator stands in opposition to metaphysical idealism. The theories of metaphysical idealism may be expressed in various ways, but in one way or another they always manage to find the divine and the infinite in the human and the finite. The "spiritual" part of man belongs to the divine life. Under such circumstances that which is human passes over into the divine. No definite line of demarcation is drawn between the spiritual aspect of man, which is "the highest human" and is in itself indestructible and eternal, and the divine. This conception is in principle differentiated from faith in God as Creator, not only because it is a metaphysical speculation, but also because the relationship between God and man in this case is not characterized and defined by the sovereignty of the divine. As far as faith is concerned all creation is finite, and therefore of a different nature than the eternal God. This is true also of man. He possesses nothing incorruptible and eternal which belongs automatically to him; he has no divine, spiritual nature. God is God, and man is *qua homo* finite, corruptible, *creatura*. There is a sharp line of demarcation between Christian faith and idealism, no matter how frequently they have been confused and commingled. As far as faith is concerned, the divine cannot be included in the finite, but instead, the eternal God meets man, speaks to him, and has fellowship with him in the finite world of his existence. The attempt of idealism to escape the finite appears to faith as a failure to realize the seriousness of the situation in which man actually stands, as visionary optimism, and as a false apotheosis of the human.

But Christian faith in God as Creator is also differentiated from a metaphysical dualism which regards this finite life as evil and separates it from the sovereign and divine love. It is well known that the ancient church in its struggle to preserve faith in God as Creator faced such a situation in its conflict with Gnosticism and Marcion, who attributed the creation of the world to a lower god. It should be pointed out that it is not at all impossible for a metaphysical dualism to pass over into a metaphysical idealism. This is made possible by the idea that man belongs to a higher sphere but has become imprisoned in the finite world. Under all circumstances metaphysical dualism regards life in this world as evil. To this idea Christian faith in God as Creator is opposed. Evil is not to be found in the finite as such. To Christian faith evil does not make its appearances in an undefined, metaphysical opposition between the finite and the infinite, but in the definite opposition between the divine will and that which is inimical to it. It does not perceive life itself as evil. The God of creation is none other than the God of salvation.

When Christian faith in God as Creator is viewed against the background of these two foreign conceptions, two fundamental features become evident. In the first place, the relationship between God and man which is characterized by this faith is one of complete dependence upon God. The relationship is, in the famous phrase of Schleiermacher, "a feeling of absolute dependence." The content of this fundamental idea is obscured when this dependence is confused with a relation of cause and effect, as Schleiermacher confused it. The religious significance of this dependence is that in relation to existence and man God is sovereign, that in every circumstance man is completely at the mercy of the power of God, and that he can trust only in God, not in something divine within himself.

It is this status of unconditional dependence, which, as an element of faith in God as Creator, characterizes the Christian relationship between God and man. But in the second place, faith in God as Creator perceives this life as something good, a gift from him who is the giver of all good gifts (Jas. 1:17). To regard life in this finite world as evil results in an ascetic view which is foreign to faith. *The finite world in which man lives is God's world.* It cannot be divided into spiritual and profane parts. Not only "the spiritual life," but also that part of existence which we call the secular is subject to the government of God. Just because life is a gift and this world is God's world, the strongest obligation and the most unconditional responsibility are involved in life.

3. The Content of Faith in God as Creator.

According to our previous exposition, creation is that work of divine love through which this love appears as the sovereign power in relation to existence. Faith perceives the divine love as that power which gives life to and in the fullest meaning of the word sustains all things; it is that power which by its continuous creative activity establishes its kingdom out of chaos. In whatever direction faith looks, it sees the same divine love: "of him, and through him, and unto him are all things" (Rom. 11:36). The proposition that creation is founded upon and is sustained by the divine will expresses the thesis that the creation is completely dependent on God. Nothing perdures which is not sustained by this divine love. If divine love is the sovereign and life-giving power of existence, then everything not connected with or sustained by this love is marked for corruption and destruction (cf. § 16. 2). When theology has designated this part of God's activity as "providence," it should be noted that this is not a different activity, but simply the continued creative activity of God. We could speak of it as a different work only if creation had been finished at a certain point of time. Since this is not the case, the idea of providence is inseparably connected with God's creative activity as a *creatio continua*.[2] God's providence is his continuous creative activity. There is, of course, a different connotation in providence than in creation. Providence suggests the maintenance of that which already exists. Nevertheless, providence must be connected with the fundamental idea of creation. When we pray God to preserve his Christian church, this preservation is in reality nothing else than the continuous, life-giving activity of divine love.

From the point of view of faith in God as Creator the divine love gives a meaning to all existence. Since existence and history are not in themselves a complete whole, this meaning is not to be found in history as such. As long as history is seen without connection with the will of God, the meaning is hidden; but it is revealed through the continuous struggle of the divine will against the opposing forces. Christian faith in God as Creator is opposed, therefore, both to that pessimistic world view which regards existence as a meaningless repetition, and to that evolutionistic and optimistic view which attempts to find the meaning in a continuous progress toward a goal of perfection attainable in this world. Christian faith finds the meaning of existence in the fact that every moment has eternal significance, since it involves a decision for or against the will of God. The divine will is not indifference to history when history is understood as the arena in which the divine will struggles against inimical forces. The attitude of the divine will toward history is not merely that of a negative condemnation, but is rather a positive desire to save and thereby to re-create. But the ultimate goal does not lie in a certain "end period" of world history, it

[2] Schleiermacher, *op. cit.*, pp. 142-49. The trouble with Schleiermacher's analysis is not that he combines the idea of providence with creation; this is in reality its merit. Since, however, the consciousness of absolute dependence upon God is combined with the insight that all things are conditioned and determined by the interdependence of nature, the idea of God's providence as *creatio continua* tends to become lifeless. Cf. 16. 2.

must rather be understood as a new creation, "new heavens and a new earth" (II Pet. 3:13).

Faith perceives clearly that such ultimate goals within history are figments of imagination, since every historical period must be subject to the divine creative activity, which is at the same time salvation and judgment. The perfection which faith contemplates implies, therefore, a radical transformation of the present order. This is symbolically expressed in the words about new heavens and a new earth (cf. § 51. 1). From this point of view the perfection cannot be referred to a certain "last" times within time, but is just as near to every time and generation. Every period must in reality be regarded as "the last times."

21. The Law of Creation

1. Creation implies order in contrast to chaos. Creation is thereby subjected to the law of the Creator. Since his loving will is the matrix of creation, the law of creation is a crystallization of this will. Its purpose, therefore, is the creation of a society in which the order of law is characterized by solicitude for the neighbor and a concern for mutual harmony. Man's vocation is to live in accordance with the order of creation.

2. The law of creation has been obscured through sin. When sin rules in human society, the order of creation is thereby changed into chaos. Through the revealed law God has clarified and interpreted the law of creation that was obscured through sin.

1. Lex creationis.

Christian faith in God as Creator is inseparably connected with the idea of God's law. In the combination, Creator–creation, there is implicit the idea of law and a definite order. For faith it is a fundamental and essential point of view that creation stands in constrast to and implies a victory over chaos. Creation in and by itself is subject to the Creator, under his dominion, and under obligation to obey that order which is contained and given in the act of creation. The law which is thus connected with creation is a universal law and is unconditionally valid.

The idea *lex naturae* has often appeared as a substitute for the *lex creationis,* or *lex creatoris,* of Christian faith. *Lex naturae,* the law of nature, could be described as a rationalized and secularized variety of *lex creationis.* The foundation of both is a universal law. The difference between them can be defined in this way, that *lex naturae* is a metaphysical conception, while *lex creationis* is a religious concept, originating in the relation to God and inseparably connected with faith in God as Creator. The idea *lex naturae* or law of nature rests on the false assumption that in a purely rational way a reasonable system of law and justice could be deduced which would be both universally applicable and definite in content. In reality there is no such fixed natural law. A rational analysis can only demonstrate the existence of various and competing systems. Christian faith has no reason whatever to attach itself to the idea of *lex naturae,* especially since it has in the concept of *lex creationis* that universal and unconditionally valid law which men try in vain to reach by a purely rational method.

The real significance of the law of creation is first of all the establishment of order in contrast to chaos. But the character of this order becomes more significant when we realize that creation has its origin in God's love. The law of creation is determined by God's love, and its purpose is to secure the realization of God's loving will within creation. The law of creation is in other words the law of love. When we speak about law, we must also consider justice, for law and justice belong together. As we have previously noted, the characteristic aspect of creation's law or order of justice is the fact that it has reference to and is defined by the demands of the loving will of God. This order which should be realized in creation is therefore an order and a society which are characterized by solicitude for the neighbor, whether this be practiced in larger or smaller associations; for instance, in the family, the nation, the state, or in humanity as a whole. Whatever associations there might be, the law of creation is concerned with the establishment and maintenance of a society of mutual love. That man belongs to creation signifies, therefore, that he is subject to the authority of creation; or, in other words, that he has received from God a vocation which he is called to fulfill; a vocation which is connected with and defined by the law of creation.

2. *Lex creationis* and *Lex revelationis*.

According to the Christian view of life, the *lex creationis* has been disturbed through sin and disobedience to God's will. This disturbance means not only that man transgresses the law of creation, but also that, through the transgression, the meaning and significance of this law have been obscured. Under such conditions there cannot be found any infallible testimony of the meaning of the divine will. Not even conscience can act as such. The Christian conception of conscience has a twofold perspective. On the one hand we have an appeal to conscience as a witness to the divine will in creation. The function of conscience, as Paul says, is "to accuse or excuse" (Rom. 2:15). But on the other hand it cannot be maintained that conscience is able to give under all circumstances an absolutely certain testimony or that it constitutes an infallible basis for action in accordance with the divine will. Conscience may be obscured, "darkened," and even the worst criminals have been able to appeal to the dictates of conscience. Conscience must therefore be "enlightened," if it is to function properly.

According to the point of view here presented sin affects human society in such a way as to create chaos instead of order. Dissolution enters instead of the order envisaged in the law of creation, and conflicts appear instead of communion. Obviously sin does not imply a dissolution of the law of creation in the sense that the will of the creator is nullified and ceases to operate; but in the sense that the purposes intended by the law of

190

the Creator are set aside in so far as human laws, the laws of human self-aggrandizement, usurp the place of the divine law.

But Christian faith is not in such a situation that it has no other guidance than the obscured and darkened law of creation. When this law has been obscured, the Creator finds another way to realize his will. The law of revelation, *lex revelationis*, defines and interprets the law of creation. The demand of God is brought forth by various messengers of God, who thus clarify its significance. This law of revelation is perfected in Christ, who, from one point of view, is the "fulfillment of the law." "Think not that I came to destroy the law and the prophets; I came not to destroy, but to fulfill" (Matt. 5:17).

This law of revelation in its essence is the law of love. There can be no doubt about this. The demand of love is the fundamental and comprehensive demand. According to the word of Jesus "the whole law hangs" on the commandment of love (Matt. 22:40). Paul writes: "love is the fulfillment of the law" (Rom. 13:10). And also: "For the whole law is fulfilled in one word, even in this: Thou shalt love thy neighbor as thyself" (Gal. 5:14). The Johannine writings, which emphasize the same point of view in regard to the significance of law, present the commandment of love as "the new commandment." It is "new" in this respect, that the significance of love has been revealed and clarified in Christ. But it is also significant that this "new" commandment is described as "an old commandment which ye have had from the beginning" (I John 2:7).

It must be strongly emphasized that this law of love which Christ has revealed and fulfilled is in principle nothing else than the law of creation. There is no contrast between these two laws. There is no other will than God's will of love undergirding this principle of order which is inherent in the idea of creation in contrast to chaos. Christian faith has always emphatically maintained that creation rests on God's love. There are at the present time special reasons for a strong emphasis on these points of view. In certain theological circles the idea of "orders of creation" has caused considerable mischief, not the least when the state has been identified as one of these "orders." It has even been suggested that these "orders" are sacrosanct, even when their appearance and activity militate against the most elementary demands of the divine will of love. It seems to have been forgotten, both that their function is to serve this will of love and that they exist under the conditions imposed by sin. Everything depends upon the fact that the law of God really rules in the ordinances of human society. If this is not the case, the agencies which were intended to serve God by controlling and defeating the destructive powers enter into the service of these diabolical forces. The theological aberrations which we have seen in our time remind us how important it is to hold fast the conviction that God's will in creation is nothing else than that will whose essence had been revealed in Christ, and that *lex creationis* is nothing else than *lex revelationis*.

22. God and the World

1. The problem of God and the world becomes particularly acute in relation to evil. Evil is of two kinds: physical evil and moral evil or sin. The latter kind of evil stands under all circumstances in radical antithesis to the will of God.

2. Christian faith does not conceive of everything that happens as a direct expression of the divine will. If this is done, it obscures the reality of evil and destroys the character of the Christian conception of God. Since existence contains also elements that are hostile to the divine will, a certain dualism is inseparably connected with the viewpoint of faith. In relation to this hostile element the divine will is sovereign in grace and judgment (cf. § 16. 2).

3. To be included in God's care or providence means neither a fatalistic submission to the inevitable course of events nor a eudaemonistic attitude which attempts to make God a servant

of man; but unconditional trust in that God who is sovereign in relation to evil. Faith in providence means, in other words, not that we "accept everything from God's hand" in the sense that God is the cause of everything that happens; but a conviction that God cares for all things, that his purpose is present in all events, and that therefore we may confidently place everything in God's care.

1. Two Kinds of Evil.

The existence of evil creates the most acute problem of the relation of the divine will to the course of this world. Evil is, however, of two kinds: physical evil, and moral evil, which in the Christian vocabulary is called sin (cf. §§ 30-32). The German language has two words to denote these two kinds: *das Übel* and *das Böse*. Evil in the first sense includes everything connected with the fact that human life is subject to finiteness and corruption. Here we think especially of physical suffering and death. In so far as this evil is *inseparably* connected with the conditions of the present life, Christian faith finds herein nothing that *in itself* is contrary to God's will, but rather accepts it as a part of the order of creation. In so far as this physical evil is inseparably connected with the fact that human life is subject to finiteness and corruption, it cannot be separated from the divine will without dethroning God as the Lord also over death and corruption, and without removing creation from its complete dependence upon God. On the other hand, Christian faith maintains emphatically that evil as sin under all circumstances stands in a radical antithesis to the will of God.

The distinction here made does not imply, however, that everything which we call physical evil can without further consideration be referred to the will of God. Christian faith refuses to be satisfied with such a simplified solution of the problem, both because the evil in the world of nature presents continually insoluble riddles, and also because there is an evident connection between physical evil and sin. This latter situation is revealed in part by the fact that sin gives a sting to physical evil which it does not possess in itself. It is also evident that in specific instances no clear distinction can be made between the physical evil which has its origin in finiteness, and that which is the result of the corrupting and destructive power of sin. It is perfectly evident that physical evil in general has its origin in sin, and therefore in a factor which stands in direct conflict with the will of God.

2. *The Will of God and the Course of the World.*

It is indubitable that the treatment of the problem of God and the course of the world has often been vague and obscure. The reason for this has been not only that faith here as everywhere else perceives "in part," but also because the most vital, inescapable, and fundamental ideas of faith have been obscured. The confusion arises because, on the one hand, it is necessary to speak of sin and its consequences, and consequently about that which is in conflict with God's will; but, on the other hand, it has been maintained, in the interest of a monistic world view, that the course of events is to be understood as a reflection of the divine will. It is self-evident that such a combination of disparate views must present a great temptation to confuse black and white. We need not here take the trouble to analyze the various attempts at rational adjustments. But it is extremely important to fix clearly in mind that faith has no interest whatever in such adjustments, simply because the attempt to find a reflection of the will of God in the general course of events results either in concealing evil, or in obscuring God's constant opposition to it, or in a denial of that God who is "pure love." All these are consequences which stand in direct and violent conflict with the fundamental viewpoint of Christian faith.

If we are to hold fast to Christian faith's conception of God and at the same time accept everything that happens as an expression of God's will, it is necessary to minimize and, as far as possible, conceal the terrible reality of sin and God's antagonism

to it. We may then speak about evil as the dark shadows of existence, or as that which is incomplete, etc. This means that the
conception of God has been naturalized and humanized. It is
also possible by rational adjustments to obscure God's continuous
opposition to evil by such vague and ambiguous expressions as
God's "sufferance" or "permission" of evil. But such expressions
in reality indicate a certain resignation or indulgence on God's
part, and fail utterly to affirm that the divine will stands in a
radical and condemning opposition to evil and is always intent
on its subjugation. If, on the contrary, evil is conceived of as
really evil while God nevertheless is made responsible for everything that happens, the inevitable result is the negation of God
as a God of love. This relationship is only slightly hidden when
in the presence of the devastation of sin we resort to arguments
about God's inscrutable will and suggest that, if we knew the
whole situation, even that which most obviously is in conflict
with love could somehow be made compatible with divine love.
To hide behind the phrase that "God's ways are not our ways"
is only a covert way of repudiating God as a God of love. Love
is given lip service, but in reality it is made responsible for that
which according to revelation is obviously evil. God's will becomes indefinable, and God himself becomes nothing but blind
and inscrutable fate. It is true that God is unfathomable to faith,
but this means that God's love meets us as an unfathomable
miracle, and that the closer it comes to us the more marvelous
and boundless it appears. It certainly does not mean that its
unfathomableness is a covering for that which is the opposite of
love. Faith holds, indeed, that divine love cannot be measured
by human standards, that this love may hide itself behind the
mask of wrath, and that to attain its purpose it may use even the
harshest means. But this does not imply that sin and the resultant evil are an expression of the divine will. We cannot attribute
to the divine will that which is contrary to the revelation and
action of this will in the work of Christ. When evil is surrepti-
tiously attributed to the divine will, it is common to *confuse* two

things which must be kept strictly separated: God can indeed turn evil into good and "compel even injury to profit us," but the conclusion must not therefore be drawn that evil is sent by God and is an expression of his will.

Islam proclaims the fatalistic doctrine that everything that occurs is the inscrutable will of Allah, but this is not the language of Christian faith. Christian faith does not refuse to admit that actual existence is not in every respect a reflection of the divine will, but on the contrary contains much that is antagonistic to this will, whether it appears as indifference or hostility. Faith refuses to attribute to God that which the Gospel attributes to Satan. It says also that the desolation and nameless suffering which follow sin are as far from God's will as the blackest darkness is from the brightest sunshine. Faith does not perceive the course of events in its entirety as a realization of the divine will, nor does it identify God's will with the course of nature. It looks upon existence as a *dramatic struggle* and sees the inner meaning of existence emerging out of this struggle where the divine will stands in conflict with hostile forces. That which faith designates as divine revelation consists precisely in this victorious struggle of the divine will. If God's will were comprehended in everything that happens, there would be no need of a "revelation." The very fact that faith points to a divine revelation indicates that it does not accept everything that happens as a reflection of God's will. The background against which faith beholds the active revelation of God is not simply that certain events do not clearly reveal God's will, but that existence is filled with such elements which, far from revealing God, are rather opposed to his will.

The reason that Christian faith refuses to be incorporated into a completely monistic system is not that it is afraid to consider the, humanly speaking, harsh means and difficult ways of divine love. The purpose is not to preserve some poor human conceptions of happiness which could not endure the misfortunes and unhappiness caused by divine love. If monism had no stronger foe than such a eudaemonistic world view, it could feel quite secure. The purpose is only to guard the purity of the Christian conception of God. Faith cannot attribute human sin and its consequences to the divine will without practicing sleight of hand and transforming black into white. Faith therefore stands before an inescapable decision. Either God discloses himself in Christ and in that spiritual life which he dominates, in which event he is divine love and his will is not reflected in every occurrence; or everything that happens is actually an expression of the divine will, in which event the characteristic features of love in the Christian idea of God are enveloped in obscurity, and nothing remains except mysterious and impenetrable Fate.

God does not will everything that happens, but he wills something *in* everything that happens. Nothing is indifferent to him. There is nothing that lies outside his sphere of interest. There is no situation in which God does not desire to realize his purpose. According to the conviction of Christian faith God does realize his will even in relation to that which opposes him. Even in relation to evil the love of God is sovereign love. This means, from one point of view, that every situation, even though it is called forth by hostile "powers," has a divine meaning, and that divine love is capable of making itself effective in every situation. No situation can arise which would overpower God, or would be able, as it were, to wrest the power from his hands and thus bring the absolute sovereignty of divine love to nought. Divine love always appears to the eye of faith as the irresistible power, sovereign in *grace* and *judgment*. Everything else that is called power, no matter how much it may have the semblance of power, is doomed to dissolution, desolation, and defeat. In vain does this "power" assault the divine power. Only of divine love and whatever belongs thereto can it be said that it "never faileth," and its goal is the only goal that is ultimately realized.

3. *God's Providence.*

When Christian faith places God's love in relation to the

course of the world, faith appears as trust in God's care, or faith in his providence. If we are to define this faith more definitely, we must differentiate it from two misinterpretations. On the one hand, faith in God's providence is something entirely different from a simple submission to the actual course of events. If every occurrence could without further consideration be regarded as a reflection of the divine will, the attitude of faith to the suffering and tribulation of the world would be abject resignation, and the only possible course of action would be to submit as gracefully as possible to the "inscrutable" will of God. The attitude of faith does contain an element of patience and steadfastness, but this does not imply that faith retires within itself with a fatalistic statement: God wills it. If faith has become aware that existence contains infinitely much that is contrary to and in conflict with God's will, it must, since it sees only "in part," again and again suspend judgment in regard to God's ways and activity. But under no circumstances can resignation be the last word of faith or the expression of its attitude. As far as faith is concerned any reference to abject resignation leads ultimately to a paralysis of courage and spiritual vigor.

On the other hand, faith in God's providence is far removed from that eudaemonistic attitude which desires to make God a servant of man. Such conceptions have sometimes appeared in Christian thought. A line of thought which makes God the servant of man reverses the relation which, according to faith, exists between God and man. The theocentric character of faith means that all eudaemonism must be radically removed from the relationship between God and man. Under these circumstances faith in God's providence cannot mean that man is thereby immune from all suffering and pain. In the presence of actual facts such an interpretation appears unrealistic and cannot be verified by faith itself. The prayer of faith for God's protection is not a prayer to be delivered from suffering and grief, but a prayer that God will preserve us *in* all danger and harm, and above all that God's dominion may be realized.

198

The meaning of Christian faith in God's care is an unconditional trust in that God who is sovereign even in relation to evil. Paul has expressed this trust in a classic word: Nothing whatever "shall separate us from the love of God in Christ Jesus" (Rom. 8:38 f.). There is nothing that can force itself between God's love and the man of faith; nothing evil is able to do so. Even if we were thrust into utter darkness, there is no situation in which we can be placed outside the sphere of divine love and care. God is near even when he seems farthest removed. We are continually in his care and under his protection. The Christian faith in providence appears therefore as confidence in relation to everything that happens. "If God be for us, who can be against us?" This is vastly different from mere resignation before the vicissitudes of life.

But the words that nothing can separate us from the love of God must not be given a wholly negative interpretation. This conviction includes the confidence that this trust is a trust in God who is *able to overcome* evil and compel even suffering and harm to serve the purpose of divine love. Faith does not deny that suffering and want are in themselves evil. If God is not permitted to take suffering and make it serve his purpose, it is not a purifying but a ravaging power, not improving but embittering. Suffering and want are not in themselves an expression of the divine will. But the sovereignty of divine love is revealed in that God's care appears as both condemning and redeeming love. Suffering in which God's love is present and active is changed from a dull and meaningless pain into a purifying and saving power. Thus it becomes a means whereby God adds new areas to his dominion, and through this act of God it receives a significance which it did not possess in itself. Although faith cannot certify God's care as immunity against all suffering, it verifies again and again the power of God to make sufferings serve as the birth pangs of a new and richer life. Faith flees to God, its Helper in all need. As far as faith is concerned there is no time when it does not flee to him for help, no difficulties which he cannot solve, and no situation in which faith is not completely dependent upon his aid. But faith in providence does not mean that the course of events is mapped out beforehand by God. This would be a deistic and inert conception of God's care and providence, dependent on the idea of God as an extra-mundane being. Faith in providence affirms on the contrary that God is living and active in that which happens, that God has resources sufficient for all emergencies, and that the sovereignty of his care is revealed by his ability to turn evil into good.[1] When faith stands before this expression of God's power it is able to confess in spite of suffering and buffeting: "This has happened that the works of God should be made manifest" (John 9:3). Faith is certain that "to them that love God all things work together for good" (Rom. 8:28), i.e., to those who are subdued by and trust in divine love. It is here that the nature of faith in providence is differentiated from mere resignation. Faith is not resignation, but a conquering conviction. The prayer of prayers, "thy will be done," is not, as it has sometimes been interpreted, an expression of resignation, but of the conquering faith in the power of God (cf. § 45. 9).

The statement that faith in God's providence means that man receives everything as from the hand of God may be subject to misinterpretation. It can easily be understood as if the divine will were the cause of everything that happens. But this attempt to explain that which is hostile to God is, as we have seen, contrary to the characteristic viewpoint of Christian faith. Furthermore, such a theory would have no power to help anyone who is suffering under the oppression of evil. Nothing is gained by a theoretical argument about its origin, and certainly not if that argument derives what is hostile to God from the divine will. Such an elucidation simply makes matters worse. Christian faith

---

[1] Cf. A. C. Turner, *The World's Order,* "To know that the world is contained in the providence of God is not to know that every minutest occurrence has been mapped out in detail in advance, but to know that every contingency in your outward relations is provided for and can be turned to good." (In *Concerning Prayer,* B. H. Streeter and others, London: The Macmillan Co., 1916, pp. 429 f.)

in providence does not attempt to give a theoretical explanation of evil. The essential element in this faith is that God *cares for all things*, that he wills something in everything that happens, and that the man of faith may confidently place everything in his hands.

23. The Legitimacy and Limitation of Dualism

1. When Christian faith combines God's will and the course of events, a tension is created which proves to be a part of that situation within which faith exists. This tension arises because faith opposes every attempt to eliminate or obscure the evil which is hostile to God's will (the legitimacy of dualism), and at the same time opposes all encroachments upon the sovereignty of the divine will in relation to existence (the limitation of dualism).

2. All endeavors to overcome this tension through a supposedly rational explanation of evil must necessarily fail. For Christian faith the problem of evil is concentrated in the question of its being overcome. The answer is given in faith's reference to God who in his struggle gains the victory. Through the victory of divine love even the vanquished evil receives finally a significance which it did not have in itself.

1. No Metaphysical Dualism.

In the previous exposition of the conception of God and his activity we have constantly found that a certain dualistic element is inseparably connected with faith's viewpoint of existence and its relation to the divine will. Existence contains elements that are foreign to the divine will and in conflict with it. Existence as such is not an adequate expression of this divine will. Faith would be tempted to find the will of God reflected in everything that happens only if it could ignore sin and its consequences, which represent a will in conflict with the divine (§ 30). But

201

faith opposes every attempt to eliminate or in any way to hide and obscure the terrible reality of evil. All such attempts to explain away evil appear to faith as unrealistic arguments which are constantly refuted by the actual conditions in existence. Faith is also opposed to every attempt to blunt and minimize God's continuous antagonism to this evil. Just because the God of Christian faith is love, all compromises with evil on God's part are completely excluded. The God of faith is that God whose only purpose is to vanquish evil and thus realize the dominion of his love.

But this viewpoint of faith implies that it is placed in a tension which proves to be a part of the conditions of its existence. Just as faith is opposed to hiding the dualistic element, so it is also opposed to an absolute dualism. As far as faith is concerned God is not a power coincident with other powers and stronger than these, but the power upon which all existence is absolutely dependent. In relation to evil he is *unconditionally sovereign*, whether this sovereignty reveals itself *in grace or in judgment*.

The dualistic element has a very central place within primitive Christianity. Every attempt to understand primitive Christianity without giving sufficient attention to this fact is doomed to failure. Nothing could be more misleading than the attempts made in the eighteenth century to dismiss the dualism of primitive Christianity by saying that Jesus "accommodated" himself to his contemporaries, or, as in the nineteenth century, by assigning a secondary significance to it by showing its connection with Parseeism. For the Gospel it is fundamental that there is a struggle between the divine will and the power of evil, however this power may be described. It is perfectly evident that Jesus' struggle for the Kingdom of God is a struggle against the power of "Satan."

A review of the history of theology from this point of view indicates clearly that theology has often attempted to suppress this dualism of primitive Christianity, and that this tendency has been connected with the endeavor to incorporate Christian

faith in a monistic world view. But we may also note that sometimes this early Christian dualism has been given a metaphysical
character which is foreign to it. This was Marcion's point of
view, and the same misunderstanding has always occurred when
a metaphysical antithesis between the infinite and the finite has
been set over against idealistic monism.

The dualism which is characteristic of Christian faith appears,
therefore, as a double antithesis. On the one hand it stands in
contrast to an idealistic monism which in one way or another
tries to minimize evil in order that it may be fitted into a monistic
scheme, and which at the same time blots out the boundary between the divine and the human. But on the other hand it stands
in an equally sharp contrast to a metaphysical dualism which
conceives the contrast between the divine and the human as an
absolute antithesis between the finite and the infinite. The intention is to make this antithesis as sharp as possible: the finite
and the infinite cannot be joined together. But in this view the
antithesis between "good" and "evil" is not as radically conceived as in Christian faith. The antithesis of metaphysical dualism is undefined. But in Christian faith the antithesis is between
the divine will, defined as love, and the hostile forces which
oppose this will.

2. *No Rational Explanation of Evil.*

The tension to which we have referred cannot be resolved,
since this would imply either a toning down of evil or an abridgment of the sovereignty of divine love. All attempts to explain
evil rationally are therefore foreign to faith. It does not feel
competent to incorporate evil into the divine government of the
world in a rational manner, any more than it attempts to present
a rational explanation of the origin of evil in general. It is not
interested in "theodicies." Neither the idea of punishment nor
the insight that God is able to make evil serve his purpose can
be used in trying to find a rational place for evil in God's government of the world. The idea of punishment is to some extent

legitimate, but it is not sufficient as a rational explanation, since it would imply a proportional relation between sin and punishment (cf. § 19. 2). Faith has, however, no deeper insight into God's relation to evil than the conviction that he is able to make evil serve the purposes of his love. But neither can this idea be used as a rational explanation of the existence of evil. Such an idea would be acceptable only if it could be demonstrated that the gain under all circumstances exceeds the loss. But this would mean that *all* evil in reality is turned into good, because every loss would be an argument against this rational explanation. To use this deepest conviction of faith as a rational explanation would lead to an easy judgment of evil, which would be incompatible with faith. But the idea of punishment as a rational explanation would, on the contrary, obscure the Christian conception of God as love.

Just as faith cannot rationally incorporate evil into God's government of the world, so neither can it give a rational explanation of the origin of evil. The problem of the origin of evil is for faith a question of the origin of sin. The attitude of faith to this problem will be discussed more in detail in a later chapter (§ 31). Here we need only state that all proffered explanations, in so far as they do not simply explain the problem away, are nothing else, and can be nothing else, than expressions of something inexplicable. There is no answer which does not present a new question, whether the reference be to "the freedom of the will," to human nature, to a pre-existent fall, or to a supernatural evil power. In reality faith perceives that a rational explanation of the origin of sin cannot be given. In so far as the meaning of existence is to faith inseparably connected with the divine will, it cannot conceive of sin in any other sense than something meaningless and irrational. But an attempt to give a rational explanation of the irrational is obviously impossible. In addition, every such explanation would inevitably take the form of an excuse, and the idea of excusing sin is altogether foreign to faith (cf. § 32. 9).

Christianity is not a religion which has an easy explanation at hand for everything that happens. On the contrary, it refuses the attempt to provide a rational world view, or in other words to incorporate faith into a monistic system of thought which is capable of solving all riddles. When classical idealism made this attempt, it succeeded only in cutting the central nerve of Christian faith. Christian faith would rather leave these problems unsolved than adopt explanations and harmonizations which can result in nothing else than explaining away that which is to faith Alpha and Omega: the divine and loving will.

To faith, the problem of evil is the problem of conquering it. This is the essential point. Faith is indifferent to all questions which do not touch on this main problem. Consequently, all the metaphysical speculations about the origin and ultimate cause of evil have no interest for faith. Even if a satisfactory explanation of the origin of evil could be given, the problem of overcoming it would not be any nearer to a solution. Faith has, however, a tremendous interest in the methods and character of evil, because these questions are inseparably connected with the problem of conquering it. It is important to have a clear view of what is to be conquered and the way in which evil works in the world. In the last analysis, therefore, the problem is the possibility and reality of the victory over evil. The fundamental religious question in view of the actual nature of existence is whether there really exists a power able to conquer evil at its deepest level. The answer of faith, given on the basis of what it perceives of God's active, redeeming, and re-creating revelation, is this: Nothing is impossible for God. If evil is unconquerable, faith in God is dead. It would then be meaningless to talk about a God. But the eye of faith sees not only evil in all its ugliness, but also and above all the God who is victorious.

The question about the way in which God wins the victory and the significance of this victory will be discussed in the next part. We would add here only a concluding word about the light which this victory of God sheds over the darkness of existence. The victory over evil gives a meaning even to that which is in itself meaningless. Evil is "justified,"[1] if we may use that word; it becomes legitimate in so far as it is overcome. Love realizes its inner riches when it breaks down indifference and hostility and captures the opposition by sacrificing itself. This is the significance of the word that there is more joy in heaven over one sinner who repents than over ninety and nine righteous persons who need no repentance (Luke 15:7). The victory of divine love removes the meaninglessness of existence. But this light in the darkness is something entirely different from a rational explanation of evil. It is only when conquered that evil becomes meaningful and legitimate.

---

[1] W. Temple, *Mens Creatrix*, p. 287, "When conquered, it is justified." In *Mens Creatrix* Temple has given an excellent exposition of the problem of evil (pp. 261-92). It should be remarked, however, that on the basis of his main theme he accepts this too readily as a rational explanation of evil.

Part III

THE ACT OF GOD IN CHRIST

DIVISION A

THE VICTORIOUS ACT OF RECONCILIATION

24. The Completed and Continuous Work of Christ

1. When we speak in the following pages of God's way to men, the work of God is to be primarily understood as a work of redemption. It must, however, be specifically emphasized that this work is also a work of judgment and creation.

2. The work of divine love is, from one point of view, once and for all accomplished in Christ and finished through the cross. From another point of view, it is a constantly continuous work, the work of *Kyrios-Christus* and of the Spirit, the Life-giver, who "proceeds from the Father and the Son."

1. The Way to Fellowship with God.

In the previous pages we have again and again encountered the problem of the relation of the divine will to evil. Our conclusion was that there is a dualistic element in the viewpoint of the Christian faith. Under the conditions of history there is a constant conflict between the divine will and the forces opposed to it. We have seen that the problem which faith perceives as central is the question of the subjugation of evil, or, in other words, the establishment of the rule of God and fellowship with God. This question, which we have merely touched upon in the previous pages (cf. § 18) must now be discussed in greater detail. This part of our exposition of the content of Christian faith is therefore entitled: The Act of God in Christ. Even this title in itself indicates that fellowship with God, as far as faith is concerned, is based entirely and completely on an act of God. This point of view has in reality a decisive significance for everything that follows. According to the viewpoint of Christian faith there is no way from man to God, no way in which man could gradually strive upward toward the divine. The way to fellowship with God is God's way to man.

Part III is divided into two general sections, A and B. The purpose of the first is to clarify the way in which the divine love itself makes possible the redemption of man. The central point here is the act of reconciliation and victory of the self-sacrificing, divine love. When the act of Christ is thus placed in the center, it cannot be too strongly emphasized that this act, in accordance with the fundamental proposition just stated, must be understood as the act of divine love itself. The purpose of the second section is to discover how the divine love re-establishes the broken fellowship between God and man through that act of forgiveness that creates faith. The background of this discussion is an analysis of the nature of sin, or of that evil which opposes the realization of fellowship between God and man.

It is clear, therefore, that the chief content of this part implies a closer exposition of that divine act of redemption to which we have alluded in previous sections. We must then add, however, that this act of redemption is at the same time an act of judgment and creation.

2. *Two Aspects of the Act of God in Christ.*

In our discussion of the idea of revelation (§ 3. 5) we stated that Christian faith perceives this revelation both as completed and as continuous. The full significance of this twofold aspect becomes clear, however, only as we analyze more fully the act of God in Christ. The revelation of God is from one point of view completed. That which has taken place is with reference to revelation decisive and definitive. Christian faith expresses this fact in various ways. It speaks of the incarnation of the divine "essence," the divine love, in Christ. This means that Christian faith does not expect another revelation of God which should supplement and correct the one already given. The Christian relationship between God and man is once and for all defined by the revelation of God in Christ. Faith can also view this matter from the point of view of activity and say: that work of God which has been done in and through Christ has been done once and for all, it is finished and it is of decisive significance. The reconciliation between God and man is here once and for all established. "God was in Christ, reconciling the world unto himself" (II Cor. 5:19). The victory over the powers hostile to God has been won once and for all.

But Christian faith perceives this revelation, or act of God, as at the same time continually in progress. It is not a question merely about something that has happened and now belongs to the past, but about something that happens continuously, *quotidie spiritualiter in quolibet christiano* (Luther). Christ is continually engaged in his work of revelation and reconciliation in the world. The victory over the forces hostile to God is won anew in a renewed struggle. Christian faith expresses this contemporaneous aspect of the work of Christ both by confessing him as Kyrios, the risen, living and active Victor; and by its proclamation of the work of the Holy Spirit who is also the Spirit of Christ. The relation between these two affirmations about Christ as Kyrios and the Spirit will be discussed further in the following chapters. Here we desire merely to emphasize that faith in Christ as Kyrios and faith in the Spirit are analogous in so far as both express the character of the revelation of God as a living and active revelation in the present. It may be added that Christian faith does not view the continuous activity of God as different in nature from the finished work. It is just this finished act which in the present is continually realized anew.

25. The Incarnation

1. The Christian confession of faith in Christ is essentially a confession that God was incarnate in the man Jesus Christ. In

this sense Christ is "of the same substance with the Father," and the Father is of the same substance as Christ. The confession of the divine incarnation in Christ is thereby a statement relative to the essential nature of the Christian conception of God.

2. The confession of faith in Christ stands in a double antithesis. On the one hand it repudiates the conception of Christ as an intermediary being (separation Christology), whether this is stated in such a way that Christ becomes some kind of half-god, or, on the basis of an idealistic line of thought, he is conceived as "the ideal man," "humanity's prototype," etc. On the other hand it rejects all attempts to identify Christ with God and thus view him as a god visiting this world (theophany). What is essential to faith is to see God "in the despised man Christ" (Luther).

3. The incarnation in Christ is something given in and through the advent of Christ, but also something which is perfected in his completed work. The confession of Christ is based, therefore, on the finished work of Christ.

Excursus. The Boundary Line of Faith. Since it is contrary to the genius of faith to attempt an explanation of the unfathomable, theology must not attempt to give a rational explanation of the possibility of the incarnation. Faith cannot do more than refer the person and work of Christ to God's eternal and sovereign love.

1. The Religious Significance of the Confession of Faith in Christ.
Faith in Christ is not something which gradually appeared within Christianity; it was from the beginning identified with Christianity itself and has continued to be so through the ages. The confession of faith in Christ is from the beginning the focal point, the symbol which identifies Christian faith. The ancient church gradually worked it out into definite, theological formu-

las, among which those of Nicaea and Chalcedon are of greatest importance. The work on Christology was of the greatest importance during this period, and the results along this line can be said to represent the essential contribution of the theology of the ancient church. They fought in the interest of these Christological formulas, convinced that here something essential to Christian faith was at stake, and that the issue was in reality the very existence of Christianity. The focal point was the idea of the incarnation. Christ is "of one substance with the Father," the "substance" of the Father is "incarnate" in Christ.

If we are to understand the issue, we must follow the principle that our task is to clarify those religious ideas which are expressed in the development of the Christological dogmas and their formulations. The reason so many discussions of the Christological problem have brought such meager results has been that they were concerned with the external forms and failed to penetrate to the heart of the matter. This is true of the attempts to defend as well as attack Christology.

The Christian confession of faith in Christ is essentially a confession of faith in the incarnation of divine love, of God, in the man Jesus Christ. It is by deliberate choice that we here accept the principal word of the ancient church: incarnation. Even if this word may be misinterpreted and has therefore resulted in some conceptions of the nature of revelation which are foreign to faith, there is no other Christological concept which has so faithfully preserved the deepest intentions of the Christian faith. This expression affirms first and last that the revelation in Christ has reference to God's approach to man and that divine love itself here enters the hostile and finite world. It affirms that the "essence" of God, or in other words the divine and loving will, "dwells" in Christ (John 1:14). It is not an accident that the idea of incarnation served as a bulwark against all external attacks and all attempts to reinterpret the faith which occurred in the ancient church. It is not an accident that Augustine, who had been strongly influenced by Neo-Platonism, per-

ceived in the "incarnation" the point at which the specifically
Christian differentiated itself from Neo-Platonism. He never
tires of repeating that the failure of Neo-Platonism lies in its inability to understand the incarnation. The concept of incarnation preserved the fundamental theme of Christianity during the
early centuries when all kinds of moralistic and speculative influences threatened to destroy the Christian conception of God.
The incarnation proclaims the gospel of the divine self-giving,
and has thus guarded the fullness of the Christian revelation of
God. It declares that no one but God, or divine love itself,
dwells in Christ and performs the work of redemption. To say,
therefore, that the Christology of the ancient church was a
"Hellenization" of Christianity is to turn the actual historical
situation upside down. It was the Christological idea of the incarnation that more than anything else served as a bulwark
against the process of Hellenization which was at work in the
church. It was "foolishness to the Greeks," to be sure, but it
was also an expression of the fundamental idea of Christian
faith. It is important to emphasize that for faith the incarnation
means the incarnation of *divine love*. When the idea of incarnation has sometimes led to ambiguous interpretations of the nature of divine revelation, the reason has been that the "essence"
of God has been understood in a more or less "physical" sense.
Even though we may note tendencies toward such an interpretation both within the ancient church and in later times, the
fathers of the ancient church did not use such "naturalistic"
concepts as their interpreters during the eighteenth century
supposed. Even if the Christological formulas of the ancient
church employ expressions that sound to us "naturalistic," it is
beyond doubt that their chief purpose was to maintain that in
Christ we meet that which is *essentially* divine. The decisive
element in the Christian confession of faith in Christ is stated in
the simple and expressive word of Luther: "We find the heart
and will of the Father in Christ." Therein lies his "unity of substance with the Father." The deed of Christ removes the veil

and reveals the heart of God. Christ is "the effulgence of his glory and the very image of his substance" (Heb. 1:3). He is not identical with God, but he and the Father are "one" (John 10:30); one in will, in heart, in purpose, and in work. This reflection of God's heart does not mean merely that faith should find here a certain likeness to God and that the love of Christ should be like God's love. "The substance of the Son" is not only *like* the Father's, it is the same; and the love of Christ is to faith the love of God himself. Where Christ is, there is God; and where Christ is active, there God is active also. The self-sacrificing and self-giving love of Christ is the love of God himself, its struggle against evil is God's own struggle, and its victory is God's own victory. In the deed of Christ God realizes his own will and love.

This view of the unity of substance does not imply a depreciation of it, but rather an emphasis on its religious meaning. The religious intention in the confession of faith in Christ is obscured as soon as something other than God's "disposition of heart" becomes essential and as soon as the idea of a more or less "physical" unity of substance appears. Just as we do not know the "essence" of a man unless we know the disposition of his heart, will, personality, and character, so faith cannot adopt any other point of view in regard to the essence of God. It can speak of the essence of God only in tentative figures, but the import of the question cannot be of anything less than the heart of God. God's essence is his loving will, not some obscure "substance" behind this will. It is meaningless to attempt to draw a distinction between God's will and his nature or his "substance." If God is "spirit" (John 4:24), then there is nothing more "substantial" and *essential* than his will and his disposition of heart. If we should speak of a substantial unity which would mean something other than this unity of disposition, we would thereby assert something less rather than something more. We would not thereby lift the question of the unity of Christ with the Father to a higher plane, but rather bring it down to a lower; a plane on which the real meaning of the question is lost.

If the terminology in these propositions differs from that of the ancient church because of their use of the concept of substance, the difference is not in essentials. The positive interest of the theologians of the ancient church was in the essential revelation of God in Christ, that revelation which creates the redemptive fellowship between God and man. When the Christology of the ancient church, with its concept of substance, rejected the expression of an identity of will between God and Christ, it did so because to the fathers this expression contained something else and something less than is contained in the theses which we have just stated, and consequently it could not be used by them to express the essential meaning of the revelation of God. The theology of the ancient church was guided by the same positive interest which has been definitive for the presentation given here. From a positive point of view that which is essential to Christology is and remains this one matter: if love is the expression for that which is the inner being of God, for *die Natur Gottes* (Luther), then Christ's unity of substance with the Father means nothing else, i.e., *nothing less than* the incarnation of the divine and loving will in Christ.

If, therefore, "the Son is of the same substance with the Father," this proposition may also be turned around. It must then also be true that the Father is of the same substance with the Son. Such a transposition of the principal statement of the Christology of the ancient church reveals its real religious significance. The question about the "divinity" of Christ cannot, as we have already stated (§ 5. 2), be put in such a way as to imply that God is the known magnitude, and that with this given concept of God we can measure the divinity of Christ. The question to which the confession of faith in Christ gives an answer is the question *what kind* of being God is, what his will is, and how he acts. The confession of faith in Christ is, therefore, not a statement about Christ, but an affirmation about that God who has revealed himself. If Christian faith affirms that Christ is of the same substance with the Father, it thereby makes a statement about the character of the Father's being. The real function of the confession of faith in Christ is then to guard the content and purity of the Christian conception of God. To a certain extent the formulas of the ancient church have really served this purpose and have stood as a bulwark against the process of Hellenization and moralization. But it is quite evident that the theology of the ancient church was not able to follow consistently this principal point of view which it had adopted in Christology, but allowed the conception of God to be determined also by other factors. This became even more the case within the later scholasticism of the Latin church. The ancient confession of faith in Christ was here accepted as a revered heritage, but its influence was greatly reduced. From this point of view the Reformation meant a reversal. The whole of Luther's work as a reformer could be explained from this point of view, that he accepts and follows the full consequence of the ancient confession of Christ. No approach can be more misleading than to suppose that the Reformation meant a dissolution of the ancient Christology. The very opposite is the truth. It is Luther who more than anyone before him takes the ancient confession seriously, and sees the "nature" of God reflected in the deed of Christ. This is the foundation of his deeper conception of the Christian relationship between God and man and the Christian conception of God.

2. *The Delimitation of the Confession of Faith in Christ.*

If we are to understand fully the real purpose of the confession of Christ, it is instructive to note how it is differentiated from two opposite lines of thought. Its struggle on these two fronts began in the early days of Christianity and has continued ever since. The two Christological types which confronted the ancient church may be designated *the separation type* and *the theophany type.* On the one hand the church opposed all tend-

encies to separate Christ from God, so that Christ would become a kind of intermediary being, a half-god, or a lower god;
and on the other hand, it opposed all attempts to identify Christ
with God, so that the appearance of Christ would be regarded
as a theophany, or as a divinity wandering around incognito and
disguised upon the earth.

The first type appears to some extent even in the Apologists,
who talk about Christ as an "other" (lower) God. It appears
later in the so-called Dynamic Monarchianism, and above all
in Arianism, which later returned in more subtle forms. This
rejected separation-Christology was strongly influenced by the
god and Logos concepts of Greek philosophy. Wherever this
philosophy has had a positive influence on Christology, it has
led to a conception of Christ as an intermediary being. The
presupposition is that God is conceived of as a being enthroned
in isolated majesty, and the philosophical idea of the Logos is
well adapted to serve this metaphysical conception of God. The
ancient church doctrine of the incarnation stands in definite opposition to this line of thought. The Son is of the *same* substance
with the Father, it is the divine nature itself which is incarnate
in Christ, not an intermediary being. It may be pointed out that
what has been said of the influence of Greek philosophy in general is true also in regard to Neo-Platonism. It might be assumed
that the situation here was different, since the idea of emanation
has a certain affinity to the idea of incarnation. But the antithesis is really the same. The fundamental idea in Neo-Platonism's
conception of God is the exalted tranquility and isolation of the
Deity. Emanation is from this point of view a cosmic process
in which the divine is attenuated and weakened as the emanation progresses. The idea of the incarnation of the divine is entirely foreign to Neo-Platonism, inasmuch as the Deity remains
in his isolated exaltation and the process of emanation is in
reality conceived of as a fall into sin.[1] It is clear, therefore, that
the influence of Neo-Platonism on Christology, and of Greek

[1] Cf. A. Nygren, *Agape and Eros*, Eng. tr., pp. 144 ff.

philosophy in general, tends to interpret Christ as an intermediary being.

The theophany type includes all endeavors to identify Christ with God in such a way that the historical is removed and the concrete human features disappear from the person of Christ. Among these are such Christological types as Docetism and Modalism, which reappear after Nicaea in somewhat milder form in Monophysitism, Monoteletism, and other related forms. If separation-Christology has been influenced by Greek philosophy, the decisive influence in theophany-Christology came from the Hellenistic mystery cults. This is the natural habitat of the ideas of theophany. It is extremely significant that the confession of Christ in the ancient church turns as decisively against this doctrine of identity as against the separation-Christology. It continues the sharp polemic which occurs already in the Johannine writings against the contemporary "Gnostics" who denied that "Jesus Christ had come in the flesh" (I John 4:2 ff). The formula of Chalcedon settled the irrelevancy of theophany-Christology. It declares that Christ is not a divinity wandering around in disguise on the earth, but that he is our brother and a man like us. The real purpose of the doctrine of the "two natures," which are inseparably and indivisibly united without change and confusion, was to maintain both his unity of substance with the Father and his "true humanity." The church declares that it is the divine being himself who meets us in the lowliness of the historical, human person. It should be emphasized that its purpose is not to explain rationally how such a "union" is possible. In this respect it differs from the subsequent scholastic theology.

This review of the struggle on two fronts in the ancient church confirms the statement previously made that the Christology of the ancient church cannot be understood as a "Hellenization" of Christianity. When we note the fundamental ideas behind the formulations of the dogmas of the ancient church, they do not appear as a Hellenization, but rather imply the most determined opposition against *both* forms of that process of Hellenization which endeavored to gain a foothold within the church. The real significance of the struggle of the ancient church is that the fundamental ideas of Christianity are maintained, both against that Hellenization which had its roots in Greek philosophy and tended toward a separation of Christ from God, and against that which had its roots in the mystery cults and resulted in an identification of Christ with God analogous to divine theophanies.

It is not our intention here to write a history of Christology. But we must present an example from the Christological discussions of a later time in order to illustrate the importance of this twofold opposition for the Christian confession of faith in Christ. Scholastic theology, both older and more recent, has never been satisfied to stop with the negative attitude of the formula of Chalcedon toward all rational explanations. On the contrary, scholasticism has always endeavored to elucidate and explain how the divine nature in Christ is connected with the human. In reality these explanations tended to favor the theophany type of Christology, or in other words to obscure the "true humanity." The human element was conceived of as a kind of abstract humanity, a cloak which the divine subject had assumed. There was no appreciation of that true humanity to which both the Gospels and the New Testament writings in general give unimpeachable testimony.

Against this scholastic theology there appeared during the eighteenth and nineteenth centuries a humanized Christology based on idealistic philosophy. The purpose was to emphasize the "true humanity," which had been neglected by scholasticism. But the result was simply a change from the theophany type to the separation type. Christ became a kind of intermediary being. The starting point was the human person, but this was idealized in various ways. Christ was regarded as "the religious prototype of humanity," "the ideal man," the incarnation of the religious or moral ideal, and so on. This meant that, contrary to the intention, the human individuality was not properly expressed, and the result was the creation of an unrealistic and fantastic being who, as an intermediary being, was in reality neither god nor man. Such a concept as "the ideal man" is nothing but a fantasy. In this process the religious significance of the fundamental idea of Christology, the idea of incarnation, was lost, and it became impossible to express clearly the idea that the divine enters and dwells in the world of humanity, and that Christ is God's way to man. The Christology of the ideal man represents, on the contrary, an apotheosis of the human. The theology of the nineteenth century is filled with unprofitable discussions between the scholastic and the idealistic, humanized type of Christology.

Against this background the real significance of the confession of faith in Christ is sharply depicted. From the point of view of Christian faith the failure of scholastic theology did not consist in its desire to take the idea of incarnation seriously, but in its inability to comprehend clearly the lowliness of the historical and human elements. The defect of idealistic Christology did not lie in its attempt to emphasize the true humanity of Christ, but partially in its inability to accomplish this intention effectively, and, even more important, in the fact that Christian faith is not concerned with an idealized humanity, but with the divine, with God. The confusion of these two is in principle foreign to faith. The characteristic viewpoint of faith is well expressed in Luther's word that it is most vital to perceive that God who is "hidden in the despised man Christ." These words contain the whole inner tension of the confession of Christ—God in the humble circumstances of man. Here no attempt is made to escape the tension by means of a Christology of separation or theophany. The revelation of God is a revelation "in secret." The eye beholds a human figure who lived under historical conditions and was crucified on Golgotha, but in this lowliness faith sees nothing less than the incarnation of divine love. Christian faith thus preserves its twofold front. It will not be induced to remove the tension by adopting the idea of an idealized humanity. Faith is not interested in a hero cult. But neither will it accept any modern versions of the theophany type of approach, which are designed to remove the historical difficulties, the *skandalon* of history, by substituting "the exalted Christ" for the historical person of Jesus. Faith cannot forget what happened outside the gates of Jerusalem. Certainly it turns its eyes toward the exalted Christ. But he is none other than the Crucified.

3. *The Theology of Incarnation and the Atonement.*

In the history of Christian thought there has appeared at times a certain tendency to pit the doctrines of the incarnation and the atonement against each other. In Anglican theology a certain polemic emphasis has sometimes been placed on the doctrine of incarnation, and support for this has been sought in the tradition of the ancient church. In more pietistic circles, however, the idea of incarnation has often been overshadowed by an emphasis on the redemptive work of Christ. Historically it is easy to show how such a conflict has arisen. But in principle such a conflict is not legitimate as far as Christian faith is concerned. Faith perceives the incarnation of the divine and loving will and the redemptive work of this divine will as an indivisible whole. Any isolation of the doctrine of incarnation would in reality only obscure the active character of the revelation of God and would fail to indicate that the divine revelation appears only in the form of a redemptive and judicial creative act. If the incarnation is emphasized at the expense of the work of Christ, the result would be a more or less "naturalistic" interpretation of Christianity. But the isolation of the doctrine of atonement would, on the contrary, obscure the fact that the work of reconciliation and redemption is altogether the work of divine love. This has often happened in theology (cf. § 26. 4). In reality the theology of the ancient church does not lend support to a one-sided theology of incarnation. The incarnation is regarded as the prerequisite, the only possible prerequisite, of the work of redemption. No other power than the divine could accomplish this. Traces can also be found of the genuinely Christian idea that the incarnation itself is completed in the accomplishment of the work of redemption. The divine and loving will becomes fully "incarnate" when the work is finished. The important thing is that there is an intimate connection between faith's affirmations about the person and the work of Christ. Theology has often severed this connection. But in so doing it has only obscured the viewpoint characteristic of faith. As far as Christian faith is concerned, everything depends on the actualization of divine love in the work of atonement and salvation. Or, in other words, Christ has brought the divine love into the world through his life, suffering, sacrifice, and victory. Through him the divine and loving will has entered the world. Luther has expressed this in a classic passage: "To blot out sin, destroy death, and remove the curse through himself; to impart righteousness, to bring life to light, and to bestow blessings; to bring the former to nought and to bring the latter into being—this is *the work of divine omnipotence alone*."[2] The confession of faith in Christ is based on his finished work. The incarnation is perfected on the cross. Here divine love appears in its unfathomableness and inexhaustible riches. In this connection these words are acceptable and true: *Christum cognoscere est beneficia eius cognoscere.*

Excursus. The Boundary Line of Faith.

In the work of Christ faith encounters the inscrutable miracle of divine love. Since faith meets Christ as the incarnation of divine love, it comprehends the mystery of his person in the eternal and divine will and in nothing else. He is, in other words, "begotten of the Father from eternity." In this matter, as in everything else, faith is unable to give a "rational explanation" of the miracle. When faith says that Jesus came "in the fullness of time," it points to a divine plan for the life of hu-

---

[2] W. A., Vol. 40, 1, p. 441.

manity, but it does not imply that his life and work can be explained on the basis of a conjunction of favorable contemporary conditions. Faith perceives, on the contrary, that the mystery of both his person and his work rests on the equipment given him by God, i.e., on the incarnation. In this sense his origin is of "holy spirit," and in this sense the words once uttered by Söderblom are true: "the miracle of his being was present already in the bosom of Mary." This is in reality the religious meaning and content of that idea of the conception of Jesus without a human father which, besides other and quite different interpretations of the Gospel of John, meet us in primitive Christianity, especially in the Gospel of Matthew. This is analogous to ideas common in antiquity about the origin of famous persons. But when in later theology the attempt has been made to use this idea as a rational explanation of the mystery of the person of Christ, it appears at once that it is impotent. Schleiermacher's exposition of this problem is still valid.[3] Theology has attempted to find in the birth of Christ without the will of man an explanation of his "sinlessness," or at least of his "freedom from original sin." It is perfectly evident that this explanation explains nothing. *If* it is desired to gain an explanation in this way, it will be necessary to be consistent and to remove "inherited sin" also from Mary. The Roman doctrine of the immaculate conception of the Virgin Mary is at least consistent. It must be added, however, that this rationalistic explanation has a semblance of legitimacy only as long as one conceives "the Son's unity of substance with the Father" in a "physical" sense, but that it loses even this semblance of legitimacy as soon as it becomes evident that the unity of substance, about which faith never ceases to speak, does not consist in some special physiological nature, but in nothing less than that we "possess the heart and will of the Father in Christ." Under such circumstances Christian faith must reject these rationalistic explanations of theology, as well as all others. The function of theology is not to explain the possibility of the

---

[3] Schleiermacher, *Der christliche Glaube,* Eng. tr., pp. 398 ff.

person and the work of Christ. In the presence of the unfathomable love of God all attempts toward a rational explanation remain useless.

26. Christus Crucifixus—Christus Victor

1. The work of Christ finished on the cross is that act of divine love through which God establishes the reconciliation between himself and the world.

2. This finished work appears to faith first of all as a victory over those demonic powers which have enslaved humanity, and is, therefore, the victorious intervention of the divine will. Since, however, these destructive powers are in part an expression of the divine judgment, the victory implies not only an altered situation for humanity, but also an act whereby God is reconciled in and through his reconciliation.

3. The way of reconciliation is the way of the self-giving, self-sacrificing, suffering, and vicarious divine love. In and through this unbroken activity of God the order of justice as the pattern of the relationship between God and man has been supplanted, but in such a way that at the same time the radical and condemning opposition of divine love to evil has been perfectly expressed.

4. The Christian conception of atonement is obscured if it is interpreted in part as a divine act and in part as a compensation to divine righteousness rendered by Christ as Man; when it is no longer understood as a divine act it is entirely destroyed. The traditional distinction between objective and subjective atonement is calculated to confuse rather than clarify the issue, and these two can in no case be proposed as the alternatives.

1. The Finished Work.

Christian faith perceives the work of Christ finished on the cross as an act of reconciliation, as a deed accomplished by divine love through which God effects reconciliation between himself and the world. The expression, "the work finished on the cross," has been chosen for a twofold reason. It is intended to indicate the central place which the cross has in Christian faith, and also to emphasize that the cross must be seen in connection with the whole life of Christ. The cross summarizes the totality of his life and work.

This formulation, therefore, accentuates a twofold antithesis. It takes issue with any theology which isolates the cross from the rest of his life, and assumes that the work of reconciliation has reference only to the cross. This approach is characteristic of some tendencies in medieval scholasticism. But it also takes issue with those tendencies which assign a secondary significance to the cross, as was done in the idealistic-humanistic theology of the last centuries. The teachings of primitive Christianity testify that the eyes of faith are irresistibly drawn to the cross. "For I determined not to know anything among you, save Jesus Christ, and him crucified" (I Cor. 2:2). The reason for this is that the cross gathers up and summarizes the totality of his life and work. The conflict to which his life and work had been dedicated was epitomized in his struggle and victory on the cross, and therefore this deed is the consummation of the incarnation.

Faith perceives the work finished on the cross as a divine deed, an act of divine love. This point of view is of vital significance for the Christian faith. If this is not given adequate consideration and other points of view are permitted to intrude, the fundamental Christian idea is obscured, and it is no longer apparent that fellowship with God is based entirely on divine love and is established entirely through its activity. It is also clear that every approach which does not perceive the entire work of Christ as an act of God is at complete variance with the central content of the confession of Christ as expressed in the doctrine of incarnation.

In the previous part we have spoken of God as Saviour

(§ 18). When we now say that the finished work of Christ is that divine act whereby God establishes *reconciliation* between himself and the world, this term is intended to indicate the nature of that salvation which we are discussing. The essential character of salvation is a reconciliation, the re-establishment of a broken fellowship between God and the world. Since the fellowship has been broken by the hostile power of evil, the reconciliation implies the destruction and subjugation of that power which separates God and the world. Faith perceives the divine act in Christ primarily as an act of reconciliation and redemption, as Luther expresses it in his explanation of the second article: "who has redeemed me, a lost and condemned creature, bought and freed me from all sins, from death, and from the power of the devil" (cf. also § 2).

A reconciliation between two partners can be effected in various ways. It can be accomplished by negotiations between the two parties, or by mediation by a third party, or by the action of one of the parties. All three of these approaches have been used by theology in its effort to set forth the nature of reconciliation. But this is a mistake. From the point of view of Christian faith the first two are excluded. Faith cannot accept the idea that man should negotiate with God as with an equal, or that the reconciliation should be based, at least in part, on some accomplishments on the part of man. Nor can the idea of a third party as mediator be accepted. To be sure, theology has often argued along this line and used the idea of Christ as "the Mediator," which occurs a few times in the New Testament. But Christian faith cannot speak about Christ as Mediator in any other sense than as the means through which divine love realizes its purpose. This is the decisive viewpoint in the New Testament. As far as faith is concerned it is imperative that this work be understood as an act of which the divine and loving will itself is the subject. Reconciliation between the two hostile parties is based entirely on the activity of one party, the God of Love.

2. Victory and Reconciliation.

If we are to investigate how Christian faith understands the significance of the work of Christ finished on the cross, we must first of all note the fundamental idea of *struggle and victory* which is here revealed. The divine will carries out its purpose through a bitter struggle with hostile forces. Christ carries on the struggle of the divine will against the evil powers, those demonic powers which have enslaved man. The cross is the victory over these powers. The cross is the chief Christian symbol because it is a symbol of victory. It is a crucifix of triumph. Those images of the Crucified which have reveled in picturing the sufferings of martyrdom in the most gruesome manner have missed what is essential to the Christian faith: the idea of victory, and have obscured the fact that suffering love is at the same time the victorious and sovereign love.

The fundamental idea of struggle and victory meets us in the New Testament in a variety of figures. The Gospels present the work of Jesus as a struggle against unclean spirits, concentrated and incorporated in the figure of Satan. The Kingdom of God is established by the defeat of those powers which are inimical to God. In this connection it is said that the Son of Man came to give his life a ransom for many (Mark 10:45). The same fundamental theme is found in the New Testament as a whole. Paul regards sin, death, and the demonic powers as the enemies whom Christ has defeated (cf. especially Rom. 4:25; 6:3 ff.; 8:38 f; I Cor. 15:3 f.; 15:24 ff.; 15:54; II Cor. 5:18 ff.; Gal. 1:4; Phil. 2:6 ff.; Col. 2:15). It is especially characteristic of Paul that he includes also "the law" among those destructive powers which Christ has conquered. The law is, from one point of view, holy and divine, but from another point of view it is a tyrannical power of destruction (cf. Rom. 7:9; I Cor. 15:56; Gal. 3:13). As such a destructive power the law, too, has been overcome by Christ (cf. Rom. 7:4; I Cor. 15:57; Gal. 3:13; Col. 2:14). Christ is "the end of the law" (Rom. 10:4). The other New Testament writings present this same theme of a redemptive act which has occurred in and through the victory of Christ over the destructive powers (cf. Acts 20:28; Eph. 1:17; I Tim. 2:5; II Tim. 1:10; Tit. 2:14; Heb. 2:14; 9:12; I Pet. 1:18; Rev. 1:5; 5:5, 12). In the Johannine writings the dualistic feature appears exceptionally strong and serves as a background to the acts of conflict and victory of Christ. Cosmos stands as an obscure power hostile to God; and the purpose of the revelation and work of Christ is to vanquish this power and dethrone the devil (cf. John 12:31). The way to death is at the same time the way to glorification (John 12:23). In I John 3:8 the purpose of Christ's coming is summarized thus: "To this end was the Son of God manifested, that he might destroy the works of the devil."

This fundamental theme dominates the viewpoint of the ancient church in regard to the significance of the work of Christ. The thought of Christ's struggle with and victory over the destructive powers occurs in constantly new variations. These powers are almost always defined as the powers of sin, death, and the devil, and the relation of Christ especially to the last of these is pictured in lurid colors. During the Middle Ages this ancient Christian theme was more or less pushed aside. There were two reasons for this: the Latin theory of the atonement finally formulated by Anselm, and the medieval passion mysticism. Yet this fundamental theme of Christianity persisted in various ways, in preaching, in hymns, especially in the Easter hymns, and in art. It returned with new power in the Reformation. As Luther has given new life to the ancient confession of Christ and its doctrine of incarnation, so he has also restored to its central position the ancient theme of conflict and victory. Luther never tires of picturing Christ's "wonderful struggle," *mirabile duellum*. It is significant that Luther not only regards the ancient triad, sin, death, and the devil, as destructive powers, but includes also the law (as Paul did) and wrath, the divine wrath. Through this insight of Luther, Christian faith is able to view the work of Christ under the most profound perspective. This will be discussed more fully later.

We must now in a few words define the significance of this fundamental, classical theme of Christianity. During later centuries it has sometimes been looked upon with suspicion, principally because it has been expressed in drastic and even grotesque forms. But if we look at the fundamental religious idea which it represents, this classic Christian theme appears in monumental simplicity. The background is the divine will and the forces opposed to it. Christ stands as the warrior and victor of the divine will in the struggle against the evil powers in every form. The antagonism between the divine will and evil comes to a focus in a decisive conflict. The evil powers appear to have won the victory. But Christ wins the victory in apparent defeat and triumphs in his death. Divine love is victorious in self-giving and sacrifice. This decisive victory creates a new situation and changes the estate of both man and the world. A new age has begun. The finished work signifies the victorious coming of divine love. Christian faith is born with a paean of victory in its heart: "In all this we are more than conquerors," no power whatsoever "shall be able to separate us from the love of God, which is in Christ Jesus our Lord" (Rom. 8:37 ff.; cf. also "Thanks be to God, who giveth us the victory through our Lord Jesus Christ," I Cor. 15:57). We need hardly underscore further that this idea of conflict and victory is inseparably connected with the central content of the confession of Christ: the victorious power is none other than God's own power.

Up to this point we have not been directly concerned with the idea of reconciliation. The analysis must now show how this victory of Christ over the destructive powers appears to faith as an act of reconciliation. As a matter of fact, the triumph of Christ is at once a victorious and reconciling act which involves a transformation of man's estate and a new situation for the world, and implies a reconciliation between God and creation. Since the divine will is radically antagonistic to evil, and since God cannot, therefore, be reconciled to evil, this reconciliation entails the destruction of the power of evil and its dominion. This reconciliation furthermore implies that the finished work of Christ has a positive significance for the divine will as such and thereby accomplishes reconciliation. In order that this statement may not be misunderstood, we hasten to add that Christian faith always perceives God as the acting subject in reconciliation. Here the classic words of Paul must be accepted without qualification: "God was in Christ reconciling the world unto himself" (II Cor. 5:19). But Christian faith can at the same time speak of God as being reconciled, that his wrath is "stayed," "is turned away," and so on. Such expressions are legitimate so long as they do not encroach upon, but are rather incorporated into, the fundamental Christian point of view, namely, that reconciliation is throughout a work of God. To Christian faith the matter appears thus, that God is reconciled in and through his reconciliation of the world unto himself.

In order to see how this line of thought is connected with the victory of divine love in Christ, it is necessary to note that these destructive powers which are vanquished stand partly in an inner relation to and are an expression of divine judgment. This is certainly not true of sin. This hostile power cannot serve the divine will except in so far as the divine will overcomes it and turns it into good. But all the other "destructive powers" of which faith speaks can be seen from two points of view. They are, on the one hand, tyrannical powers which enslave humanity, and on the other hand the instruments of divine judgment. This is the case with those two powers, death and the devil, which the ancient church placed side by side with sin. Death in this case is not simply physical death. The ancient church combined death with sin, and even regarded these two as different expressions for the same thing. Both denote separation from God. The separation from God caused by sin is *eo ipso* death. But this death may also be regarded as an expression of divine judgment. That sin is death is in accordance with God's will and judgment. Even the devil can similarly be placed in relation to the divine will. He is, of course, from one point of view, the incarnation of that which is hostile to God. But, from another viewpoint, it is in accordance with God's will that because of sin men have been placed under the dominion of the devil; he has thus, as the saying goes, acquired a certain legitimate dominion over men. If we are to understand the primitive conception of Christ's struggle with and victory over the destructive powers, we must keep clearly in mind this inner relation between death and the devil on the one side and the divine will on the other. It then becomes clear that the victory over the destructive powers is at the same time a reconciliation. The religious point of view which is hidden behind the drastic figures is that the loving will of God prepares a way for itself through judgment. The victory of Christ through his self-giving is the means whereby God reconciles the world unto himself and is at the same time reconciled.

When the law and wrath are included among the destructive powers the concept of reconciliation becomes even more profound. This is especially the case when divine wrath is considered in this connection. It was for this reason that Luther could speak so profoundly about the atonement. While death and the devil can be used only indirectly as instruments of the divine will, the "law" is very closely connected with this will. The law as such is holy and good, and a direct expression of the divine will. But the demand of the divine will expressed in the law becomes at the same time a destructive power. The law cannot save man from the power of sin; the way which the law indicates is nothing but salvation of self by self. The sharp words which Paul and later Luther spoke about the law must be understood from this point of view. The law stands as the condemning power, it is connected with the curse (Gal. 3:10), and it even drives men to sin (I Cor. 15:56), since it leads men into the way of salvation of self by self, which in reality is a way that leads away from salvation into sin. Under these circumstances the victory over the law means that divine love in Christ breaks through the legal order of justice and establishes a new order in the relationship between God and man.

The tension in the divine will appears, however, most intensively when divine wrath is regarded as one of the destructive powers which are vanquished through the self-giving of divine love in the work of Christ. The question here is not simply about an instrument of the divine will, but an essential element in this will. "Wrath" is God's direct and immediate reaction to sin. But at the same time it is, according to Luther, a destructive power and a tyrant, even the worst of all tyrants. When wrath is separated from love it assumes this character. Thus, the conflict is carried into the divine nature itself. Luther expresses this idea in picturesque language: "The curse, therefore, which is God's wrath resting over the whole world, struggled with the blessing which is God's eternal grace and mercy in Christ. The curse encountered the blessing and wanted to destroy it, but it was not able. The blessing is divine and eternal, and consequently the curse must give way. If the blessing in Christ could be made to retreat, then God himself could be overcome. But this is not possible." [1] The overcoming of wrath means, according to this analysis, that the inmost nature of God, the divine love, "the blessing," makes a way for itself through wrath, "the curse." This occurs when Christ submits to wrath and bears the burden it imposes, or, in other words, through the self-giving sacrifice of love. Divine wrath is thus "reconciled"; it is, so to speak, fused with love. But this act of atonement through which wrath is reconciled is at the same time a divine act, the act of divine love itself. It is hardly possible to penetrate deeper into the mystery of the atonement. The act of reconciliation appears with crystal clarity as the victory of divine love itself. But it remains nevertheless a mystery, the mystery of divine love. It is not dissolved and rendered superficial as in the Latin theory of the atonement (cf. § 4). God is reconciled in that he reconciles the world unto himself through the self-giving sacrifice of love. From this point of view we must now examine further how Christian faith comprehends this sacrificial act of love.

[1] W. A., 40, 1, pp. 441 ff.

3. *Propter Christum.*

There is an abundance of expressions in the vocabulary of Christian faith which, if rightly understood, reveal what it cost divine love to effect this reconciliation. If these, however, are not understood from this fundamental point of view, the result is a caricature of the work of Christ and of the relation of the divine will to the act of reconciliation. From the beginning of Christianity and down through the ages Christian faith has recurrently proclaimed the self-giving sacrifice of divine love in the crucified Christ. Paul speaks of this freely and frequently. "He that spared not his own Son, but delivered him up for us all" (Rom. 8:32). "God commendeth his own love toward us, in that, while we were yet sinners, Christ died for us" (Rom. 5:8). Christ "loved me, and gave himself up for me" (Gal. 2:20; 1:4). "One has died for all" (II Cor. 5:14), and Christ "became a curse for us" (Gal. 3:13). God has made Christ "to be sin on our behalf; that we might become the righteousness of God in him" (II Cor. 5:21). The same fundamental theme, the self-giving of divine love *for us,* recurs in constantly new variations in the other writings of the New Testament. "Herein is love, not that we loved God, but that he loved us, and sent his Son to be the propitiation for our sins" (I John 4:10). Christ is "the Lamb of God, that taketh away the sin of the world" (John 1:29). It is reiterated again and again that the act of Christ was for our sakes, or on our behalf. But the expression "for us" imperceptibly passes over into and assumes the significance of the expression of "in our stead." It can rightly be said that no idea has had a stronger position within the life of faith or has been dearer to the Christian heart. But it cannot be denied that this fundamental Christian theme has become strange and incomprehensible to many within Christianity in these later times. The reasons for this have been many and need not here be elaborated. We should note, however, that one of the principal reasons has been that this fundamental Christian theme has frequently been subjected to grotesque interpretations which have obscured its

Christian character. This Christian character can be revealed only when the self-giving of love "for our sake" is firmly connected with *divine* love, or, in other words, when the sacrifice of Christ is understood as the self-giving of divine love. When this point of view is obscured or lost, the expressions mentioned here become false symbols.

Christian faith has used many and varied figures in its attempt to express the content and significance of the self-giving action of divine love. We shall consider here three fundamental ideas which have played prominent parts in the history of Christian thought. These three illustrate our fundamental theme from various points of view: the act of love as a sacrifice, as an endurance of punishment, and as a vicarious act.

It is not at all surprising that Christian faith looks upon the finished work of Christ as a *sacrifice*. The idea of sacrifice is common in all religions and not least in the Old Testament. The primitive Christian view connects the sacrifice of Christ directly with the Old Testament sacrifices. The Letter to the Hebrews, which is more interested in this line of thought than any other writing in the New Testament, declares that the offering of Christ signifies both the fulfillment and the abolition of all sacrifice. The idea of sacrifice occurs frequently in the New Testament even when the word itself is not used. It is present in those passages which speak of "the blood of Christ." "The new covenant in my blood" (I Cor. 11:23 ff.), "a communion of the blood of Christ" (I Cor. 10:16), "being now justified by his blood" (Rom. 5:9), "for our passover also hath been sacrificed, even Christ" (I Cor. 5:7). When Christian faith perceives the work of Christ as a sacrifice, the reference is not simply to the death on the cross. It refers rather to his whole life, since in him self-sacrificing love pours itself out in willing obedience (Phil. 2:8). But this whole sacrifice is summarized and perfected in the sacrifice on the cross, since his whole life is there offered. When Christian faith declares that this sacrifice implies the perfection and abolition of all other sacrifices, the reason is that this sacri-

233

fice is directly connected with divine love. The sacrifice is in the last analysis the sacrifice of divine love itself. Divine love does not remain outside and apart from that which takes place here; it is active in this offering, it brings the sacrifice, it offers of its own, yea, even itself (cf. Heb. 9:15; §§ 3, 4). This sacrifice affirms that there is no limit to the self-giving of divine love; it gives itself without measure or restraint. Since it is in the last analysis the sacrifice of divine love itself, the Christian idea of sacrifice has radically reversed all non-Christian conceptions, in which the purpose always and everywhere is to seek to influence the divine power by human gifts and sacrifices. The sacrifice of Christ signifies, therefore, the abolition of all such sacrifices. There is no longer any justification for their existence. But this abolition occurs because the sacrifice of Christ, being the sacrifice of divine love, is perfect and complete. But Christian faith can speak of this sacrifice, too, as a sacrifice to God (Heb. 9:14). This statement is possible because Christian faith looks at the act of reconciliation from two points of view: God is reconciled in that he reconciles the world unto himself. This means that the sacrifice of divine love in Christ has a reconciling significance also for God himself. But it would lose its Christian character, if, as has often happened, it is separated from this connection and conceived of as a compensation given to God by man.

When Christian faith has understood the finished work of Christ as a suffering or an *endurance of punishment* on the part of divine love, this approach is closely connected with the struggle of Christ against those demonic powers which hold men captive. When divine love becomes "incarnate" and is subjected to the conditions of sin and death, the result is that it must become a suffering love. It has to live under those harsh conditions and consequences which are the results of sin. Through its radical opposition to the sinful life it reveals the nature of sin as hostility to God and the unconditional character of divine judgment. But most significant for Christian faith is the fact that divine love in complete solidarity with men assumes the burden of all the suffering, guilt, and condemnation which has been occasioned by sin. The divine love reaches the very limits of suffering in the fact that its burden is imposed by divine wrath. The divine wrath which rests on humanity strikes at the very heart of divine love. It must, however, be emphasized that this affirmation of Christ's suffering under divine wrath does not imply that this wrath is directed to Christ and his work. It means rather that divine love in Christ enters into complete solidarity and suffers with the world toward which divine wrath is directed. When divine love bears the burden of divine wrath, the wrath is transformed into and fused with love.

The idea of sacrifice and the bearing of the burden imposed by sin lead directly to the significance of his finished work as *vicarious*. The vicarious suffering of divine love is to faith the most evident and the most inscrutable of all spiritual realities. The older theology often obscured this reality by grotesque misinterpretations, and later theology has often rejected it because of its superficial view of the nature and conditions of divine love. But this vicarious love is dear to the heart of every Christian. We have deliberately chosen the most direct and questionable word, vicariousness. It is clear, however, that the affirmations of Christian faith to the effect that the work of Christ was "for us," "for our sake," ultimately include the conception "in our stead." The first expressions tend to be superseded by the latter. This approach to the work of Christ is intimately connected with the idea of his struggle and victory over the demonic forces. This struggle and victory have occurred for our sake, for our salvation and redemption. But since we have been unable to accomplish this work ourselves, it has manifestly been done in our stead. But this vicarious victory is seen in its depth and power only when we note that it is at the same time an act of reconciliation whereby God reconciles and is reconciled, and thus a new relationship between God and the world is established. Our situation is what it is *propter Christum*. Divine love in Christ has done what no human power could accomplish. When God meets man with reconciling and forgiving love, it is *propter Christum* and *per Christum*. In this connection one could use the old and much misinterpreted expression, satisfaction, but in a sense widely different from that which it has in scholastic theology. For Christian faith it is clear that Christ has "made satisfaction." The term *satis*, "sufficient," is, to be sure, entirely too weak to express the significance of the work of Christ. But ignoring this, it can well be said that Christ has satisfied God, viz., in the sense that he has adequately accomplished the reconciling and victorious work of divine love; and in so doing he has also made complete satisfaction for us.

The word vicarious is, however, connected with certain dangers. It has sometimes been interpreted as a mechanical and automatic transfer of our burden to him. This is the interpretation which emerges whenever the organic connection between the work of Christ and divine love is even slightly ignored. When this unspiritual interpretation is avoided, however, we gain a new perspective of the vicarious act of suffering and triumphant love. The vicarious aspect of Christ's victory cannot be interpreted to mean that we are set free from the struggle against sin and from the suffering that it entails. Such a viewpoint would be completely unrealistic. The vicarious element in the work of divine love is its creation of a new situation while it simultaneously releases in human life a constantly active and quickening power. The vicarious suffering of divine love does not automatically remove the burden, but it gives new power to bear it; vicarious love does not end the struggle, but it furnishes a new possibility to carry on the struggle. Its act is not only a completed act, but a continuous activity. We stand here at the point where *propter Christum* becomes for Christian faith also *in Christo*. It must be added, however, that the act of forgiveness based on the work of reconciliation is not motivated by this renewing power which flows from vicarious love. The basis of forgiveness is to be found solely in that divine love which in giving itself reconciles the world to itself (cf. §§ 33, 34).

We need only add to what has already been said about the work of divine love as a sacrificial, suffering, and vicarious act that these ideas must be incorporated into and characterized by the fundamental theme of reconciliation and atonement. The subject of our previous discussion, throughout, has been suffering love. But nothing is more essential to Christian faith than the conviction that this suffering love is at the same time a victorious and, in relation to evil, a sovereign love. Suffering love does not simply passively endure evil, it vanquishes this evil in victorious activity and is revealed as sovereign even in apparent defeat. Every viewpoint which one-sidedly presents only the passive side, or emphasizes this over against the active, creates a wrong conception of the relation of divine love to evil.[2] Nothing is more vital to Christian faith than that the act of reconciliation in Christ is a victory.

In this victorious act of self-giving love the system of legal justice as a pattern of the relationship between God and man is abrogated. Spontaneous and "uncaused" love is not confined within a purely legalistic system when in sovereign power it creates the new order. But this abrogation of the order of justice takes place in such a way that the radical and condemning opposition of love to evil is most fully expressed. The wrath against sin does not cease, but it is fused with love and in this sense canceled.

4. The Demarcations of the Christian Doctrine of Atonement.

The Christian doctrine of atonement as here presented is differentiated both from the scholastic and from the idealistic theories.[3]

We may define first the *classical* idea of the atonement by

---

[2] Cf. B. H. Streeter, "God and the World's Pain," *Concerning Prayer* (New York, 1921), p. 39. "If Christ is truly to us the portrait of the unseen God, the Crucifixion is not merely an event which happened once during three hours of time, it stands for something that is eternal in the life of God—but so also does the Resurrection. Therefore everlastingly in the life of God 'death is swallowed up in victory.'"

[3] Cf. G. Aulén, *Christus Victor*.

saying that here *the divine act is unabridged and the order of justice breached*. Even when it is stated that God is reconciled, the meaning is not that divine love has ceased to be the acting subject of atonement, but rather that God is reconciled in and through his act of reconciliation. This is one continuous and divine act accomplished through Christ. But this divine act breaks through the system of legal justice. The self-giving of love creates a new and higher order.

The fundamental character of the scholastic theory of the atonement is: *an unimpaired order of justice and an impaired act of God*. It has often been argued that, according to the theory of Anselm and later scholasticism, God is simply the object of reconciliation and nothing more. But this is false. God is also the subject in so far as he takes the initiative and sends the Son into the world. But at the decisive point in the act of reconciliation, the rendering of satisfaction, the emphasis is placed on the service which Christ *qua homo* renders. But the act of God is thereby impaired. The atonement is no longer, as in the classical theory, that act in which God at the same time reconciles and is reconciled, but on the contrary, partly a divine work and partly a compensation which Christ as man offers to God on behalf of man. In this way also the order of justice is preserved unimpaired. The whole theory indicates that the work of reconciliation is securely placed within the system of legal justice.

In the third type, where the theory of the atonement is based on idealism, the idea of the atonement as an act of God is more completely set aside. Even when the significance of the work of Christ is emphasized, it is in terms of Jesus as the religious "archetype" of humanity, "the ideal man," or the incarnation of the religious and moral ideal (cf. § 25. 2). Here, even more than in the scholastic type, the emphasis is placed on human activity, and consequently this viewpoint represents, even as far as Christ is concerned, a line from below upward, from man to God. The idealistic theory of the atonement is sharply critical of the legalistic aspect of the scholastic theory. But this does not mean a breach in the order of justice along the line of the classical theory, but in reality only that legalism is replaced by a moralistic and ethical point of view, since the emphasis is shifted from the divine act to that which is accomplished by man.

When we regard these three different types from the point of view of the *confession of faith in Christ,* it becomes clear that the classical theory of the atonement stands in intimate relation to the central content of this confession: the incarnation of divine love in Christ. This connection is evidenced by the fact that the atonement is throughout the work of divine love, and that it cannot be accomplished by any other power. This connection is broken in the scholastic theory, since here the emphasis is placed on the fact that compensation is given to God through Christ *qua homo.* The "divine" in Christ is significant only in so far as it gives added value to the work of the "human nature." The idealistic type has to an even greater degree lost the appreciation of the central content of the confession of faith in Christ.

If we look at the three types from the point of view of the *conception of God,* the observations may be summarized in the following statements. In the conception of God connected with the classical theory we note a twofold tension. In the first place, God is sovereign, but he is also the God who is engaged in a struggle under historical conditions. In the second place, God struggles against hostile powers, but among them are also powers which represent and dispense divine judgment. It is characteristic that these tensions are not dissolved by rational adjustments. On the contrary, the principal point of view is that divine love wins the victory through self-giving and sacrifice (*crux triumphans*). Wrath is overcome by being fused into divine love. But at the same time the radical opposition to evil on the part of the divine will appears in much clearer light. The scholastic type knows of such a tension, although in a weaker form, but

239

this tension between divine mercy and righteousness is resolved through a rational process: righteousness is given due compensation and is thereby satisfied. This line of thought indicates that neither "righteousness" nor love is here understood in its complete Christian sense. That this is true in regard to love is quite clear. In regard to the opposition of righteousness to evil, the intention is to emphasize the seriousness of sin and guilt, but the idea of satisfaction indicates only too clearly that this intention has not been realized. An opposition to evil which can be satisfied with a compensation is not very radical. In the idealistic type, finally, there is in reality no tension. This type wants to maintain a "pure" and "unified" concept of God, characterized by unchangeable love. But this unity has been gained at the price of weakening the radical opposition of the divine will to evil. The concept of God has become humanized, and love has become something more or less self-evident and stereotyped. When this occurs, the theory of the atonement has lost its Christian character.

The distinction here made between the three theories of the atonement replaces the traditional distinction between an "objective" and a "subjective" theory. This latter distinction has usually been understood to mean that the scholastic type has been called objective, and the idealistic and humanized type subjective. The idea has been that in the objective atonement God has been regarded as the object, and in the subjective the reconciliation takes place in man. It is immediately clear that this distinction does not at all agree with the classical idea of atonement. The concepts, objective and subjective, are not germane to the subject, since there can be no theory of the atonement which does not include both an objective and a subjective element. The alternative of an objective or subjective atonement therefore becomes misleading. It should rather be stated that the atonement includes both objective and subjective elements. In regard to the classical theory it is clear that this is to an imminent degree "objective," since the finished work of Christ

appears to faith as something objectively given. But it is just
as clear that this idea of the atonement contains a subjective
element, since the divine act of reconciliation continually realizes itself anew in human life, or, in other words, the finished
work is at the same time a continuous activity in the present.

27. Kyrios-Christus

1. The continuous work of Christ receives its content from the
finished work, and implies a realization of the latter. In his
continuous work Christ appears as the Lord of the Christian life,
as Kyrios. The existence of this life is *propter Christum* as well
as *in Christo*.

2. When his finished work through the exaltation becomes the
continuous work, this exaltation implies at the same time the
revelation of the significance of the former.

3. The various expressions of the exaltation contained in the
primitive Christian confession—risen, ascended into heaven, sitting on the right hand of God the Father Almighty—reveal the
significance of the exaltation from various points of view: Christ
lives, he is set free from the earthly limitations of space and time,
and belongs entirely to the divine life. He therefore exercises
his dominion (*regnum Christi*).

Excursus. The Boundary Line of Faith. Any affirmations concerning the *how* of the resurrection which seek to reach beyond
the scope of what has already been said, lie outside the boundary line of faith.

1. The Continuous Work of Christ.

In the previous paragraphs we have endeavored to view the
work of Christ finished on the cross in the light of Christian
faith; or, in other words, we have tried to understand the essen-

tial significance of this work as it appears in the light of that which continually takes place in the Christian life. When we now turn to that which continually occurs and view it as the continued work of Christ, it is necessary to note how this continuous work is anchored to and inseparably connected with the work once and for all finished on the cross. When Christian faith is directed toward Christ, it implies that it is directed toward One who is active in the present; and when it uses the combination Jesus Christ or Christ Jesus, it implies that this continuous work is inseparably connected with the work accomplished in history.

Christian faith exists as faith in Christ (cf. § 5). We are not interested here in the various factors which determined the formulation of this faith in Christ, nor in the various elements which it may contain. We are concerned with the significance of the fact that Christian faith *exists* as faith in Christ. The very center of this faith in Christ is the conviction that Christ as the object of faith is the living Christ who is active in the present, and that he is the central power in the life of Christian faith. The cohesive and governing force in Christianity is not a certain set of doctrines or statutes which have once been formulated, nor anything that belongs merely to past history; it is rather the Lord of the church who is present with his own "even unto the end of the world" (Matt. 28:20), and who through his presence rules the souls of men. This effective presence is to faith the essential element in the Christian life and the factor which makes it *Christian*. The inner history of this Christian life appears, therefore, from the most profound point of view as a history of the works of Christ. Faith in Christ stands inseparably connected with Christ as the one who is active in the present. It would lose its meaning if it were a question simply of something belonging to past history. Faith lives primarily in the present since the inner nature of faith implies being gripped and controlled by something which positively declares itself to be a divine revelation. Without this contemporaneity faith in Christ would be reduced to an intellectual assent to certain events in ancient history, or to certain "religious ideas" formulated and delivered in the past. Faith would then lose its religious character, and it would be quite meaningless to speak of faith in Christ. This character of being continually in the present is not something secondary or accidental; it is essential to Christian faith.

The contemporaneity of faith in Christ characterizes the entire life and culture of the Christian church. Christian faith has from the beginning and down through the ages affirmed the presence of Christ and in a variety of expressive figures has declared: *in ipsa fide Christus adest* ("in faith itself Christ is present"). We need only remind ourselves how strongly this is emphasized in primitive Christianity. Christ is the Head, we are the members (Paul); Christ is the vine, we are the branches (John); our life is a life "in Christ"—"it is no longer I that live. but Christ liveth in me" (Gal. 2:20), we must abide in Christ as he abides in us (John 15:4 ff.). This presence of Christ is the foundation on which the whole cultus of the church is based. It is abundantly present also in Christian psalms and hymns.

If, then, it is essential for Christian faith to speak of the continuous work of Christ, it is also just as essential that this activity of Christ be anchored to the work finished on the cross, and that its concrete content and character be derived from this vital connection. Through this connection the act of Christ is preserved from becoming simply an abstract principle. It is true that the living faith in Christ is based on the whole, continuous activity of Christ. It is also true that through the exaltation the historical life is set free from the merely temporal and historical accidents which may have belonged to it. But this does not alter the fact that the continuous activity of Christ receives its decisive and abiding character from the work finished on the cross. This means that the character of the living and continuously active Christ is defined by self-giving victorious and sovereign love. The act of Christ retains at all times and under all circumstances this character. In the continuous work this victorious act of love is raised above all temporal and local limitations (cf. § 3). There is a continuous reciprocity between that which has occurred and that which continually occurs. It is very significant that in the testimony of faith there is a constant interchange of the present with the perfect, and vice versa. The significance of this disregard of time is that to faith the past is never simply past, but something which is continually present in the continuous work. The victory of divine love through self-giving is continually realized in the present. It is realized in a continuous struggle. Luther describes very drastically how Christ always "beats and chokes" in us those enemies which were the object of the one decisive struggle, and how he thus appears as *Kyrios*, as "my Lord." Everything is dependent on this fact that we have him in our midst who is the victorious Lord. "But for us fights the Valiant One whom God himself elected." "When you look at this person," Luther writes, "then you see sin, death, wrath, hell, the devil, and everything evil vanquished and killed. In so far as Christ rules in the hearts of believers, there is no sin, no death, no curse." The work of the atonement once finished is continually realized anew "in the hearts of the believers." The victory is an "eternal" victory, and therefore also a victory in the present. The existence of the Christian life, therefore, is both *propter Christum* and *in Christo*. Any opposition between these two points of view is in principle excluded. Everything depends on the finished work of divine love in Christ; from this point of view the watchword *propter Christum* is unconditionally valid. But everything depends also on the work which is continually being done in the hearts of men; and in this sense the watchword *Christus in nobis* is just as unconditionally valid. But *Christus pro nobis* must nevertheless precede *Christus in nobis*, since God's act of forgiveness does not rest on the work of Christ "in us," but on the contrary is based entirely on the divine act of atonement *propter Christum* (cf. § 26. 3).

2. The Act of Exaltation.

The work finished on the cross becomes through the exaltation a continuous activity. Christ as *Kyrios* is "exalted" and "glorified." This exaltation (Phil 2:9; Heb. 2:9 ff.) is the birthday of the Christian church and of Christian faith. Christianity comes into existence through the discovery and conviction of faith that the apparent defeat was in reality a victory. That Christ appears as the Exalted, *Kyrios,* does not mean, therefore, that the work finished on the cross must be complemented by something which occurs later, nor that the victory was something subsequent to the sacrifice of self-giving love. It means rather the revelation of that victory which was contained in the sacrifice of love. His work does not become a victory *through* the exaltation, but this unveils, reveals, and realizes the victorious deed contained in his finished work. In reality the exaltation is included in that which appears to be its exact opposite, in the deepest humiliation. When the day of his departure approached (John 12:23), we read: "The hour is come that the Son of Man shall be glorified." When we speak of exaltation as a revelation of victory and of the Crucified as the victorious Lord, we are dealing with something which is revealed only to the eye of faith. It is not a question of an external manifestation of victory comprehensible to all men. The triumph of the cross and of Easter was completely hidden from the chief priests and the scribes.

The exaltation means that the Crucified and his work are raised above all the limitations of history, but this implies at the same time a revelation of the meaning and significance of this work, and of its character as the victorious deed of divine love itself. If this point of view is not given due consideration, the result is a conception of the cross which is foreign to Christian faith. It would then appear only as a *martyrium*. But for Christian faith *theologia crucis* is at the same time *theologia gloriae,* but not in the sense of a glorification of the human. What we have now said may also be expressed in this way: that Good

245

Friday appears in its right perspective only when it is lighted by the glory of Easter. If the note of triumph is not present in the preaching about the passion, this preaching has lost its Christian character. It is significant that the hymns of Easter, rather than the passion hymns, have been able to express more clearly the Christian view of the cross.

3. *Various Aspects of the Exaltation.*

The fact that the work finished on the cross becomes the continuous activity appears to faith as God's act of exaltation, whereby the purpose of this work is revealed. When faith beholds the completed work in the light of that which continually occurs, it is confronted with the fact of the exaltation, or more accurately with the exaltation as an act of God, and is compelled to make the confession which the ancient church formulated thus: "God hath made him both Lord and Christ, this Jesus whom ye crucified" (Acts 2:36). The conceptions which set forth this act of exaltation are summarized in the threefold affirmation of the Apostolic Creed about the resurrection, the ascent into heaven, and the sitting on the right hand of God. The continuous work is carried on by this exalted Christ. If we look closer at these three expressions, we note that none of them can be isolated from the others, but that all three together furnish the background against which the continuous work and the dominion of Christ appear to the eye of faith. Faith in the resurrection, the living Christ, Christ set free from the power of death, is to be sure the starting point and the foundation of the other two conceptions of faith, and the resurrection must, therefore, from this point of view be regarded as fundamental. But the idea of the living Christ is by itself not a sufficient background for his continuous work. This background is obtained only when the living Christ is also the One exalted above the temporal and spatial limitations of earthly life, and belongs completely to the divine sphere. This is the significance of the two affirmations about his ascent into heaven and his sitting on the right hand of

God. The figurative expression, "the right hand of God," is naturally to be understood in accordance with the ancient formula, *dextra dei ubique est*, "the right hand of God is everywhere." The exaltation, therefore, does not imply a *separation* from the life and struggle on earth, but on the contrary *nearness, presence.* It is an affirmation that Christ is continually and everywhere active in and through his spirit, or, in other words, a statement about his continuous work.

Christ enters upon his dominion, his Kingdom (*regnum Christi*), in and through the exaltation. The name *Kyrios,* Christ is Lord, signifies that he has such a kingdom. This dominion of Christ continues, according to the New Testament, until the consummation of the Kingdom, and it extends over the whole of creation. Everything is subject to Christ. "He must reign, till he has put all his enemies under his feet" (I Cor. 15:25). The universality of this dominion is asserted in Matt. 28:18: "All authority hath been given unto me in heaven and on earth." It is significant that these words are an introduction to the great commission: "Go ye therefore, and make disciples of all nations." Even if the dominion of Christ in principle can be said to include the whole visible and invisible world (cf. I Pet. 3:22), it is nevertheless concentrated in the church, "the Body of Christ" (cf. § 37). It is especially here, in and through the church, that the rule of Christ is realized. The church as the Kingdom of Christ "constitutes the limited, earthly locus of *regnum Christi,* which Christ, the Lord of creation, has selected to be his earthly body."[1]

Excursus. *The Boundary Line of Faith.*

In regard to *how* the exaltation takes place, theology cannot make any statements beyond the assertion that it is an act of God. This is true in regard to the resurrection as well as to the other formulas: ascended into heaven and sitting on the right hand of God. Theology cannot, without exceeding its function

---

[1] O. Cullmann, *Köningsherrschaft Christi und Kirche im Neuen Testament,* p. 32.

in either case, make any statements which are not organically connected with the relation of faith to the continuous work of Christ. It is, therefore, entirely outside the sphere of systematic theology to make decisions in regard to those historical and exegetical questions which are connected with the resurrection faith of the first disciples, or with the empty tomb, or with the manner in which Christ made himself known to his own. Theology can state only that, according to the evidence, different conceptions of *how* the resurrection took place were current in primitive Christianity. Sometimes it is asserted that the risen Christ appeared to his own in virtually the same form as in the days of his flesh, and at other times it is said that one body is buried in the earth and another, spiritual organism arises (I Cor. 15). Paul does not conceive of a continued bodily existence of the same nature as the earthly. But in neither case do we find a purely spiritualized conception. It is evident that the primitive Christian resurrection faith is of a different nature from the philosophical doctrine which regards the "soul" as in itself immortal, and immortality as the liberation of the soul from the prison house of the body. Such a distinction between "soul" and "body" is absolutely foreign to the resurrection faith of the early church. It is evident that in the New Testament we meet various ideas of the manifestation of the risen Christ, but it is also evident that the disciples regarded him as having a certain "corporeality," however spiritualized and "transfigured" this might have been. These ideas emphasize the contrast to the philosophical and idealistic conception of immortality. At the same time it is clear that the main concern is to assert the identity between *Kyrios-Christus* and Jesus of Nazareth, and to present the resurrection as God's act of exaltation.

Under all circumstances that which is essential to faith is the conviction that the exaltation as a whole is an act of God. The essential matter is that he who was "crucified, dead, and buried," was raised by God and installed in his eternal realm. Since this is essential, the problems which would compel us to choose between the "subjectivity" or "objectivity" of these visions are eliminated. Neither of these obscure terms expresses the characteristic viewpoint of faith. If "objectivity" should here mean that the resurrection can be demonstrated as any other empirical fact, it would be contrary both to the primitive Christian testimony of faith according to which the risen Christ manifested himself to his own, but not to a Caiaphas, a Herod, or a Pilate; and also to the present Christian experience which affirms that faith alone has fellowship with the exalted and glorified Christ. In this sense we are dealing with something "subjective," since it is not a question of an empirical verification but of an affirmation of faith. The whole sequence of the exaltation, however, possesses at the same time the greatest possible objectivity, since faith asserts that this sequence is an act of almighty God through which the completed work of Christ manifests its power in his continuous activity and his reign is thus extended (Rom. 1:4; 4:25).

28. Christ and the Spirit

1. When Christian faith conceives of God's act of salvation as the work of the Holy Spirit, it does not in reality intend to distinguish this work from the continuous activity of Christ. The presence and activity of Christ is a presence and activity in the Spirit. The combination of these two expressions guards the characteristic quality of the Spirit and at the same time protects the presence of Christ from unspiritual misinterpretations.

2. It is clear from the foregoing that faith does not conceive of the Spirit as a being distinguished from God. On the contrary the Spirit makes known the immediacy and continuous activity of the revelation of God. The statement that the Spirit "proceeds" not only from the Father but also from the Son is a legitimate Christian concept, since it affirms that through the victorious act of divine love in Christ the Spirit comes "in fullness" (John 1:16).

1. The Work of Christ and the Work of the Spirit.

It is essential that Christian faith in God is a faith in Christ; it is also essential that it is a faith in the Spirit. This statement expresses something decisive in regard to the nature of faith (cf. § 2). Christian faith has spoken about the Spirit and his work especially in connection with the origin and development of the church in the world. The Holy Spirit "calls, gathers, enlightens, and sanctifies"; and through "the means of grace" he establishes his communion of saints in which he "begets and fosters" every individual Christian. The work of the Spirit has reference first and foremost to the church, and consists in this that he creates, establishes, and maintains the church. The church is the temple of God in which the Spirit dwells. The fellowship with God which he establishes is designated as "being born of the Spirit" (John 3:6, 8) and it continues to exist because the Spirit "dwells in" man (Rom. 8:9; I Cor. 3:16; I Thess. 4:8; II Tim. 1:14). The Spirit "is life" (Rom. 8:10), and "makes alive" (John 6:63; II Cor. 3:6). Those who "are led by the Spirit, these are sons of God" (Rom. 8:14). The Spirit opens the eyes and "searches out" the things which belong to God's revelation: "But unto us God revealed them through the Spirit: for the Spirit searcheth all things, yea, the deep things of God. . . . The things of God none knoweth, save the Spirit of God. But we received, not the spirit of the world, but the spirit which is from God; that we might know the things that were freely given to us of God" (I Cor. 2:10 ff.). As the Spirit of truth he bears witness to this revelation of God (Rom. 8:16; I John 5:6; Heb. 10:15).

It is clear from our previous discussion (§ 27) that Christian faith can derive the church and the fellowship with God from Christ and attribute its origin and existence to his work. It can be said of Christ, too, that he is "life," that he "makes alive," and that he "dwells in our hearts through faith" (Eph. 3:17). Christian life can be described as a life "in the Spirit," but also as a life "in Christ." Consequently there is no real difference between the work of the Spirit and the continuous work of Christ. We are not dealing with two different acts, but with the same divine act of love described in different terms. This inseparable connection between Christ and the Spirit is evident in the designation, the Spirit of Jesus Christ. The Spirit of God cannot be named with the name of anyone else except Jesus Christ; and he must be given this name, if the essential character of the Spirit of whom faith speaks is to be properly designated. If the Spirit is the Spirit of Jesus Christ, it implies that Christ is active in and through the Spirit. It is not surprising, therefore, that the language of Christian faith speaks interchangeably of Christ and the Spirit, and permits the one expression imperceptibly to pass over into the other. Paul can say "the Lord is the Spirit," and he can also speak of the transformation into "the image of the Lord" which takes place when the Lord who himself is the Spirit is active (II Cor. 3:17). In regard to the Johannine writings we may remind ourselves that the Gospel of John reports Jesus as speaking in the same context in the so-called farewell discourses about the sending of the "Paraclete," "the Spirit of Truth," and then saying: "I will not leave you fatherless, I will come unto you" (John 14:16 ff.).

When Christian faith uses interchangeably these two expressions, *Kyrios-Christus* and the Spirit, the significance of this usage must not be obscured or denied. This variation serves a twofold purpose. On the one hand the characteristic quality of the Spirit is preserved. That the Spirit is the Spirit of Jesus Christ indicates something very definite about the nature and work of the Spirit. All spiritualistic movements, which separate the Spirit from Christ and transform him into something indefinite, obscure the significance of the Christian faith in God. We cannot appeal to "the Spirit" in behalf of something that is foreign to the work of Christ. On the other hand, when the continued activity of Christ is viewed as the work of the Spirit, the presence of Christ cannot easily be misinterpreted in a mechanistic and unspiritual manner. It serves to emphasize the spiritual nature of the presence of Christ. But this does not mean to faith a lessening of the reality and effectiveness of the presence of Christ. When the presence of Christ is designated as "the real presence," this is in reality a characteristic expression of the intentions of faith. It would be misleading, however, if theology should (as has sometimes been done) present the alternative: real presence *or* spiritual presence. Theology would then obscure the fact that to faith the spiritual presence is in the deepest sense of the word the real presence (cf. § 44). The localization of the presence of Christ in "the means of grace" may be defended only on the condition that what is called means of grace is not so defined as to obscure the fact that Christ is effectively present wherever his Spirit in word and deed actualizes the divine, self-giving, and sovereign love.

2. Faith in God as Faith in the Spirit.

Since the object of faith is God alone, "the Spirit" cannot be conceived of as separated from God or as a being independent of him. Any tendency to regard the Spirit as a separate being co-existent with God would mean that faith has as its object partly God and partly something distinct from him, which in that case competes with him. This would destroy the nature of faith as completely dependent on God. When Christian faith refers to the Holy Spirit, its real purpose is something entirely different. To speak of the Holy Spirit is to see God from a positively defined point of view and to actualize certain essential features in the Christian conception of God. What "the Spirit" actualizes is first and foremost the presence of God as an *immediate* and *active* presence. Where the Spirit of God is, there God himself is effectively present. "The Spirit" assures us that God is not distant and that he is not in reality an extra-mundane being who sits enthroned in exalted eminence, and who from this eminence possibly sends a few messages down to the world; but, on the contrary, that God is near to us and that he is immediately and effectively active in our life. The expression that

God "reveals himself" in and through his Spirit is intended to indicate the mode of God's "personal" revelation in contrast both to those tendencies which interpret God's activity as some kind of higher natural process, and to those attempts to mechanize in one way or another his self-disclosure and deprive it of its active and living character, in which he immediately realizes his loving will (cf. § 3. 5). It is also evident in the history of Christianity that whenever the concept of the Spirit is not given a central place, in contrast to primitive practice, but is set aside, the obscuring of the dynamic features of the idea of God follows as a consequence. Thus God is removed into the abstract distance and divine revelation is apt to be limited to a certain point in the past. The content of the conception, "the Holy Spirit," is the same as the content of the conception of God. The Holy Spirit is as such the Spirit of Love, and consequently also that Spirit who stands in unabridged opposition to evil and is active with all the sovereignty which belongs to divine love. It is significant that the combination "Spirit and power," or "the Spirit of power," occurs so frequently in the primitive Christian testimony of faith, and likewise that the "Nicaean" confession gives the Spirit the characteristic designation: the Giver of life. We cannot say anything about the Spirit which we cannot at the same time say about God; and neither can we give a content to the conception of God which cannot at the same time be given to his Holy Spirit. The Spirit is the appearance of divine love in the present; he is God as he reveals himself to us in active deeds. Wherever God works, he works in and through the Holy Spirit. When faith conceives of "sanctification" in the sense of the realization of divine fellowship as the work of the Holy Spirit, the intention is to emphasize that sanctification is an act in which God himself is *immediately* and *effectively* active.

The Holy Spirit is therefore the Spirit of God and of Jesus Christ. There is a deep significance in the ancient theological formula which states that the Spirit proceeds also from the Son. That which has occurred in history, the completed work of

Christ, is the condition for the coming of the Spirit in purity and "fullness." From the viewpoint of Christian faith the whole content of the work of Christ finished on the cross can be summarized in this one statement: the Spirit comes "in fullness" (John 1:16). The Spirit comes when Christ has been "glorified." The statement that the Spirit proceeds from the Son cannot be interpreted to mean that the Spirit is not altogether a divine Spirit. The Spirit which "proceeds from the Son" proceeds also "from the Father," since the work of salvation here accomplished is throughout the work of the Father. The statement that the Spirit "proceeds from the Son" means not only that the work of Christ is the condition for the coming of the Spirit in fullness, but also that the work of "the Son" is not only a work completed and finished once and for all. On the contrary, it is a continuous work in the Spirit. In reality it is interpreted through the continuous activity of the Spirit, since the real significance of the finished work is manifested to faith only through the inner testimony of the Spirit. Thus Paul says significantly: "No one can say: Jesus is Lord, but through the Holy Spirit" (I Cor. 12.3). To this we may add one more witness: Luther's explanation to the third article of the Apostolic Creed in his Small Catechism.

29. The Trinitarian Element in Christian Faith

The essential purpose of the ancient church's doctrine of the Trinity is to maintain both the definitive and dynamic content and the unity of Christian faith in God. Although the terminology used, "three persons in one Godhead," has tended to threaten the unity of faith in God, especially as the concept of person has become more definitely fixed, nevertheless the threefold and unified viewpoint of Christian faith is contained in the meaningful and living revelation of the one true God in the world of men.

Excursus. The Boundary Line of Faith. This mode of God's revelation has its basis, as far as faith is concerned, in the eternal being of God. All speculations about the "immanent trinity" which go beyond this proposition lie outside the boundary line of faith.

When at this point we consider the problem of the trinitarian element in the Christian faith, the purpose is not to add anything to our exposition of the way of divine love already presented, but only to define more accurately certain affirmations about the mode of God's revelation which have already been noted. The theology of the ancient church regarded the doctrine of the Trinity as a summary of the content of the Christian revelation. We are not concerned here with the question of the origin of the trinitarian formulas, but with the essential significance of this conception and its meaning for Christian faith.

The significance of the Christian doctrine of the Trinity is twofold. On the one hand, it serves to indicate the living content of Christian faith in God, and on the other hand, it serves to maintain the unity of this faith. It affirms that Christian faith receives its characteristic content from the fact that it is a faith in Christ, and its living and immediate character from the fact that it is a faith in the Spirit. Faith in Christ gives to the divine revelation its historical anchorage and its inner richness, and faith in the Spirit indicates its character as a continuous, present, and living revelation (cf. § 28). Faith in Christ and in the Spirit are, therefore, essential elements of the Christian faith in God, and cannot be eliminated without rendering this faith indefinite and superficial. Faith knows God through the work of Christ as intimately as it is possible to know him under earthly conditions, but it comprehends the essential significance of this work of Christ only because it is continually realized in and through the continuous activity of the Spirit. At the same time that the ancient doctrine of the Trinity thus clarifies the significance of the Christian faith by maintaining this threefold viewpoint, it also guards the unity of Christian faith in God, or, in other words, affirms its pure monotheism. It declares that when it speaks of

Christ and the Spirit, the reference is always to the revelation of the one true God and to nothing else (§§ 5, 28).

It cannot be denied, however, that this terminology, "three persons in one Godhead," endangers the unity of faith in God, and that this formula, therefore, may point in an entirely different direction from the one intended. We must note carefully that the term person (*persona*) at the time of the formulation of this doctrine did not possess the fixed and definite significance of independent individuality which it has today. The ancient church understood the word person in such an indefinite and vague sense that it could readily be combined with a most thoroughgoing monotheistic conception which was very firmly held. If we were to explain to the men of the ancient church what we mean by person and personality, these ancient church fathers would no doubt deny us the right to use their trinitarian formula according to *our* concept of person; they would brand us as tritheistic heretics.

The seed of tritheism lies in reality in the expression "three persons." It is interesting to note how theology has tried to avoid the division of the conception of God which seems to be caused by the doctrine of the Trinity. We find one example of this in the statement that "the external works of God are indivisible" (*opera dei ad extra indivisa sunt*). No divine act can be ascribed to a certain person of the Godhead, to the exclusion of the others. The purpose of this affirmation is evidently to refute the suspicion of tritheism. Every divine act is an act of the entire Deity. Luther, who has spoken many a critical word about the term "trinity" and consents to keep it only "on account of the weak" (*pro captu infirmiorum*), asserts emphatically the unity of God: "whatever person in the Godhead is named, it designates the real and true God" and "in the Godhead there is the highest unity." But in spite of these attempts to maintain the unity of God, the pressure of the concept of person became too strong for theology. Theology was forced to adopt interpretations which were foreign to its original purpose. It was not possible to maintain the proposition of the indivisibility of God's work. The development of the doctrine of the Trinity tended, for example, to ascribe the work of salvation more to the Son than to the Father, or, in other words, the loving will of God was not always given its place as subject of the redemptive act of Christ, which, however, was the intention of the confession of faith in Christ (cf. § 26. 4). In the same way the work of the Spirit was separated from the work of the Father and the Son. The result was that the idea of God's living and continuous revelation was obscured and the conception of grace became mechanized. The grace of God became something else than divine love directed toward men, and this undefined conception of grace became in Latin scholasticism a substitute for the Spirit. But in this way the living, unified, and organic view of the revelation of God, which the doctrine of the Trinity was meant to preserve, became obscured. In comparison with this danger of dividing the conception of God into a tritheism, the numerous abstract speculations about the "immanent" Trinity and the mutual relation of the three divine persons are relatively harmless. These speculations have a detrimental influence only in so far as they draw the attention away from that which is essential to faith, viz., God's concrete revelation of himself in his work. But the tendencies toward tritheism attack the very foundations of the purity and majesty of Christian faith in God. It is evident that these tendencies become stronger as the concept of personality becomes more definite and elaborate. To repeat verbatim the trinitarian confession of the ancient church, "three persons in one Godhead," is under such circumstances contrary to the original intention of maintaining the unity of faith in God, and leads to conclusions which the trinitarian formula was intended to guard against. Faithfulness to the letter in that case becomes faithlessness toward the spirit and purpose of the ancient confession.

But the intention itself contains something essential and inalienable to the Christian faith. *Both* of the fundamental ideas that produced the doctrine of the Trinity belong to the deepest convictions of the Christian faith. The whole previous presentation of the way of divine love is a proof of this. It is not an accident that Christian faith in God is at the same time faith in Christ and in the Spirit. Neither can be eliminated without destroying Christian faith, since the act of Christ involves the self-realization of divine love and the Spirit reveals God's immediate and continuous work. This threefold viewpoint of faith expresses, therefore, the meaningful and living revelation of the one true God, and at the same time prevents faith from being impoverished by deistic and pantheistic influences. A faith in God which is at the same time faith in Christ can never become pantheistic; and a faith which is at the same time faith in the Spirit cannot become deistic. Consequently, all so-called unitarian interpretations tend inevitably to become pantheistic or deistic and impoverish the content and vividness of faith in God. But as long as Christian faith in God preserves this threefold viewpoint, it also maintains its unified and organic character. The work of Christ is throughout the work of God, and the Spirit is not an independent being at the side of God, but the expression of God's immediate and continuous activity.

Excursus. The Boundary Line of Faith.

The trinitarian element in Christian faith has reference to the revelation of God. These affirmations of faith deal with the *modus* of revelation. Since faith is completely dependent upon the revelation, it cannot make any affirmations which are not based upon this revelation. Faith can, therefore, say nothing else about the revelation in Christ and in the Spirit except that it originates in the eternal being of God. Faith has attempted to express these eternal relationships by the symbolical statements that the Son is "born of the Father before the worlds," and that the Spirit "proceeds from the Father and the Son." With these statements faith touches that line of demarcation which it cannot cross without passing beyond the area of revelation and thereby becoming something else than faith. Luther had a clear conception of this fact and also of the line of demarcation between Christian faith and metaphysical speculation. He consequently warned against all speculations about "God as he is in himself." Such speculation about the exalted, divine Majesty is nothing but human presumption.

One point in this subject demands further clarification; that is, the question of the extent and center of revelation. When faith affirms that the revelation of God in the Son and in the Spirit is founded in the eternal being of God, it implies that faith does not dare to prescribe a limit to the scope of divine revelation. When the loving will of God became incarnate in Christ, this did not constitute its first appearance. In this connection the idea of pre-existence has a legitimate place as indicated in the conception of the Word who was eternally with God and has made himself known in various ways. But these ideas of the universality of the divine revelation are legitimate only in so far as they do not encroach upon the idea of the incarnation. The viewpoint of Christian faith in regard to revelation is, as has already been stated (§ 3. 3), both universal and exclusive. Faith does not set a limit for the revelation, but neither does it recognize any other God than that divine Love which has become incarnate in Christ.

DIVISION B

THE BROKEN AND RESTORED RELATIONSHIP WITH GOD

30. The Nature of Sin

1. Sin is a concept which cannot be used except in a religious sense. The significance of the knowledge of sin can be known only as divine revelation illuminates the fact of sin.

2. Sin is that which breaks the fellowship with God. The essence of sin can therefore be more closely defined as unbelief. If in faith man is ruled by the loving will of God, the essence of sin

consists in that man is not dominated by God, but by something separated from him. This other power is the ego. The essence of sin is, therefore, negatively unbelief and positively egocentricity.

3. Sin from this point of view is not simply isolated deeds or something imperfect, but a perverse direction of will, which implies a deviation from the essential destiny given to man by God. Sin is, therefore, a specifically defined magnitude, and it cannot be referred to the indefinable contrast between the finite and the infinite.

4. It is clear from the foregoing that Christian faith knows of no division of man into a lower and sensuous part which is the seat of sin, and a higher and spiritual part which would lie outside the area of sin. When man is designated as a sinner, it is a religious judgment which has reference to man as a whole.

Excursus. The relation of the consciousness of sin to faith cannot be psychologically schematized, either in the sense that a "mature" faith would be a prerequisite for the consciousness of sin, or that a "mature" consciousness of sin is a prerequisite for faith. The words of Luther are here applicable: *quo sanctior quis est, eo magis sentit illam pugnam.*

1. Sin as a Religious Concept.

It cannot be sufficiently emphasized that sin is a concept which belongs entirely to the religious realm. As soon as it is removed out of this sphere, it loses its essential significance. We do not speak of sin in a juridical environment or in criminal justice. There it is simply a question of crime and transgression of law. To inject the concept of sin in this connection would be to introduce an irrelevant category. In the same way a non-religious philosophy of morals and ethics cannot use the word sin, even if, in following Kant, it speaks of evil as a "radical evil." As long as one is concerned only with ethical points of view, one does not need the concept of sin, in fact cannot find any use for it. If it is used, it has lost its essential significance. In the ethical field the question is about good and evil, right and wrong, but not about sin. When the concept of sin is removed from the religious sphere, it becomes weak and enfeebled, as even the common usage of the language indicates.

On the contrary, faith cannot avoid speaking about sin. The problem of evil becomes acute in relation to the problem of sin. This means that sin is a concept that is inseparably connected with the relationship to God. There is no sin which is not sin against God. It is meaningless to talk about sin if it has no relation to God. From this point of view the words of the 51st Psalm are unconditionally valid: "Against thee, thee only, have I sinned" (Ps. 51:4). From the viewpoint of Christian faith it would be meaningless to divide sin into two classes: sins against God and sins against the neighbor. There is no sin against the neighbor which is not sin against God. The sin against the neighbor becomes sin just because it is sin against God. If we were to talk about some sins which are not sins against God, the concept of sin would have lost its meaning. It has then been moved outside the religious sphere. To say that the concept of sin belongs entirely in the religious sphere is the same as saying that all sin is sin against God.

Under such circumstances it is evident that the significance of sin is apparent only against the background of divine revelation. Without a divine revelation there can be no concept of sin. The divine revelation reveals sin. The clearer the eye of faith has perceived the divine revelation, and the more brightly its light illuminates the meaning and significance of sin, the more completely the essential nature of sin is disclosed. Consequently, Christian faith perceives sin most clearly in the light of the revelation of divine love in the work of Christ.

2. Sin as Unbelief and Egocentricity.

If sin is a concept that belongs entirely to the religious sphere, it follows that the significance of sin is to be found in that which is contrary to the fundamental religious relationship. The concept of sin is therefore dependent upon our understanding of this fundamental relationship. If religion is interpreted in a moralistic sense, as for example in Pharisaism, and the essential element is the keeping of certain statutes and precepts, sin then consists in the transgression of these precepts. If, however, religion is intellectually interpreted and the essential element is to hold fast to certain religious formulas, "heresy" becomes the chief sin. Both of these tendencies, as is well known, have frequently appeared in Christianity. It is evident, however, that neither of these approaches reaches the heart of the matter. If the fundamental religious relationship according to Christian faith is fellowship with God, it follows that the essence of sin is everything that breaks and hinders this fellowship and causes a separation between man and God. Therefore, when the reformers asserted that the essence of sin was unbelief, they gave the concept a pertinent definition (cf. Rom. 14:23).

This interpretation of sin, however, needs to be more closely defined. It is indubitable that the definition of sin as unbelief, which is almost purely negative, appears rather unrealistic, and that it seems to be difficult to gain from this definition a more positive determination of the significance of sin. We find, therefore, that when theology speaks of unbelief as the mark of sin, it has often complemented this interpretation by adding other definitions and has designated egocentricity and sensuality as the two other chief forms of sin, together with godlessness. But it has been difficult to find any organic connection between these three chief forms of sin. Under these circumstances one is forced to face the question whether it is legitimate to speak of unbelief as a fundamental definition of the essence of sin. If in principle we are to interpret sin as unbelief, we must attempt to prove that there is an inseparable connection between this negative definition and a more positive definition of the essence of sin. The meaning of sin as unbelief is therefore the chief problem.

It is clear that the connection we seek cannot be found as long as the concept of faith is given a purely intellectual interpretation. If "faith" consists primarily in an intellectual acceptance of certain statements about God, it is misleading and even meaningless to talk about sin as unbelief. From such unbelief there is no connecting link to the positive content of sin. When the definition of sin as unbelief has appeared unrealistic, it has been due to the influence of this intellectualistic concept of faith. The relation between faith and sin becomes more profound when faith is conceived of as trust and confidence in God. Then it becomes possible to find a connection with the positive content of sin. It is questionable, however, whether even this definition of faith can demonstrate clearly and unequivocally how and why the positive content of sin is comprehended in sin as unbelief.

But the connection between what we have called the negative and positive aspects of sin becomes abundantly evident as soon as we consider, not a specific aspect of faith, but faith in its entirety, faith as fellowship with God; or, in other words, when faith is interpreted to mean that man is subdued and dominated by divine love (cf. § 2. 2). As far as faith is concerned God is unquestionably the Lord in this fellowship between himself and man. If faith means to live under the dominion of God, then sin as unbelief means that *God does not have dominion,* and that something else than God's loving will exercises this dominion. Thereby sin is both negatively and positively defined. This other power which rules man in sin is nothing else than his *own ego.* Indifference or hostility to the divine will [the former must be emphasized as well as the latter] is *eo ipso* egocentricity. When the divine will does not rule, man is, as Luther says, *incurvatus in se,* selfishly directed toward himself. But if the character of sin, therefore, appears from a

positive point of view as egocentricity, this is not a new fundamental form of sin coincident with unbelief or "godlessness."
Sin as unbelief and sin as egocentricity are one and the same
thing seen from different points of view. Egocentricity is opposition to the divine will, and therefore "unbelief." Wherever
this power rules, the fellowship with God is destroyed.

The concept of sin is hereby defined from the point of view
of divine love. If it is a characteristic of this love that it "seeketh not its own" (I Cor. 13:5), the exact opposite is true of sin.
The essence of sin appears in this that man "seeks his own."
Sin is always concerned with a *quaerere quae sua sunt*. This
egocentric seeking of one's own may appear in various forms.
It may appear as egocentricity in a strict sense when it is a question about one's own ego, but it may also appear in a wider
sense. There is a nationalistic egocentricity, a class egocentricity, and so forth. In the widest sense egocentricity appears
as "a seeking after that which belongs to this world," and as an
attachment to the things of this world in general. But no matter
how much it is expanded, it does not cease to be egocentricity.
It can manifest itself in grosser or more refined forms. It appears
in its most refined and sublimated form when "the search after
God" is incorporated under its aegis. It might be assumed that
seeking after the divine, after God, would be the very opposite
of sinful egocentricity. If, however, this seeking after God is in
the interest of making God serve one's own ego and to secure
something for one's own personal benefit by divine help, this
does not imply a turning away from sin, but rather that sin here
is present in its most sublimated and deceptive form. Sin reveals itself in that it does not recognize God as sovereign, as
Lord, but instead desires to make him the servant of human
desires and purposes.

It has sometimes been suggested that sin be defined as disobedience. From a purely factual point of view this does not
imply any deviation from the twofold definition: "unbelief–
egocentricity." If sin means that the loving will of God does

not rule over man, the relation of man to this will is one of disobedience and rebellion.

We may add that sin has sometimes been defined as sensuality. If this concept is understood in its strict and narrow sense, it may be regarded as the result of egocentricity, a "seeking one's own." If, on the contrary, it is understood in a metaphysical sense as identical with finiteness, two possibilities emerge. It may then be asserted that man's nature consists of two parts, one sensual and finite, and another spiritual and infinite. Sin would then be connected with the finite part of man. But in so doing the fact that sin concerns the whole man is obscured (cf. § 4). If, on the contrary, it is asserted that man as a total being is finite and thereby stands in opposition to the divine as infinite, the qualitative difference between the loving will of God and the sinful will of man has been replaced by an indefinable opposition which in reality obscures the real nature of sin.

3. Sin as a Perversion of the Will.

If the nature of sin is both unbelief and egocentricity in a narrower or wider sense, it means that sin is in reality a perversion of the will. Sin cannot be understood as consisting simply in individual and isolated thoughts and acts. Such an atomistic conception of sin, which is characteristic of Pelagianism, is both superficial and unrealistic. Sin *expresses* itself in individual thoughts, words, and deeds, but sin itself is of a more profound nature. The various sins depend on the condition of "the heart," as the Bible expresses it. That which comes from the heart "defiles the man, for out of the heart cometh forth evil thoughts, murders, adulteries, fornications, thefts, false witness, railings" (Matt. 15:18 ff.; cf. Matt. 5:28; 12:34; Luke 16:15, etc.). Sin is not something simply "accidental" which is more or less loosely connected with man and which we might be able to separate from us, but it is, on the contrary, something that involves and characterizes man's inmost being, his "personality," since after all there is nothing which is more essential to man than the inclination of his will.

It is, therefore, clear that sin cannot be regarded as something incomplete or as something which has not yet reached perfection. Sin is a perverse will, and therefore the opposite of that which it ought to be. Whether it appears as indifference or hostility to the loving will of God, sin is the opposite of this will. Where sin and egocentricity hold sway, there a power rules which is hostile to divine love, the sovereign power of the universe, and which, therefore, inevitably brings desolation and destruction.

Sin is revealed to the eye of faith, therefore, as a deviation from the essential destiny given to man by God. Faith understands this destiny to be that life in which the ego with its many desires no longer is the tyrannical master, but in which the loving will of God rules. Faith discovers that the purpose of God is that man should live a life characterized and defined by his will and love, and that consequently this is a God-given destiny. That man has this destiny is the significant element in the idea that he is created in the image of God. This concept of the image of God cannot be demonstrated or established independently of faith; it is an affirmation *of faith* which becomes meaningful in and through the revelation of God and in the measure that man grasps what fellowship with God means. It emerges in and through the encounter with God's condemning and restoring love. It then becomes apparent that man's destiny is to live under God's dominion, that sin is that which separates man from that kind of life God intended him to live. But the concept of the image of God is used in a way that is foreign to faith if theology attempts to define this "image" as some "residue untouched by sin," which would explain the possibility of salvation by supplying a motive for God's saving love, and eventually also explain how man is able to accept the proffered salvation. This use of the conception of the image of God is foreign to faith both because Christian faith knows of no "explanation" of salvation except on the basis of the loving will of God, and also because it does not try to explain the activity of divine love by pointing to some certain quality in man. From the point of view of sin the concept of the image of God sets forth the lost destiny of man, and from the point of view of salvation it reveals the divine purpose in creation.

This definition of sin as a perverted inclination of a will that is hostile to God emphasizes still further the difference between the conception of sin represented by Christian faith and the metaphysically oriented conception which identifies sin with finiteness. In opposition to these idealistic conceptions there has sometimes appeared in the history of Christian thought a tendency to shift from a volitional and qualitative to an indefinite and metaphysical conception of sin. The intention has been to emphasize as strongly as possible the antithesis created by sin between the divine and the human. It is especially opposed to the disposition of idealistic metaphysics to blot out the distinction between the divine and "the highest human" and its inclination to regard sin simply as imperfection. In contrast, the anti-idealistic metaphysic desires to view man as a totality when it speaks of him as a sinner. But in comparison with the conception of sin in Christian faith this indefinable metaphysical viewpoint blurs rather than clarifies the concept of sin. The questionable element in this approach is not that it proposes to deal with the whole man—Christian faith does that also (cf. § 4) —but that sin is a constitutive part of human nature, viz., finiteness. In spite of its opposition to idealism this approach blunts the point of sin, because sin consists exactly in the antagonism between the divine will and the human egocentric will. The metaphysical conception of sin both obscures the essential meaning of sin and exercises a baneful influence upon the conception of salvation. From this point of view a fellowship with God such as is envisaged in Christian faith is excluded, since the chasm between "the infinite" and "the finite" cannot be bridged. But for the Christian faith fellowship with God becomes both possible and actual through the forgiving and saving act of the loving will of God.

4. A Total Conception.

When Christian faith understands sin as unbelief and ego-centricity, and consequently sees sin as a perverse will hostile to the divine will, it follows that faith cannot divide man into a lower part which would be the "seat" of sin and a higher part which would remain outside this sphere. Such a division has often been suggested. Such theories may vary, but the main principle is that sin belongs to the "sensual" part of man, while his "spiritual" part has remained untouched by this corruption. This theory has in reality appeared in Christianity even from most ancient times, and has come from the Greek mysteries and idealism. We meet it in its typical form in Gnosticism, with its theory that the material and corporeal is the prison house in which the "divine" part of man is held captive. Thus medieval mysticism talked about "the fundamental essence," das Funk-lein, etc., as that part of man in which the divine resided. Essentially the same idea is found in Schleiermacher, when he makes a distinction between the lower and sensual and the higher and spiritual consciousness, and in his proposition that sin consists in the fact that the sensual consciousness has "outreached" the higher or the consciousness of God. Between this highest spirit-ual element in man and the divine there is no definite boundary.

From the point of view of faith this division of man is mis-leading because sin is attributed to man's lower nature, to some-thing external and peripheral, while his "inmost" being is free from the tyranny of sin. But for Christian faith it is evident that sin is located just in this inner recess, in the inclination of the will. The theory of division leads to a false idealization of human life and to a minimizing of the seriousness of the human situation. The conception of sin is weakened and destroyed as soon as it is separated from the inner nature of man. Luther expressed the characteristic Christian conception of sin when he turned so decisively against this theory of division and its attempt to locate sin in an external part of man. There is nothing more evident to faith than that man does not possess an area which is immune from sin and to which he could point as something acceptable to God. The judgment that man is a sinner is a total judgment, it applies to the whole of man, and therefore also to "the inner" and "spiritual." Consequently salvation also applies to the whole of man; it does not mean that a certain part of man is set free, or that the "spiritual" is released from the oppression of the "sensual." When man stands face to face with God, *coram deo,* he stands as such under the judgment of God and this judgment pronounces him a sinner.

In this connection it is important to emphasize the statement with which this chapter began, viz., that sin is a concept which belongs entirely within the religious sphere, or in other words that it is applicable only *coram deo.* If we do not hold fast to this religious context, the viewpoint of Christian faith in regard to man's situation would be misinterpreted. It could then easily be accused of painting the situation in too dark colors and of being therefore monotonous and unrealistic. It is significant that Luther, who strenuously asserts the total judgment implied in *coram deo,* at the same time speaks of another aspect of human life, viz., *coram hominibus.* On this plane the absolute verdict which is applicable *coram deo* is not valid. *In naturalibus* there is room for a variety of human moral actions. It is only in respect to religion, *coram deo,* that all such relative judgments cease. *Coram deo* all human boasting ceases (I Cor. 1:29), man stands before God uncovered, naked, without protection and without any possibility of justifying himself.

Excursus. Rejection of Psychological Schematizations.

When in this chapter we have connected the consciousness of sin with faith, this connection cannot be psychologically schematized, either in the sense that a certain amount of faith would be a prerequisite for the consciousness of sin, or that a certain degree of consciousness of sin would be a prerequisite for faith. The latter has been by far the most common. Both in ancient and modern times (for example W. Herrmann) it has been asserted that the way to faith leads of necessity through that crisis to which the "moral demand" drives man, and that the reception of divine grace depends on having passed through the depth of consciousness of sin. The questionable element in this theory is not simply that "the moral" as such does not by any inner necessity lead to a religious crisis, but principally the idea that a complete and mature consciousness of sin serves as a preliminary step toward faith. Such a scheme is contrary to the nature of the Christian life in faith. Both the theory that regards consciousness of sin as a preliminary stage, and that conception which, like Schleiermacher, asserts that the consciousness of sin disappears in the measure that the consciousness of God is realized, are foreign to Christian faith. Christian faith accepts rather the statement which Luther with his clear insight into the actual human situation formulated thus: *quo sanctior quis est, eo magis sentit illam pugnam.* The nearer God comes to man and the more completely the "fellowship" between God and man is realized, the more acute becomes the consciousness of sin. On the basis of this fundamental rule all psychological schematizations of the relation between faith and the consciousness of sin become impossible.

31. The Solidarity of Sin

1. Individual and specific acts of sin are not isolated and unrelated to each other but are rooted in the inclination of man's will; likewise, the sinful will of each man is not isolated but exists within a context of comprehensive human interrelationships. The idea of original sin, in contrast to atomistic conceptions of sin, is significant because it expresses a total view both of individual man and of the human race.[1] This significance is

---

[1] In our translation of the author's discussion of this subject we have found it

obscured if the conception of sin is transferred from volitional to physical and finite categories.

2. This universality of sin, embracing the will of all mankind, appears in the last analysis as a solidary interrelationship of evil which encircles and as a demonic power enslaves humanity.

3. This solidary interrelationship of sin does not nullify or minimize the character of sin as a perversion of the individual will. From the point of view of Christian faith sin has the character of both inevitability and volitional activity.

4. The solidary interrelationship of sin cannot be used to explain the origin of sin. The purely speculative question about the origin of sin is foreign to faith. The interest of faith is concentrated on the problem of the nature of sin and its subjugation.

1. *The doctrine of original, or inherited, sin.*

We cannot obtain a real insight into the nature of the Christian conception of sin except by noting how Christian faith perceives sin as a solidary interrelationship. This meets us as the idea of original sin. In regard to the common distinction between original and actual sin it must be stated that this does not imply two different categories of sin. The expression original sin has reference to all sin. From the point of view of Christian faith all sin is "original sin." "Actual sin," therefore, is an ex-

---

necessary to employ terms which are not direct translations of the words used by the author. The following formulation may therefore serve to clarify this procedure:

1. The atomistic conception of sin:
    a. Individual acts of sin are independent and unrelated.
    b. Individual sinners are independent and unrelated.
2. The solidary interrelationship of sin:
    a. Individual acts of sin are interdependent and interrelated.
    b. Individual sinners are interdependent and interrelated.

We have translated the author's expression "*syndens överindividuella sammanhang*" as "the solidary interrelationship of sin," and "*syndens överindividuella makt*" as "the demonic power of sin" (cf. § 31. 2, 3).—Trs.

pression which denotes the external manifestation of original sin. Since the term "original sin" can easily be misinterpreted and lead to conceptions which are foreign to Christian faith, it is necessary first of all to bring to our attention those points of view which theology has endeavored to reject by means of this conception if we are to be able to understand the Christian significance of the idea of original sin, or, in other words, the fundamental religious ideas which are herein expressed.

When the doctrine of original sin was formulated in the ancient church in opposition to Pelagianism, the intention was to overcome the casuistic and atomistic Pelagian view of sin. The weakness and unreality of the Pelagian view were its isolation of the individual and sinful decisions of will. This was a twofold isolation. On the one hand, the sinful acts of will were understood as independent one of the other, and the will was considered free to decide either for or against sin. There was no feeling for the continuity of volition, nor for the fact that the nature of sin is a corruption of the will. On the other hand, men were regarded as isolated individuals without any consideration of their solidarity with humanity as a whole. In either case this is an abstract conception which does not correspond to the viewpoint of Christian faith relative to the actual situation. Personal decisions are not isolated one from the other, but are closely connected and stem from a certain definite character of the will. Nor are individual human beings isolated from the race, but stand rather in a very close and intimate relationship. The significance of the doctrine of original sin consists in its opposition to this twofold and unrealistic isolation and in its emphasis that sin is a perversion of the will and a solidary interrelationship. In both of these respects the intentions of the doctrine of original sin express realistically faith's conception of the character and extent of sin.

In the first place, therefore, the doctrine of original sin is concerned with man as a whole. Sin does not have reference to something external and peripheral in man, nor to something "accidental"; it has its "seat" in his inner being, in the inclination of the will, and applies, therefore, to man as a whole. Luther has given a clear expression to this idea, which is contained but not clearly and fully expressed in the term, original sin, when he translates original sin by "personal sin." "Original sin, natural sin, or *personal sin* is the principal sin. If it did not exist, neither would there be any actual sin."[2] In reality personal sin expresses much more clearly than original sin that idea which the latter is intended to convey.

But, in the second place, the concept of original sin is also intended to view humanity as a whole. Sinfulness does not belong simply to separate individuals, it is characteristic of the whole human race. Individual man as a member of society participates in the sinfulness of the race. This brings to the fore the idea of the inevitability of sin. Man stands through an inner necessity under the power of sin. The context of sin surrounds him and determines his life. If, from this point of view, we use the expression "original sin," or inherited sin, it must be said that this expression really is designed to emphasize this total view of man. The word original sin tells us that the solidarity of the race is a solidarity in sin. There is in humanity a sinful inclination which is reproduced from generation to generation. The sinful interrelationship places a terrific burden on the life of humanity and appears as a demonic power in relation to individual man. It must be emphasized, however, that this "inheritance" consists not simply in inherited sinful dispositions and tendencies; in fact the whole inner inheritance is a sinful inheritance, and therefore this sinful interrelationship affects the individual in the most varied manner and through innumerable means. In the final analysis the view of Christian faith regarding this sinful relationship is adequately expressed only when the idea of the sinful interrelationship of the race passes

---

[2] W. A., 10, I, 1, 508, 520, quoted by K. Holl, *op. cit.*, I, 66. Cf. also, *"dass also die Reue gehe nicht stücklich über etliche Werke, die du öffentlich begangen hast wider die zehen Gebot——sondern* über die ganze Person *mit alle ihrem Leben und Wesen."* E. A., 11, 282.

over into the concept of that spiritual power of evil which is active in relation to the human will (cf. § 2).

We have now tried to define the two fundamental ideas which have been expressed in the concept of original sin. If, therefore, it is essential for Christian faith to use the concept of original sin in the sense previously explained, it must at the same time be added that this term involves certain very evident dangers. Ever since the days of Augustine the concept of original sin has tended to refer sin to the purely physical and has thereby obscured the nature of sin as volition and as a corruption of the will. When this occurs, the concept no longer serves as a profound perception of sin, but has rather injected an element which is foreign to Christian faith.

In view of what we have now said about the solidary interrelationship of sin and the inner inheritance of sinfulness, it should be added that Christian faith knows not only about an inheritance of sin, but also knows and reckons with an *inheritance* of blessing and a relationship of blessedness. As far as faith is concerned, the situation of the race and of the individual is characterized by the continual conflict between these two powers: the blessing and the curse. Man is the arena where this conflict takes place.

2. *The Power of Evil.*

We have already suggested that Christian faith did not stop with the idea of an interrelationship of sin in which individuals are united with one another. At the same time that sinfulness in human life is always defined as volitional, it also appears to faith in the form of a demonic spiritual power which commands and subjugates the human will. The solidary interrelationship of sin concretizes itself in inscrutable and obscure powers, a mysterious complex which cannot be accurately delimited and defined, and which slips away and becomes shadowy as soon as one tries to grasp and comprehend it. Nevertheless it shows its power in the most fearful manner and by the most cruel oppression of human life. Evil is in possession of a sphere of power which stretches beyond individuals and their direct and definable relationships. In the New Testament we often meet more or less mythologically formulated expressions for this complex of evil powers (cf. Rom. 8:38; Gal. 1:4; Col. 2:15; Eph. 6:12). In the last analysis Christian faith perceives this evil as concentrated in the satanic power which is in conflict with the divine will. Man is placed in a vast conflict between the two magnitudes, the Kingdom of God and that kingdom which is from below. The divine will contends with the hostile spiritual powers which also tyrannize man. When the New Testament and the Christian church have spoken about the devil as the incarnation of this concentrated evil power, it is necessary to distinguish between the fundamental idea and its expression. The use of the conception of the devil is not in and by itself the least guarantee of a profound insight into the nature and terrific power of evil. Many examples can be cited which show that the idea of the devil has been used in such a way that the conception of evil has been weakened. It is of greatest importance for Christian faith that the dualistic element contained in this conception be not obscured, or, in other words, that the element in creation which is hostile to God be allowed to appear with all the realism and intensity which it possesses for faith. It is not a demonic mythology which is important, but an insight into the nature of evil, its power and extent. Thus Luther, with a clear insight into the imperfections and dangers of these conceptions, pictures the contrast between the divine and the satanic as the contrast between love and hate. *"Denn wie die Liebe ist ein Bild Gottes, und nicht ein tot Bild noch auf Papier gemalet, sondern ein lebendig Wesen in göttlicher Natur, die da brennet voll alles Guten, also ist wiederum Hass und Neid ein recht Bild des Teufels . . . dass man den Teufel nicht besser malen könnte denn wenn man könnte eitel Hass und Neid malen."* [8]

---

[8] E. A. 18, p. 366.

3. Sin as Inevitable and Volitional.

When reference is made to the solidary interrelationship of sin it may seem to suggest a contrast between sin as a demonic power (original sin) and sin as a volitional act of the individual (actual sin). It might be interpreted to mean that sin regarded as a demonic power minimizes its character as perversion of the individual will; in other words, if sin is conceived of in terms of a demonic power it cannot be attributed to the individual will. But if this is done and sin is attributed to the individual will only in the measure that it is *not* dependent upon this demonic power, a conception is introduced which is foreign to faith, i.e., it does not correspond to the judgment of the religious self-consciousness (cf. § 32. 1). But from the point of view of faith and of the judgment of the religious self-consciousness there exists no such contrast. Sin as personal sin is always a perversion of the will, and all individual sin is a result of the fact that not the loving will of God but the ego separated from God holds sway. No matter how much personal sin stands in an intimate connection with sin as a demonic power, this personal sin is nevertheless something which adheres to and determines the personal will as such and is a result of this personal will and a reflection of its character.

Christian faith perceives sin, therefore, both as inevitable and volitional. The solidary interrelationship of evil is a demonic power which man cannot escape. Humanity stands under the power of egocentricity, and its life is characterized by this fact. But sin has at the same time the character of volitional activity. As soon as one or the other of these points of view is suppressed, the conception of sin becomes either moralistically superficial or naturalistically obscured. It is evident that there lies herein a certain tension-filled relationship between different viewpoints. But it is not a question about a "paradox" or an "irrationalism" in the sense of a combination of logically conflicting concepts. From this point of view it is interesting to note how Luther, who so energetically maintained the twofold character of sin as inevitable and volitional, critically examines the two concepts, necessity and freedom, which he employs. Necessity and freedom seem to be opposite concepts, and it would then be a question of a purely logical contrast. But in reality the two mentioned concepts are, according to Luther, both ambiguous and in this connection inadequate. "Necessity," says Luther, belongs to "physics" not to theology. If this concept is to be used in theology we must "bathe and wash it." The word freedom is also ambiguous. In this connection it cannot be a question of freedom in the sense of freedom of choice. What Luther wants to emphasize is that sin, at the same time that it is inevitable in reference to "natural" man, nevertheless must not be understood as a natural defect, but must always be conceived of as the result of a volitional act of the individual.

4. The Solidary Interrelationship of Sin and the Problem of its Origin.

In the history of theology the question of the solidary interrelationship of sin has frequently been combined with the problem of the origin of sin. The attempt has been made to use the idea of this interrelationship as an explanation of the origin of sin. But if the solidary interrelationship of sin, according to the viewpoint of faith, does not nullify or even minimize the character of sin as a corruption of the will, it follows that faith cannot easily find an explanation of the origin in this interrelationship. In reality the confusing ideas which have been connected with the doctrine of original sin have been the result of attempts to use this doctrine for speculative purposes which are foreign to faith and to explain the ultimate origin of sin. In regard to these attempts it should be said, both that they have not been able to give a satisfactory explanation, and that they have come into conflict with certain vital interests of faith. They have not, in other words, reflected the characteristic viewpoint of faith in regard to the relationship between the demonic and the individual factors of sin.

The doctrine of original sin has usually been employed in the interest of such an explanation by making a distinction between the sin of the first man, which was occasioned by the misuse of his freedom induced by the misleading suggestion of an evil, superhuman power, and all other sin which then is due to the change in the nature of man which was the result of this first sin. It is clear, however, that this is not a real explanation, but simply removes the question one step further back.[4] To attribute the cause of sin to a free will is in reality nothing else but a retreat to something unexplained and inexplicable. This becomes even more inexplicable if it is maintained that the will of the first man was originally a good will given to him by God in creation. Nor can we obtain an adequate explanation by going back to a superhuman evil power which acts as the tempter. Such an explanation places us simply before a new question, unless we are satisfied with an ultimate dualism. But the most serious defect in this theory is not that it offers an inadequate explanation, which is no explanation at all, but that it obscures the nature of sin as this is understood in the light of faith. According to this theory only the first sin was in reality a "personal" sin. All other sin must then be regarded as a certain physical element in man, a sinful "substance," which exists independent of man's personal character. This approach is, therefore, in conflict with the purpose which the doctrine of original sin was intended to serve against the Pelagian atomistic and casuistic conception of sin; or, in other words, it conceals the fact that sin is a corruption of the will. It should be added that such a conception of the relation between the first sin and all subsequent sin leads to a division of responsibility which does not correspond to the Christian consciousness of sin (cf. § 32. 1). If, after the first act, sin is separated from the personal will, this implies that there is an excuse for all subsequent sin. This leads inevitably to a contrast between the solidary interrelationship of sin and individual sin.

---

[4] Cf. Schleiermacher, *op. cit.*, pp. 291 ff.

But if we cannot combine the doctrine of original sin with the idea of an original state and the fall in order to provide a rational explanation of the origin of sin, it does not follow that Christian faith finds the ideas of the original state and the fall useless. "The original state" and "the fall" are not simply myths, but neither are they an event in human history which belongs to a definite period. As creation is not something once and for all finished, but a continuously ongoing activity (cf. § 20), so the original state and the fall are not an individual event, but belong to humanity as a whole. When the idea of the original state and the fall is combined with Christian faith, the "original state" reveals to every man the destiny given him by God, and "the fall" declares that the solidary interrelationship of sin does not remove the character of sin as an act of will; or, in other words, when sin becomes actual in our lives, we are engaged in destroying the destiny given us by God.

When Christian faith, therefore, deliberately rejects all attempts to furnish a rational explanation of the origin of sin in human life, the reason is not only that all these explanations fail and every answer places us before a new question, but especially because these explanations obscure that which faith perceives as the essential in regard to the nature of sin and the relationship between sin as a demonic power and individual sin. Theology is content to leave the problems of the origin and first appearance of sin in the world to that speculative "philosophy" which is delighted to deal with them. But the interest of faith itself is concentrated on the problems of the nature of sin and its subjugation, for these are to faith the most vital questions.

32. Sin and Guilt

1. The Christian consciousness of sin is a consciousness of that which separates man from the divine will and consequently places him under the judgment of God. It implies, therefore, also an immediate consciousness of guilt, which appears as an

awareness of man's unworthiness before God. Every attempt to make guilt dependent on the connection between individual sinfulness and the solidary interrelationship of sin leads to a casuistic and relative conception of sin which is foreign to Christian faith. This makes it evident, furthermore, that guilt cannot be rationally motivated.

2. Since the religious conception of sin refers to man as a whole, and since the judgment of God is unconditional, it follows that from a religious point of view there can be no degrees of guilt. The decisive element lies entirely in the different relations of men to the divine and gracious will. From this point of view the "hardening" appears as the definite rejection of the divine and gracious will characterized by the suspension of the consciousness of guilt.

3. A relative point of view is justified, however, when the mutual relationships of men in this world are made the object of judgments based on empirical and psychological premises. In that case different degrees of guilt can be established, and the evaluation does not then depend only on the character of the individual acts but also on the environmental conditions. When we pass over to the religious sphere, this relativistic conception loses its validity.

1. The Consciousness of Sin and of Guilt.

When man stands face to face with God and is compelled to see his sin as a contrast to the loving will of God, the consciousness of sin manifests itself as an awareness of his own unworthiness before God. The divine judgment under which man then enters is a judgment on his life as opposed to the divine will, and on that egocentric corruption of will which is the essence of sin. This judgment reveals man's distance from God and his unworthiness to stand in his presence. There is no other word which so immediately and genuinely expresses the significance of the consciousness of guilt as this word *unworthiness*. When we read in the parable of the prodigal son: "Father, I have sinned against heaven and in thy sight, I am *no more worthy* to be called thy son" (Luke 15:18 ff.), these words express the characteristically Christian consciousness of guilt. This note is sounded wherever the consciousness of guilt manifests itself spontaneously and unreflectively. It is found in the confession of sin in the Swedish church: "We are worthy, therefore, to be cast away from Thy presence, if Thou shouldst judge us according to our sins." The religious consciousness of guilt always says: Because I am what I am, I am unclean (Isa. 6:5), defiled, separated from God and unworthy to stand in his presence.

It is clear from what we have now said that the religious consciousness of sin, which always expresses a relation to God (cf. § 31), immediately and unavoidably appears as a consciousness of guilt. The religious self-consciousness unites sin and guilt in an inseparable connection. As soon as man stands face to face with God and his judgment is pronounced upon him, every sin becomes also guilt, and every sin points to and is a result of that sinfulness which determines our will and characterizes our life as unworthy and guilty before God. The consciousness of guilt in the real and religious meaning of this word is the consciousness that this self in its present state is worthy of rejection from God's presence.

It must be especially underscored that the consciousness of guilt implies that man knows and submits to *God's* judgment. The idea is not that men set up certain "ideals" which pronounce a more or less severe judgment upon them. It is not human ideals, but God who judges. Nor can man's conscience be the court of last appeal. It is undeniable that in this connection there has been much obscure and confusing talk about conscience as a judge, as if man here without further consideration had recourse to an infallible standard. That conscience cannot lay claim to such an infallibility is altogether too plain when we consider what judgments have been pronounced in the name of "conscience." A reference to conscience as a judgment seat cannot even be considered, if it means that conscience of and by itself determines what is and is not divine justice, and the power of judgment is thereby transferred to the human. If we are to refer to conscience in this connection at all, it cannot be a question of conscience as a unique and constant factor, but only of that conscience which has been "awakened," "enlightened," and dominated by God. Under all circumstances it is clear to Christian faith that it is the divine will itself which subjects man to its judgment and reveals his unworthiness.

When the consciousness of sin directly appears as a consciousness of guilt, it is already evident that the question of guilt cannot be made dependent upon the relation between the individual sinfulness and the solidary interrelationship of sin. If sin is at the same time inevitable and voluntary, the inevitability cannot remove its character as guilt. No appeal to the solidary interrelationship of sin is able to erase or reduce the guilt. When man stands face to face with God and meets his judgment, he does not analyze whether or not his sins have been committed willfully and deliberately, nor does he hide behind some theories about the lesser or greater bondage of the will in order thereby to minimize and possibly excuse his sin. He can no more appeal to the solidary interrelationship of sin as the cause or basis for God's forgiveness than he can seek shelter behind this interrelationship as a protection from the accusations and judgment of the voice of God. It is not only a matter of man's inability to seek such a shelter, he does not *want* to do so. The religious consciousness does not seek excuses for sin. Nothing can be more foreign to a man in that situation than to try to argue with God about the significance of "dispositions," "environment," and training, or about the boundary of willful, deliberate, and intentional sins and the point where guilt begins. When man finds himself "guilty" and unworthy in the presence of God, it does not mean simply that he finds a certain act inexcusable, but that *just as he is,* because of his hostile and egocentric will which results in individual sins, he is "worthy to be cast away from the presence of God." In the judgment of the religious self-consciousness man discovers that he is guilty, not only when he can determine that he has acted with full freedom, if it were ever possible to do so, but also that he is responsible and guilty because sin cannot be separated from his will. Sin is an expression of and reflects the actual disposition of this will. It makes very little difference to the religious consciousness of sin whether our sinful acts were more or less dependent on the solidary interrelationship of sin. No dependence, however strong, can remove the volitional element from personal sin, or obscure the fact that I—just I—am unworthy to stand before God. It is noteworthy in this connection that those who have spoken most frankly about the guilt of sin have also spoken most emphatically about the bondage of the will. If my consciousness of sin were to be made dependent upon the higher or lower degree of conscious freedom and intention with which these sins have been committed, it would lead directly to a casuistry which would destroy *all* responsibility and *all* profound consciousness of sin. That which is essential in the judgment of the religious self-consciousness is simply this—that my will, such as it actually is, and that I, just as I am, are unworthy to stand before God. With his clear insight Luther has here expressed the heart of the matter when he places these two alternatives before us: either man is responsible for nothing, or else he is responsible for his life as a whole. This is true, since the judgment of the religious self-consciousness always refers to the ego as a whole, is always absolute and never seeks to excuse itself.

Since the consciousness of guilt is thus practically identical with the consciousness of sin, it is in reality not concerned with the question whether and to what degree the individual sins (actual sin) are dependent upon the solidary interrelationship of sin. When it is a question about the religious self-consciousness and that judgment which God pronounces on our sin, it is misleading to draw a sharp distinction between sin and guilt, which was so often done in the theology of the nineteenth century. It was then asserted that we could speak of guilt only in regard to those sins which have been committed willfully and deliberately; but that there could be no question of guilt if the individual sins were dependent on and the result of the solidary interrelationship of sin. If this were the only valid conception of sin, it would inevitably lead to that casuistry which has been mentioned before, and would in reality dissolve the concept of guilt, since in every situation it would be possible to seek protection behind the solidary interrelationship. This approach ignores the fact that the religious self-knowledge can never regard the individual sinful act as an isolated deed, but on the contrary understands it as a reflection of the actual condition of the ego. It also overlooks the fact that the judgment which is pronounced is absolute and does not recognize any relative excuses. As soon as the total viewpoint which is characteristic of Christian faith is noted, it becomes absolutely impossible to motivate the guilt rationally by a division of responsibility. To the man who stands face to face with God, guilt is an inescapable fact.

We may add here that, if the idea of the solidary interrelationship of sin becomes meaningful for the religious self-appraisal, this can occur only when this interrelationship is allowed to impose an increased responsibility and a greater guilt on the Christian man. It makes our responsibility and our guilt more acute and convinces us that our guilt is not simply the guilt of our own sin, but a guilt of that solidary interrelationship in which we participate and to which our own sin has been added.

2. *The Religious Consciousness Knows of No Degrees of Guilt.*

It is clear from our previous presentation that the religious consciousness of guilt cannot differentiate between higher and lower degrees of guilt. Since, according to the viewpoint of Christian faith, the concept of sin always has reference to man as a whole, and furthermore, since God's judgment on sin is always an unconditional and radical rejection, in the presence of God it is meaningless to differentiate between serious sins which entail serious guilt and lesser sins which cause lesser guilt. The consciousness of guilt and the awareness of our own unworthiness do not become weaker because a sin, according to human estimation, is less serious. In this connection there is in reality no place for a gradation of sins as greater or lesser. The religious self-appraisal is indifferent to all such endeavors. Our unworthiness before God, as the Sermon on the Mount unequivocally declares (Matt. 5:22, 28), is the same whether sin expresses itself in the most secret thought or in the most hideous act, whether it is a question of omission or commission, and whether it is a question of an unconscious act or one committed deliberately and on purpose. However, "small" a sin may appear according to a human estimate, to the religious consciousness awakened by the divine judgment it gives evidence of that disposition which is hostile to God's loving will and renders us worthy to be cast away from his presence.

Consequently all the casuistic distinctions of scholasticism disappear which are intended to determine the degree of peril and guilt which is connected with various kinds of sin. Such a graduated catalog of sins serves only to obscure the Christian concept of sin and guilt. The distinction of scholasticism between "deadly" and "forgivable" sins has no justification. There is no sin which is not "deadly," but neither is there any sin which, as far as the divine will is concerned, is not forgivable.

If, therefore, God's judgment on sin is unconditional and radical, there is from the point of view of sinfulness no distinction between men. The word, "all have sinned and fall short of the glory of God" (Rom. 3:23), is here valid. From the religious point of view the difference lies in men's relation to the saving and gracious will of God; it is a question of their receiving or rejecting the divine grace. When this line of demarcation is established, two things must be noted: first, that the line cannot be drawn so that it becomes visible from an external point of view, in reality it is known to God alone; and second, the line must in reality be drawn, so to speak, within man, since sin does not cease under the conditions of this earthly life, and since fellowship with God exists only in the form of a struggle against that which is opposed to the divine will.

When Christian faith speaks of a state of "hardness of heart," it understands thereby a definite rejection of the divine and gracious will characterized by the suspension of the consciousness of guilt. This state is designated in the New Testament as "sin against the Holy Spirit." When this sin is defined as "unforgivable," it is not because God ceases to be willing to forgive, but because divine love does not operate through external coercion but through inner conviction, and because the conditions making such a conviction possible have ceased to exist in this state of hardness of heart. But whether a person has committed this sin or not, God alone knows. *One* thing is certain: where there is any consciousness of guilt, there the sin has not been committed.

3. *The Relative Point of View.*

When man stands face to face with God and permits his judgment to fall upon his own ego, he becomes conscious that he is really unworthy in the sight of God. Here there is no graduated scale of guilt. But it does not follow that it is impossible to speak of different degrees of guilt, or greater and lesser guilt. Guilt can be understood in different senses. The central, religious conception of guilt which we have hitherto discussed is not the only one. We *can* speak of guilt also in a narrower, purely moral sense. The failure to distinguish between these two meanings has been the cause of much confusion. It is, of course, possible to use the concept of guilt with reference to the specific conditions of individual acts and to adopt an empirical and psychological point of view, provided it is made perfectly clear that the concept is then not used in its deeper, religious meaning. "The problem of guilt" in this narrow sense appears again and again in the intercourse with our neighbors when we adopt the viewpoint of *coram hominibus,* as Luther calls it. Man *coram deo* can no more reckon with relative standards than he can avoid doing so *coram hominibus.* In this respect we must take into account the influence of such things as heritage, milieu, and so on, and even the connection between individual guilt and the solidary interrelationship of guilt. Here the idea of different degrees of guilt has a place. If, however, it is evident that our judgment in reference to our neighbors, and our own judgment in reference to our relation to them, is dependent upon the connection between individual evil and the solidary interrelationship of evil, it is just as evident that the judgment we pronounce is *relative* in character. The problem of guilt is from this point of view insoluble. The more we try to penetrate its mystery, the more impossible it becomes to review all the pertinent factors and to make a satisfactory division of guilt.

If we then distinguish between a purely religious point of view (man *coram deo*) and a moral (man *coram hominibus*), the distinction between these two cannot be so defined that in the former case we deal with the "person," disposition, and the inclination of the will, and in the latter case, with actual deeds and the moral conduct as such. In the first place, through such a distinction the *coram deo* point of view would be unduly restricted. *Coram deo* it is also a question about deeds, about human life in its entirety, and about both the disposition and the acts. Further, it is not possible to ignore the disposition and regard it as irrelevant, as moralism is inclined to do. Both the external acts and the disposition must be considered. It must be established that we are not concerned with a delimitation which would place a certain area of human life in the "religious" and another in the "moral" sphere, but rather that we are dealing with human life from two distinct points of view. As the two Latin expressions which we have borrowed from Luther indicate, in one case it is a question of man's relation to God, and in the other, man's relation to society. This may also be expressed in another formula: in one case it is a question of man *in loco justificationis*, and in the other, man *in naturalibus*.

When in the relation between men the different degrees of guilt must be taken into account, this gradation can be motivated from two points of view. To some extent the degree of guilt can be measured by the quality of the act. A certain act can imply a greater degree of evil in human society than another, and can be the result of greater or less malice. But at the same time it is necessary in the appraisal of all these human acts to take into serious consideration the conditions under which these acts have been performed. From this point of view the guilt increases in the measure that man has been surrounded by conditions favorable to a moral life, and in the measure that his training, disposition, milieu, and the like, have placed him in a more favored situation from a moral point of view.

When we pass over to the religious point of view, *coram deo*, these relativistic considerations lose their validity. The scholastic casuistry which has had such baneful influence on the conception of the relation between God and man is the result of a confusion of these two points of view. *In loco justificationis* nothing else than a total view of man has any place; here nothing matters except on the one hand human sin and guilt, and on the other, the grace of God alone.

33. Divine Fellowship Realized through Forgiveness

1. When forgiveness is designated as the means through which fellowship with God is realized, it must not be understood as a unique[1] act of God, but rather that which constitutes the fundamental basis of Christian life. The forgiveness of sin is that divine act through which divine and sovereign love subdues sinful man and incorporates him into fellowship with God.

---

[1] The word "unique" translates the Swedish *engångshandling*, which means literally an act which occurs only once. It is synonymous with the German *einmalig*. —Trs.

2. The "paradoxical" character of forgiveness is expressed in the fact that divine love, which stands in unabridged opposition to sin, receives sinful man into its fellowship. Man thereby becomes *simul iustus et peccator*.

3. If forgiveness thus supersedes all purely ethical points of view, it implies also the strongest possible expression of God's opposition to evil. It is especially in forgiveness that divine love appears as a radical judgment of sin, and the fellowship of for giveness makes the consciousness of the distance between God and man more acute.

4. The Christian concept of forgiveness presents, therefore, a threefold antithesis. Forgiveness cannot be rationally motivated through a *legalistic* interpretation of Christ's work of reconciliation. Nor can it be moralistically motivated by citing as a condition of forgiveness some quality possessed by man as such, or some human attitude, or the future results of the act of forgiveness. Finally, it cannot be motivated through *humanizing* or *hyperevangelical* conceptions which imply a minimizing of the act of forgiveness as a judgment. Faith discovers that the basis of forgiveness is found only in God's spontaneous and inscrutable, saving and condemning love, as this realizes itself in the act of God in Christ.

1. The Concept of Forgiveness.

With our discussion of the Christian concept of sin in the three previous chapters we have noted that factor which separates man from God. In this and a few of the following chapters we shall investigate the Christian conception of the realization and the nature of fellowship with God. The presentation will naturally center around two chief words: forgiveness of sin and faith. Fellowship with God is realized in and through God's act of forgiveness, and it exists as a relationship of faith.

When forgiveness of sin is here used as the principal word in setting forth how fellowship between God and man is realized, the chief reason is its rich content and expressiveness. "Forgiveness" stems from the area of the most intimate personal life and indicates, therefore, that it is a question of nothing less than the re-establishment of that fellowship and filial relation with God which was broken through sin. This concept, therefore, is much more suitable for our purpose than all those which are taken from the juridical sphere, since it sets forth that we are here dealing with an act of *God's love*. Forgiveness does not imply *simply* a remission of punishment. As long as the relation between God and man is conceived of in juridical terms, the question is principally about acquittal and freedom from punishment. The law is the only connecting link between the judge and the accused: they have no personal connection with each other. The question is only whether the accused can be acquitted according to the law. Even if a "pardon" is granted, it need not imply a more intimate personal relation between the accused and the presiding judge. What happens is simply that the punishment is remitted and the accused is set free. It is quite a different situation when it is a question about a purely personal relationship, for example, a friend's relation to a friend, and a child's to his father. When these relations are disturbed, the question is not simply whether legal action is to be taken and punishment shall be meted out, but what is now at stake is the elimination of that which separates and threatens to destroy old ties of affection. The question is whether the former confidential and intimate personal relationship can be re-established and continued anew. This can be done in only one way—forgiveness. The juridical categories prove to be inadequate when it is a question of interpreting the inner character of the relationship to God. Just because the relationship between God and man is so intimate and personal, "forgiveness" becomes the most immediate and expressive word for that act of God's love whereby he vanquishes and subdues sinful man and incorporates him into a fellowship with himself. The divine fellowship is realized through forgiveness—the only way possible, because God is love and man is a sinner.

Although the concept of forgiveness, therefore, is extremely useful in the presentation of that act of God through which the fellowship between God and man is established, it is also subject to certain misinterpretations, which would, of course, be true of whatever concepts might be used. According to the testimony of the history of Christian thought the principal danger is that forgiveness might be interpreted negatively as simply a remission of punishment. Such an interpretation is not satisfactory and does not exhaust the rich content of this idea. The essential element is the positive re-establishment of the broken fellowship. When Luther so consistently uses forgiveness as the principal word in his Catechisms and elsewhere, he pours into it this full positive significance: where there is forgiveness of sins, there is also life and blessedness.

Among the expressions which might be used in this connection the word "justification" occupies the chief place. From a positive point of view, when this word is used in its deepest meaning, its content is the same as "forgiveness of sins." It might well be said, however, that the word justification does not possess the naturalness and intimacy of the word forgiveness. "Justification" is in reality a technical theological word which was originally used in a polemical situation which must be clearly understood if the connotations of the word are to be appreciated. This is true in regard to both Paul and Luther. It is not, to be sure, subject to the danger of being interpreted negatively, as forgiveness has been; it has a very positive connotation. But "justification" can easily be interpreted in a sense that is foreign to Christian faith, since it is unquestionably easy to understand it as implying that man in a real and positive sense becomes righteous and free from sin. Under all circumstances the history of theology after the Reformation indicates that the concept of justification readily loses its Reformation content and is misinterpreted in various ways. It has been difficult to utilize and preserve the insights which were contained in the deeper interpretation of Christianity furnished by the Reformation. The word has therefore largely become more or less meaningless and strange. The positive content of Christian faith has been expressed much more effectively by the term, forgiveness of sins.

Finally, it should be emphatically stated that forgiveness of sins cannot be restricted merely to the beginning of Christian life. Forgiveness is not an act that occurs only once, at a certain time, and establishes once and for all the basis on which the Christian life exists. On the contrary, forgiveness belongs to the whole of Christian life, since this life depends on the fact that "the grace of God is new every morning." If forgiveness is the basis of the realization of fellowship with God, it means that forgiveness is both the essential foundation of the Christian life and its continually active power. We cannot, therefore, divide the Christian relationship to God in such a way that forgiveness should belong to the beginning of Christian life and faith to its continuation. If we distinguish between forgiveness as representing the realization of fellowship with God and faith as representing its continuous existence, it must be made clear that this is not a distinction between different stages of the Christian life, but a conceptual differentiation which is intended to present forgiveness as the principal foundation of Christian faith in the sense that faith owes its existence and its content to the divine act of forgiveness.

2. *The Paradox of Forgiveness.*

The divine act of forgiveness appears to faith as an inscrutable miracle. It does not occur in accordance with human thinking and expectation, but contrary to all that we may expect or think. It can, therefore, be said that in a certain sense forgiveness has a paradoxical character. This appears in the fact that *God* meets the sinful and *unworthy* man with *full* forgiveness. 1) The one who forgives is that God who stands in an unabridged and implacable opposition to sin. He does not for-

give on the premise that to understand all is to forgive all. He
cannot pass by, ignore, or condone sin. The opposition is irrevocable, and the judgment is final. *This* God now enters into
association with sinful man and receives, not the worthy but the
unworthy and condemned man, into fellowship with himself. If
we listen to the Christian testimony of faith where it is given in
its deepest and clearest form, it is abundantly evident that the
essential element is just this: God's forgiveness is given, not to
the one who is sufficiently qualified to receive it, but to one who
is entirely unworthy. 2) Another factor in the matter emphasizes even more strongly the strange and unexpected activity of
divine love. God's forgiveness does not appear to faith, like so
much of human forgiveness, as a half-measure; a forgiveness
which has an element of suspicion and still remembers the of-
fense. It is a *full* and restoring forgiveness which unites man
with God. God's forgiveness meets us as a forgiveness through
which the old has passed away, has been erased, and all things
have become new. Just because forgiveness has this character
faith can say that "where there is forgiveness of sins, there is
also life and salvation." Because God's act of forgiveness implies
that he receives unworthy man into fellowship with himself,
the act appears to the eye of faith as an inscrutable miracle
which is contrary to all human calculations and expectations. Its
character is supra-ethical. It transcends everything which is
merely moral; it is the inmost and deepest mystery of religion.
3) The inexplicable element in the divine act of love is en-
hanced still more by the fact that faith well knows that sin and
unworthiness do not disappear so long as earthly conditions obtain. If freedom from sin were the immediate or gradual result
of the fellowship with God established by forgiveness, the inexplicable character of forgiveness would at least to some extent
be removed. But this is so far from being the case that man's
incorporation into this fellowship with God rather makes the
consciousness of sin more acute, and even, from one point of
view, expresses itself as a much keener consciousness of sin and

guilt. Luther illustrates this situation by his famous statement that the forgiven sinner is *simul iustus et peccator*.

When we speak of the "paradoxical" character of the forgiveness of sin, it is necessary to guard this expression against misinterpretations. The fact that we use it with quotation marks is meant to indicate that it can be used only with certain reservations, or, in other words, that we use it simply in want of a better expression. It is not a question of a paradox in the sense of two logically opposite ideas, but rather of something "paradoxical" in the original sense of this word, i.e., something that is contrary to what we might intend or expect. This is true both of the nature of the divine act of forgiveness and the statement, *simul iustus et peccator*. When we say that God's act of forgiveness is "paradoxical," we mean, therefore, that this, God's Agape, which here meets us cannot be rationally motivated, and that every attempt to assign a cause for the divine act of love as it meets us in the deed of Christ obscures its essential character. Nor does the clause, *simul iustus et peccator*, contain a logical contradiction. That would be the case only if the word *iustus* were interpreted to mean that man has been made just in the sense of sinless perfection. But this is not the meaning. The man who has received God's forgiveness carries on a continuous and unceasing struggle against sin. Man during his earthly life is and remains completely *peccator*, but he becomes at the same time completely *iustus* in the sense that he is *propter Christum* accepted and approved by God. *Simul iustus et peccator* expresses, therefore, the inexplicable fact that in spite of man's sin God receives him into fellowship with himself through forgiveness of sin.[2]

---

[2] Cf. A. Nygren, "*Simul iustus et peccator* in Augustine and Luther," *Till Gustaf Aulén,* Lund, 1939, pp. 257 ff. "The justified man is according to Luther *completely* just, but at the same time *completely* a sinner; *totaliter iustus* and at the same time *totaliter peccator*. This conception of Luther has often been characterized as paradoxical [meaning logically contradictory, *Aulén*]. It must appear such to one who attempts to solve the problem by division. In that case *iustus sum* must mean *peccator non sum*, and if one should insist on keeping the two propositions *iustus sum* and *peccator sum*, this could be done only by interpreting

3. *Forgiveness Does Not Nullify God's Opposition to Evil.*

It is clear from the preceding that the divine act of forgiveness cannot be contained within the order of justice, and that in reality it transcends all merely ethical points of view. The forgiveness of divine Agape cannot be motivated by ethical considerations. Faith *cannot* find any other basis of forgiveness than inscrutable, divine love. In this sense God's Agape is "uncaused" (cf. § 14). But this must not be interpreted to mean a discount or a weakening of God's opposition to evil. No approach could be more foreign to faith than the assertion that forgiveness has the character of laxity and palliation. Even though human forgiveness often may have this character, divine forgiveness is immensely different. On the contrary, it is clear to faith that forgiveness does not weaken or cancel God's opposition to evil, but that this is expressed most emphatically in the very act of forgiveness.

This matter becomes evident in various ways. In the first place, the reconciling and forgiving love has adopted the way of self-giving sacrifice in its struggle against evil. Just because the way of divine love is the way of Christ and the work of Christ bears the mark of the cross (cf. § 26), it is inescapably clear to faith that God's forgiving love has nothing in common with laxity and extenuation of evil, which we human beings so often put in the place of forgiving love, but which is nothing but a caricature of forgiveness. In the second place, God's unabridged opposition to evil is expressed in that forgiveness also contains a judg-

---

it to mean *partly* just and *partly* a sinner. The propositions *totaliter iustus* and *totaliter peccator* seem to be mutually exclusive. But the situation is quite different in the case of Luther. From his point of view there is no contradiction between these two propositions. If man's righteousness before God should consist in his own works or inner quality, he could never be designated anything but a sinner. In justification man does not receive forgiveness for his past sins so that he can subsequently live on the righteousness which he has thus received. On the contrary, the justified person must live by forgiveness just as much in the present as in the past. There is *nothing* in man to which he could point and say: in this respect I do not need forgiveness. And yet he is entirely just, but this righteousness is a *iustitia aliena*. *Christ is his righteousness, and this righteousness* received in faith is perfect. To assert that this righteousness is not whole and perfect, but fragmentary, would be to despise and blaspheme Christ."

ment. No judgment strikes deeper than the judgment of a love that subdues through forgiveness. Consequently God's act of forgiveness is inseparably connected with man's remorse and penitence. Forgiveness comes to man in this particular way. It must be underscored, however, that forgiveness is not dependent on remorse and repentance in the *sense* that these are the causes of the divine act of forgiveness. They are, on the contrary, created by forgiving love. Just because forgiveness has this character of judgment at the same time that it creates fellowship, it strengthens the consciousness of the distance between God and sinful man. In the third place, the opposition between God and evil is apparent in the fact that forgiveness becomes a regenerating power in human life (cf. § 34). Since forgiveness is the establishment of fellowship with God, it implies that divine love becomes the ruling force in human life and reveals its renewing power. *Iustificatio* is, as Luther says, inseparably connected with *sanctificatio*. But this inseparable connection cannot be understood in such a way that regeneration should be the cause and explanation of God's act of forgiveness. Forgiveness cannot be explained on the basis of regeneration, but is caused solely by divine love and includes regeneration.

4. Further Definitions of the Concept of Forgiveness.

The Christian conception of forgiveness has often been obscured and misinterpreted. In regard to what has happened in this respect in the history of Christian thought the concept of forgiveness as defined in the previous sections must be differentiated from three common reinterpretations. These three have one thing in common. They seek in one way or another to explain it rationally and to assign a certain *cause* or causes to it. In the first place, the nature of forgiving love is obscured by a *legalistic* interpretation of Christ's work of reconciliation. In the second place, the idea of forgiveness has been reinterpreted in a moralistic and ethical direction by trying to find in man certain conditions which could be interpreted as causes of divine forgiveness. In the third place, an explanation has been sought by an *anthropomorphic* conception of God which weakens the radical opposition of divine love toward evil.

The essential character of divine Agape becomes obscured when, on the basis of the scholastic theory of the atonement, the work of Christ is interpreted as a compensation given to divine righteousness (cf. § 26. 4). Even if one does not go so far as the nineteenth-century theologian Philippi, who drew the conclusion that man was entitled to receive forgiveness after God had received the compensation, the scholastic theory contains an apparent tendency toward a rational explanation of the possibility of divine forgiveness. The compensation is understood as a logically possible compromise between the demand for punishment and its remission. The chief element in the idea of forgiveness is thereby obscured, viz., the "uncaused" and inscrutable character of that forgiving love which is directed toward sinful and unworthy men. That God forgives is no longer the unfathomable miracle of divine love, since he has already received due recompense for the transgression. But the positive content in the idea of forgiveness, the establishment of fellowship between God and man, is also obscured. When the gift of forgiveness is understood in an external and juridical sense, it loses not only its paradoxical character but also its inner power. It is no longer clear that forgiveness includes both judgment and renewal. The real objection to this interpretation, however, is that the work of Christ is not understood as the work of divine love in its self-giving sacrifice. As long as we adhere to this fundamental idea of Christianity, it becomes impossible to incorporate the work of Christ in a moralistic context and to dissolve the "paradoxical" character of divine forgiveness by an explanation of the possibility of the divine Agape.

In the moralistic and ethical reinterpretation of the concept of forgiveness we may distinguish between three types. One can seek to motivate God's forgiveness by assuming that man has a certain quality, a certain given "value" which God takes into consideration. One can also fix the attention on the attitude of man and interpret faith, remorse, and penitence as the conditions which motivate and explain the divine act of forgiveness. Finally, one can point to the effects of renewal and regeneration in human life which have their origin in forgiving love and assume that God forgives in view of these effects.

We meet the first of these three types wherever idealistic thought has influenced Christianity. Whenever this happens, the conception always appears that man is in possession of a certain "divine" quality, a certain "infinite value" which belongs to human nature as such, and that this "value" is in reality the reason that God forgives man. From this point of view sin belongs to the external part of man, it does not affect his inner life because that constitutes the "core of personality" which God values. We find an example of this in recent literature in F. C. Krarup's book, *The Understanding of Life.* The fundamental theme to which he returns again and again is that forgiveness implies a recognition on God's part of our personality in spite of our failings. Forgiveness must be regarded as an evaluation of the whole being on the basis of the whole personality. Forgiveness implies God's recognition of the inner core of human personality and an acknowledgment of man "as he is in himself."[3] Such a conception is contrary both to the Christian consciousness of sin (cf. § 30) and to faith's consciousness of forgiveness. The Christian consciousness does not regard sin as something external or incidental, so that the core of personality would remain untouched, but, on the contrary, sees it as a cor-

---

[3] F. C. Krarup, *Livsforstaaelse, The Understanding of Life,* pp. 97 ff. "The forgiveness of sins implies from God's side a recognition of our personality, so that he accepts this in spite of all our failings. In his judgment . . . God disregards our imperfections and holds fast to the core, to the essence of our personality; or, more correctly, he does not overlook our imperfections, but as a father in regard to his son his verdict is determined by an evaluation of the whole personality. Together with the rejecting judgment which we assume that God pronounces upon us, we can also conceive that he recognizes us as *we are in ourselves*" [italics by Aulén]. Krarup says, however, in one place that this does not "explain" forgiveness, but his words cannot be interpreted in any other sense than as an attempt to furnish just such an explanation.

ruption of the will, and consequently of the very core of personality. The sinner cannot approach God and say: You know that I have many "faults" and "imperfections," but do not look at these, but to my personality as a whole, to the inner "core"; he must say rather: I, just as I am in the inner recesses of my soul, am unworthy to be called your son. It is for this reason that the Christian concludes that forgiveness cannot be based on anything else than God's unmerited love.

The second moralizing type points to certain attitudes of man as the condition and cause of divine forgiveness. Lutheran scholasticism moved gradually in this direction, as it maintained that God justifies man *ex praevisa fide.* In contrast to Luther's view of the significance of faith, and in contrast to its own intentions, this scholasticism was compelled to regard faith as the human condition of the divine act of justification. That man's attitude is designated by the word *praevisa* and that it is seen under the aspect of God's foreknowledge do not alter the fact that it is a question here of a human cause of divine forgiveness. Another variation of this type occurs often in Pietism, especially in its legalistic form. In this case the divine act of forgiveness is motivated, at least to a certain extent, by man's remorse and penitence. The questionable element in this conception does not consist in the fact that remorse and penitence are inseparably connected with the act of forgiveness—that viewpoint is essential to Christian faith—but that this remorse and penitence inevitably come to be regarded as human accomplishments which furnish an acceptable motivation for the divine act of forgiveness.

The third of these moralistic and ethical types appears in the conception that the forgiveness of God can be at least partially explained on the basis of the results which divine love will produce in human life. This is a most insidious conception. When God forgives, he does so with a view to what the forgiven man will become through divine grace, he looks forward to the time when the person will appear righteous in the actual meaning of that word, because the divine powers are at work in him. In the last analysis this would be the cause of the divine act of forgiveness. When Luther has been cited in support of this view, it has been because he makes justification include also sanctification. But in the measure that this sanctification is conceived of as the cause of justification, the most profound and purely religious conception of Luther's interpretation of Christianity is lost. The matter can be expressed in this way: it is not sanctification that "explains" justification, but God's unfathomable justification which explains sanctification.

Finally, the significance of the Christian idea of forgiveness has been obscured by a weakening of the radical opposition of divine love to evil. We will consider here especially two types: the so-called hyperevangelicalism and the humanistic interpretation of Christianity during the eighteenth and nineteenth centuries, which was influenced by idealism. These two are in many respects quite different, but in relation to our present discussion they exhibit a certain kinship.

The "hyperevangelical" Pietism was generally opposed to the legalistic trend in Pietism. In contrast to the tendency to prescribe a certain amount of remorse and penitence as a condition of forgiveness, hyperevangelical Pietism was concerned that no humanly constructed hindrances should be placed in the way of divine love. The slogan was: "Come, just as you are." Its weakness does not appear in this slogan, which in reality is taken from the very heart of the Gospel, but in the difficulty it encounters in combining the idea of judgment with forgiveness. This is partly explained by the fact that this kind of Pietism is closely connected with a legalistic interpretation of the work of Christ. The humanistic and idealistic interpretation of the Christian conception of God is generally connected with one of these types, viz., that type which finds in man a certain value or quality that motivates divine love. It is characteristic of the anthropomorphic type that it weakens the opposition between the divine will and sin. In the measure this occurs, the "paradoxical" character of divine forgiveness is lost.

In contrast to all these reinterpretations of the Christian idea of forgiveness, Christian faith finds the basis of forgiveness only in God's spontaneous and unfathomable, saving and condemning love. Forgiveness is not based partly on something human and partly on God, its "possibility" and *reality* depend entirely on God's Agape. But this "possibility" cannot then be either rationally explained or motivated. Every such explanation would in reality deprive Christian faith of the foundation on which faith in the forgiveness of sins rests. In regard to the human "possibility" Christian faith can say nothing more than: "With men this is impossible; but with God all things are possible" (Matt. 19:26). Forgiveness is entirely God's work, a gift of God. But this does not mean that in this fellowship with God we cannot speak of human activity. Christian faith speaks without hesitation about man's seeking and receiving, of his turning toward and committing himself to God, and his bold *yes* to divine love. But this does not in the least imply that forgiveness is motivated by man's attitude. From the point of view of faith this human activity is only the result of the divine activity in human life (cf. § 35. 2). According to the viewpoint of faith salvation is entirely God's way to man.

34. Forgiveness of Sins, Life and Blessedness

1. Sin as separation from God means *death*. Forgiveness of sins, being received into fellowship with God, means *life*, participation in the eternal life of God.

2. The fellowship with God established in and through forgiveness contains within itself regenerative power. This expresses itself negatively in a struggle against sin and positively in the fact that man is commissioned as the servant of divine love. The spontaneous ethics of love are fundamentally different from and supplant every other form of ethics.

3. Forgiveness of sins as fellowship with God includes blessedness. Even though this blessedness cannot be fully experienced in this life, it appears nevertheless as peace.

Excursus I. The significance of the spontaneous ethics of love is misunderstood if the spontaneity is interpreted psychologically. It must be pointed out that we are here speaking of the work of the Spirit, and that the "freedom from the law" which is mentioned in this connection means in reality obedience to the commandments which through the Spirit become real and meaningful to man.

Excursus II. A false idealization of the Christian life appears when the fact that the Christian is at the same time *iustus et peccator,* new and old, is not sufficiently emphasized. The Christian as the "old man" lives continually under the law.

Excursus III. A false idealization of the Christian and his situation in the world appears also when it is assumed that God can realize his will only through the regenerated man.

1. Salvation as "Life."

We may begin with the frequently cited words of Luther: "Where there is forgiveness of sins, there are also life and blessedness." We must first note the word *life.* For Christian faith salvation implies *life.* Just as sin not only leads to death, but *is* death, since it is separation from God, so also the fellowship with God established through forgiveness not only leads to life, but *is* life.

There are good reasons for emphasizing this aspect of salvation. It cannot be denied that this aspect has often been unduly ignored, especially by the leading theology of the nineteenth century. It is very characteristic that the representatives of this theology looked with suspicion and a certain air of superiority on the thinking of the early church which was concentrated around this idea of salvation as life. The fathers were accused of holding a "naturalistic" or "physical" conception of salvation. It seems almost to have been assumed that to ignore the idea of life in favor of the idea of forgiveness was a sign of an evangelical and purified Christianity. It was maintained that the emphasis of the ancient church on "life and immortality" indicated that the interpretation of salvation was not sufficiently "ethical."

These accusations leveled against the ancient church by the nineteenth-century research into the history of Christian thought are to a large extent unfounded and based on misinterpretations. In reality it is not a question of ignoring the idea of salvation from sin while emphasizing exclusively the idea of immortality. It is characteristic rather that salvation is conceived of as a salvation from both sin and death. Sin and death are inseparably connected, and, as Irenaeus says, are really two aspects of the same thing, namely, separation from God. If we object to the strong emphasis on Christianity as "life," we would have to object to the point of view that is represented in the whole New Testament. A few of the many examples will suffice to indicate this. The narrow way of salvation is "the way of life" (Matt. 7:14), to participate in salvation is to "enter life" (Matt. 19:17; Mark 9:43) and to "inherit eternal life" (Mark 10:17). It is well known that the Johannine writings are filled with references to this idea. "In the Word was life" (John 1:4); Christ is "the bread of life," "the light of life," "the resurrection and the life," he that believes on him "has life" and has "passed from death into life" (cf. John 5:24; 6:33, 35, 53; 8:12; 10:10; 11:25; I John 1:2; etc.). But this is not a theme peculiar to John, it is one of the fundamental ideas in all the other New Testament writings. Justification is "justification of life" (Rom. 5:18); the Christians are "alive from the dead" (Rom. 6:13); through the Gospels they are "begotten in Christ" (I Cor. 4:15); they have life "through the Spirit" (Gal. 5:25), who is himself "life" (Rom. 8:10); the names of the Christians are written "in the book of life" (Phil. 4:3); those who have "been raised with Christ" have

died and their "life is hid with Christ in God" (Col. 3:1 ff.);
death has come into the world through Adam, but life has come
through Christ (Rom. 5:12-21): death has been conquered:
"O death, where is thy sting?" (I Cor. 15:55); the choice is death
or life (II Cor. 2:16). Christ is "the Prince of life" (Acts 3:15):
he has "abolished death and brought light and immortality to
light through the gospel" (II Tim. 1:10); in the book of Revelation we read about "the crown of life," "the book of life," "the
water of life" (cf. 2:7, 10; 3:5; etc.). We have not tried to give
a complete list of the passages referring to this subject. But the
passages quoted show clearly how vital this idea of salvation as
life is to the New Testament.

Christian faith cannot ignore this aspect of salvation without
distorting its perspective. The antithesis between a "naturalistic"
and an "ethical" conception of salvation is not germane to this
discussion. It is not a question of a choice between these two.
The Christian idea of salvation is certainly not "naturalistic,"
but neither is it merely "ethical." The conception of salvation,
just as the conception of sin, is entirely religious. Two factors
seem to have been the cause of the neglect of this idea of salvation as life. In the first place, the starting point has generally
been the idea of "the immortality of the soul" as a quality belonging to the "nature" of man, an idea which is foreign to faith.
It is easy to understand that from this idealistic point of view
the idea of salvation as life would be minimized. Death in this
sense has lost the profound seriousness which it has in Christian
faith. The passing from death to life has become something
natural and self-evident. In the second place, this tendency
represents a negative conception of the forgiveness of sins. The
insight that forgiveness implies primarily the establishment of
fellowship with God is not recognized.

When Christian faith conceives of the salvation obtained
through forgiveness as life, the meaning is not that "life" is
something added to forgiveness, so that we might speak of two
separate "gifts." On the contrary, the fellowship with God es-

tablished in and through forgiveness is *eo ipso* life, a participation in the eternal life of God. This life is an unmerited gift, it is not a self-evident, human prerogative. But under historical conditions this life is "hidden," "hidden with Christ in God," and is not yet "revealed." "When Christ, who is our life, shall be manifested, then shall ye also with him be manifested in glory" (Col. 3:3 ff.). When salvation is understood as life, it means that the eschatological perspective of faith is given due consideration (cf. § 36. 2).

2. Forgiveness as Power.

Forgiveness implies fellowship with divine love. This means that divine love itself becomes a power in human life. It exercises this power in a twofold manner: by a struggle against evil, and by making man an instrument for the activity of divine love.

We have already indicated (§ 33) that forgiveness implies a judgment on sin and that the consciousness of sin becomes more acute in the presence and through the activity of divine love. But God's forgiving love is not only a discoverer and judge of sin, its power is revealed also in a continuous struggle against evil. Christian faith does not reckon with a condition of sinlessness during this earthly life (I John 1:8), nor does it conceive of the Christian life as a continuous progress toward such a goal. When Schleiermacher speaks of salvation as consisting in both a continuous strengthening of the consciousness of God and a corresponding diminishing of the consciousness of sin, such reasoning appears to faith as unrealistic and as a false idealization of Christian life and its situation. His incorporation of the Christian life into a monistic and evolutionistic world view has led Schleiermacher to suppress the point of view which Luther describes so graphically when he says that fellowship with God increases the consciousness of sin. The Christian perspective is decidedly dramatic. All idealizing of human life is foreign to faith. It recognizes only a lifelong struggle against that sin which would always separate us from him and which continually places us before him as unworthy. The old man must daily die from sin, and the new man daily come forth and rise. Fellowship with God is not a permanent treasure which we possess and with which we can settle down in peace; it can be possessed only by being continually obtained anew. *Der Christ steht nicht im Sein, sondern im Werden*, as Luther so often says. "The new man" is not something finished and perfect; under the conditions of human life on earth he is continually becoming. The active presence of divine love in and through forgiveness signifies for the Christian life a continuous struggle against that which would again destroy the fellowship, but its presence means also that this struggle is not hopeless, since an inexhaustible supply of power is given to the Christian by the sovereignty of divine love.

But this activity of divine love in human life expresses itself not only in a struggle against evil, but as a realization of its own intentions and purposes. In the measure that divine love subdues man, it makes him an instrument for its own activity. God's Agape finds its way out into human life through the human instrumentality. The man who has been subdued by God through forgiveness is called upon to reveal, i.e., realize, God's loving will in relation to the neighbor. No one in Christendom has spoken more emphatically and profoundly about this "vocation" of the Christian than Luther. The Christian is to be "a Christ" to the neighbor, and Luther can even say that he is to be "God" to him. "We are Gods through the love which makes us benevolent toward our neighbors; for the divine nature is nothing else than pure benevolence." [1]

This very radical statement would be entirely misinterpreted and the conception of the life in faith would be thoroughly misunderstood if it were assumed that this involves a surreptitious apotheosis of human life and human love. This manner of speaking does certainly not imply that the man of faith is able to

---

[1] W. A., 10, I, 1, p. 100.

point to and rely upon his own love. It is never a question of any other love than God's Agape whose "power is made perfect in weakness" (II Cor. 12:9 ff.).

From this point of view the celebrated words of Luther that "blessedness is necessary for good works" are seen in their true meaning. When Luther enunciated this proposition, he had in mind that poison which is deadly both for salvation and for the works of love, viz., the securing of personal "merits." He wants to maintain, not only that blessedness cannot be gained through "meritorious works," but also that the constant concern with self and this poisonous egocentricity paralyze and frustrate man's opportunity to become an instrument in the service of divine love. But Luther's radical proposition, as E. Billing has conclusively shown, did not have simply a contemporary significance, but is universally valid. Peace signifies participation in a power which cannot be obtained in any other way. So long as enmity rules in the depth of the human heart, or so long as man is selfishly inclined toward self (*incurvatus in se*), "everything that happens to us serves only to intensify this selfish inclination." Man is compelled to hunt continually for new substitutes for the lack of inner blessedness. Peace is the only remedy. "Only when we are conscious of inner riches which surpass everything else, which not even death can take away from us, and about which we need not contend with others, since they are given to us strictly by grace and increase by being shared with others, only then has the heart something to hold, something that sets it free from its convulsive grasp on itself. Where peace and blessedness really are present in the heart of man, he finds that he has power to spare, not only to defend himself against the unclean powers, but also to share with others." [2] In order to underscore the chief thought in the quotation from Billing, and in order to guard against a rather obvious misinterpretation, I add here a few words by A. Nygren. "Only when we have under-

---

[2] Einar Billing, *Herdabrev,* An Episcopal Letter, pp. 22 f.

stood that Christian love, according to Luther, is God's own love which through the Christian finds its way out into human life, can we understand the deepest meaning of the frequently quoted statement by Luther that a man must be blessed in order to perform the good. This is commonly interpreted exclusively in a eudaemonistic direction. When a man is blessed and his own interests and affairs are secure in his assurance of God's grace, only then is he rich and free enough to be able to serve his fellow-men in love. The truth in this interpretation is that blessedness delivers a man from his egocentric activity, but not in the sense that all egocentric interests are satisfied, but rather because they are vanquished and destroyed. For Luther blessedness means fellowship with God. But consequently only one who by faith lives in this blessed fellowship is able to receive that supply from above which enables him to dispense it in love." [3]

The "ethics" which have been expressed here are fundamentally different from and supplant every other form of ethics. They are different from all "legalistic" ethics, since it is a question here simply of love working spontaneously. They are different from all "utilitarian" ethics, since it is not a question of any other motive than that contained in love itself. Since, furthermore, the decisive element is the activity of divine love itself, these ethics are differentiated from "intuitionalism" which regards the ethical quality as inherent in human nature. The radicalism of "Christian ethics" appears most clearly in the fact that it is not a question of human "merits," nor of human obligations of one kind or another. We are dealing here with a kind of ethics which implies that the human ego recedes, man is removed away from himself and becomes an instrument in the hands of God's Agape. To use New Testament vocabulary, it is a question of nothing else but "the fruits of the Spirit" (Gal. 5:22; cf. Rom. 7:6; 8:4).

---

[3] A. Nygren, *"Den kristna kälekstanken hos Luther,"* Svensk theologisk kvartalskrift, 1930, p. 29.

3. Blessedness and Peace.

We have already touched on this theme: forgiveness as blessedness and peace. If it is true for Christian faith that where there is forgiveness there is also blessedness, the reason is to be found in the positive and unifying significance of forgiveness. Fellowship with God is blessedness, and blessedness is fellowship with him. If the connotation of the word blessedness is primarily eschatological, it nevertheless appears in the present as peace. We might say that peace is the specific category of forgiveness. Forgiveness overcomes that inner anxiety which is found in the heart of every man as long as he is inclined toward self (*incurvatus in se*), or as long as the tyranny of egocentricity is intact. As sin is a continuous source of anxiety, so forgiveness is an inexhaustible source of inner peace. Forgiveness creates peace. Christian faith from the beginning and down through the ages testifies unanimously that the peace of God is the unique gift received through forgiveness. Paul gathers together all his wishes and prayers for his congregation in the word about "the peace of God that passeth all understanding" (Phil. 4:7), and in the Gospel of John the work of Jesus is summed up in the word "my peace I give unto you" (John 14:27). Everything that the disciples have received is comprehended in the word peace. It is significant that the apostolic greeting reads: "Grace be unto you and peace from God." Peace is the central content of the Christian life received through forgiveness. But it is necessary to emphasize in this connection that the significance of this fact is not that the Christian life is always characterized by strong and continuous feelings of peace and blessedness, nor that peace disappears when these feelings subside. The gift of peace through forgiveness is not simply a variation in feelings.

When Schleiermacher interprets "blessedness" in a more or less stoic sense and understands it as a certain uninterrupted harmony, or a feeling of being at home in the cosmos, it is a re-interpretation of the viewpoint of Christian faith that depends

309

on his general, monistic world view. But for Christian faith life in this world is neither a harmony nor an idyl. Peace does not depend on the fact that everything appears to faith in the last analysis as "harmonious," it is a peace "in spite of all" and in the midst of the struggle. Because the forgiveness which brings peace is an act of God received and held by faith, or, in other words, because peace depends on fellowship with God, it can exist in the midst of darkness and tumult, and it can dwell in a human heart filled with storm and stress. Peace, as E. Billing says, is not "a tender treasure which we must anxiously guard in order to protect it against the world, but that mighty power which guards us and in whose company we may pass securely through the world; not a perishable sentiment which comes and goes, but the secure and objective reality which surrounds us wherever we go, from which we cannot in a sense escape; not the last, final and highest in the Christian life, but the first, the basic—and the highest." [4]

Excursus I. The Significance of Spontaneity.

In and through justification man is received into a new fellowship with God. This new fellowship which is based on forgiveness is a relationship of grace and adoption, the opposite of the legalistic relationship to God. As long as man's relationship to God rests on law, he strives to secure righteousness before God and to produce in himself that religious quality which will win God's favor and be acceptable to him. When God's act of forgiveness now becomes the sole basis of fellowship with God, all these endeavors on man's part to qualify for this fellowship are eliminated. This is the significance of the statement that the legalistic relation to God has ceased to exist for the Christian. But this release from the way of self-righteousness does not mean that the Christian is passive in reference to the demand of love and the works of love. Rather the opposite is true. The release implies that man is received into the sphere of divine

---

[4] E. Billing, *op. cit.*, p. 17.

love and becomes an instrument in the service of God's Agape.

When we speak of the spontaneous activity of love, it can easily be misunderstood in a psychologizing manner. It might seem that the Christian life, from a purely psychological point of view, should be characterized by a free and unhindered spontaneity and that there would be no opposition to overcome. Such an interpretation is a false idealization of the Christian life. It must, therefore, be underscored, that this spontaneity is not a newly acquired human trait, attribute, or act; but that spontaneity is connected entirely with divine love and with the Spirit which subdues man and is active in him.

The freedom from the law, which we speak of in this connection, is described in the New Testament as a freedom of the Spirit. "Where the Spirit of the Lord is, there is liberty" (II Cor. 3:17). But this freedom signifies at the same time obedience to that which is demanded by this Spirit, or, in other words, to those commandments of God which become real and meaningful to men through the Spirit, as he introduces man into the continuous, creative activity of God. Freedom implies being free to serve and in obedience to God to render to the neighbor that service which love demands. "The commandment does not disappear with the legalistic relationship to God. On the contrary, when conscience now finally has found rest in reliance on the Gospel of God, man understands that he has never before really sought after God's will and his commandments, but has been driven into one unrealistic activity after another in his endeavor to become sufficiently religious. Now when he believes, he finds a simple and direct commandment." [5]

Excursus II. A False Idealization of the Christian Life.

What we have now said about spontaneity and obedience is complemented and made more acute when we note that the Christian man in this world is not only "the new man," but continually remains also as "the old man," *simul iustus et peccator.*

---

[5] G. Wingren, *Luthers lära om kallelsen, Luther's Teaching About Vocation,* p. 210.

No interpretation of the Christian life could be more unrealistic than that which ignores this fact and speaks of "the old things" as having passed away when man was received into the new fellowship with God. The old has indeed disappeared in so far as the forgiveness of God is complete and unconditional and man stands before him *totaliter iustus*. But this change does not imply a change in the nature of man in the sense that he now should be able to do God's will completely and thereby can point to his changed life as providing access to and security before God. On the contrary, he cannot point to one single act which is without sin. He can speak with gratitude of the power of God that is active in his life, but he is also conscious of the fact that this God's power is made strong through his weakness, as Paul says. Sin clings to man's life as a whole, and he cannot point to a single act for which he must not ask God for forgiveness. In so far as the Christian remains "the old man," he stands continually under the demand, discipline, and judgment of the law. This function of the law becomes actual and concrete in and through that vocation given him by God and in the demands which love places upon him in reference to the neighbor. The struggle against evil, therefore, becomes inseparable from the Christian life, and penitence belongs "to the whole of the Christian life," as Luther stated in the first of his celebrated ninety-five theses.

Excursus III. A False Idealization
  of the Christian's Relation to the World.

The idea has sometimes been advanced that the will of God can be accomplished only through those who have received the Gospel in faith, and that it is also in reality carried out by them. This idea is deeply rooted in the pietistic conception of Christianity. Such a point of view can lead to various consequences in regard to the relation between the Christian and the world. On the one hand, the result may be that the world is regarded as entirely profane, as an area in which the will of

God is not done. In this connection there arises a tendency to isolate the Christians from the world. This approach has contributed momentum to the secularizing process which has been going on during the last centuries, even though the real causes of this process have been of another kind. On the other hand, the conclusion has also been drawn from this premise that all the problems and difficulties of the world would be solved it all men became Christian and as such did God's will.

If we examine the thesis that the will of God can be done only by those who have received the Gospel in faith, and that it is also carried out by them, it must be stated that neither of these propositions is valid. The latter statement is, as we have seen, a truth which must be qualified, since the Christian is *simul iustus et peccator.* The first proposition, however, is not true, since God has other means which he can use to realize his will. We must here remind ourselves of what was stated in section 21 in regard to the law of creation. We advanced there the thesis that the tasks and orders of this world are not profane, but are given by God and are the bearers of his law, and that the vocation and the functions which belong to men are given to them by God. In these vocations and functions the divine law operates and its purpose is to suppress evil, subdue the recalcitrant, and thereby to realize God's will. It is also important in this connection to note the relation between the law of God and that order of justice which is the foundation of human society. It cannot be denied that God's will is accomplished within the framework of the law even though it is done under compulsion and not spontaneously.

Under these circumstances it is plain that the Christian life must not be isolated from the world. The Christians have also their temporal functions which they must carry out in accordance with the vocation given to them. But it would be just as misleading to assert that all earthly tasks and problems would be solved if all men became Christians. Such reasoning does not agree with the conditions in the world or the situation of the

Christian life. It would indeed involve a monstrous arrogance on the part of the Christians. This insight does not imply a denial of the fact that when the Gospel is received in faith, it supplies new demands and possibilities in regard to the vocation, nor of the fact that the Gospel extends and enriches the content of this vocation (cf. § 47. 1).

35. The Divine Fellowship Exists through Faith

1. That fellowship with God which is based on forgiveness exists as a relationship of faith. Its content and character are determined solely by the activity of divine love relative to man. On man's part it is therefore characterized by unconditional trust. Since God is the Sovereign in this relationship, all eudaemonism is excluded from the life of faith. Whereas divine love radically condemns sin, the idea of an identity which blots out the distance between God and man is excluded.

2. The activity of divine love is the sole foundation of faith, therefore faith is completely a work of God and a divine gift. This does not exclude, but rather includes, the fact that faith involves the whole volitional activity of man. From this point of view faith is a turning and a commitment to God. The slogan "by faith alone" (*sola fide*) is a genuinely Christian watchword, since it rejects the thought that this activity implies "human merit" or service and that it therefore is rooted in something other than God's subduing love (*sola gratia*).

1. The Relationship of Faith.

The fellowship with God established on the basis of forgiveness has its continued existence as a relationship of faith. Faith is, as we have already stated (§ 2), the characteristic word of the Christian relationship between God and man. Christian life exists as a life "in faith." Fellowship with God is a fellowship "in faith." This expresses both its riches and its limitations under the conditions of life here on earth (cf. II Cor. 5:7).

We must first emphasize that both the content and character of this fellowship of faith are determined and defined by the activity of divine love relative to man. The idea that faith may be regarded as a human condition for the divine fellowship is thereby excluded. Faith is not a human achievement or quality that can be isolated from the activity of divine love. By its own estimate faith is *nothing* in itself. It is what it is through that divine and loving will which calls it into being. The relationship to God is created, maintained, and determined by divine love. In this sense God is the subject of faith.

But this does not exclude the fact that faith is a phenomenon which belongs to human life. Faith as a creation of divine love implies that man is received into a definite relationship with God. From this point of view God appears as the sole object of faith, and man's relation to this object is then characterized by an unconditional trust. In so far as faith rules in and characterizes the life of man, man stands in a relation of unconditional trust to that divine and loving will which has subdued and subdues him. This relationship of trust implies also an unconditional *yes* to that God who reveals himself. From this point of view it is meaningless to distinguish between trust (*fiducia*) and assent, as if it were a question of two different things. Trust involves an "assent" to the content and message of the divine revelation. Furthermore, assent has the character of full and complete trust (cf. § 2. 1).

We have spoken of faith as a creation through the act of forgiveness on the part of divine love, and as an unconditional trust on man's part. But redemptive love is at the same time a condemning and sovereign divine will (cf. §§ 15, 16). This gives the Christian relationship of love its character. In this relationship God is the Sovereign, the Lord. Faith implies that man is placed under the divine government. As Luther says, "It snatches us out of our own line of vision and places us outside ourselves." There is nothing more essential to this relationship of faith than that it involves the sovereign dominion of the di-

315

vine and loving will which breaks down that human will which is separated from God and ruled by the ego. A fellowship with God cannot exist in the sense that the divine will would enter human life as a magnitude coincident with other factors. Wherever a fellowship with God is established and exists, it implies that the divine will dominates and exercises that sovereign authority which belongs to divine love. When the relationship of faith is realized, it means that God breaks down and overcomes egocentricity. While sin as unbelief is egocentricity and inclination toward self (cf. § 30. 3), the relationship of faith is characterized by the fact that the ego has ceased to be the center around which man revolves in selfish bondage, and that God has become man's center and Lord.[1] Christian faith conceives of the relationship between God and man as a relationship of adoption; man has become a "child of God" (cf. Rom. 8:14, 16; Gal. 3:26; I John 3:1, 2, 10; etc.). But this "adoption" would be interpreted with profane familiarity foreign to Christian faith, if the fact were even slightly obscured that God "the Father" is also the sovereign Lord and that this relationship of faith implies that life is placed under his sovereign government. To live in faith means, as Paul says, a crucifixion of the selfish ego and a liberation from the slavery of self (Gal. 2:19 ff.). *In the measure that* man lives in faith, he is not *incurvatus in se* and is not selfishly contained within himself. In the realm of faith everything has its center in God as the Lord of human life.

As the relationship of faith is defined by the sovereignty of divine love, it is likewise determined by the judicial activity of this love. The man of faith stands also under judgment and under God's unconditional condemnation of sin. The Christian relationship of faith is, therefore, radically differentiated from those conceptions which tend to interpret it as a relation of identity between God and man. Since all pure mysticism tends in

---

[1] Cf. Wm. Temple, *Fellowship with God,* pp. 73 f. "You cannot have salvation as long as you want it. Only when God has so drawn you into the embrace of his love and into obedience to his will that in devotion to him you cease to care about yourself, can you be saved."

this direction, there arises a twofold contrast to the Christian faith: mysticism destroys both the fellowship with God and the remoteness. It might otherwise seem that mysticism would surpass Christian faith in regard to the emphasis on fellowship when it speaks of man's immediate entrance and absorption into the divine. But in reality the relationship ceases to be a fellowship. The "god" whom man reaches on this way and the "infinity" into which he is plunged do not carry him outside the charmed circle of egocentricity. Just as the God of mysticism becomes simply the unfathomable, about which nothing can be said, so this "god" loses the power to lift man out of himself and to "remove him from his own line of vision." Absorption into the divine becomes in reality nothing but absorption into self. But at the same time, in spite of its talk about man's "negation of self," mysticism removes the "distance" between God and man which is a fundamental fact for Christian faith, and which increases in and through this fellowship with God, as we have had occasion to point out several times. Since divine love also includes judgment, and since man here on earth never ceases to be a sinner, the Christian life in faith is characterized by a peculiar twofold perspective. Fellowship with God is obtained in and through the divine act of forgiveness, but this fellowship is not an inalienable possession; it exists rather as *becoming* and perdures in a continuous struggle against that which is hostile to God (cf. § 36). Faith speaks of the existence of "the new man." This is not empty and meaningless talk. The new man is not, as has been said (Gogarten), only *ein Fabelwesen*. "If any man is in Christ, he is a new creature" (II Cor. 5:17). To deny the existence of "the new man" would be the same as to deny that act of forgiveness of divine Agape which creates fellowship with God. This would be to wound faith in its inmost heart. But to regard "the old man" as vanquished and gone would be from the point of view of faith the most terrible arrogance. During this earthly life man stands in all respects under the judgment of God, and "the new man" of which faith speaks is not an ego

317

separated from "the old man." The words of Luther are here valid: "the old man shall daily be drowned and destroyed, and the new man shall daily come forth and rise."

The Christian faith is, therefore, characterized by a peculiar twofold perspective. Faith includes both struggle and peace, self-denial and assurance of victory. It makes man conscious both of his unworthiness before God and of his participation in "that victory which overcomes the world." In faith man is at the same time nothing before God and "a lord over all things." "If God be for us, who then can be against us?" (Rom. 8:31). But this confident consciousness of victory which is characteristic of Christian faith is the very opposite of egocentric arrogance. It would be entirely misleading to characterize faith's consciousness of victory as "exaltation of self." Faith knows of nothing else than an "exaltation of God"; its "self-consciousness" is *ein vollkommen selbstloses Selbstgefühl*.[2] It trusts God above all things.

2. Faith as the Work of God and as Human Activity.

We have already pointed out in our preliminary definition of the concept of faith (§ 2) that faith can be considered from two points of view: on the one hand, that God subdues and dominates man, and on the other, that man turns toward and commits himself to God. This problem which we then touched upon must now be analyzed in more detail. It is clear from what we have already said that the most fundamental and vital viewpoint of faith is that its origin and existence depend entirely on the loving will of God and on nothing else. Faith knows that it exists as a result of the work of God and as his gracious gift. The relationship of faith exists as a relation of complete dependence on him who overwhelms and dominates man.

It is the glory of evangelical Christianity that by its watchword, *sola fide, sola gratia*—by faith alone, by grace alone, it turned with determination against all who would obscure this fundamental character of the relationship of faith. But it cannot

---

[2] K. Holl, *"Was verstand Luther unter Religion?"* *op. cit.,* p. 84.

be denied that in maintaining this watchword of faith as altogether a work of God, theology, and not least Lutheran theology, has obscured the fact that faith also, from one point of view, represents human activity. Theology has thereby given a quietistic character to the life of faith, which in reality does not agree with its nature and threatens to paralyze its power. This theology assumed that it was possible to assert the viewpoint of grace and the *sola gratia* of the Reformation only by avoiding as much as possible any reference to activity on the part of man. The divine and the human were considered as two magnitudes which would balance each other. Whatever was added to the human would then detract from the divine. Under these circumstances theology was driven into a hopeless dilemma from which it could not escape. If God really "does everything," then, of course, man "does nothing." If it be assumed that man can do something toward his salvation, then it could not be interpreted in any other way than as "co-operation," and this implied a "synergistic" or "semi-Pelagian" conception which is opposed to the "by grace alone" of the Reformation. Since no one was willing to say that God works in men by means of an external force as a power of nature, it became necessary to grant, however unwillingly, a certain degree of receptiveness in man, which naturally implied a certain amount of human activity. But this activity must then be reduced to the smallest minimum, when it was not possible to eliminate it entirely. But however severely it was limited, as soon as any activity on the part of man was admitted, the principle at stake had to be surrendered, according to this understanding of the matter. The proposition of Lutheran scholasticism that God justifies *ex praevisa fide* is significant. Faith in this case is understood as a human condition. It was a hopeless situation, for it was impossible even to maintain that principle which it was most important to affirm, namely, the Reformation principle "by grace alone"; and at the same time it was considered necessary to avoid everything which might be interpreted as a challenge and an appeal to man. The words of Paul must appear very strange to such a theology: "Work out your own salvation with fear and trembling; for it is God who worketh in you both to will and to work, for his good pleasure" (Phil. 2:12 f.). Here the idea of faith as throughout a work of God does not stand in opposition to an appeal and an unreserved challenge.

It is clear, however, that the quietistic approach with its fear of everything that suggests a human activity is not in accord with the actual situation of faith. It is very significant that the "activistic" aspect of faith has found a much stronger expression in preaching and in hymns than in theology. This aspect could not be suppressed in the practical life of piety, even though it could be done more or less successfully in theological theories. The evangelical injunction to seek, pray, and knock re-echoes in the direct and immediate expressions of the Christian life. Faith appears from one point of view as activity; it even places the greatest possible demands on man's spiritual energy. Faith implies a choice, a decision, a venture, perhaps a timid but at the same time a bold *yes* to God. And as faith in its origin has an active character, so its whole existence is activity. The heroes of faith have testified hereto in all ages. Luther, at the same time that he speaks of faith as a work of God, has also described faith as a continuous and persistent struggle, and has spoken of its bold *dennoch*, its "nevertheless." Faith exists as a militant and praying faith, which can exist and continue only by being constantly won anew. There is always something of this element in faith: Lord, I will not let you go unless you bless me.

But is not the watchword of the Reformation, *sola gratia*, disclaimed when such references are made to the activity of faith? It may so appear but only as long as God is conceived in terms of an extra-mundane magnitude who is separated from the world. Such a conclusion is not possible when God is seen from the viewpoint of faith as the one who is seriously involved in current events and who, in order to establish his dominion of love, contends with those forces which are inimical to his will.

From the point of view of this active conception of God's work of redemption everything is seen in a new light. It is no longer possible to talk about the choice of faith and its *yes* to God as a human activity apart from God. This whole problem with which an older theology struggled fruitlessly and to its own detriment simply vanishes. It is perfectly clear to faith that what we call our seeking is nothing else than the Father *drawing* us to himself, and the bold *yes* of faith is nothing else than God's subduing of man. Faith knows that here if anywhere it is necessary to seek, pray, and watch. But in the midst of this activity nothing is more certain to faith than that all this is God's work and his unmerited gift. Our "conversion" implies that we are overwhelmed by God and are "born anew" through his loving will. When faith turns to God in prayer, it means that God is about to prepare a way for his dominion (§ 45). "We know not how to pray as we ought; but the Spirit himself maketh intercession for us with groanings that cannot be uttered" (Rom. 8:26). God "draws" us unto himself, he subdues us, in forgiveness he removes that which separates us from him and enters upon his dominion. That which we call the struggle of faith is nothing else than the struggle of the living God to realize his dominion. This struggle continues through the ages, and in the midst of it stands Christ as the great Victor whose struggle and victory are on our behalf, and of whose fullness we all receive—grace for grace (John 1:16). "Salvation" is entirely the creative act of divine love; we are redeemed *sola gratia*, through God's Agape alone.

The watchword of the Reformation remains, therefore, as the principal word of Christian faith. But the human activity of faith is not obscured. *Sola gratia* does not lead us into passivity and quietism; it presents rather, as Paul indicates in Philippians, the strongest appeal to men to work out their own salvation "with fear and trembling." The significance of the watchword of the Reformation is that it irrevocably stands guard against all attempts to separate human activity from God's own activity and to consider it as "merit." The deadly poison lies in this idea of merits. Even if it appears in a sheltering disguise, as so often happens, it remains a deadly poison to the life of faith. To speak about human merit in the presence of God introduces an irreligious element into the religious life. God and our merits, these are like fire and water. But this guarding against the idea of merit is at the same time a protection against all egocentric piety. As long as we are concerned with our own ego and its merits, there is no possibility of obtaining that freedom from the tyranny of the ego and that withdrawal "out of ourselves" which constitute salvation. *Sola gratia* is a watchword not only against the idea of merits, but against all conceptions which pretend to find the cause of divine love in human efforts or value (cf. § 33. 4). It stands guard against all attempts to conceive of the way of salvation as man's way to God. It tells us that there is no other way to God than God's way to man. In this sense the term *sola gratia* is eternally and universally valid. It was not significant simply for a certain period of Christian history when it was so strenuously emphasized; nor is it a self-sufficient word of evangelical Christianity, it is rather a touchstone for Christianity as such. The principle, *sola gratia,* stands guard against all tendencies to make the ego and personal blessedness the central concern in the realm of faith, against all *Selbstbehauptung,* etc. It maintains unceasingly and irrevocably the theocentric character of faith. In the realm of faith everything has its center in God and his dominion, and faith originates and lives in that loving will of God which realizes itself in the human world.

36. Faith as Possession and as Hope

1. When man in faith receives the unmerited gift of divine love, faith implies a present possession of this gift. Since the life of faith here and now is lived under the conditions imposed by sin, this "proprietorship" is radically distinguished from self-confidence and exists only by being continually renewed.

2. Since fellowship with God exists only as a becoming, in struggle and conflict, faith appears as hope in that consummation which occurs when all that is "partial" passes away. From this point of view fellowship with God in the present appears as an earnest of that which is to come, and the expected consummation as something "wholly other" than the present.

3. These two aspects of faith lend mutual support one to the other. Faith rejects both that emphasis on the present which obscures the eschatological perspective, and that metaphysical eschatology which obscures the present reality.

1. Faith as Possession.

Just as faith may be defined both as a work of God and as a human activity, so it may be seen also from another twofold viewpoint. It is, on the one hand, a fellowship with God established on the basis of the act of forgiveness of divine love, and, on the other hand, a living hope (I Pet. 1:3 f.).

If faith means that man is incorporated into fellowship with God, it possesses an abundance which cannot be overestimated. Faith has "the pearl of great price." "He who believes, has," says Luther. Faith receives the gift which is God's own love, or God himself. Everything that faith "possesses" is included in this one thing. Christian testimony has from the very beginning given the strongest expressions to this fellowship and "possession" of faith. The life of faith is a "life in the Spirit," "in Christ," a life of God and in God. Faith does not live in anxiety, but in undaunted trust, as Paul says: *nothing* can separate us from the love of God which is in Christ Jesus" (Rom. 8:39). And John says; "our fellowship is with the Father, and with his Son Jesus Christ" (I John 1:3), "we have boldness toward God" (I John 3:21; cf. 4:18; 5:4; etc.). The matrix of this boldness of faith is the fact that the fellowship rests on God's love and on nothing else. If this foundation is weakened and the existence of faith is made dependent on something else in addition

to divine love, the boldness and confidence of faith are under-
mined. In the common piety and theology of the Middle Ages
the Christian life appears, therefore, as a balance between hope
and fear. When the Reformation brought back the confidence
of faith, the reason was that divine love became again the sole
basis of faith. The emphasis on the "possession" of faith was
renewed. "Where there is forgiveness of sins, there are also
life and blessedness."

This character of faith as "possession" may even be expressed
in such a way that faith speaks about "blessedness" and "eternal
life" as something which the man of faith enjoys even under the
conditions of earthly life. Where God is, there are blessedness
and eternal life: "He that heareth my word, and believeth him
that sent me, *hath* eternal life, and cometh not into judgment,
but *hath* passed out of death into life" (John 5:24; cf. 3:36).
Eternal life is not only something that shall be given to the
believer at some future time, but something which already exists
in and through faith's fellowship with the eternal God. It must
be added, however, that such expressions about eternal life must
not be separated from the eschatological perspective.

But if this relation of faith to divine love exists in the present, this "possession" about which faith so boldly speaks is not
a secure and permanent property. The boldness of faith is radically distinguished from *securitas*. All self-confidence is excluded. Such an attitude would imply a self-exaltation which
would be diametrically opposed to the humility of faith. Faith
itself exists as a becoming. The possessing of this gift on the
part of faith must be constantly and continually renewed. The
life of faith is a life in constant peril, an unceasing struggle
against opposing forces. Consequently the boldness of faith is
accompanied by fear and trembling. The opposition of the Reformation to the mixture of hope and fear of the Middle Ages
does not consist in that the Reformation knew nothing of "fear."
To stand face to face with God is to fear him, according to Luther, but this fear is now fused with trust and ceases, therefore,

to be a *timor servilis*. Trust itself includes a trembling which does not cease during this life, because man is man and God is God.

2. *Faith as Hope.*

Faith is directed not only toward the present and active God but also toward that which does not yet exist. It is essential to faith that it stretches forward to "the things that are before" and "presses on toward the goal" (Phil. 3:13 ff.). Faith exists as hope. The hope of faith is rooted in the act of divine love, it arises from the contrast between the costliness of the gift and the imperfections of life. As we have already pointed out, the life of faith is a constant struggle against the powers of sin which intend to destroy the fellowship of faith with God and rob it of its inner peace. Christian life is a constant becoming, and it has the character of that which is imperfect and unfinished. This imperfect and unfinished state does not disappear during this life, rather it becomes more apparent as faith grows strong and vigorous. The more faith perceives and understands what fellowship with God means, the more clearly the unfinished character of life here on earth appears. But at the same time faith emerges as a living hope. The inner riches of the life of faith and the fellowship with the exalted, living, and eternal God transcend the framework of earthly life. Faith cannot be contained within a this-worldly perspective nor within the boundaries of this life, since God cannot be contained within these limits. Christian hope is, therefore, throughout the hope of *faith*. It does not rest on any theories of the indestructible nature of man or on "the immortality of the soul," but entirely on faith's encounter with God. If the God of faith is a living God, then life with him is a life that cannot be enclosed within the narrow confines of the conditions of this earthly life. Faith looks beyond that which is "partial" toward a consummation, the content of which is the undisturbed and pure life with God exalted above

325

all opposition and imperfection, where God's dominion is unabridged and unhindered (cf. § 51).

If we now note more closely how faith speaks about this
hope, we encounter two lines of thought which strangely contend one with the other. On the one hand, "that which is to
come" appears as the completion of that which now is. That
which is to come is, so to speak, in line with the present, i.e.,
the "possession" of faith is to be exalted to a higher dignity. The
present is an outer court of "life in the world to come" and an
earnest of that which is to be. On the other hand, the present
appears as only a faint shadow of the future. The future is understood as a new creation, as something "wholly other" than
that which now is, and as something about which faith can
speak only in groping figures. "It is not yet made manifest what
we shall be" (I John 3:2). It is not simply a question of a perfection of that which now is, and not only a liberation from the
limitations of the present life of faith, but of something that is
in the essential meaning of the word "wholly other." This twofold perspective of hope and the conflict between these two
lines of thought indicates clearly that the content of Christian
hope appears to faith as an unfathomable mystery which lies
outside the capacities of human thought.

3. *The Relation between Faith as "Possession" and Faith as Hope.*
    The life of Christian faith is characterized by a certain inner
tension between these two aspects, which reflects the inner
rhythm of faith. At certain times in the history of Christian
thought this tension has turned into an antithesis in which faith
as "possession" has been emphasized to the exclusion of faith as
hope, or vice versa. In other words, faith has sometimes been
understood as exclusively this-worldly and sometimes as metaphysical eschatology. Both of these misconceptions are due to
the fact that the inner richness of faith has not been fully
understood.

When faith is conceived of as exclusively this-worldly, the

intention is to emphasize as much as possible the present ethical functions of the Christian life. The danger is that faith may be understood as a relation to the world rather than as a relation to God. The theology of the later half of the nineteenth century furnishes many examples of the tendency to reduce "the Kingdom of God" to an ethical and cultural ideal. The defect of this line of thought is not that it takes the present into account, nor that it emphasizes that the life of faith exists for the purpose of spending itself in love. This emphasis is a sound counterbalance to that eschatology which issues in quietism and passivity. But the danger is that the essential element of faith is obscured, viz., that faith is committed to a kingdom that is not of this world. Without the eschatological perspective the fellowship with God becomes limited and the power of faith paralyzed. When faith becomes concentrated on temporal goals, it becomes unable to accomplish its work in the world. If faith is to be active in the world, it has to be "free from the world"; it must live in God and be anchored in the hope of his eternal Kingdom.[1]

If the exclusively temporal perspective has a certain optimistic view of the course of this world as a constant progress, which does not conform to the actual situation, the view of metaphysical eschatology represents a pessimism which results in quietism and passivity in reference to the affairs of this world, and conceives of faith as a flight from the world rather than a victory over it. Faith here closes its eyes and dreams of being separated from the world "that lieth in evil." The reason for this attitude also is its failure to appreciate the inner richness of faith. If faith is in reality fellowship with God, it cannot avoid relating the divine will to the affairs of this world, and cannot, therefore, sink into inactive pessimism. It knows that fellowship with God implies responsibility and inexhaustible possibilities. It "hopeth

---

[1] Cf. W. Temple, *Fellowship With God*, p. 69: "The man who will do most to move the world is not he who concentrates all his attention upon the needs of the world and dedicates all his energy to reforming labors. The man who will do most to move the world is he who truly dwells with God; for through him there will operate in the world the sources of omnipotence."

all things," because fellowship with God means submission to the government of the sovereign power of existence.

The more faith appears as unconditional trust in the loving will of God, the more closely the possession and the hope of faith will be united. These two aspects of the life of faith will then no longer exclude each other. There is, to be sure, a tension between them. Faith lives in the present. If God is near and with us, then we live now in the Father's house. Life here on earth is not something indifferent and of less value, it is filled with significance and responsibility in the service of the heavenly Father. Every passing moment becomes from this point of view filled with eternal meaning. But faith places us also as "strangers and pilgrims" in this world, and it speaks of "those using the world, as not using it to the full" (I Cor. 7:31). Faith has "its citizenship in heaven" (Phil. 3:20). Faith is at home in this earthly sphere, because God is there; and faith is a stranger in the world because sin is there. But this inner tension does not mean that one of these viewpoints must curtail the other. These two aspects of faith strengthen each other. When faith "possesses" in a rich and full measure, its hope rises triumphantly. And conversely, when the hope of faith is living, its light penetrates into the present and transforms it so that the treasures of faith appear in a new and transfigured form.

Part IV

THE CHURCH OF GOD

DIVISION A

THE NATURE OF THE CHURCH

37. The Church as the Dominion of Christ

1. The finished work of Christ is the foundation of the church, and in and through the exaltation the church appears as his continuous work. The church is, therefore, the reign or dominion of Christ on earth (*regnum Christi*), as this is exercised and perdures until the consummation.

2. The church and Christ are correlative. Christ has become embodied in the church. Various biblical expressions illustrate this relationship: the church is "the body of Christ," "the vine," "a holy temple in the Lord."

3. The church is, therefore, a creation through the act of God in Christ. This may also be expressed in this way: the church is a fellowship created by the Holy Spirit. Since the church is a divine creation, its nature cannot be comprehended within sociological categories; it is revealed to faith alone.

1. The Dominion of Christ on Earth.

In the previous part we have spoken of the work of God in Christ. This work of God is accomplished in and through the church. The chapters which discussed the questions of God's act of forgiveness and his act of creating faith are therefore in a certain sense an introduction to the following discussion of the church of God and its work.

The problem of the relation between Jesus and the church

has long been a subject of discussion. There has been a wide difference of opinion. The exegesis which flourished at the beginning of the present century generally assumed a negative attitude. The church, so it was said, is a later creation which has no relation to the historical Jesus. But the attitude of present-day exegesis is different. The reasons for the attitude of the older exegesis were rooted in an unhistorical misjudgment of Jesus' messianic claims and their significance, and a similarly unhistorical interpretation of his work on the basis of personal points of view. The problem of the measure in which the church has its foundation in the teaching and work of Jesus, and the measure in which it corresponds to his intention, is a complicated question which cannot be discussed fully in this work. If we listen to what the exegetical research of the present has to say, it should be underscored that the solution of the problem does not depend entirely on the interpretation of those passages in the Gospels which speak directly of the church. It is much more important to note how frequently the idea of the establishment of a new fellowship, a new *koinonia,* occurs in the Gospel reports of Jesus' words and work, and how this idea characterizes the Gospel as a whole. It was Jesus' desire to gather and "organize" a new people, a true Israel of God, a *koinonia* prepared for the Kingdom of God. Among the great number of passages in the New Testament which deal with this subject we call attention to the following: Jesus as the bridegroom, the prepared wedding feast, the temple which is to be built, the cornerstone which is laid, and so forth. Some of his acts reveal the same intention: the call of the twelve, the commissioning of the disciples, the feeding of the five thousand, the last supper, and so on. The idea of the church as a communion and fellowship gathered around the Messiah is inseparably connected with the messianic idea. From this point of view it can hardly be denied that the church which appeared at Pentecost not only had its historic roots in Jesus' teaching and work, but that it also is consistent with his intention. The continuity between Jesus and the apostolic church is unbroken.

But however significant these historical questions may be, it is in principle much more important to note how inseparably the New Testament associates Christ and the Church. The decisive point in the question of the relationship between Jesus and the church is in the final analysis the fact that the foundation of the church is the finished work of Christ and that the church appears as a living reality in and through the exaltation (cf. § 27). The Christian church is the church of Easter and Pentecost. If the exaltation is the starting point of the continuous work of Christ, this continuous work is directly connected with the church, and the church is in the final analysis nothing less than this work continuing through ages and generations. We might state the matter thus: the church is the result of the finished work and is identical with the continuous work of Christ.

The church may therefore be defined as the dominion of Christ, *regnum Christi,* as this obtains under the condition of this life on earth. In § 27. 3 we remarked that according to the viewpoint of the New Testament that kingdom which Jesus accepted in and through the exaltation was of a universal character, but that it is concentrated in the church as far as life here on earth is concerned. When this reign of Christ is established, it means the beginning of a new age, a new aeon, the new "time of fulfillment." The old age remains, but in the midst of this old aeon the church as *regnum Christi* represents the new age. The church lives in this world, but is not of the world. It participates in two worlds. It is the messianic fellowship, the true Israel, the new covenant, *Kyrios-Christus* united with his own in the world. The church is thereby placed within the eschatological perspective and has its eyes focused on that consummation which is to come when the old aeon has definitely passed away and the glory of the Kingdom of God will be revealed. But even though the eschatological perspective is essential for the church, this does not remove or minimize the significance of the fact that the church already here on earth lives in that new age which has come as a result of the victory of Christ over those destructive powers which have kept men in servitude. To participate in *regnum Christi* is to live in that new age which because of the victory of Christ is the new age of life.

2. *The Church and Christ.*

The church and Christ belong together. They constitute an inseparable unity. The church exists in and through Christ. Just as the church cannot be conceived of without Christ, so neither can we think of *Kyrios-Christus* without his dominion and the connection with that fellowship which belongs to him. Where Christ is, there is the church. This proposition can also be reversed: where the church is, there is Christ. Fellowship with Christ is a fellowship with him in and through the church. *Christ has become embodied in his church.* Under the conditions of this earthly life the church is the mode of the living and active revelation of Christ. There he meets us and deals with us. One could even say, Christ is incarnate in the church.

This fact that Christ is embodied and incarnate in the church is the significance of the description of the church as "the body of Christ" which occurs so often in the New Testament. This figure, which to Paul is in reality much more than a figure, reveals in a concrete way the inseparable unity between Christ and the church, and tells us that Christ lives in and gives life to his church. When Christ in Ephesians and Colossians is called "the head" ["he is the head of the body, the church" (Col. 1:18)] the intention is not to designate that which separates him from the church, as has sometimes been suggested. "When the church is called the body of Christ and Christ the head of the church, the meaning is not to give *one* part to Christ and another to the church, but rather to emphasize their inseparable relation and unity. Christ is not merely the head, he is the head of the church. And the church is not merely the body, but the body of Christ. The body of Christ is Christ himself. The church is

332

Christ as he after his resurrection is present with us and meets us here on earth." [1]

We find the same fundamental view of the relationship between Christ and the church in a number of other biblical expressions such as the vine and the branches (John 15:5), and the church as a holy temple in the Lord: "Christ Jesus himself being the chief cornerstone; in whom each several building, fitly framed together, groweth into a holy temple in the Lord" (Eph. 2:20-21). In both of these passages the church is one with Christ, and he is at the same time the Lord and unifying power of the church. It may be added that all three of these figures express both the inseparable unity of the church with Christ and the Christian fellowship within the church. The body has various "members" which have different functions (I Cor. 12), but they all belong to one and the same body. The branches belong to one and the same vine and therefore have fellowship one with another. The stones of which the temple is built do not lie separated from each other. "As living stones" they are "fitly framed together." These figures speak, therefore, of the inner fellowship in the church. But everything depends on the fellowship with Christ. Fellowship with him is at the same time fellowship in the church.

3. The Fellowship of the Spirit.

The church as the dominion of Christ is the church of God. Its origin is in the finished *work of God* in Christ, and it perdures as the creation of the continuous *work of God* in Christ. On the basis of what we have already said about the relation between the Spirit and the continuous work of Christ (§ 28), the church as the dominion of Christ is at the same time a fellowship created by the Holy Spirit. These two definitions of the nature of the church must be considered as parallel. The gift of the Spirit and his work are the sign of the coming of the new age and of the

---

[1] A. Nygren, *Corpus Christi*, in *A Book about the Church* by Swedish theologians, p. 20.

fulfillment of the promise to the fathers. The Spirit is also the earnest of the coming consummation. That the church is a fellowship created by the Spirit emphasizes the eschatological perspective which is inseparably connected with the church.

The Spirit is, therefore, just as inseparably connected with the church as *Kyrios-Christus.* The Christian confession relative to the church in the third article of the Creed is a confession of faith in God the Holy Spirit who "calls, gathers, enlightens, and sanctifies," and thereby establishes a temple of "living stones" and creates that spiritual fellowship which is "the communion of saints." The confession of faith in the church does not imply, therefore, that it is a confession of faith in something in addition to God; or, in other words, that the church stands as some intermediate reality between God and man, or a magnitude coincident with God, so that faith would be directed in part to God, Christ, and the Spirit, and in part to the church. The confession of faith in the one, holy, ecumenical church expresses an essential and precious element in our Christian faith in God, because it confronts us with that activity of God which is the continuous work of Christ, and with that Spirit who calls, gathers, enlightens, and sanctifies.

Under these circumstances it would be misleading if, with Schleiermacher, we were to conceive of the Spirit as a kind of *Gemeingeist.* This would mean that faith is no longer concerned with the Spirit, but with the human spiritual life. The church is distinguished from all other "spiritual fellowships" because everything in it depends on the creative and sanctifying activity of the Holy Spirit. The church originates and grows in the measure that the Holy Spirit through the Word and the sacraments (cf. §§ 40-46) accomplishes the work of sanctification in the souls of men; or, in other words, as the forgiving and condemning love of God realizes itself. In this fellowship of the Spirit everything depends on the fact that God's love is allowed to rule. Luther describes very pointedly the inner life of the church when he calls it "a kingdom of grace," a *regnum gratiae,* and when in the

Large Catechism he asserts that the life of the church is characterized by "a continuous and unceasing forgiveness of sins, both that which we receive from God and that which we exercise mutually in forbearing and edifying one another."

According to this analysis the primary viewpoint of Christian faith relative to the church is that it exists as a divine creation in the world of men. Under such circumstances it is clear that one cannot rightly understand the nature and function of the church as long as one follows a sociological approach. If the church rests on the foundation of the finished work of God in Christ and the new age thereby introduced, and if the church exists in the world as the dominion of Christ on earth and a fellowship created by the Spirit, it would not only be unsatisfactory but directly misleading to define the church in terms of human endeavors and efforts. The church is then something entirely different from a mere human organization, or a human society and association for the satisfaction of certain religious needs and interests. Only the eye of faith can discover the innermost and deepest nature of the church. The church appears as a living reality only when faith directs its attention to Christ and discovers the inseparable connection and unity between his finished and continuous work and the church. From this point of view the historical communions are seen in their true light. But this will not lead to an idealization of these churches, nor to a romanticism which deifies the frail human reality and is blind to its defects. Faith's clear view of the nature of the church condemns unreservedly everything within the historical communions which does not bear the stamp of the activity of the Holy Spirit. Faith knows that these communions do not have and must not be given any other function than to serve Christ and his Holy Spirit. But it knows also that it is not a question of organizations and associations of men, but, in spite of all frailty and human weakness, we stand here in the presence of the dominion of Christ and the fellowship created by the Spirit —the Church of God.

38. One Holy, Ecumenical, and Apostolic Church

1. The one, holy, ecumenical, and apostolic church is that church which appeared as a living reality in and through the exaltation of Christ, and which since that time has perdured through ages and generations.

2. Since the church is the dominion of Christ, and since it has, therefore, only *one* Lord, there is only one church. The unity of the church is manifested in the Word and the sacraments. Consequently this unity is not a uniformity of organization, doctrine, or life. The various church communions are different expressions of the one, ecumenical church.

3. The holiness of the church rests on the finished and continuous work of Christ, which is the power sanctifying the church. It is not dependent on the subjective "holiness" of the members. The church is "a communion of saints" only through God's act of forgiveness.

4. The church is ecumenical because the act of God in Christ has a universal significance and purpose. This universality is expressed in the great commission: "Go and make disciples of all nations." The church exists as continually becoming. Its boundaries, which are continually shifting, are defined only by the extent of the activity of Christ, the Spirit and the Gospel among men. They cannot be fixed in such a way that definite limits are drawn around certain qualified individuals.

5. The church is called apostolic because that Gospel by which the church is built was given to it as an apostolic message, and because this message is continually proclaimed anew by other messengers following in the footsteps of the apostles.

1. The Living Church.

In the preceding paragraphs we have spoken of the church

as a church of God, a divine creation in history and in the life of men. That church which the old confession describes as one, holy, ecumenical, and apostolic church is not an abstract idea, or an "invisible" church, or the "essence" of the church, in contrast to another, concrete, actual, and historical church. It is not strange that such a distinction has been attempted. Men have looked at the various denominations and have found it difficult, not to say impossible, to apply to them the exalted predicates which the confessions ascribe to the church. The church ought to be one, but in reality it is separated into many denominations which have often bitterly fought against one another. The church ought to be holy, but its defects, weaknesses, and sins are only too apparent. The church should be inclusive and characterized by the open arms of the Father, but its actions have often been narrow and exclusive, and it has drawn limits which belie the claim to universality. When all this has taken into consideration, it has seemed natural to distinguish between two kinds of churches, and to place the ideal and essential church in contrast to the concrete, empirical, and historical denominations. The former would then be an invisible church, and in contrast, the latter a visible and tangible reality. This approach has been fairly common among Protestants during latter centuries, not least under the influence of Pietism, and the claim has sometimes been made that this represents simon-pure "protestant" Christianity.

These theories have had baneful results. They have not served to clarify but rather to obscure the problem of the church. But the most serious result of this division has been the dissolution and destruction of the consciousness of the church. The more "important" church, the invisible church of the essence, became nothing more than a pale and flimsy ideal, an abstraction; and the so-called visible church, the historical denominations, came to be regarded more and more as human institutions and organizations. This meant that the "visible church" lost (one could say was deprived of) more and more of its religious

337

content and its character as a church. The most evident result of this supposedly higher spirituality, which regarded it as unspiritual to apply these high predicates to the actual churches, was that these churches came more and more to be regarded as profane. The spiritual and "invisible" church had no living reality, and the "visible" church was no church at all.

The idea that these speculations about the church can find support in the Reformation is entirely false. Luther would have rejected them as spiritualistic errors. When he spoke about the visible and invisible church, the significance is something entirely different.[1] His view of the church was infinitely more realistic and absolutely free from such a depreciation of the actual, historical church. However sharply and violently he criticizes Rome, he can nevertheless say that the Roman church is "holy," because in this church there still remain "baptism, sacrament, the word of the Gospel, the Holy Scriptures, the churchly office, and the name of Christ and of God."

Neither does this theory of division have any support in the conception of the church found in the New Testament. Primitive Christianity knows nothing about two kinds of churches. It knew no other church than that of Easter and Pentecost, in which the apostles were the authorized messengers of the Lord and which brought the message of *Kyrios-Christus* out into the world. This church is "the body of Christ" and "a holy temple in the Lord." We have every reason to hold fast to the testimony of primitive Christianity. This primitive conception of the church corresponds accurately to the viewpoint of faith in general: faith finds the superhistorical and the revelation of God in history (cf. § 4), and it finds, therefore, also the dominion of Christ and the fellowship created by the Spirit in that church which was born at Easter and Pentecost and has continued its life through the ages. Faith knows of no other church. This does not imply an idealization of the church and its life (cf. §

---

[1] Cf. H. Olsson, *"Kyrkans synlighet och fördoldhet hos Luther,"* ("Luther's Teaching about the Visible and Invisible Church"), in *En bok om Kyrkan*, pp. 306-26.

37. 3); but it means that faith does not lose sight of that which belongs to the real nature of the church.

2. *The Unity of the Church.*

The church is one. The unity rests on the fact that the church is the dominion of Christ. The unity is a unity in Christ. There is no positive difference if this unity also be defined as a unity in the Spirit of Jesus Christ. The unity is given in the very existence of the church, it is, in other words, an existential unity. There may be different forms of Christian fellowships, but these do not destroy the existential unity of the church. This could be destroyed only if the church had several Lords. Since the church has only one Lord, *Kyrios-Christus,* and one Shepherd (John 10:16), the unity of the church is based on a secure foundation.

It is a different matter that this unity has been only partially achieved in the church. It has been hidden and damaged by schisms and contention. It is, therefore, the inescapable duty of the church to overcome these differences and to realize more and more fully the actual unity inherent in the church (cf. § 49). This twofold view of Christian unity meets us constantly in the New Testament; on the one hand an actual, inescapable reality; and on the other hand, exhortations to realize and preserve this real unity. Thus the Letter to the Ephesians exhorts the readers to "preserve the unity of the Spirit in the bond of peace"; and it does so on the basis of the unity which actually exists: "*one* body and *one* Spirit even as also ye were called in one hope of your calling; *one* Lord, *one* faith, *one* baptism, *one* God and Father of all, who is over all and through all, and in all" (Eph. 4:3-6).

The unity, which is an indestructible unity in Christ and his Spirit, manifests itself in that Gospel which has been entrusted to the church and by which it is edified. This Gospel appears in different forms, as Word and as sacraments. The reference to the Gospel as the basis of unity of the church does not imply, however, that another basis has been found in addition to Christ and the Spirit. The Gospel creates unity because Christ and the Spirit are active through the Word and the sacraments as "means."

The Word and the sacraments are the bearers of the unifying and homogeneous message which centers in *Kyrios-Christus*. This message can indeed be perverted by men, and such perversions cause schisms, injury, and havoc. But the Gospel remains. It cannot be changed by men and made into something else. It is and remains "a faithful saying" (I Tim. 1:15), and it appears, therefore, as the bearer of the unity of the Christian church.

Consequently, the unity of the Christian church is a unity in and through the Word and the sacraments. It is, however, not a unity consisting in organizational uniformity. The unity does not demand that the Christian church should at all times and in all places have identical forms and orders of organization. Even if this were the case, it would not in the least guarantee that unity which is essential and decisive for faith. On the contrary, *this* unity may exist under different external forms. This means only that the Holy Spirit can accomplish his creation of fellowship under various forms. To maintain the opposite would, according to faith, mean that we place the forms above the Spirit. The organization is important, but it is important only in so far as it serves as an instrument of the Spirit. The office of the ministry is one of the instruments of the activity of the Spirit through the Word and the sacraments, and because of this function it serves as one of the constitutive factors of the church (cf. § 46). In this capacity it belongs also among those factors which create unity in the church. But this does not mean that a demand may be made for uniformity in everything that belongs to the organization of the church, nor that the organization of the New Testament congregations should be regarded as some kind of ideal and as legal authority for all time to come. The organization of the church must rather have a certain amount of elasticity to adapt itself to changing conditions. The principle is then always that the organization must be of such a character that under various conditions it serves in the best possible manner as an instrument of the Gospel for the establishment of the fellowship.

The unity of the Christian church is not a uniformity in doctrine. The Gospel is the unifying factor of the church, but it is not a finally formulated, doctrinal authority. If a finally and irrevocably fixed system of doctrine were proposed as the basis of unity, it would lead to an intellectualized orthodoxy and a false objectivity. But such false objectivity invariably turns and becomes the exact opposite (cf. § 49).

Finally, the unity of the Christian church is not a uniformity of life. It is not a purely subjective matter. It is true that the nature of the life which God bestows upon men in and through the church is determined by God's act of forgiveness, and participation in this new life is, therefore, a participation in a common treasure. But this does not mean that the unity of the church demands an identity of experience and practice, or a fixed religious and ethical quality. As the light passing through a prism breaks into a variegated system of colors, so "the new life" appears in a variety of experiences and patterns of life. It cannot be imprisoned in a legal straitjacket. The demand for a uniformity in life is contrary to the variety of human life in the world and would serve to disrupt rather than to unify the church.

3. The Holiness of the Church.

As a dominion of Christ the church is holy. This holiness rests on the finished work which Christ makes effective through his continuous work. The holiness of the church is not an external, hierarchical, and institutional holiness, nor does it consist in the character of the members of a closed and limited society whose claim to holiness rests on their own qualifications. The holiness of the church depends entirely on that Holy Spirit who is active in the Church. If faith is to be certain that there is "a communion of saints" in the world, this certainty cannot be based on the existence of a relative degree of human holiness, and much less on any human perfection. Such a conception is contrary to the fact that the justified possesses no subjective holiness of his own; from the subjective viewpoint he is at the same time *iustus* and *peccator*. Just as faith's certainty of fellowship with God rests entirely on his forgiving love, so its certainty about the holiness of the church cannot rest on anything else than the saving power of divine love, i.e., God's act of forgiveness. With his intuitive insight Luther saw that what is here determinative for the individual life of faith is also determinative for the church. In the large commentary on Galatians he declares that the confession of faith in a "holy" church is a confession of faith in the victory of Christ. Luther vigorously distinguishes between the view of faith and empirical perception. Only faith can see the holiness of the church. "Reason and the eyes" perceive the imperfections of Christian life and conclude that the church is unholy. But, says Luther, "I deny the truth of this conclusion. If I look at myself or my neighbor, the church would never appear holy. But if I look at Christ who reconciles and sanctifies it, the church appears as entirely holy, for he has taken away the sin of all the world." [2] We may add another word from the same source, where Luther says that the reason for the holiness of the church is that we "have God's work among us, i.e., the word and the sacraments, and these make us holy." [3] It is not a question of a holiness of our own or of the church itself, but of the fact that there are powers which sanctify us. When in this connection Luther points to the Word and the sacraments, it is significant that he thinks of these as powers in action. They are not conceived of as an inalienable treasure belonging to us, as they are apt to be considered as soon as "the means of grace" through which the Spirit works are interpreted in a more or less mechanistic manner (cf. § 40). The

[2] W. A., 40, 1, p. 445.
[3] *Ibid.*, p. 70.

church exists where men are being "sanctified," and where the Spirit is active through his "means." The holiness of the church rests on the activity of this Spirit, and on nothing else. In the midst of everything in the world that seems to belie the existence of a holy church, faith is certain of this holy church, because it perceives the continuous activity of Christ and the Spirit who fulfill God's loving will and in so doing build and sanctify the church.

If the church is holy, it implies that it is "not of this world." "The holiness" places us in the presence of the other-worldly, eschatological perspective. The church lives and works in this world. But it is not of this world. "The holiness" stands guard against all tendencies to confine it within this world and transform it into a power coincident with other earthly powers. The temptation to do this lies near at hand. The intentions may be most generous, pointing to the many earthly tasks which confront the church of Christ. The temptation is that the church becomes absorbed in and limited to the affairs pertaining to this world. But the "holy" church cannot be merely a society for the promotion of better social conditions, and the like, or a proponent of a future social utopia. That holiness stands guard against such tendencies does not mean that the pressing problems of this world are not important for the church. It is rather connected with the insight that the ability of the church to serve the purposes of divine love and righteousness here on earth depends entirely on the fact that the church is "not of this world" and that its "citizenship is in heaven."

4. The Ecumenicity of the Church.

The church is ecumenical or *catholic* because the finished work of Christ is universal. "God was in Christ reconciling the *world* unto himself" (II Cor. 5:19). Both the finished work and the continuous work of Christ are universal in character. This is seen clearly in "the great commission" according to which Jesus sends out his messengers to make disciples of all nations.

The Spirit working through the Gospel wants to penetrate as far and as deeply as possible into the human world, and his activity does not stop before any boundaries of time or space. He is no respecter of persons. "There cannot be Greek and Jew, circumcision and uncircumcision, barbarian, Scythian, bondman, freeman; but Christ is all, and in all" (Col. 3:11). The ecumenicity of the church expresses the universal scope of the victory of divine love in Christ, of the reconciliation of the world, of the free access to forgiveness, and of the open arms of the Father.

"Ye are all one in Christ Jesus" (Gal. 3:28). When, therefore, all boundaries of race, religion, and social status are eliminated it means that there is a universal brotherhood in the church. "One is your teacher, and all ye are brethren" (Matt. 23:8). "Through him we have our access in one Spirit unto the Father" (Eph. 2:18). The gift is the same for all. The access to the Father is the same for all. All are called to the family of God. No one has preference before the other. No one has any occasion for boasting. It is true of everyone that he possesses nothing which has not been given to him as a gift of grace alone.

Since the ecumenicity of the church implies a universal purpose which does not cease as long as life on earth lasts, it means that the church is continually in a state of becoming and of change. Christian faith cannot, therefore, draw any boundaries around the church. About this problem of boundaries the Christian faith can say nothing more than that the church extends as far as the activity of Christ, the Spirit, and the Gospel reach, that the church of God is being established where the Spirit of Christ is active, and that because of this work of the Spirit the boundaries of the church are continually changing. It might seem that the result of this conception would be the blotting out of the boundaries of the church, but in reality this definition is the only one which does *not* erase these boundaries. All other boundaries are imaginary. If an externally fixed boundary is substituted for that which is fixed by the activity of the Spirit through the Gospel, faith would interpret this as a removal of the actual and decisive boundary.

The church cannot, therefore, be defined, as it were, from below on the basis of the individuals who belong to it. Such a sociological point of view which fixes certain human qualifications as prerequisites for the formation of the church have lost sight of that which according to faith is the creative and constitutive factor of the church as a creation of God. This conception assumes, consciously or unconsciously, that the church is a society, an association, an organization of certain qualified persons. Their right to membership in the church would rest on their own qualification. In principle it makes no difference whether these qualifications are understood in one way or another. One may, for instance, say that the church is the sum total of all true believers, and thus make the Christian confession the principle governing the formation of the church; or the boundary may include all who have been baptized. In the first case the qualification is "true believers," and in the second "baptized." [4] In either case this represents a different conception of the church than that which came into being at the inception of the Christian church. In both cases limitations are imposed which encroach on the universality of the church. Just as it is true to say that everything in the church has its center in faith, because the center is Christ, so it is false to assert that the church can be built on the human qualification of personal faith, or that the church may be defined as the sum total of all true believers. Just as it is correct to say that baptism is an act of God through which he creates the church and that we become members of the church through baptism, so it is wrong to say that the church is the sum total of all baptized. The church is not the sum total of the believers, nor of the baptized. It is the dominion of Christ on earth and the fellowship created by the Spirit (cf. § 39. 2, regarding membership in the church).

---

[4] Cf. R. Josefson, *"Kyrkan och dopet,"* ("The Church and Baptism"), in *En bok om kyrkan,* p. 333.

We may add here a remark about the word catholicity. The "catholicity" of the church is the classical Christian expression of the universality of the church. But in evangelical usage the word "catholic" has unfortunately become associated exclusively with the Roman church. That this glorious appellation of the church has been reserved for the Roman communion represents a certain danger in view of the power of language over thought. It has tended to weaken the consciousness of evangelical Christianity as being an expression of that which is universally Christian. That the Roman church cannot claim to be the sole representative of the universality of the church is perfectly clear. The various denominations are all members in that one, holy, catholic, and apostolic church, because and in so far as the constitutive factors are active in each one.

5. *The Apostolic Church.*

When the ancient confession calls the church "apostolic," it has reference to a constitutive element of the Christian church. This name implies first of all a reference to the significance of the apostles as the authorized messengers of the Lord and of the fundamental work which they accomplished. The sure and unchangeable Gospel which has been entrusted to the church and by which the church lives was given to it as an apostolic message. But the word apostolic tells us also that the Gospel needs messengers for its activity. It is not accidental, or simply a matter of convenience, that the church has a ministerial office in the service of the Gospel. Such a service is essential for the church and belongs to its nature (cf. § 46). The apostles were the first messengers of the Lord. But the message must thereafter be carried on further. When the church is called apostolic it implies a twofold perspective. It means that the Word is a living word, proclaimed continually by new messengers; and it emphasizes also the apostolic continuity, the unbroken connection in the life of the Christian church.

39. The Church and the Christian Life

1. The Christian life exists in and through the church. The individual Christian is not isolated, nor is he antecedent to the church. The church is "the mother who bears and fosters every individual Christian."

2. Membership in the church rests on the call of God, not on human qualifications. It is realized and actualized in the measure that man becomes what God's call intends him to be: a living member of the body of the church.

1. *"The Mother Who Bears and Fosters*
   Every Individual Christian."

All Christian life has its roots in the fellowship created by the Holy Spirit, or, in other words, in the church. The church is, therefore, according to Luther's well-known words in the Large Catechism, "the mother who bears and fosters every individual Christian." This statement expresses in a forceful way the dependence of the individual Christian on the church and the antecedence of the church in reference to the individual believer. Whether we are concerned with the beginning of faith or its continued existence, the relation to the fellowship created by the Spirit is of fundamental importance. The church appears as the bearer of the divine revelation which continues in and through the activity of the Spirit, because the church itself is created and maintained through this living and active revelation of God. The church meets and enfolds the individual as a *solidary interrelationship* of blessing (cf. § 31. 1) which is opposed to and struggles against the solidary interrelationship of sin. This interrelationship of blessing is, to use an expression from the Gospels, that holy fire which Christ has lighted and which burns unceasingly in the world. It need hardly be said that when the church is described as an interrelationship of blessing and a kingdom of grace (cf. § 37. 3), this does not mean that faith is

347

concerned with something human, or with a purely human "spiritual life"; it is concerned only with that Holy Spirit who creates this interrelationship of blessing and thereby brings man to Christ in order that man might find in him the One who continually realizes the redemptive activity of divine love. That the man of faith is dependent on the church is the same as saying that he is dependent on Christ who is active in the church. The church cannot be separated from Christ any more than Christ can be separated from the church. Faith does not find Christ *outside* of or coincident with the church as the interrelationship of the divine blessing, but rather *in* this interrelationship. There is no room here for a proposition that would compel us to choose between Christ and the church. It is just as meaningless to predicate Christ without the church as to affirm the church without Christ. The former would mean that we seek the living among the dead; and the latter, that we take the soul away from the church and thereby destroy its life.

The character of the church as "the mother who bears and fosters every Christian" has often been obscured by the so-called individualistic movements. It is understandable that such movements have appeared as a reaction to institutional and legalistic reinterpretations of the idea of the church. Against the institutional conception a subjective reinterpretation of the idea of the church has appeared, which places the individual Christian life as antecedent to the church and regards the church as an association of a greater or smaller number of individual Christians. In evangelical Christianity "individualistic" ideas have often appeared which obscure the actual significance of the Christian fellowship. It has even been asserted that the essential meaning of the Reformation was that the emphasis was shifted from the church to the individual. That this is a gross misinterpretation of Luther's view is clear from the words already quoted from the Large Catechism. That such a misinterpretation could appear may be explained in part as due to the varied meanings of the word "individual," and also to the fact that "individualistic Christianity" has been interpreted to imply an assertion that in the relationship between God and man we are dealing with a relationship between "God and the soul," as Augustine expressed it, or, in other words, an immediate and direct relationship between God and man. If, however, the word individualism is used in its ordinary meaning and individualistic Christianity is made to imply that the individual is independent of the church, that he is isolated from the fellowship with others, and that he is antecedent to the church, such an individualism is unrealistic and contrary to the conditions under which faith lives. "Individual Christianity" is in reality a *contradictio in adjecto*. The Christian life in faith is not isolated from the fellowship; it lives and is nourished, "is born and nurtured" in that solidary interrelationship of blessing which the Holy Spirit creates through the ages. He who desires to separate himself from this relationship condemns himself to exist on a very restricted diet. In fact, such a course indicates an egocentric isolation, self-sufficiency, and "inclination toward self" which is the very opposite of faith. We may, therefore, state the following propositions as self-evident. If individualism means isolation of the individual, it is in reality that sin from which man is delivered in and through faith. If individualistic Christianity means that from the point of view of the individual Christian the church is secondary, such a conception is to faith unrealistic and contrary to the actual conditions under which faith lives.

In view of this relation between the church and the individual it must be said that Schleiermacher's famous formula of the relation between "Catholicism" and "Protestantism" is not very illuminating. "The antithesis between Protestantism and Catholicism may provisionally be conceived thus: the former makes the individual's relation to the church dependent on his relation to Christ, while the latter, contrariwise, makes the individual's relation to Christ dependent on his relation to the church." [1] According to this formula the church in Protestantism would be

---

[1] Schleiermacher, *op. cit.*, p. 103.

secondary in relation to faith, and the emphasis on the church as primary would be characterized as something specifically belonging to Rome. Much unrealistic, "Protestant" individualism has been dependent on this formula of Schleiermacher. That it is completely contrary to the words of Luther which we have quoted is apparent, and even on that basis we may assert that Schleiermacher has not expressed the relationship which is characteristic of evangelical Christianity. It is remarkable that his formula is really contrary to what he himself says in another place in his work. He asserts that the difference between evangelical and Roman interpretation of Christianity must not be stated so that the Roman emphasizes the priority of the fellowship and the Protestant stresses the individual life in faith, because the antithesis lies in the different conceptions of the nature both of the individual and the church's life.[2] The antithesis in regard to the conception of the church appears especially in the fact that Rome identifies the Christian church with the Roman Catholic church.

2. *Membership in the Church.*

Membership in the church rests on the call and election of God. The words of the Lord in the Gospel of John apply to the whole church: "Ye have not chosen me, but I have chosen you" (John 15:16). No one has received or can receive membership in the church in any other way. This call and election occurs especially through baptism. Baptism is a concrete and evident expression of God's call and an act through which man is consecrated to participation in the church of God. As baptized persons we possess our Christian membership in and have been incorporated into the church. But this aspect of baptism as the fundamental act of God through which he creates the church does not mean that the call of God is inseparably connected with baptism so that he could use no other means. It is clear that the call of God can also come through the Word. The church can-

---

[2] *Ibid.*, p. 360.

not, even from this point of view, be identified with the sum total of the baptized. But in whatever way the call of God meets man, it is unquestionable that, as far as faith is concerned, man's membership in the church rests on nothing but the call and election of God.

We have already stated (§ 38. 4) that membership in the church rests on no human qualifications of any kind. This must now be further clarified. It is clear that the conception of the church which holds that membership in the church is bestowed through God's call is of a different character from that which conceives of the church as an association of people with certain definite religious qualifications and achievements manifested in faith, confession, and conduct. Underlying these various notions are the intentions of producing as far as possible a "pure" church, a church made up of true believers and persons with a true Christian experience, in contrast to the church as "a mixed fellowship." This conception implies that, by becoming a personal Christian, man becomes a participant in the church. If this line of thought is consistently carried out, the result would be that membership in the church becomes dependent on what can be determined in regard to a person's Christian life and whether this person's Christian experience is of such a character that it can be accepted.

It is clear, however, that this conception of the church is not consonant with but rather foreign to that conception of the church which we find in the New Testament. Here we do not meet the idea of a "pure" church in the sense previously indicated, nor the idea that certain distinct qualifications constitute the basis for membership in the church. In regard to the former it may be sufficient to refer to the parable of the tares among the wheat, where the idea of establishing a congregation of only "sanctified" and "pure" members is definitely rejected. "Wilt thou then that we go and gather them up? But he saith, Nay; lest haply while ye gather up the tares, ye root up the wheat with them. Let both grow together until the harvest" (Matt.

13:28-30). We hear sometimes of the conception that the so-called pure church is the ideal, but that actual conditions are such that it cannot be realized. The later part of this statement is undoubtedly correct, but according to the New Testament a pure congregation is not an ideal to be sought during this earthly existence. It is rather a utopia; and, what is worse, a utopia that is dangerous and fatal for the Christian church.

Nor do we anywhere in the New Testament meet the idea that a person can qualify for membership in the church by any religious achievements. If we desire a really decisive proof of how foreign this idea is to the New Testament, we need only consider the account of Jesus' relation to the children and his word that to such belongs the Kingdom of God (Mark 10:13-16; 9:33-37). When Jesus admonishes the disciples to become as little children, it does not mean that he ascribes certain qualifications to children. On the contrary, it is perfectly evident that the children have no qualifications and that they receive their place in the Kingdom only through the call of God. Consequently, the baptism of children is fully consonant with the whole spirit of the Gospels (cf. § 43). Jesus does not as a rule issue his call to those who are properly qualified; he had come, not to call the righteous, but sinners. A theory which would place human qualifications as the foundation for membership in the church is not only foreign to the New Testament, it is contrary to the fundamental view of salvation which is there presented.

But what we have now said about the conception of the church and membership in the church must not be so interpreted as to obscure and depreciate faith, confession, sanctification, and a life of service in love. The idea is sometimes advanced that the conception of the church which makes membership dependent on definite religious qualifications places a stronger demand on the Christian life than that conception which starts with the call of God. But this represents a false statement of the problem. Through the call of God the Christian is incor-

porated as a living member in the body of Christ. He is called
to realize and actualize this membership. The relation between
the gift of membership and the obligation it imposes meets us
in the words of John 15:16: "Ye did not choose me, but I chose
you, and appointed you, that ye should go and bear fruit, and
that your fruit should abide; that whatsoever ye shall ask of the
Father in my name, he may give it you." The call of God and
his reception of man into the fellowship of his church confront
man with the most serious obligations. There is no challenge
greater than that which comes from God's revealed will to receive man into fellowship with himself in the church (cf. § 47).
To change the question of the conception of the church into a
question of stronger or lesser demands is to by-pass the heart
of the matter. It is not a question of an antithesis between a
stronger or weaker emphasis on faith, sanctification, and the
service of love, but of something entirely different, viz., the foundation of our membership in the church and how this membership is obtained. This foundation, at least as far as the New
Testament is concerned, is not human achievements, but God's
call and election in Christ through the Word and the sacraments.

DIVISION B

THE CONSTITUTIVE FACTORS OF THE CHURCH

40. "The Means of Grace"

1. The activity of the Holy Spirit which creates the church takes
place through "the means of grace." These constitutive factors
of the Christian church are God's holy Word, the sacraments,
and prayer.

2. "The means of grace" must not be understood in a mechanical
way as factors which as a third element stand between God and
man. Anything which to the Christian faith is "a means of
grace" is so only because and in so far as the love of God thereby
enters into a direct relation to man.

3. The conception of the means of grace possesses both elasticity and stability. On the one hand, the boundary of the means of grace cannot be externally drawn, and on the other hand, all means of grace are defined by the work of Christ.

1. The Constitutive Factors of the Church.

In the preceding discussion the church has been defined as the dominion of Christ and as a fellowship created by the Spirit. The essential nature of the church is thereby indicated. No other definition can supersede this interpretation or come into conflict with it. If we speak of the church as "the communion of saints," the significance of this phrase becomes clear only when we note that it does not refer to any subjective holiness which might serve as a starting point for the establishment of the church. The church can be called the communion of saints only because the Holy Spirit here accomplishes his sanctifying work in the world. The phrase, "a fellowship created by the Spirit," indicates that which is essential for the Christian church, if we thereby maintain that this Spirit is the Spirit of Jesus Christ, and that the Christian church through this creation by the Spirit is also a creation of the finished and continuous work of Christ.

Even though the nature of the church is thus clearly indicated, it is necessary to define more closely those factors which are essential to the work of the Spirit and which therefore have a constitutive significance for the church. Theology has commonly called these constitutive factors of the church the "means of grace." Several well-founded objections may be made against the use of this phrase. It has become apparent that it has given rise to a certain mechanistic conception of the ways in which the Spirit of God works in the creation of the church. The very expression *means of grace* easily leads to the view that we are here concerned with something separated from the divine Spirit, or with some external means which the Spirit employs. But the phrase also has the merit of emphasizing that the purpose of everything in the church is the establishment of "the kingdom

of grace" (§ 37. 3), a kingdom in which God realizes the dominion of his love. The phrase may be used, therefore, as long as
it is clear that the Spirit is not separated from the means of
grace, but constitutes their living power (cf. § 2).

When we try to identify these means of grace and centers of
power in the church, we encounter various conceptions within
Christianity. The Roman church has usually referred to the sacraments as the essential, not to say the only, means of grace.
The older evangelical theology has generally emphasized two
chief forms of these means: the Word and the two sacraments,
baptism and the Lord's Supper. It is evident that this evangelical definition, which does not limit the means of grace to the
sacraments, but strongly emphasizes the significance of the Word,
contains a richer and broader view. The truth of this affirmation
is evident when we note the classical statement of Luther about
the Gospel and its various forms in the Smalcald Articles (III,
4): "God is superabundantly rich in his grace. *First*, through
the spoken word, by which the forgiveness of sins is preached
in all the world; which is the peculiar office of the Gospel. *Secondly*, through Baptism. *Thirdly*, through the holy Sacrament
of the Altar. *Fourthly*, through the power of the keys, and also
through the mutual conversation and consolation of brethren."
Two things are worth noting in this statement by Luther: first,
that Luther does not, as was done later in orthodox scholasticism, limit the Word simply to the Bible, but strongly emphasizes the "spoken" and living word, the word as proclaimed; and,
second, that he adds to these other means of grace also "the
mutual conversation and consolation of brethren," or that means
of grace which Pehr Eklund used to call "the word of conversation." [1] There are, of course, some real dangers connected with
this idea of Christian conversation as a means of grace. The
danger is that the attention is drawn to something merely human.
As far as Christian faith is concerned it is axiomatic that nothing
can be a means of grace except that through which we encoun·

---

[1] Pehr Eklund, *Evangelisk Fadervärsdyrkan*, p. 285.

ter *God's own grace*. Nevertheless, it is entirely appropriate to speak of "conversation" as a means through which the grace of God is active. The dangers should not eliminate the correct use of this idea. The question is not about some human work as such, but only about that grace of God which is active in human weakness (II Cor. 12:9). In this sense one can say, in agreement with the intention of Luther, that the Word as a means of grace appears also in the form of "conversation."

But to these two chief forms—the Word and the sacraments —we now add a third: prayer. Even though theology in general has not regarded prayer as one of the chief forms of the means of grace, it cannot be seriously denied that prayer is an essential "mark" of the church, or, in other words, a center of spiritual power, nor that in reality it must be regarded as a means of grace. In this respect we may join with Schleiermacher in *Der christliche Glaube,* when in the section dealing with "the essential, unchangeable, and fundamental features of the church" he closes his exposition of the means of grace with a section on the subject, "prayer in the name of Jesus." The reluctance with which prayer has been regarded as a means of grace has doubtless been due to the fact that prayer has been interpreted as an exclusively human act in which man turns to God, and therefore, it is argued, prayer cannot have the character of a means of grace. It is quite evident, however, that this argumentation is not very cogent, since prayer is not only our turning to God, but also God's approach to us, and a mode through which God accomplishes his loving will (cf. § 45). It is therefore a means of grace. It should be added that the real character of prayer becomes apparent only when it is regarded as a means. Prayer is a real prayer only when it is an approach of God to us. If on the contrary it were only our turning to God, it would not be prayer in the real Christian sense.

2. The Means of Grace as the Form
of the Immediate Activity of the Spirit.

We have already stated that the expression, means of grace, tends toward a more or less mechanical conception of the work of the divine Spirit. The means of grace are understood as a third element which stands between God and man; while in reality these means are nothing less than the modes of God's immediate fellowship with man. In the history of Christianity we may note a certain conflict between a mechanical conception of the means of grace and an opposition to the idea of any kind of means. This latter viewpoint asserts that the conception of means of grace tends to destroy the immediacy of the Christian fellowship with God. Man does not really come directly to God, but comes in contact with certain "means of grace" which take the place of God. Thus the question can arise: does God work immediately or through means? The fanatical, mystical, and spiritualizing approach holds to the first of these alternatives. It can easily be explained why this opposition to the means of grace has appeared again and again within Christianity. The cause is that hardened and mechanical conception of the means of grace which has appeared not only within the church of Rome but also in evangelical theology and which utimately rests on a conception of God as an extra-mundane being who sits enthroned in exalted majesty and therefore can deal with men only through some intermediary means. But the Christian faith has had good reasons to reject a conception which gains immediacy for the relationship between God and man at the price of surrendering the means of grace. This way leads to a suppression of the living revelation, not to the desired immediacy. The danger is that the relation between God and man loses its content, and that we cannot escape from the charmed circle of our own ego. The mechanical conception of the means of grace cannot be replaced by negations, but only by a deepened insight into the character of these means. It will then become apparent that this problem is not actual and that God works immediately when

357

he works "through means." The idea that the means of grace could be understood as an independent factor between God and man is completely foreign to faith. The means of grace are nothing but those modes through which God continually realizes his loving will. In the means of grace God does not merely give certain gifts, he gives nothing less than himself. Wherever faith encounters a means of grace, it encounters God himself, who is the immediately and effectively active God. The means of grace tell us that God is not only the distant and hidden God, he is the living God who is active in the present and works "immediately" wherever he works. Therefore Christian faith is opposed to a false conception of the means of grace on two fronts: it rejects a mechanical objectivity, and also a spiritualizing dissolution of the means of grace.

3. The Elasticity and Stability of the Means of Grace.

It is clear from the previous discussion that the means of grace possess a relatively high degree of elasticity. Christian faith has no interest in circumscribing the compass of the means of grace. On the contrary, it must oppose all such attempts, inasmuch as it would inevitably eventuate in a diminution of the rich connotations inherent in the concept of the means of grace. In regard to the elasticity it may be said that there is a certain degree of difference between these means, since this elasticity is less marked in the case of the sacraments. But the means of grace also possess a definite stability. If they cannot be circumscribed by external boundaries, they can so much the more readily be identified on the basis of that inner character which distinguishes them as means of grace. The stability in the concept of the means of grace rests on the fact that Christ is the Lord of the divine revelation and that the establishment of the church by the Spirit signifies throughout a realization of the reign of Christ. The Word as a means of grace, both the Scripture and the oral word, has its center in him who is "the Word." The sacraments are also inseparably connected with the work of

Christ. Baptism is a baptism in the name of the Father, the Son, and the Holy Spirit, and the Lord's Supper receives its content from that deed of Christ in which divine love became victorious through sacrificial self-giving. If the mutual conversation and consolation of the brethren is a means of grace, it is so because in this way the work of Christ is realized and in so far as these persons become something of "a Christ to their neighbors." And prayer as a means of grace is a prayer in the name of Christ. As such it is connected with the answer to prayer; or, in other words, as such it is God's approach to the souls of men. Christ is, therefore, the ruling power of the means of grace. We have already stated this by saying that the means of grace are the modes of the activity of the Holy Spirit, since the Holy Spirit is also the Spirit of Christ.

41. The Word of God

1. "The Word" as a means of grace is the self-impartation of divine love in the form of a message. This message authenticates itself as the Word of God through the testimony of the Spirit. The criterion is not that man autonomously decides what is "the Word of God," but, on the contrary, that the Spirit in and through the content of the Word subdues man and places him under "the reign of the Word."

2. In and through the incarnation of Christ, the Word of God is a word given once and for all, and anchored in the holy Scriptures. But in and through the continuous work of Christ it is at the same time living and continually active in the present.

3. The Christian conception of the Word as a means of grace must be distinguished from two extreme viewpoints: in the first place, from that approach which through theories of inspiration and proofs mechanizes the Word and ignores the fact that the Word comes to us in the form of human testimony; and in the second place, from that approach which conceives of man as

autonomous in relation to the Word and thus destroys the character of the Word as a divine message: the Spirit is separated from the Word.

4. The Word of God is in part law, in part gospel. Both of these are essential to the church. The church lives by the Gospel. But it must also guard the sanctity of God's law.

Excursus I. The position of the Old Testament is determined by the fact that the revelation of God in Christ at the same time fulfills and abrogates its testimony. The Old Testament is the prerequisite for the New, and the New is the standard for the interpretation of the Old.

Excursus II. The living and active Word appears also as "a word of conversation," in so far as it is given to the believer to be "a Christ" to the neighbor. If we speak of this as a means of grace, we are not concerned with something human, but with the power of God which is active in the weakness of men.

1. *The Word as a Message.*

When the Reformation through Luther emphasized the Word as the central means of grace in the church, this implied a new discovery as far as Christianity of the Middle Ages was concerned. The medieval church conceived of divine grace as being completely associated with and active through the sacraments. The Word was significant only as doctrine and law. It is noteworthy that when the theologians of the older Franciscan school presented the idea of the Word as "prevenient grace," they were thinking of that law which produces a certain contrition in man and thereby prepares him for the "real" grace which comes through the sacrament. Luther regarded the whole medieval conception of the means of grace as a degradation of the Word. It can be asserted that the entire work of the Reformation is connected with the discovery that the Word which God speaks to men is the means through which his grace, i.e., his condemning and forgiving love, comes to men. Even though this was a discovery of something that had been obscured in the Latin theology of the Middle Ages, it was nevertheless a rediscovery of that which is essentially Christian and from the beginning had constituted the center of Christianity, since in the primitive church everything was concentrated in "the Gospel."

The Word as a means of grace signifies for Christian faith the self-impartation of divine love in the form of a *message*. It is not simply a question of the impartation of a doctrine which man could theoretically appropriate, or that certain subjective "religious experiences" are induced by the Word. The Word appears as a divine message. It is important to emphasize this point of view in contrast both to an intellectualized reinterpretation of the Word and to a psychological dissolution of it.[1]

If the Word as a means of grace has the character of a message addressed to men, it must be further underscored that this message is to faith a direct expression of the voice of God speaking to men. It is not a question of an impartation of the divine and saving will through certain intermediaries; it is divine love itself which is active in this message and which in grace and judgment directly approaches men. The Word comes to man, not as a word from man himself, or originating within himself, but as a strange Word, a voice from "above." It comes indeed in the form of a human word, but it is not the word of men but of God himself. Faith does not receive the Word "as the word

---

[1] During recent times the concept of the Word has been the object of much theological research. The dialectic theology has used the Word as a principal concept, and has strongly emphasized that the Word is God's direct word to men, *senkrech von Oben*, which confronts man with the necessity of making a decision. It has turned its polemic especially against the psychologizing dissolution of the concept of the Word common in the theology of the nineteenth century (cf. E. Brunner, *Die Mystik und das Wort*; K. Barth, *Dogmatik I, Die Lehre vom Worte Gottes*). As far as Swedish theology is concerned, these conceptions of the Word do not contain anything new. Long before the rise of dialectic theology E. Billing, in his work, *De etiska tankarna i Urkristendomen,* and elsewhere had emphasized the character of the Word as a message. He conceived of the preaching both of Jesus and the apostles from this point of view. The view of Billing is preferable to that of dialectic theology, since in his conception the character of the Word as a means of *grace* is much more clearly expressed. The concept of grace is in fact weakened in dialectic theology, at least when this theology first appeared.

of men, but as God's word" (I Thess. 2:13; Gal. 1:11). God is in the Word. It authenticates itself as a divine word through "the testimony of the Spirit." "God must tell you in your heart: this is God's word" (Luther). The conviction does not come through any external demonstration. It occurs inwardly, because the Word comes with an authority which man cannot escape, and which overtakes and subdues man. The conception of faith in regard to what here occurs would be completely obscured if it were asserted that man himself according to his own pleasure decides whether or not he will accept the Word as the Word of God. According to the viewpoint of faith man has no standard whatever whereby he can presume to judge and decide whether or not a certain word is the Word of God. The "conscience" of man cannot be regarded as such a standard. Conscience cannot be the court of last appeal, nor can it render an infallible decision. On the contrary it must be said that conscience is captive "under the obedience to the Word." The authority is not in man, but in the Word itself. The Word confronts man with an authority from which there is no appeal. If man submits to the Word and receives it as a word from God, it is not on the basis of subjective discretion, but because he cannot escape its inner compulsion. The Word convicts through its own content and character. If faith says that the conviction comes as a result of the inner testimony of the Spirit, it is the same as saying that it occurs through the content of the Word and through its inner power. Because the Word is a direct expression of and actualizes the divine will, there is, in the words of the older evangelical theology, a *mystica verbi cum spiritu sancto unio intima et individua.*[2] The old evangelical theology was guided by a correct intention, which agrees with the viewpoint of faith itself, when in the Rahtmann controversy it rejected the idea that the word of Scripture contains God's will but not God's power, and that the power comes from the Spirit who works in the souls of men in co-operation with the Word. This was rightly

---

[2] Holazius, *Examen theologicum acroamaticum,* II, 452.

regarded as undermining the conception of the Word as a means of grace. This conception obscured the inherent and convicting power of the Word. The *way* in which this older evangelical theology maintained the presence of the Spirit in the Word, by its doctrine of verbal inspiration and the idea that the Spirit "apart from the use of the Word" dwells in it, was quite unsound and led to a mechanical conception of the means of grace. But the intention and purpose were legitimate. These theologians perceived that the character of the Word as a means of grace is intimately connected with the fact that the testimony of the Spirit cannot be separated from the convicting and subduing power which is inherent in the content of the Word and through which man is placed under "the government of the Word" (Luther).

2. The Sure and Living Word.

The active Word as a means of grace is at the same time a sure and living Word. The certainty of the Word rests on the fact that "the Word" has become embodied and incarnate in Christ. "The Word became flesh and dwelt among us" (John 1:14). The Word is certain both in the sense that its content is clear and definite, and that, as once and for all given, it remains steadfast and applicable to all times and generations (cf. I Tim. 1:15; II Tim. 2:11; Tit. 1:9). The incarnate Word is at the same time a living Word, not only because it appears in a living person, but especially because "Jesus Christ is the same yesterday, today, and even forever" (Heb. 13:8) or, in other words, because his finished work unceasingly becomes living and active in his continuous work (cf. §§ 27, 28). Both of these points of view, the Word as certain and as living, apply to the word of Scripture as well as to that oral message which Luther emphasized so strongly in the Smalcald Articles.

Since the Word is incarnate in Christ, it is anchored to the Scriptures. Christian faith regards the Word of Scripture as the fundamental and normative Word of God. The message which is proclaimed through the ages is received from and determined by this word of God. The dominant place which Scripture occupies in the Christian life of faith does not rest on theories which attempt to demonstrate the divine authority of Scripture, but its positive foundation is the fact that Christian faith is Christocentric, that Christ is the central content of Scripture, and that every message about the act of God in Christ is derived from and determined by the message of Scripture. To set aside the scriptural Word of God would be the same as setting aside Christ and the Word incarnate in him.

The New Testament has throughout the ages abundantly demonstrated its right to this foremost place. It has authenticated itself as the incomparable and inexhaustible source of power of the Christian church; one might be tempted to add, as a source which has become richer because it has been active in each generation. There has been no renewal of Christian life which has not received its power from the New Testament, and which has not *become* a renewal just because it received its power from this source. When Christian life has been removed from this center of power, it has been weakened and has lost its inner strength. This indicates more clearly than anything else the significance of the New Testament as the center of spiritual power for the Christian church. When the message of the biblical Word of God is not isolated but is seen in its connection with every living Christian message, the Bible demonstrates its superiority as the Christian Book of Life above all others and as the central Word of God.

3. Two Misconceptions.

The viewpoint of faith in reference to the Word as a means of grace must be distinguished from two misconceptions: a mechanistic objectivization and a spiritualistic dissolution.

The mechanical objectivizing of the Word appears as soon as the attempt is made to support or demonstrate the character of the Word as a Word of God by rational arguments, thus obscuring the fact that the Word always manifests itself in the form of a human testimony. We meet such a mechanical objectivizing in the theory of verbal inspiration, which originated in the Middle Ages and has been associated with all scholastic theology. But it appears not only in this special theory, but in all theories of inspiration in the measure that these involve a rational demonstration, thus obscuring the human aspect of the Word. This mechanical objectivizing is contrary to the actual attitude of faith and to the real character of the Word. It is contrary to the attitude of faith, since faith does not submit to the Word because its divine authority has been demonstrated, but because the power of the Word itself compels submission, or, in other words, because of the inner testimony of the Spirit. From the point of view of faith it is a completely foreign approach which obtains when Melanchthon and later scholasticism add to the testimony of the Spirit a number of arguments which are intended to support and prove the divine authority of Scripture. Here things are joined which do not belong together. Where the testimony of the Spirit is found, all other arguments are superfluous and irrelevant; and where it is not found, no other arguments can serve as substitutes. The mechanical objectivizing is contrary also to the nature of the Word, since the Word always appears as a human testimony. From the point of view of faith the Word has a twofold character. From one point of view it is in its entirety a human testimony. Scripture is a collection of historical documents of religion. But in the midst of all this human and incidental in these religious documents of man, faith discerns the divine voice, the Word of God, speaking with unconditional and inescapable authority directly from God to man. The Word of God comes in the "form of humiliation." These conditions under which the Word of God exists cannot be improved or overcome by any kind of theories of inspiration, or by arguments that are designed to protect the Bible from its "humanity." Faith always discovers the revelation of God in "secret," in the human covering that hides it. This universal and fundamental rule applies also to the Word of God, both in Scripture and in preaching.

The point of view of Christian faith with reference to the Word as a means of grace must also be distinguished from a spiritualistic dissolution of the Word. This approach may appear in various forms: as mysticism, rationalism, and humanizing idealism. However much these types may differ from one another, they have this in common that they in one way or another separate the Spirit from the Word. When this occurs, the Word loses its character as a divine revelation. The Word becomes a human word. The boundary between "the highest human" and the divine becomes uncertain, and the human becomes "autonomous" in relation to the Word of God. The supposedly higher immediacy of mysticism in the fellowship with God means in reality that "the divine" is sought and found in "the depths of the soul," consequently in "the highest human." In rationalism the eternal rational ideas inherent in the nature of man become the standard whereby "the Word" is measured and evaluated. Man appears as autonomous in relation to the Word also within the humanistic interpretation of Christianity influenced by idealism. There is no line of demarcation between the Spirit of God and the spirit of man. This is reflected most clearly in the fact that Christ is no longer regarded as the incarnation of the divine Word, but as the "religious archetype" of humanity, "the ideal man," who embodies in himself the religious and ethical ideal of humanity. The Word then ceases to be regarded as a strange word that comes to man and invites and compels him to submission.

4. Law and Gospel.

The Word of God comes to us as law and gospel. Both of these forms are connected with the Christian church, but in different ways. The law, as we have already pointed out, belongs to creation. It was an expression of the divine, creative will (cf. § 21). It was, therefore, in action "from the beginning." But the Gospel is in a different category. It has its foundation in God's "promises," but it appears as a living reality only in Christ and in his finished work. The Christian church is founded on the message of the Gospel. It is born of the Gospel. The Gospel is the power that gives it life. The Gospel and the church constitute, therefore, one inseparable unity. It is the Gospel which makes the church what it is. But this does not mean that the law is set aside, or that it has only a secondary significance for the church. In reality the law is just as indispensable to the church as the Gospel. This is due not only to the fact that the "justified" man is never only a "new" man, but during this earthly life is also the "old" man—*simul iustus et peccator*—and that as *peccator* he lives under the law and is subject to its accusation and judgment. It is due also to the fact that man's earthly tasks and his calling have been given to him by God and are the bearers of the divine law. The law has therefore a universal significance, and in reference to human society it becomes extremely important for the church to guard the sanctity of God's law. This obligation includes also the duty to interpret the significance of the divine law in accordance with the revelation of his holy will in the church (cf. § 48).

Excursus I. The Position of the Old Testament.

When the Christian church received the Old Testament into the biblical canon, it did not mean that the Old Testament occupied a position of equality with the New. The viewpoint of Christian faith in reference to the Old Testament rejects both the approach which would deny it a place in the canon, and that approach which places the Old on a par with the New. The relation of Christian faith to the Old Testament is twofold and determined by the fact that the revelation of God in Christ at the same time fulfills and abrogates the Old Testament testimony (cf. § 3. 4). Both of these aspects, the fulfillment and the abrogation, must be emphasized. The fulfillment expresses the fact that the New Testament stands in a positive relation to the

Old. The Old Testament is an introduction to the New. The way of the divine revelation in Christ goes through the Old Testament. Without the Old Testament the revelation of God in Christ could be without foundation and could not be understood in its essential significance. When the connection between the Old and the New Testaments has been severed, as in Gnosticism and by Marcion, it becomes clear that the fundamental Christian theme in the New Testament has been either dissolved or grotesquely reinterpreted. But on the other hand, Christian faith declares emphatically that the fulfillment of the law, the promise and the sacrifice, implies an abrogation of these three factors in their Old Testament significance. From the point of view of Christian faith, therefore, the New Testament becomes the touchstone for evaluating the Old. In other words, the Old Testament can serve as a means of grace within the Christian church only when it is illuminated by the revelation of God in Christ. It must under no circumstances be allowed to osbscure the new relationship between God and man created through the act of God in Christ, nor the Christian conception of God therein given.

Excursus II. The Word of "Conversation."

When Luther in the Smalcald Articles calls "the mutual conversation and consolation of the brethren" a form of "the Gospel" or a part of the Word as a means of grace, it indicates how vividly and richly he is able to perceive the work of the Holy Spirit. It cannot be said, however, that this valuable suggestion of Luther has borne much fruit within evangelical theology, at least not in earlier times. Post-Reformation scholasticism ignored this suggestion of Luther, with the result that its treatment of the concept of the means of grace became narrow and lifeless. The narrowing of the concept of the means of grace within the older evangelical theology can easily be explained. The explanation is to be found in its twofold opposition: to Rome and to the fanatics. Roman theology spoke in its way, through its theory of saints, about a means of grace in "conversation," even though it did not refer directly to the saints as "means of grace." Evangelical theology regarded Rome's attitude in regard to the saints as disastrous, especially since common piety did not respect, and was not asked to respect, the more reserved pronouncements of theology, but could freely turn its expressions of honor and reverence into a cult of saint worship. The opposition to "the fanatics" and their dissolution of the Word as a means of grace caused evangelical theology to concentrate more and more on a narrow definition of the concept of the means of grace. In contrast to Luther's emphasis on "the living Word," scholastic theology confined the Word as a means of grace to the Bible and conceived of this Word almost as a divine record or protocol. But in so doing "the mutual conversation and consolation of the brethren" disappeared as a means of grace, and evangelical theology could take only a negative attitude to the Roman doctrine of the saints. It was inevitable that the dynamic conception of the revelation and the means of grace was thereby obscured. If a purely negative attitude relative to the Roman doctrine of the saints involves the surrender of interests vital to faith, it is even more important that the means of grace through "brotherly conversation" is so defined that it corresponds to the characteristic viewpoint of faith and that the misleading and disastrous interpretation of Rome is removed. In the first place, we note that the Roman definition of saint is external, legalistic, and too narrow. The legal hierarchical authority of Rome decides on the basis of fixed rules what persons are to be regarded and venerated as saints. This involves not only a usurpation of a judgment which does not belong to man, but also an improper restriction of "brotherly conversation" as a means of grace. This must not be limited to certain persons who in one way or another are more prominent in the church. Faith is not concerned here only with certain spectacular and well-advertised deeds, but also with that which is done in secret by ordinary people who in a limited sphere have served to reveal the living God to their neighbors. If faith speaks about "saints" in connection with this "brotherly conversation," these can be described only as those who have been permitted to reveal clearly and fully that God is the living God.[3] In the second place, it is entirely foreign to faith to regard those who have been permitted to be something of "a Christ to the neighbor" as holy in the sense of being perfect. The decisive element is not a supposed human perfection, but that power of God which is active in human weakness (II Cor. 12:9). Those who in this sense have been and are "saints" would be very reluctant to speak about perfection. They have rather been most conscious of their sins and have clearly perceived their unworthiness before the Holy One. Faith accepts their testimony in regard to themselves, it knows that they speak the truth. In the third place, when faith speaks about this personal means of grace, there is no tendency toward worship of human beings. "The saints" do not attract attention to themselves, but desire that faith may see God who lives and works and thus "glorify the Father who is in heaven" (Matt. 5:16; cf. Ps. 147: 1-2). If they are a means of grace, it is because they are "a Christ to the neighbor," or, in other words, that the neighbor through them apprehends something of the blessings of divine love. It is true here also that God works directly even when he works through means, and even when he uses sanctified persons as means. That other people, for our comfort and consolation (II Cor. 1:3 ff.; Heb. 12:1), have been able to show to us something of the living God does not mean that our faith depends on them, so that it would be a secondary faith, a faith dependent on men. If God uses men as his instruments, it means that just in this way God comes directly to us, and that we believe, not on the basis of the words of others, but because we ourselves have seen (John 4:42).

42. The Sacraments

1. The sacraments are the self-impartation of divine love in the form of action. Among the holy rites which have been mentioned

---

[3] Cf. N. Söderblom, *Ett bidrag till den kristna uppenbarelsetrons tolkning*, p. 15.

in this connection two are of special importance: baptism and the Lord's Supper. Their special significance is not simply historical, but is due to the fact that both in their own way embody the central content of the Gospel.

2. The sacraments as means of grace do not mediate a different kind of grace from that received in the Word. Their significance lies rather in the peculiar form of these means of grace, and in the certainty and concretion with which the sacraments actualize the Gospel.

3. The Christian idea of the sacraments must be distinguished from two extreme views: partly from a mechanical materialization, and partly from a spiritualizing dissolution. In the former the grace of the sacrament becomes something other than the self-impartation of divine love, and in the latter the sacraments cease to be means of grace.

1. *The Gospel in the Form of Action.*

In addition to the Word as a means of grace certain holy rites or sacraments must also be included among the centers of spiritual powers of the church. These holy rites have occupied an important place in the Christian life from the very beginning. The exegetical research of the last few decades has emphasized this fact. When we come to determine which rites are to be here included, we must note that no unanimity on this question has been attained within Christendom. In the Orthodox as well as in the Roman church the number of sacraments has been fixed as seven: baptism, penance, confirmation, the eucharist, marriage, ordination, and extreme unction. In evangelical Christianity we find both an enlargement and a limitation of the concept of sacrament. On the one hand Luther speaks of the sacrament in such a wide sense that every deed whereby a man becomes "a Christ to his neighbor" can be called a sacrament. On the other hand, when it is a question of the sacraments as constitutive factors of the church, he restricts the number to baptism and the eucharist. During the early part of his life he often included penance as one of the sacraments, but already in *De captivitate babylonica* it is stated that penance cannot be regarded as a sacrament in the same sense as baptism and the eucharist.[1] In evangelical Christianity the concept of sacrament was restricted to these two acts. It may be worth noting, however, that in evangelical Christianity there are acts which correspond to all those which the Orthodox and Roman churches call sacraments, with the exception of extreme unction, which to a large extent has been replaced by the Lord's Supper.

When evangelical Christianity has thus restricted the sacraments to baptism and the eucharist, theology has usually defended this action, by asserting that only these were instituted by Jesus himself. But this assertion cannot without further consideration be regarded as decisive. The purely historical question whether baptism and the eucharist were directly instituted by Christ during his earthly life contains some uncertain elements. This applies not only to the institution of baptism which the Gospels do not ascribe to Jesus during his lifetime, but to the exalted Christ; but it applies also to the eucharist, since it may be questioned whether the act of the last evening was intended to create a permanent institution in the church, continuing generation after generation. From the purely historical point of view it is clear, however, that both baptism and the eucharist have a secure place in the Christian life from the very beginning, and that they occupy a really dominant place in the church. Both the Pauline and the Johannine writings testify that the Christian life was virtually constituted by the fact that Christians were baptized into Christ and that together they celebrated the Lord's Supper. The Christian life in the primitive church as far back as we can trace it is constituted and characterized by these two acts. No other rites can even approximately be compared with them.

[1] Luther, W. A., 6, pp. 549, 972.

But even if the secure position of baptism and the eucharist can be thus historically demonstrated, the decisive argument for these rites as constitutive factors of the church cannot rest on such historical considerations. If baptism and the eucharist as means of grace in the Christian church are to be established on a secure foundation, this foundation can be nothing else than the peculiar character of these holy rites and their inner connection with the fundamental fact of Christianity. Purely historical reasons cannot in the last analysis be decisive. Even *if* it cannot be historically and critically demonstrated that these rites were instituted by the historical Jesus, ordained and established by his teaching, it is not thereby proved that they do not belong within the church as its center of spiritual power. Even if it can be shown that the sacramental idea was widespread in the time of Jesus and that there are certain evident connections between the Christian sacraments and similar rites which are found outside Christianity, it is not thereby proved that the sacraments are invalid and should be rejected as means of grace. The question about the validity of the sacraments is not a question about the origin of the sacramental idea, its development, and the elements which are possibly to be found in the primitive Christian conception, but the question concerns the meaning which the sacraments have for faith and their significance for the Christian life of fellowship.

That which in the last analysis determines the Christian nature and legitimacy of the sacraments is nothing other than their own content. The criterion consists in this—that the sacraments in the form of action furnish a comprehensive expression of the central content of the Gospel and are organically connected with the work of Christ. The sacraments appear to Christian faith as the self-impartation of divine love in the form of action. The two principal features which, as we have already indicated (§ 14), characterize this divine love, are concreted in baptism and the eucharist. Baptism reveals the character of divine love as spontaneous and prevenient: it is the sacrament of prevenient love.

The Lord's Supper reveals the self-giving of divine love in the work of Christ: it is the sacrament of suffering and victorious love. When the essential significance of the two sacraments is thus defined, their Christian character is firmly established.

From this point of view the question of the divine institution of the sacraments appears in altogether new light. This question lies entirely outside the sphere of historical investigation. The divine institution cannot be demonstrated on historical grounds. But in the measure that baptism and the Lord's Supper express something which is fundamental in Christianity and thereby prove that they possess an abiding significance for the Christian fellowship, faith perceives them as divinely instituted and at the same time as instituted by Christ. Their abiding foundation and their legitimacy lie in the self-realization of the divine will in the work of Christ.

2. The Significance of the Sacraments.

When Christian faith regards the sacraments as means of grace, it does not mean that the saving work of divine love could not be realized without sacraments. Such a point of view could be maintained only if the gift which is bestowed through the Word would be regarded as of a different kind and less valuable than the gift given in the sacraments. The assertion that the sacraments are means of grace does not in the least curtail the other possibilities of divine love, a fact which the older evangelical theology clearly perceived.[2] But faith is not on this account led to despise the value of the sacraments. Faith is not interested in rationing the grace of God. It does not ask whether it is possible to dispense with one or the other of the means of grace; it asks rather what "means" the divine and loving will appears to use in order to realize its purposes. It finds that there is such a treasure in the sacraments as means of grace that the Christian fellowship cannot without detrimental effects neglect their use.

---

[2] *Non defectus sed contemtus sacramenti damnat.*

If we are to define the meaning of the sacraments as means of grace, we must first definitely assert that their significance does not lie in the fact that they mediate a special kind of "grace," or any other grace than that which comes to man through the Word. All attempts to attribute a special kind of grace to the sacraments lead to a weakening and disqualification of divine grace. Christian faith knows of no other grace than that which consists in the self-impartation of divine love, or, in other words, that God gives himself. It is therefore clear that the sacraments could not be regarded as means of grace unless it is a question of the self-impartation of divine love, and that all notions about other gifts do not imply an addition or a higher gift, but rather a subtraction and something less. Faith cannot think of a greater gift than God himself. In that gift all other gifts are included, and without this gift all others are from the point of view of faith of no value. The legitimate element in the oft-repeated statement of the old evangelical theology, *idem est effectus sacramenti et verbi* ("sacrament and Word have the same effect"), lies in the fact that the gift of both the Word and the sacrament is nothing else and nothing less than the divine love which saves and unites men to God. If, therefore, Christian faith cannot credit the sacraments with bestowing a gift different from that received through the Word, it is clear that their specific significance for the Christian life depends on that special form in which the loving will of God here is expressed.

The question of the significance of the sacraments for the Christian life cannot at this point be discussed in detail; the final answer must be given in the discussion on the significance of baptism and the Lord's Supper (§§ 43, 44). The general point of view should here be emphasized, however—that the importance of the sacraments is connected with the fact that the central content of the Gospel meets us *concentrated in the form of an act*. The uniqueness of the sacraments lies in the peculiar form, an act, but this form is important because the sacramental act reveals the inmost nature of the Christian Gospel. The significance lies in that certainty and concretion with which the sacramental act objectifies the Gospel. The Word as a means of grace manifests its richness by presenting the Gospel in the multifarious form of a personal testimony, but in the sacraments the loving will of God appears in the simple act, in a direct and certain form. This difference between the Word and the sacraments must not be emphasized too one-sidedly. If we say that divine love meets us as a message in the Word and as an act in the sacraments, these two forms must not be exclusively separated. In a certain sense the message of the Word is also an "act," and as a divine message it is the most powerful act of God. The sacramental act also has the character of a message. Just because this act reflects the inmost core of the Gospel, it is the most concentrated Gospel message which can be given. It is nevertheless proper to emphasize the peculiar character which the sacraments have because the divine and gracious will here expresses itself in active form.

Evangelical theology often speaks of the sacraments as a *verbum visibile*, "a visible word." The combination has the merit that it unites the Word and the sacraments, and emphasizes that the sacraments have the character of a message. It may be argued, however, that the formula, "a visible word," too strongly emphasizes the visual element, and that it does not call to attention the most essential character of the sacraments, viz., the action. If the Word is made the principal expression for the means of grace, it would be better to speak of the sacraments as "the Word of action." In regard to the treatment accorded the sacraments by evangelical theology, it can be said that it reveals a certain monotonous repetition. The theologians have been satisfied to emphasize the very important fact that the gift received in the sacraments is the same as that received through the Word without trying to analyze the significance of the fact that the Gospel here meets us in a concentrated form as an act.

It should also be noted that the sacramental act inseparably unites individual and congregational points of view. The sacramental act is always directed toward the individual, but it is at the same time a corporate act. These two points of view are also present in preaching, when sometimes one and sometimes the other point of view appears more prominently. But it cannot be denied that this union of individual and congregational viewpoints is constitutive for the sacraments. Baptism is an act concerning the individual child, but at the same time an act through which the church is established. The Lord's Supper edifies and strengthens the church at the same time that it concerns the individual believer.

3. Two Misinterpretations.

The Christian conception of the sacraments must be differentiated from two misinterpretations: from a sensuous mechanization of sacramental grace, and from a spiritualistic dissolution of the sacraments as means of grace.

The history of the Christian sacraments indicates clearly that from the very beginning there have been certain dangers in the direction of mechanization connected with the sacramental idea. It is also evident that these dangers originate outside Christianity. The most serious danger is that the sacraments are conceived of as working *ex opere operato,* i.e., through the mere performance of the act. Traces of this idea meet us already in Paul (I Cor. 15:29). This conception is always more or less connected with the idea that the sacraments work in a physical way, or, in other words, that the sacramental grace is reduced to a plane below the personal and spiritual fellowship with God. It is not the task of systematic theology to trace the influence of these "magical"[3] ideas on the sacraments through the centuries, which appear not least in the Roman conception of Christianity. Evan-

---

[3] In this connection it would be in place to utter a warning against a too facile use of the word magic. Later evangelical theology has been too ready to use this word. Its statements seem to imply that any thought of the presence of Christ in the Lord's Supper (cf. § 44. 4) must be branded as magical. But, as von Hügel rightly says (*Essays and Addresses,* p. 241): "Magic begins only when and where things physical are taken to effect spiritual results apart altogether from minds transmitting or receiving."

gelical Christianity has not escaped this influence. In spite of
the fact that from the beginning it was intent on guarding the
spiritual purity of the relationship between God and man, the
ex opere operato idea has not only stubbornly remained, but
even enjoyed a certain renaissance during the nineteenth century due to influences of an entirely different nature (cf., as far
as Scandinavia is concerned, Martensen's *Dogmatics*).

The mechanistic and materialistic conception of the sacraments arises when the sacraments are interpreted as "realistic"
rather than "symbolic." The divine grace becomes a substance.
The gift received is conceived of as something else, and therefore something less, than the self-impartation of divine love. A
dissolution of the character of the sacrament as a means of grace
occurs when the sacramental act is conceived of as "symbolic"
in contrast to "realistic." The emphasis is then placed on the
human activity as such and the sacrament loses its character as
a divine gift and an act of grace.

The sacramental act is to Christian faith at the same time a
symbolic act and a deed of God. When the question is asked:
are the sacraments symbols *or* are they real acts of God or of
Christ? the question itself is entirely misleading. It is not a
question here of an either – or, but of a both – and. The one
does not exclude the other. To maintain the "symbolic" view in
contrast to the "realistic" implies the abrogation of the sacraments as means of grace. To maintain the realistic in contrast
to the symbolic implies a materialization of the presence of God.
Neither of these approaches, the Roman or the extreme Reformed (Zwinglian), expresses the characteristic viewpoint of
faith. Just as all our words about God have a symbolic character, it is clear to faith that the same is true also of the sacramental acts. But this does not imply a denial of the real and
effective presence of the divine will. As far as faith is concerned,
the essential element is that the loving will of God realizes its
purpose in these symbolic acts.

43. The Sacrament of Prevenient Love

1. Baptism is an act of God's prevenient grace and therefore at the same time bears witness to the obligation of the Christian life to die from sin. The significance of baptism both as a congregational act and as an act directed to the individual lies in the fact that the essential content of the whole Gospel is concentrated in this sacrament.

2. Since baptism implies man's reception into fellowship with the Christian church, its principal form is the baptism of infants. Membership in the church is thus independent of all human judgments and dependent only on God's loving will. It removes all man-made hindrances from the way of fellowship with God, and is at the same time a living testimony to the obligation and responsibility of the church to care for and nurture the baptized.

3. The Christian idea of baptism must be distinguished from a mechanical interpretation of the effect of baptism, as well as from interpretations which nullify the primacy of grace.

1. The Significance of Baptism.

In the treatment of baptism systematic theology cannot enter into the problem of its origin, nor of its connection with more or less analogous rites outside Christianity. The interest is concentrated on the question of what is essential to baptism as a Christian sacrament, or, in other words, the significance of Christian baptism. If the legitimacy of Christian baptism shall be established, it must be done by showing that an inner connection exists between the act of baptism and that which is constitutive for Christianity. The act must reveal, not only something relatively secondary, but that which is fundamental. It must reveal the very essence of Christianity. Baptism does so by being the most unequivocal expression of that which theology since ancient times has called *God's prevenient grace.* What the sym-

379

bolical act of baptism demonstrates is nothing else, and nothing less, than God's love which is directed toward and seeks man. Baptism is an expression of the open arms of the Father. This act is symbolic, but its symbolical character does not exclude the fact that at the same time it is a real act of God. God uses this symbolical act to declare and realize his loving will. Divine love meets man in the act of baptism as "prevenient grace," or, in other words, the act of baptism testifies that God's love is always prevenient love (cf. § 14. 2). Baptism declares that this love of God directed toward us is the foundation of the Christian life, the only and sure foundation, and that our salvation out of "the power of darkness" and our fellowship with God is in God's hand and originates in his seeking and restoring grace. Baptism incorporates man into "the kingdom of grace." It signifies, therefore, a "regeneration," which does not imply, as in Pietism, a change in man, but a change in his status. But at the same time that it calls attention to the foundation of the Christian life, it demonstrates also that the obligation of his life is to die from sin, or, to use the biblical language, "to die with Christ" (Rom. 6). The gift which is contained in the fact that man is consecrated to divine love contains both a judgment against that which opposes the loving will of God and the obligation to overcome it. From this latter point of view baptism means, as Luther says, that "the old Adam in us, together with all sins and evil lusts, shall be drowned by daily sorrow and repentance, and be put to death; and that the new man shall daily come forth and rise, to live before God in righteousness and holiness for ever." We encounter, therefore, the whole of Christianity in concentrated form in the act of baptism with its gift, its judgment, and its obligation. Baptism is not connected simply with some individual Christian ideas, it is the essential element in Christianity which is embodied in the act. This central position of baptism is the starting point for the evaluation of its significance as a congregational act and as an act directed toward the individual.

2. *Baptism of Infants as the Principal Form of the Sacrament.*

The value which baptism has for the Christian life appears most clearly when it is regarded as a congregational act. From this point of view baptism means that man is received into membership in the church. It is an act which is significant for the establishment of the church. But the value of baptism as the means of grace that establishes the church can be fully appreciated only when baptism occurs in the form of baptism of infants. Infant baptism is from the point of view of faith far from a secondary or less worthy form; it is on the contrary its highest, purest, and most perfect form, that form in which its inner meaning is most clearly apparent. The nature of baptism is such that it should be an infant baptism, and it is as such that it demonstrates its inner power. No other form of baptism is so effective or so essential for the Christian life. Even *if* baptism was not originally infant baptism, it does not mean that the latter is a degeneration from a higher form. It means rather that the necessary congregational conditions were not yet present which would make it possible for baptism to develop its fundamental connotations in the form of infant baptism.

The reason that infant baptism must be regarded as the ideal realization of the idea of Christian baptism lies in the fact that infant baptism, more than any other form, demonstrates the reality and is the result of God's prevenient and unmerited love. The significance of infant baptism for the congregation lies in the fact that it shows how membership in the Christian church is based entirely on the loving will of God and consequently is entirely independent of the caprice of men. The foundation of the church is God's gracious will, and the church is, therefore, a fellowship created by the Holy Spirit (cf. § 37). Infant baptism demonstrates more clearly than anything else the seeking, inexhaustible, and unmerited grace of God. Nothing, therefore, can take the place of infant baptism as a means of grace through which the church is founded. Everything else is a substitute.

Situations may arise in which a substitute must be used, but it remains even at best a substitute.

As the creative factor of the church infant baptism removes all the man-made hindrances from the way to fellowship with God. It is the Magna Charta, which tells us that the membership of the individual in the church must not be made dependent on the examination and approval of men. No human caprice must be allowed to decide whether or not we may belong to the church of God. Infant baptism removes such guardianship and the heavy oppression which it places on the spiritual life. It testifies that our membership in the church of Christ does not depend on the approval and acceptance of our fellow-men, but is founded on the loving will of God. We belong in the church of God on this basis alone, and we obtain what we possess in the measure that the divine love subdues us and our fellowship with God is realized. It is possible that in our search and our spiritual struggle we may find the hearts of our fellow-men closed to us and the way of salvation obstructed by their precepts and ordinances. If we were then dependent only on human judgments, we would stand on the outside rejected. But infant baptism tears aside all these man-made hindrances, and testifies that we do not find the heart of God closed, and that even though faith is weak and the flame burns low, we nevertheless find room within the church of God.

But infant baptism is at the same time *the living conscience of the Christian church*. Infant baptism assumes that it is possible to bring the baptized person into contact with the Christian spiritual life, and it stands as a living testimony of the obligation of the church to bring about this contact. Where this possibility is not present, baptism cannot be practiced in its highest form as infant baptism.

When in the previous paragraphs we have endeavored to elucidate the value of baptism, especially infant baptism, our attention has been directed toward baptism as a congregational act. This has been done because the value of baptism as a means of grace is thereby most easily and clearly seen. By its removal of all man-made hindrances infant baptism expresses the open arms of the Father and serves at the same time as the living and responsible conscience of the church. But in emphasizing this phase there is no minimizing of the value which baptism has for the individual. On the contrary, this value is included in what we have said about its importance for the fellowship. Here no sharp line of demarcation can be drawn between individual and congregational viewpoints. A distinction can be made, however, between the value baptism has for a person who simply ignores it and for one who consciously takes his place within this means of grace. Whether the individual Christian considers this or not, infant baptism stands as the Magna Charta of the church and the individual, creating those conditions of fellowship which directly benefit the individual. This is the strongest possible proof of the significance of baptism as a means of grace. In the measure that the individual Christian assumes the place which baptism has given him, baptism appears both as an act of God's prevenient grace, and as an act of election and promise which is irrevocably secure and to which man can return again and again for renewed strength. But baptism also involves a great responsibility. He must take baptism and its gift seriously. Baptism makes the demand of conversion and repentance actual. It involves the obligation "to die with Christ."

Since infant baptism, therefore, gives most emphatic expression to the prevenient grace of God and consequently appears as the principal form of baptism, there can be no reasonable objection to its validity. The question whether infant baptism occurs in the New Testament is of relatively minor importance. There is nothing that actually contravenes, but much that clearly indicates that infant baptism belonged to the practice of primitive Christianity. The decisive element is that infant baptism is consonant with the whole spirit of the Gospel (cf. § 39. 2), as this spirit is revealed especially in Jesus' own treatment of the children in Mark 10:13-16. This pericope has a legitimate place in the ritual of baptism.

3. *The Delimitations of the Christian Idea of Baptism.*

The Christian idea of baptism must be distinguished from two misinterpretations: from that interpretation which speaks of the effect of baptism as mechanical and deals in ideas which lie below the spiritual plane; and that which speaks of the human prerequisites for the reception of the grace of baptism in such a way that it abrogates the primacy of grace. We may add to this principal statement a few remarks about certain theories of infant baptism.

If infant baptism signifies man's reception into the Christian church, this cannot mean that the child before baptism was not the object of God's love, and that baptism, therefore, should constitute the act whereby God is persuaded by men to open his fatherly arms. It cannot be denied that such ideas have been found even within evangelical Christianity, especially in connection with the so-called emergency baptism. But such ideas are in conflict with the fact that baptism is an act of God and that this act in itself expresses and is the result of the loving will of God. But it is also evident that the membership in the church founded on baptism does not mean that this membership is fully and completely realized in and through baptism. The membership founded on the act of divine love in baptism is realized in the measure that the gift of baptism is received in faith, or, in other words, in the measure that the fellowship of faith with God is actualized through God's continued work in man. In order to guard against all more or less "magical" conceptions, the Reformers rightly emphasized that the gift of baptism is received only in and through faith. It has been less fortunate when evangelical theology, in dependence on ideas which Luther at one stage of his life advocated, has sometimes drawn the conclusion that some form of faith must be present in the infant or given to him in order that the significance of the act might not be lost. The danger of this idea is that it leads directly back to that conception, below the personal and spiritual level, which it was intended to avoid. This involves the most vulnerable point: the conception of faith itself. At the same time this talk about a faith given to or "infused" in the little child through baptism serves to undermine and obscure the real significance of infant baptism. It produces the impression that it concerns unrealistic and unverifiable assertions. If the value of baptism is inseparably connected with an ability on our part to discover some faith in the child, it cannot be said that its value rests on any sure foundation. In reality this discussion about "faith" in the little child obscures entirely that which to Christian faith is the very heart of the matter, viz., that infant baptism is the act of election by divine love through which the baptized person receives and is assured of his right to membership in the church. This is the "objective" gift of baptism which exists before and independently of faith. It is a different matter that this membership given and secured through baptism is realized only in the measure that the fellowship with God in faith actually is realized. Just because the membership in the church is founded on baptism, the significance of infant baptism appears in the most concrete and unmistakable manner.

44. The Sacrament of Suffering and Victorious Love

1. The Lord's Supper is the sacrament of suffering and victorious love. The characteristic and fundamental ideas of the Lord's Supper in Christian faith—remembrance, sacrifice, fellowship (communion), and eucharist—are all comprehended under this point of view.

2. The Lord's Supper as an *in memoriam* celebration brings the faithful back to "that night in which he was betrayed." Participation in this memorial feast has, therefore, the character of a confession.

3. The idea of remembrance brings with it the idea of *sacrifice*, since that which is remembered is the sacrifice of self-giving, divine love. This idea of sacrifice is also expressed in the fact that the Lord's Supper emphasizes that our lives, too, are to be broken and given in the service of love. The idea of sacrifice becomes a caricature as soon as the sacrifice is separated from divine love and is regarded as a performance presented to God.

4. Since suffering love is also victorious love, Christ appears in the Lord's Supper as the One who in the present makes his work dynamic and effective, and thereby enters into *fellowship* with man. His presence is spiritual, but for that reason it is also a real presence. The conception of the Lord's Supper in Christian faith is differentiated in two directions: against a realism which rejects symbolism, and against a symbolism which rejects realism. The idea of communion is present also in the sense that fellowship with Christ implies fellowship among the believers. In both of these respects the communion idea has an eschatological character.

5. As the sacrament of victorious love, the Lord's Supper is also a *eucharist*, characterized by thanksgiving and praise.

1. The Fundamental Idea of the Lord's Supper.

The Lord's Supper includes a multitude of ideas. But all these are characterized and defined by the fact that the Lord's Supper is the sacrament of the cross, of suffering and victorious love. The Lord's Supper brings us, therefore, into the inner sanctuary of the Gospel.

When the Lord's Supper is designated as the sacrament of *suffering* and *victorious* love, both of these points of view should be emphasized. They are in reality inseparably connected, since the way of suffering is the way of victory of the saving and reconciling divine love. The self-giving sacrifice of love not only leads to victory, it is victory. If this point of view is not sufficiently emphasized, the Lord's Supper loses something of that which is its most important element; the idea of communion is obscured and the eucharistic element disappears. The Lord's Supper is the sacrament of the cross, but the significance of this fact becomes clear only when it is realized that for Christian faith the cross is a crucifix of triumph.

If theology shall properly interpret the significance of the Lord's Supper, it must clarify the various ideas which are connected with the Christian celebration of the sacrament. It must be stated in this connection that the theological analysis of the Lord's Supper has frequently been narrowed and perverted because the old controversies have been allowed to determine the approach, and the attention has been drawn to the controversial issues to the exclusion of other essential elements.

A review of what the Lord's Supper has meant to Christian faith during the centuries indicates that the interpretation centers around four principal ideas: remembrance, sacrifice, fellowship (communion), and eucharist. All these ideas are found even in primitive Christianity. They have subsequently appeared throughout the entire history of Christianity, but it must be admitted that some of them have at times been suppressed and others frequently misinterpreted. In the following discussion we will pay greater attention to the ideas of sacrifice and fellowship, both because these are the most important and because they are the points most frequently subject to misinterpretation.

Christian faith perceives the Lord's Supper as a means of grace, or, in other words, as an act of divine love imparting itself to men. But this principal point of view does not exclude the fact that the Lord's Supper can also be subjectively regarded as a human act. This twofold perspective must be carefully noted if the Lord's Supper is to be rightly and fully understood.

2. *The Idea of a Memorial.*

The starting point of Christian faith in its interpretation of the significance of the Lord's Supper is the fact that it appears as a memorial celebrating the completion of Jesus' work. The idea that the Lord's Supper is a memorial feast has been connected with its celebration since the days of primitive Christianity (cf. Luke 22:19; I Cor. 11:24 ff.). Paul writes: "As often as ye eat this bread, and drink the cup, ye proclaim the Lord's death till he come" (I Cor. 11:26).

The significance of this memorial aspect lies in the fact that it gives to the sacrament a secure, historical foundation. It places us in the presence of that historical life which was the embodiment of the saving and reconciling act of divine love. The remembrance brings to mind what once happened and makes it live again. This last element—that what has happened lives again —must be emphasized in this connection, because it is just this point of view which is directly connected with the primitive significance of "remembrance." This idea serves as the foundation upon which the other ideas rest. If these other ideas are separated from the memorial aspect and emphasized so as to minimize it, there is danger that the Lord's Supper would be reinterpreted in terms of mystery theories which are foreign to Christian faith. That which separates the Christian celebration of the Lord's Supper from all mystery cults is just this fact—that we are not concerned with a mythical figure. The Lord's Supper has reference to that historical work which was finished on the cross.

There is consequently no reason to despise or set aside the idea of a memorial. On the contrary, it is of highest importance that this point of view should characterize the interpretation and also find expression in the celebration. But the interpretation of the Lord's Supper would be restricted and impoverished if this idea were emphasized to the exclusion of other ideas in the sacrament. This has occurred in certain areas of Reformed Christianity, and not least in the theology which flourished during the latter half of the nineteenth century. Such an isolated presentation of the idea of remembrance which involves an interpretation of the "memorial" as a commemoration of something historically past leads to an emphasis on the martyrdom, to the exclusion of the victory, of the cross. The Lord's Supper then becomes a human memorial celebration which ignores the idea of the sacrament as a means of grace. In reality the memorial aspect points to the other ideas here mentioned, and its real significance can be perceived only when these others are given full recognition.

The Lord's Supper as a memorial is connected with the fact that as a human act it is a *confession* of the Crucified. This is expressed also in the words of Paul already quoted. The Lord's Supper is a proclamation of his death until he comes. It must be added, however, that this act of confession becomes deeper and more significant in association with the other ideas, especially the idea of fellowship. The confession is a confession of faith in that Lord who meets his own in the Supper.

The Lord's Supper is an act of confession. When we speak of a confession, we think primarily of an oral confession. But there are also confessional acts, such as that of the Lord's Supper. It might be said that this confessional character has become more and more prominent. In the measure that attendance at the Supper ceases to be enforced and compelled, the confessional element becomes stronger. This confession is not secondary to an oral confession. Just because the Lord's Supper is concerned with that which is essentially Christian, this confession must receive the greatest significance. This act is a confession that is concerned with the inner personal life and declares that the confessor desires to belong to the Lord of the Supper. As such it is connected with self-examination in the presence of divine love. If in this connection we speak of being "worthy and well prepared," this "worthiness" and "preparation" consist only in this: that we are willing to have God judge our unworthiness.

3. *The Idea of Sacrifice.*

As the sacrament of the cross the Lord's Supper is the sacrament of sacrifice. Even during primitive Christianity various ideas of sacrifice were connected with the Supper. The gifts given in connection with the celebration of the holy meal were designated as "sacrifices." It was also said that the celebration included a "sacrifice" of thanksgiving and praise. At this point the idea of sacrifice becomes that of *eucharistia*. Furthermore, the Supper involved an obligation of sacrificial service in love. But pre-eminently the idea of sacrifice has been connected with the cross to which the Supper calls attention. The idea of memorial automatically carries over into the idea of sacrifice and thereby receives its essential content. The words "given for you" and "shed for you" make the sacrificial act of self-giving love dynamic. The idea of sacrifice is thereby validated as a genuinely Christian idea, inseparably connected with the Christian celebration of the Supper. The Lord's Supper is the sacrament of suffering love. It confronts the believers with the love that gives itself to the utmost. It reveals the Gospel and permits it to appear directly without explanations and interpretations, concentrated in the form of an act.

But if the idea of sacrifice in the Lord's Supper leads Christian faith to the saving and reconciling act of divine love in Christ, this idea is obscured and perverted as soon as the act of sacrifice is separated from divine love. This history of the sacrament indicates that very grave dangers have been present at this point. A perverted reinterpretation of the Christian idea of sacrifice appears in those theories which originated chiefly in the Latin church and led finally to the fully developed doctrine of "the sacrifice of the Mass." These theories are very closely connected with the reinterpretation of the doctrine of the atonement in Latin Christianity. It is extremely significant that the first traces of the doctrine of the sacrifice of the Mass appear in Cyprian, or, in other words, contemporaneously with the interpretation of Christ's act of reconciliation as a compensation given to God by Christ *qua homo*. The Latin theory of the atonement is the prerequisite for the doctrine of the Mass. "The sacrifice of the Mass" implies a bloodless repetition of the sacrifice on

Golgotha. The renewed sacrifice is presented by the priest as a meritorious performance before God. Even if the sacrifice of the Mass has never been officially established within Roman theology, it has dominated and characterized the Roman sacramental conception and practice. The Reformation directed its sharpest protest against this approach. Luther attacked this point more vigorously than anything else in the Roman worship, because it involved a gross perversion of the Gospel. The intention of Luther's work in connection with the reformation of the Roman Mass was to eliminate everything that had any connection with the theory of the sacrifice of the Mass. The rejection is motivated by that fact that the sacrifice of Christ is "eternal" and valid for all time, and that the idea of an achievement of man to be presented to God is excluded. Behind this argumentation there lies a view of the reconciling work of Christ which differs from that of Latin scholasticism, since this work is an act of self-giving sacrifice of divine love (cf. § 26. 3, 4).

The reaction against the perverted reinterpretation of the idea of sacrifice has resulted in a minimizing of this idea on the part of evangelical theology. In certain places there seems to be a fear even of using the word sacrifice. It is clear that this is not consonant with the thought of the Reformation, and that the perverted use should not be allowed to discourage the rightful use of this idea. The idea of sacrifice is in reality inseparably connected with that Gospel which has its center in the cross. To eliminate the idea of sacrifice from the Lord's Supper would mean that the Supper is separated from the cross. The defect of the Roman theory of the Mass was not that it emphasized the sacrifice, but that it separated the act of sacrifice from divine love and understood it as a human achievement. Furthermore, it was not that it emphasized the sacrifice as a present act, but that the theory of the Mass by its talk of a "repeated" sacrifice obscured the fact that the sacrifice made once and for all is an eternally valid sacrifice, and that the act of reconciliation is not only something that has been done, but something that continually occurs because Christ unceasingly realizes anew his finished work. But from this point of view the idea of sacrifice carries over into the idea of fellowship. As we pass from the idea of remembrance to the deeper idea of sacrifice, this latter conception brings us to the idea of fellowship and to the thought that Christ in the Supper meets his own and gives them a share in the fruits of his life and work.

The idea of sacrifice in the Lord's Supper has reference primarily to the sacrificial act of divine love in the finished work of Christ. But the gift which is here given to the believers involves at the same time an obligation. As the Lord's Supper places us in the presence of the self-giving of divine love, the celebration of the Supper implies a consecration to a life in sacrificial love. The Lord's Supper tells us that the sacrificial act of self-giving love must never depart from the Christian life. The Lord's Supper serves in this respect as the conscience of the Christian life. Participation in the Lord's Supper is a consecration to Christ, and therefore also a consecration to self-giving love; it is true of our lives also that they are to be broken and given in the service of love (Rom. 12:1). It may be added that in this case the idea of sacrifice passes immediately into the idea of fellowship, since sacrificial love creates fellowship.

4. The Idea of Communion.

The idea of communion may be said to represent the climax of the celebration of the Lord's Supper. This communion is primarily a fellowship with Christ. In and through the Supper Christ himself enters into communion with his own. But this communion implies also a fellowship of the believers, since it is through their fellowship with Christ that they are united with each other.

If from the point of view of communion the Lord's Supper appears as an *act of Christ,* the reason is that suffering love is also *victorious* love. The Lord's Supper is not a service of sorrow, not a funeral mass. It is, indeed, the sacrament of suffering love, the sacrament of the cross. But the cross is not only a symbol of ignominy and martyrdom, but primarily the symbol of victory and triumph. Christian faith, therefore, perceives the Lord's Supper as an act in which the victorious and exalted Lord is actively present as the One who invites and entertains the guests, and gives to them of his own, even himself. The act is not simply the act of the guests and the priest; there is a greater One present. Christ, the Lord of the Supper, is here active and bestows his inexhaustible gift, which is "the bread of life" for all times and all generations. The Lord's Supper is, therefore, not a funeral mass, but the great festival of joy of the Christian church, when the celebrating congregation hails the Lord of the sacrament with the greeting: "Blessed is he that cometh."

When theology has frequently spoken of "the real presence" of Christ in the Supper, this idea expresses the characteristic view of faith in regard to the Lord's Supper as a means of grace. This sacrament is a means of grace because of "the real presence" of Christ. The idea of the real or effective presence of Christ is deeply rooted in the Christian faith and stands in intimate connection with the fundamental view of faith in regard to the way in which divine love realizes the work of reconciliation. The manner in which this idea has been expressed in theology is a different matter. Here it is important to distinguish between the fundamental idea and the expression. Theology has been more occupied with the question *how* Christ is present than with anything else regarding the Lord's Supper. This has occasioned much discussion and disagreement. As far as Christian faith is concerned, the most serious objection to these speculations has been the fact that they have drawn the attention away from the essential element—the act of Christ—to various theories of what happens or does not happen regarding the bread and the wine.

The history of the doctrine of the Lord's Supper, which we must touch upon briefly here relative to the problem of the presence of Christ, has usually been presented as a struggle between "symbolic" and "realistic" conceptions. It is then asserted that the "realistic" conceptions, which originated in pagan mystery cults, have crowded out the original "symbolic" interpretation, and that the final result of this process is to be found in the Roman doctrine of transubstantiation. It is claimed that Luther took a compromising and mediating position, while the Reformed doctrine represents a purely "symbolic" and therefore "purer" interpretation. This whole traditional conception of the history of the Lord's Supper needs a revision. In part it is too much dependent on typical Roman points of view, and in part it fails to differentiate clearly between the fundamental religious ideas and their expression.

In reality it must be maintained that the conception of the Lord's Supper both in the primitive and in the ancient church was both "symbolic" and "realistic." We meet sometimes expressions which seem at first to be grossly "realistic," but together with these we also find expressions which are entirely "symbolic." The Gospel of John is a typical example. On the one hand we read: "Except ye eat the flesh of the Son of Man and drink his blood, ye have not life in yourselves" (John 6:53); and on the other hand: "It is the Spirit that giveth life; the flesh profiteth nothing" (John 6:63). This vacillation between "symbolism" and "realism" is in reality very characteristic also of the theology of the ancient church, especially in the leading Greek theology. Even today this combination of symbolism and realism can be found in "Orthodox" Christianity.[1] If we are to analyze the essential significance of the doctrine of the Lord's Supper in the ancient church, it is not sufficient to say that realistic conceptions may

[1] Cf. Stefan Zankow, *Das Orthodoxe Christentum des Ostens,* p. 104. The liturgy of the Eucharist, says Zankow, is "the symbolic presentation and observance of the life of Christ and the sacrifice on Golgotha. But it is at the same time the exalted mystery of the continual return of Christ to his own and his true and intimate union with them. In the liturgy we behold most clearly and movingly the realism of the symbolism and the symbolism of the realism of the Orthodox church, the mystic and symbolical intercourse between heaven and earth, from God to man, from Christ to the church." Zankow points out that the Roman doctrine of transubstantiation has had considerable influence within the Orthodox church, but that it has not become dominant. The words we have quoted indicate the presence of the typical conception of the ancient church in modern Orthodox Christianity.

be explained as the influence of pagan mystery cults, and that a "spiritual" interpretation would indicate a more "pure" Christian viewpoint. This proposition follows too rigid a scheme. There may have been some influence from pagan sources in the ancient church. But the realism may also be due to the endeavor to emphasize the divine revelation as a revelation in *history*, in contrast to a Platonic and spiritualizing dissolution of the characteristically Christian idea of revelation. It is evident that the so-called symbolic interpretation of the Lord's Supper cannot without further consideration be regarded as a more "pure" Christian interpretation. Behind this idea, when it is presented in contrast to "realism," lies this Platonic spiritualism, which appears for example in the Alexandrian theology.

The Roman doctrine of transubstantiation, which gradually became dominant especially in the West, must not be regarded as a consistent development of the interpretation of the Lord's Supper in the ancient church. The gross "realism" of this doctrine is rather a deviation from the characteristic combination of "realism" and "symbolism" in the ancient church. When scholastic theology advocates a realism in *contrast* to all symbolism, it is one indication that scholasticism constitutes a deviation in the history of Christian thought and that the Latin theology of the Middle Ages represents a side line in this history.

Luther rejected the doctrine of transubstantiation, but he maintained the personal presence of Christ in the bread and the wine. This means in general that Luther resumes the connection with the main tradition of the ancient church, in so far as he rejects both a gross realism and a symbolism that is contrasted with realism. The fundamental religious idea, which lies behind those expressions in which Luther formulated his conception of the Lord's Supper, appears in his struggle with Zwingli. The question is concerned with two fundamental ideas. In the first place, Luther wanted to maintain that the Lord's Supper is a gift, a means of grace. This point of view was ignored in Zwingli's thought, which centered in the human act of remembrance. In the second place, Luther wanted to emphasize that the act of revelation and reconciliation by divine love took place and continues in *history*, in the world of humanity. The background of Zwingli's theory is the ancient opposition between the spiritual and the corporeal. To Luther the decisive contrast between "the spirit and the flesh" was not an antithesis between the spiritual and the corporeal, but the antithesis between the Holy Spirit of God and sinful humanity. In opposition to all spiritualistic and idealistic attempts to dissolve the revelation of God, Luther contended that the revelation of God takes place *in history*. The decisive element was for him that God's act of salvation and reconciliation took place and continues to occur in and through a historical and human life, and that the divine love meets us in human poverty and weakness. The purpose of insisting on the presence of Christ in and with the bread and the wine was, therefore, to assert that this Christ, who as the incarnation of divine love acts in the Supper and gives himself to his own, is none other than the Crucified whose life was broken and given for our sakes. Luther's emphasis on "the real presence" is thus connected with the idea of incarnation and is explained by this connection. He is concerned with "the Word that became flesh."

When the fundamental religious ideas of Luther's interpretation of the Lord's Supper have been thus clarified, it must be added that the discussions about this subject during the Reformation period were connected with serious aberrations which stemmed from inherited problems and conceptions. This is true especially about the concept of *materia coelestis*, the concept of the heavenly and transfigured body of Christ. This introduced a scholastic element which was foreign to the interpretation of the Lord's Supper in the ancient church, and which led to insoluble difficulties not only for Luther but also for Zwingli and Calvin. When Calvinistic theology asserts that the body of Christ is confined to a certain place in heaven, it is dealing with conceptions which are just as difficult as Luther's speculations about ubiquity, and which from a religious point of view are inferior to Luther's conception of a "ubiquity" which rests on the fact that "God's right hand is everywhere."

In the interest of clarifying the significance of the Lord's Supper it is, therefore, of fundamental importance that the analysis of the idea of communion is separated from all scholastic speculations; and at the same time that the attention is fixed on the religious intentions which lie behind the realistic point of view which is essential to Christian faith. When the Lord's Supper in the form of an act comprehends the central content of the Christian revelation, it appears both as a "symbolic" and a "realistic" act. It is a real act of Christ in the form of a symbol. As far as faith is concerned the emphasis lies in the fact that the Lord's Supper is an act of Christ, an act *in which the living Christ is active*. Christian faith, therefore, objects to the idea of contrasting the symbolic with that realistic point of view which concentrates everything in the effective presence of Christ. As soon as this occurs, the Lord's Supper becomes a feast of death and a sorrowful celebration. That which makes the Supper a means of grace is obscured and the act of divine love in history is hidden. If then legitimate and central interests of faith are to be found in speaking of the "real" presence of Christ in the Supper, it must nevertheless be said that the nature and essential significance of this presence are obscured in the measure that the realistic point of view is allowed to supplant the symbolic. When in this connection ideas approaching transubstantiation are permitted to enter, that which is essential and decisive for faith becomes obscured. For Christian faith everything is concentrated in this one thing: that Christ is effectively present with his own in the power of his spirit and thus realizes in them that *communion* with God which he has established through his work and which includes "forgiveness of sins, life, and blessedness." The blessed bread and wine are the instruments which he uses in this act. They point back to what has once occurred, and they also express the inner connection between the finished and the continuous work. If reference is made to a presence in a physical sense, it does not mean a higher degree of his presence. It is not through a purely external connection with Christ, but through his spiritual and active presence, that the fellowship of the believers with God is realized. The spiritual presence is to faith the highest form of presence; and in its inscrutable mystery it is the only "real," regenerative, and life-giving presence.

The gift of the Lord's Supper is the fellowship with Christ and with God established in and through the forgiveness of sins, or, in other words, "the forgiveness of sin, life, and blessedness." The two last words, life and blessedness, must be given due consideration. The viewpoint of Christian faith in regard to the gift of the Lord's Supper is differentiated in two directions: in part in contrast to a reinterpretation in a physical sense, and in part in contrast to an essentially negative conception of the significance of forgiveness (cf. § 34. 1, 3). When the ancient church early began to speak of the Lord's Supper as "the medicine of immortality," this expression was full of dangers, since it could easily be interpreted in a physical sense and since it tended to obscure the essential significance of the Christian conception of the means of grace. But in so far as the purpose was to assert that the gift of the Lord's Supper is "life," this easily misinterpreted formula expresses something of extreme importance for the Christian faith. This aspect should be emphasized in contrast to a certain tendency in evangelical Christianity to interpret forgiveness predominantly in a negative way by which the interpretation of the sacrament is perverted. The celebration of the Lord's Supper then assumes the character of penance. In opposition to such a restriction of the content of the sacraments Luther's words ought to be underscored: "Where there is forgiveness of sins, there are also life and blessedness."

The idea of communion has, as already indicated, another aspect. The fellowship with the Lord of the Supper involves also a fellowship of the believers among themselves (cf. I Cor. 10:17;

John 15:1 ff.). As a constitutive factor of the Christian church and as the sacrament of love and concord, the Lord's Supper is both an expression of the Christian fellowship, an obligation to establish such fellowship, and a power creating unity.

This character of the Supper as a mark of and a power creating Christian unity is not nullified by the fact that the various theories about the sacrament and the way it should be celebrated have caused schisms among Christians. Even if men have done their utmost to tear this bond of unity asundei, they have never quite succeeded. *Theories* about the Lord's Supper can divide and have divided the faithful in a disgraceful and humiliating way, and from this point of view the Sacrament of the Altar stands as the accuser and the conscience of Christianity. But no devisive theories can bring to nought that demand for unity which is contained in the Lord's Supper and which is derived from the fact that it is a communion with the Lord of the Supper. The Sacrament is and remains a power of unity from which the Christians may receive strength to a new and richer fellowship. Just because the eucharist brings us into the holy of holies of Christianity, into the presence of the victorious act of divine love by self-giving sacrifice, and into the presence of Christ, we are also brought to the deepest and most immovable foundation of Christian unity.

Just as the Lord's Supper brings us to the deepest foundation of the Christian fellowship, it permits this fellowship to appear to its widest extent; it opens the door into the wide communion of the saints. The communion is not only a fellowship with those who together bend the knee at the table, it is a communion with those who generation after generation among all peoples and tongues belong to the Lord Jesus. The communion which is effected in the Lord's Supper does not stop with that which is and that which has been. It transcends the boundaries of this earthly life. The fellowship is a possession, but it is also a hope which is directed toward the fulfillment of communion, a participation in "the great supper in heaven" (Matt. 26:29; Luke

14:15; cf. § 51). The *eschatological* perspective is inseparably connected with the celebration of the Lord's Supper. Its inner character appears as an eschatological banquet.

5. The Idea of Eucharist.

All the various ideas in the Lord's Supper are gathered together and expressed in the idea of the eucharist, in thanksgiving and praise. This idea is from the very beginning intimately connected with the celebration of the sacrament, "they took their food with gladness and singleness of heart, praising God" (Acts 2:46 f.). The order of service of the sacrament contains numerous eucharistic ideas. In the Swedish Mass the celebration of the Lord's Supper is surrounded with thanksgiving and praise (*sursum corda, prefation, sanctus,* prayer of thanksgiving, and *benedicamus*). It must be said, nevertheless, that the eucharistic ideas have often been suppressed in the evangelical celebration, and even in the Roman Mass. The reasons for this suppression in evangelical practice have been various. Most prominent of these have been the neglect of the positive significance of the forgiveness of sins (cf. § 44.4), and the elevation of the confessional service to a place which even dominates the celebration itself instead of being a *preludium* and a servant in relation to the sacrament. The celebration has thus assumed a certain dull and somber character which is not in harmony with the nature of the sacrament. Such a point of view not only differs from that of the ancient church but also from that of Luther. It is significant that Luther urges that the preface shall be sung in the glad spirit of the Gospel, since it is here a question of the very core of the great message of joy. It is undeniable that the Lord's Supper as the sacrament of suffering love is characterized by the deepest seriousness. But suffering love is also victorious love. The gracious act of victorious love fills the believers with thanksgiving and jubilation. The Christian character of the Lord's Supper is weakened when this eucharistic element is neglected.

45. Prayer

1. Prayer is a constitutive factor of Christian life. The character of prayer as a means of grace derives from the fact that prayer is both man's turning to God and God's approach to man.

2. Prayer expresses both the conflict and the possessive character of faith. From the first point of view the most profound and dominant purpose of prayer is the realization of the divine and loving will: "Thy will be done"; from the latter viewpoint prayer is thanksgiving and worship.

3. Prayer is the means by which God who answers prayer realizes his loving will; indeed, the most profound interpretation conceives of prayer as God's own act: "The Spirit himself maketh intercession for us" (Rom. 8:26); "Christ liveth to make intercession for them" (Heb. 7:25; Rom. 8:34; I John 2:1).

1. Prayer as a Means of Grace.

Prayer is an essential element in the Christian's spiritual life, and a vital condition of life for the Christian church. When prayer is excluded from the life of the Christian church, the church ceases to exist. It is therefore eminently a constitutive factor of the Christian church. The various means of grace, to which previous reference has been made, are indissolubly connected with prayer and become effective means of grace only in this connection. It is thus impossible to present the constitutive factors of the church, its spiritual centers of power, and omit from consideration the subject of prayer. In any presentation of Christian faith prayer of a necessity demands a place.

But if it is undeniable that prayer is an essential element in the life of the Christian, it is not on this account alone that prayer can and ought to be designated as a "means of grace." There has been a certain understandable reluctance to place prayer in this category. This reluctance has been motivated, as we have seen (§ 40.1) by the tendency to conceive of prayer as entirely

401

a human function. On closer examination this argument is found to be entirely untenable because, for Christian faith, prayer is combined with the answer to prayer, and because it involves not only man's turning to God but includes also an act of God. It may, however, be objected that the answer to prayer does not necessarily prove that prayer itself is an act of God, and therefore a means of grace. With reference to this objection it must be asserted that prayer is a means of grace not *only* because it is connected with the answer to prayer, but principally because prayer itself cannot be interpreted by Christian faith as simply and entirely a human act of turning to God. Prayer *is* indeed a human act of turning to God, but it is at the same time a divine act by which God draws man unto himself. As a matter of fact, prayer does not only have its matrix in the quest of divine love for man, but in its inner nature it is an expression of this loving will as it subdues man. From this point of view prayer is indubitably a means of God's active "grace," a means of grace. It is noteworthy that when Luther speaks of prayer he maintains that prayer is evoked as God's benefactions are presented to the one who prays, and that prayer is thereby initiated and vitalized. According to this viewpoint the benefactions of God are not only conditional for the possibility of prayer, they also create genuine prayer. Prayer, in other words, is simply a means of grace, a way in which the divine and loving will realizes itself in the spiritual life of the Christian.

2. *Prayer as Man's Approach to God.*

By an inner necessity faith expresses itself in prayer. The twofold aspect of faith, which consists in the fact that faith is at once a present possessing and a constant becoming, that is to say, a militant faith (cf. § 36), is reflected in prayer. Prayer reflects both the militancy and the possessiveness of faith. Militant faith expresses itself in militant prayer which asks and seeks something from God; the prayer of possessive faith is the prayer of thanksgiving and in its highest form becomes worship.

The ultimate purpose of the prayer of militant faith is the realization of the loving will of God. This is the constitutive element in all militant prayer. Whatever the prayer of Christian faith asks for, its ultimate goal points in this direction. Faith cannot and does not desire anything else than the realization of God's loving will. Therefore the prayer of all prayers is always "Thy will be done." Prayer is a petition that God's will shall overcome all opposition and shall realize its unabridged dominion. But this concern for the dominion of God's will on the part of prayer does not imply a spirit of resignation in the fact of that which happens. On the contrary, from this viewpoint prayer is seen as conquering prayer.

The purpose of prayer is not to effect a change in the divine will, but that the will of God *shall be done*. Since Christian faith conceives of God as pure love, and the purpose of the divine will is the realization of the aims of this love, it is meaningless to attempt to change God's will. Such a prayer would be nothing but an expression of a defective confidence in the divine and loving will and its wisdom. Since God is love, all prayer must be characterized by the desire to realize in unabridged measure this loving will. Prayer, therefore, is principally a petition that we might grasp and understand fully and clearly this divine will and its purposes, and that this will shall entirely subdue us. Prayer becomes a means of perceiving God's will. The comprehension of the will of God is the condition upon which it is realized in the experience of him who prays.

Prayer proposes to effect a change, not of God's will, but in ourselves and in the circumstances of life. It endeavors to open the doors to the power of divine love. It is indubitable, however, that the prayer, "Thy will be done," has often been interpreted in terms of resignation. This would imply that the purpose of this prayer is to express the submissive resignation of him who prays to surrounding circumstances, as if these circumstances were in themselves a direct expression of the divine will. In this way prayer loses its expansive power and its most profound content. Such a misinterpretation of the significance of prayer occurs because of the tendency to accept everything that happens, without further question, as a direct expression of the divine will, ignoring the fact that existence comprises within itself much which is not expressive of God's will, but is actually in open conflict with it (cf. § 22). If this is inescapably clear to faith, then the prayer, "Thy will be done," cannot be uttered in the spirit of resignation. On the contrary, this prayer then becomes in the highest degree a militant and conquering prayer of faith, a prayer which wages war upon all forces inimical to the will of God, and a prayer which calls down the sovereign power of God's love. It is precisely because everything in prayer is concentrated upon the accomplishment of God's will, that prayer is a world-winning power.

The prayer of militant faith has a twofold background: on the one hand the fact of that evil which opposes the will of God, and on the other the sovereignty of divine love even in relation to evil. When this dualistic element is suppressed prayer loses its militant character. Both Schleiermacher's position and Ritschl's in this connection are illustrative. When Schleiermacher inserts Christendom into the framework of a monistic world view, the result is that the only kind of prayer which he will accept as valid is that of submission and gratitude. As a matter of fact, in the final analysis, he conceives of the prayer of submission and gratitude as simply a corridor to that higher stage of existence which is distinguished by the characterization of Christian life in terms of an unbroken harmony and of perfect peace and joy in God. The unrealistic element in this conception is not that Schleiermacher designates Christian life as joy in God, but that he attempts to remove from the realm of prayer its essential tension and militancy. In this connection, P. Althaus is right when he declares that this conception of Schleiermacher implies an unwarranted anticipation of the situation of the "triumphant church"; "the conflict is swallowed up by victory *prematurely*, the Christian dualism has been submerged . . . in the monistic conception of the world and of history."[1] As a matter of fact, the militant prayer which opposes all evil can never be eliminated from Christian faith as it exists in the circumstances of life on earth. But this prayer is empowered by the sovereignty of the divine and loving will even in its relation to evil.

Militant prayer must be distinguished from two misinterpretations: from the transformation of prayer into a passive resignation, and from an egocentric orientation which makes man the master and God the servant of the various desires and demands of man. As has already been pointed out, prayer is concerned with the realization, not of man's but of God's will. This certainly does not exclude the fact that the one who prays, to use the words of Paul's letter to the Philippians, lets his request "be made known unto God by prayer and supplication" (Phil. 4:6), and thereby commits his whole life with its needs into the hands of his heavenly Father. But egocentric importunity is certainly excluded from this militant prayer, and it is likewise clear to him who prays that he does not rightly understand what is best for him and that his best is decisively dependent upon his relationship to God.[2] Thus our petitions are dominated by the all-inclusive prayer for the realization of the divine and loving will. This fact is also expressed when Christian faith speaks of prayer as "prayer in the name of Jesus Christ." This expression, which has reference primarily to prayer as a prayer of the Christian church, reveals at the same time something of the nature of Christian prayer. In every case Christian prayer is uttered with Christ in mind. The spirit of Christ is the power which deepens and sanctifies prayer, removes impure motives, and guards the direction of prayer so that it is in harmony with the loving will of God.

Because of an inner compulsion, the scope of militant prayer

---

[1] P. Althaus, *De yttersta tingen*, p. 83.

[2] W. Temple, "Prayer and Conduct," in *The Pilgrim*, 1921, p. 337: "Prayer which is mainly occupied with a result to be obtained is comparatively powerless to obtain results."

expands to include intercession. Intercession is therefore not a secondary or incidental element in the prayer of Christian faith. Christian prayer must of necessity become intercession simply because prayer is primarily concerned with the realization of the divine and loving will. When Christian faith is isolated, it withers. When prayer dwells in the presence of divine love, it cannot be concerned simply with me and mine; it becomes necessarily also a bearing of the burdens of others. Thus prayer expands into intercession.

As an expression of the possessive character of faith, prayer manifests itself as thanksgiving and praise to God for his unspeakable gift, which at its most profound level involves the gift of himself. In its highest and purest form this prayer of thanksgiving becomes worship, *adoratio*. The one who prays bows in worship before the unsearchable majesty of divine love which condescends to draw near unto those who are dust and ashes and are unworthy to dwell in his presence. Faith worships him who alone is "worthy to receive praise and glory" (Rev. 4:11; 7:12).

3. Prayer as God's Approach to Man.

Prayer is not only man's turning to God, but is at the same time primarily God's approach to man. As far as faith is concerned, prayer is not a transaction in which man alone is active; it is rather a communication between God and man. Prayer is not simply man speaking to God, but it is also God giving an answer. Luther has characteristically put it thus: "It is a conversation; on the one hand *we* speak to God, and on the other, *he* speaks to us. To speak to him means to pray, and this is something great and glorious—that the exalted majesty in heaven condescends to us who are miserable worms, in order that we might be permitted to open our lips in prayer before him and that he willingly hears us. But it is even more glorious and precious that he speaks to us and that we may listen to him. . . . What he has to say is much more comforting than anything we

have to say." [3] The viewpoint which is primary to faith asserts
that God hears our prayers and answers them. When faith speaks
in such terms about divine answer to prayer it does not imply
that all the "wishful prayers" which man may utter are to be
fulfilled by God, but rather that prayer is not without its answer,
and that such an answer to prayer always involves at its deepest
level the realization of the divine and loving will. According to
faith, God employs prayer as a means through which he accomplishes his purposes in victorious conflict against inimical forces.
And what is true of other means through which God works is
also true of the "means" of prayer, namely, that God works immediately even when, according to man's viewpoint, he works
through some means. In and through prayer God draws man
into subjection to the dominion of his will, he enlightens man
as to the purpose of this will, how it wins its victories, and com-
missions man to be an instrument in the service of this will.
Thus, from faith's most profound point of view, prayer appears
as God's own work in man's soul. The God to whom we pray is
not merely a distant, extra-mundane deity, but the God who is
living and active in the historical process and who in prayer directly related himself to us, indeed, who is nearer to us than we
are to ourselves. This conception of the effective presence of
God in prayer has been expressed by faith both by reference to
the way in which the Spirit of God makes intercession for us
and to the intercessory prayers of Christ. "Ye have received the
Spirit of adoption, whereby we cry, 'Abba, Father'" (Rom.
8:15); "And in like manner the Spirit also helpeth our infirmity:
for we know not how to pray as we ought; but the Spirit himself maketh intercession for us with groanings which cannot be
uttered" (Rom. 8:26). But the Spirit who prays is also the Spirit
of Christ. From this viewpoint, therefore, the continuous work
of Christ appears to expectant faith as a continuous prayer of
intercession. Prayer in the name of Christ is at once a prayer in
which Christ continually realizes his work and in which the in-

---

[3] Quoted by F. Heiler, *Das Gebet*, 2nd ed., p. 231.

tercessory prayer of divine love is mighty on our behalf. "Since the labors of all men in the service of God's Kingdom are directed by the work of an eternally active God, therefore the presentiment emerges that even the prayers of men in the final analysis are directed by a deeper, never-ending intercession, borne and evoked by it." [4]

46. The Christian Ministry

1. The Christian ministry also belongs to the constitutive factors of the church. It has its basis in the commission of Christ and is a necessary instrument in the activity of the Gospel that establishes the church. The primary function of the ministry is the preaching of the Word and the administration of the sacraments. In this respect it appears as a ministry of reconciliation.

2. The religious point of view of the ministry as a service under the divine commission is obscured when the ministry is misinterpreted in an objective or a subjective manner.

1. The Ministry as a Commission Given by Christ

In the previous chapters we have spoken of the means of grace as the constitutive factors of the church. But the Christian ministry must also be included among these constitutive factors, since the ministry is a necessary instrument in the activity of the Word and sacraments that establish the church. It has sometimes been discussed whether the ministry belongs to the *esse* or to the *bene esse* of the church. In the latter case it would be assumed that the ministry is an appropriate and practical institution, but that it is not "essential" for the church and does not belong to its constitutive factors. The idea has sometimes been added that this represents the evangelical viewpoint in contrast to the Roman. This is incorrect, however, in the measure that Luther's conception of the matter is of guiding conse-

---

[4] E. Billing, *op. cit.*, p. 103.

quence. There is, to be sure, an antithesis between Luther and Rome in regard to the ministry, but this lies, as we shall see later, on an entirely different plane. It does not touch the question whether or not the ministry should be regarded as a divine institution. In reality Luther has emphasized even more strongly than Rome that the ministry is a divine ordinance which rests on a divine commission. He motivates the ministry on the basis of the saving work of God in Christ. The service of the ministry, he says, is "a service which goes *from* Christ, not to Christ, and which comes *to* us, not from us."

The ministry has the same secure position also in the New Testament. Its fundamental point of view can be summarized in a few propositions. The ministry is inseparably connected with the church. Its basis is the commission of Christ, and it is consequently a divine commission. It possesses, therefore, an authority given to it by Christ, but his authority is not a personal possession of the minister. The ministry is a ministry of service, a *service* in the church. Its function is to serve the brethren by serving the Gospel.

That the ministry implies a commission from God is emphasized in the whole New Testament, in the Gospels as well as in the letters. The Lord sent out his disciples with the message: "As thou [God] didst send me into the world, even so send I them into the world" (John 17:18; 20:21). The messengers are invested with authority by the Lord. They have authority to forgive sins in his name. "What things soever ye shall bind on earth shall be bound in heaven; and what things soever ye shall loose on earth shall be loosed in heaven" (Matt. 18:18; cf. Matt. 16:19; John 20:22-23). But this is not a personal authority. They are entirely dependent on Christ, they are his instruments and servants. Everything depends on the fact that they serve. "Whosoever would become great among you shall be your minister . . . even as the Son of man came . . . to minister" (Matt. 20:26-28). The function is to make disciples of all nations, and it is done in his name. "He that receiveth you receiveth me, and he that receiveth me receiveth him that sent me" (Matt. 10:40). In Acts and in the letters we see how this ministry developed in the church. But the religious viewpoint is the same. The decisive element is the commission which has been given and which is to be faithfully administered. We find that Paul, often in the strongest terms, emphasizes the commission, ministry, and service which have been given to him. But he emphasizes just as strongly that the authority is not his, and that he is nothing in himself. "What then is Apollos? and what is Paul? . . . Ministers" (I Cor. 3:5). He wants to be known as "a servant of Christ and a steward of the mysteries of God" (I Cor. 4:1). His confidence does not come because "we are sufficient of ourselves, to account anything as of ourselves; but our sufficiency is from God" (II Cor. 3:5). His boldness rests on the fact that the ministry has been given to him by God's grace. "Therefore seeing that we have this ministry, even as we obtained mercy, we faint not" (II Cor. 4:1). The ministry is entirely a service of Christ. Consequently it is at the same time a service of the church, the congregation. The ministry can serve the church only by being entirely a service to Christ. "If I were still pleasing men, I should not be a servant of Christ" (Gal. 1:10). The service to the congregations consists in this—that the messengers bring forth the message about Christ. "We preach not ourselves, but Christ Jesus as Lord, and ourselves as your servants for Jesus' sake" (II Cor. 4:5). Consequently the messengers are helpers of the joy of the congregations. "Not that we have lordship over your faith, but are helpers of your joy" (II Cor. 1:24).[1]

When we consider the ideas of the ministry expressed in these quotations, it is clear that the starting point with reference to the ministry is the commission. The Lord himself has given this commission, in the first place to his apostles who thus have a special position, but also through them to all those who during the centuries have been authorized as the messengers of Christ

---

[1] Cf. O. Linton, "The Church and the Ministry in the New Testament," in *En bok om kyrkan, A Book about the Church*, pp. 100-131.

in the footsteps of the apostles. This means that the commission of Christ is continually given through the church, and that, from the point of view of faith, the ministry is maintained in the church through the activity of the Holy Spirit. From this point of view it becomes quite misleading to ask whether the commission comes from the church (the usual word in this connection is the congregation) or from the Lord himself. From the point of view of faith this alternative is meaningless, since a commission from the church cannot be such unless it is a commission from that Lord who is the Head of the church.

Paul defines the ministry of the church as a *ministry of reconciliation*. Its significance can hardly be expressed in a more vivid manner. "But all things are of God, who reconciled us to himself through Christ, and gave unto us the ministry of reconciliation: to wit, that God was in Christ reconciling the world unto himself, not reckoning unto them their trespasses, and having committed unto us the word of reconciliation. We are ambassadors therefore on behalf of Christ, as though God were entreating by us: we beseech you on behalf of Christ, be ye reconciled to God" (II Cor. 5:18-20).

That the ministry of the church is a ministry of reconciliation implies that it has its foundation in the finished work of Christ, in the atonement. If the reconciliation is a work of God from above, then the ministry of reconciliation is also a gift from above, and a ministry given by God. The reconciliation demands a ministry. This is not because the atonement needs to be complemented or repeated. It has been done once and for all. It remains for all times and generations. But the reconciliation demands a ministry because it addresses itself to every new age and every new generation. The victorious act of reconciliation must be carried out in new struggles. The victory of self-giving love does not mean that the struggle has ceased. The ministry of reconciliation is a ministry of struggle and conflict. As God's act of reconciliation in Christ was carried out in a struggle against the destructive powers, so the messengers of reconciliation are called upon to participate in this struggle. It is carried on in the consciousness that human power does not avail anything here, for "everything is from God," but also in the consciousness that Christ is the victorious Lord and that his messengers go forth under his authority.

The ministry of reconciliation must proclaim the message of reconciliation. All the tasks which may belong to the ministry are gathered together in this one essential function: the word of reconciliation has been entrusted to us. This aspect must be carefully noted. The message which has been entrusted to the messengers must be proclaimed as it really is. The attention must be drawn to the message, not to the messenger. The messenger serves the cause whose servant he has become. The messenger is an instrument, nothing else, but also nothing less than an instrument. It is the cause itself that is to speak, *majestas materiae,* as Luther says. The Word and the sacraments are the bearers of the message of reconciliation. The ministry belongs to the constitutive factors of the church because the Word and the sacraments are the constitutive factors of the church. This means likewise that the activity of the ministry has its center in the worship life. It has been thus from the very beginning in the Christian church, and so it must remain. Ordinances and forms may change, but the church is the same throughout the ages. The fellowship of the church is a fellowship in the Word and the sacraments, a fellowship which expresses itself in the worship life. The worship is the center of the church, because the decisive element is fellowship with Christ, and because this fellowship is realized in the worship life. "Where two or three are gathered together in my name, there am I in the midst of them" (Matt. 18:20). This fellowship with Christ is especially connected with the Lord's Supper, which is the seal of the new covenant. The function of the ministry appears, therefore, as something secure and irrevocable, however the forms of activity may change. There is no other church than the historical, actual, and concrete church which stems from Christ and his apostles, and which is founded on the Word of God and the sacraments in whose service the ministry of the church is engaged.

2. *Misinterpretations.*

Misinterpretations of the significance and status of the ministry arise when the religious point of view is not preserved pure and inviolate. Such misinterpretations have either an objective or subjective character, and lead to either a mechanical or a spiritualizing conception.

The first of these types appears both in the Roman and in the evangelical tradition. That the ministry in the Roman church is understood in a mechanistic way is to a large extent due to the theory of the sacrifice of the Mass (cf. §44. 3), which in turn is directly connected with the Latin conception of the atonement. Just as Christ in his sacrifice stands before God as the representative of man, so the priest stands as the representative of humanity in the repeated sacrifice of the Mass. Through the cultic rite he presents an achievement to God which is intended to benefit men. The ministry thereby becomes a mediator between God and man. In and through this mechanical conception of both the sacrament and the ministry, the ministry of reconciliation has been interpreted in a way that is foreign to faith. In spite of the fact that Christ's act of reconciliation is the unique sacrifice through which all human sacrifices that are intended to influence God are abrogated, the priest here appears as a "sacerdotal priest" in a sense which belongs to the pre-Christian period. It was not an accident that Luther's criticism of the Roman Mass was concentrated on the sacrifice of the Mass. By this criticism he struck also at the Roman perversion of the office of the ministry.

An objective and mechanical intepretation has at times appeared also within evangelical Christianity. While the Roman interpretation was attached to a mechanization of the sacrament, the evangelical viewpoint was occasioned by the mechanization of the Word as a means of grace. The change appears as orthodox theology begins to identify the Word with sound doctrine. It is significant that in regard to the function of the ministry the emphasis came to be placed on doctrine and its impartation rather than on proclamation, message, or *kerygma* in the primitive Christian sense of that word. By this intellectualization of the Word the purely religious aspect of the ministry was weakened and obscured, and the way was opened for a conception which was closely akin to institutional bureaucracy.

It is, therefore, not strange that a reaction begins in connection with Pietism. Here the pendulum swings to the opposite extreme. The question about the ministry and its status now becomes a question about the personal and religious qualifications of the minister, and results in a dissolution of the concept of the ministry. When the emphasis is placed on personal piety, the function of the ministry to proclaim the message is obscured, and a burden is placed on personal piety which it is not able to bear. This subjective tendency which occurs in Pietism received a curious development in romanticism and its cult of personality. In this connection it is interesting to see what Schleiermacher has to say about the ministry in *Der christliche Glaube*. The chapter is entitled "The Ministry of the Word of God," but the central point is the distinction between a stronger or weaker religiosity: the stronger influences the weaker through self-presentation. This occurs through *Selbsdarstellung*. "There can be no self-communication except through self-presentation acting by way of stimulus; the imitatively received movement of the self-presented person becomes in the receptively stimulated person a force that evokes the same movement" (*Der christliche Glaube*, § 133.1). When we have once noted that Schleiermacher looks at the ministry from this point of view, it is of less interest to mark that with customary skill he later seeks to combine this idea with the title of the chapter. But one does not need to be in doubt about his approach, especially since his idea about the Holy Spirit as *Gemeingeist* constitutes the link between his talk about the ministry of the Word and the "self-presentation" of the spontaneously active persons.

The Christian conception of the ministry is reinterpreted and perverted when the priest is regarded as a sacrificing priest, when the task is restricted to the impartation of certain fixed doctrines, or to a sharing of personal religious experiences. The idea of the ministry is delivered from all these objective and subjective reinterpretations when the essential element is that commission of Christ given in and through the church, and when the function is completely defined by that message which is to be proclaimed in the service of the Word and the sacraments. Here there is no room for the pendulum to swing between an objectivism which places the messenger apart from his message, and a subjectivism which substitutes for it one's own personal religious experiences. The message, the living Word of God, contains an appeal which is directed to the messenger as much as to those who may hear him. Nor can it be accepted that the function of the ministry is a certain religious "self-presentation." If the messenger places himself in the foreground, he offends the "majesty of the clause." Everything depends on the fact that the message is proclaimed as the living Word of God which it actually is.

DIVISION C

THE CHURCH IN THE PRESENT AGE

47. The Obligations of Church Membership

1. The goal of those who have been called by God to membership in the Christian church is to become more and more living members in the Body of Christ and to serve Christ by serving the neighbor in love, being nurtured and strengthened through the means of grace.

2. The two principal forms of churchly activity are evangelism and social missions. In relation to society the churchly activity

is designed to prepare a way for the influence of Christianity within the various areas of life.

1. Living Members in the Body of the Church.

The church of Christ is not of this world, but it has its existence in this world. The church belongs to the new age, but it lives at the same time in the old. This means that the church is a contending church, an *ecclesia militans*. Its life is characterized by the unceasing struggle between the loving will of God and those destructive powers which in this age oppose God's will. Membership in the church must be seen from this point of view. To be a member in the church of Christ means to be incorporated into that new solidary interrelationship in which the Spirit is active. Under those circumstances the meaning and goal of the membership are perfectly plain. This new man who has been incorporated into the new relationship of the Spirit shall more and more become a living member in that church which is the Body of Christ. What this signifies has already been described in those chapters which dealt with the Christian fellowship with God as existing on the basis of God's act of forgiveness and as expressed in the life of faith (§§ 33-36). When we now resume the discussion of the significance and obligation of this membership, the intention is to clarify the matter further from the point of view of membership in the militant church.

The meaning and purpose of the membership are, therefore, that man shall become a living member in the Body of Christ. The necessary condition is that man receive nourishment for his spiritual life from those means of grace which are offered in and through the church. In accordance with what has already been said (§ 35) we cannot speak of faith as involving an obligation. Faith is a gift of God and the living form of that new life which is given by God. But the use of the means of grace may be regarded as an obligation which accompanies membership in the church, even though it must be added that this "obligation" is at the same time the great privilege which the church offers. The Christian life of faith is edified, purified, and strengthened through the use of the Word, the sacraments, and prayer as means of grace. There is no rivalry between the individual use of the Word and prayer and the congregational usage of these means of grace and the sacraments in the worship life of the church. On the contrary, these two mutually assist each other. Since the Christian life in principle is a life in the fellowship of the church, the significance of the worship life of the church with its climax in the Lord's Supper is of highest importance for every member in the church.

Because the membership in the church rests on the call and election of God, it involves the strongest challenge to man. He must prepare himself for the struggle against those destructive powers which intend to bring this membership to nought. The apostolic watchword is relevant in this connection: "Work out your own salvation with fear and trembling; for it is God who worketh in you both to will and to work" (Phil. 2:12 f.). The Christian life is never, under the conditions of earthly life, a secure and inviolate possession. What has been won can be lost. But the armor which man must put on for this struggle is, as the Letter to the Ephesians says, the armor of God. "Wherefore take up the whole armor of God, that ye may be able to withstand in the evil day, and having done all, to stand" (Eph. 6:13).

Membership in the church, therefore, imposes an inner obligation on man himself which directs him to use the means of grace whereby the Christian life is nurtured, disciplined, and strengthened. But there is at the same time an outward obligation, which concerns man's conduct and appears in the demand that he shall "bear fruit." This is the practice of love in relation to the neighbor. This love arises, to be sure, out of God's Agape, which is the life-giving center in the Christian life, and it is therefore spontaneous. The fruit of the Spirit is first of all love (Gal. 5:22). But we have already seen (§ 34.1) that it is not

417

a question here of a spontaneity in a psychological sense, but rather that the Spirit opens the eyes of man to see what God in each case demands, and consequently it is not improper in this connection to speak of the obligation of membership.

The whole "Christian ethics" is characterized by the dominant directive of a service in love on behalf of the neighbor in the struggle against the destructive powers. This Christian view of life is misinterpreted if in its place the ennobling and perfecting of one's own personality is regarded as the principal ethical task. This has often been the case especially under the influence of romanticism. But to place Christian sanctification under this aspect means in reality to concentrate on egocentricity. The goal that is sought in this way is just like happiness, which escapes the one who tries to capture it. It is not a question of developing one's own personality into an ideal, but to walk in the new order of love into which man has been placed, and to obey and follow the commandments which God gives in the various situations in life and which are intended to serve the neighbor.

In the measure that man now discovers and obeys God's will in the various situations in life, his calling, which is connected with those ordinances of life, given in creation and connected with the law of creation, is deepened and enriched. The calling receives a richer content and becomes free and flexible. Man becomes more personally concerned in the call, and new possibilities are opened for works which do not lie within the framework of the law.[1] What the Sermon on the Mount says about

---

[1] Cf. G. Wingren, *Luthers lära on kallelsen, Luther's Teaching about the Call,* pp. 76 f. "When God deals with man in his ordinances, he desires two things: he wants to save him for his heavenly kingdom, and he wants him to serve the neighbor. In *the law,* which appears in the call, God compels man to serve his neighbor even though unwillingly, and thereby the old man is crucified. Thus the neighbor is served and man himself through his cross is impelled toward heaven or salvation in one single, concrete act of God. In *the Gospel* the portal of heaven is opened, but now the miracle occurs that the man who in faith enters heaven immediately loses himself lovingly in the call as in an 'open prison,' and in compassion for his neighbor concerns himself for his welfare. Consequently God carries this twofold work further in a concrete act through the Word and the

the works of love is not to be interpreted as "a new law" with a multitude of fixed ordinances for every circumstance in life, but is rather an expression and an example of what the Gospel can accomplish in various situations.

2. *The Activity of the Church.*

In a previous chapter we have discussed the Christian ministry. What we said there does not imply that the ministry alone should represent the activity of the church, and that the church can be divided into an active and a passive part. The ministry has its particular task, but the demand for activity on the part of the church applies in just as large a degree to all the members of the church. It is not a demand addressed to certain qualified groups among the members. Not even in this way can the church be divided into an active and passive part. The demand for activity applies to all members on all levels. But it is perfectly natural that this demand is met more fully in the measure that the members more and more become living members in the Body of Christ.

The significance of this demand is evident from what we have said about the twofold obligation: the inner and the outer. In this connection we are concerned especially with the latter, which has its basis in the new order of love. From this point of view the activity of the church expresses itself in two chief forms: evangelism and social missions. Both of these must then be understood in their widest sense. Evangelism is directed toward the non-Christian peoples. But it must at the same time be concerned with the non-Christian and secularized multitudes within Christendom. Social missions includes the Christian service of love in all its forms. It must be carefully noted that it is not a question here of simply external works, but of an activity which has its foundation in and is characterized by love. Con-

---

Spirit, not outside of, but within the heart. The freedom of faith does not dissolve the call, but on the contrary undergirds it and gives it new life" (cf. further pp. 210-41).

sequently, whatever can be said about the activity of the church must be characterized by the fact that here we are concerned with the actualization of "conversation as a means of grace" (§ 41.2). The inmost character of the activity of the church is revealed in Luther's statement that the Christian is to be "a Christ for the neighbor." The cure of souls is then not a function which belongs solely to the ministry; even though the minister has here his special task when under the seal of the confessional he hears confession and in accordance with the command of Christ pronounces absolution.

The activity of the church which is directed toward society is designed to bring the Christian influence to bear on the various areas: in legislation, in social life, in the education of youth, and so on. The people who belong to Christendom have all been subject to such influences since the day Christianity came to them, and this has to a large degree determined their social life. What this has meant and means can best be seen when we note what happens in a land where the Christian influence is eliminated and the state maintains principles which are contrary to Christianity. The present time furnishes fearful examples of this. Membership in the church involves an obligation to guard the Christian social and political heritage. In reality it cannot be preserved except by being cultivated and by gaining new victories in the struggle against opposition.

48. Church and State

1. According to Christian faith the state has a function given to it by God. Its primary function is to maintain the order of justice. In this function the state is the bearer of God's law.

2. Church and state have each their peculiar functions which must not be confused.

3. Since it is the function of the church to guard the sanctity of

God's law, the church must function as the conscience of the state in case the state violates this law.

1. *The Function of the State.*

The Christian view of the state and its order of justice is radically different from the secular and profane point of view. Even though there have appeared tendencies within Christianity to consign the earthly functions to the realm of the secular, this has only demonstrated a lack of appreciation concerning the significance of the Christian faith in creation and of the universality of the divine law. From the Christian point of view there is in reality nothing that is "secular." Life cannot be divided into two parts, the secular and the spiritual. God's will and law meet man in all the situations of life.

If we note what the New Testament has to say about "government" and its function, it is clear that Christian faith from the very beginning has placed what we call the state in direct relation to the will of God. The state has a function given to it by God. It exists in order to serve God. It is, in other words, an expression of a divine demand, i.e., God's law has been embodied in the order of society. To be a citizen of a state means to encounter in a specific form the demand of divine law and to be subject to its authority. The obligation of citizenship is at the same time a divine obligation.

According to the Christian view, the basic and primary function of the state is to preserve justice and order. As the bearer and preserver of the order of justice, the state is an expression of that creative will which desires order in contrast to chaos. The order of justice exists primarily to prevent violence and unrighteousness. It is, therefore, that foundation on which all secure human intercourse must be built. It is that means which God uses to war against the evil, demonic forces and to establish peace and justice in society. Where the order of justice prevails, there the will of God is realized in accordance with those demands which are contained in this law. It is realized whether the demand is met willingly or under compulsion. The question of spontaneity is not germane in this connection. Spontaneity has reference to the Gospel, while the state operates within the area of the law.

If the state is to maintain the order of justice, it must possess power. The power of the state is the protection of the order of justice. At this point the state appears as that organized power which does not hesitate to use force when it is necessary. Justice and power are from this point of view very closely related. The power is a prerequisite for the state to function as a state of justice. But at the same time there is a demonic temptation included in this power, a temptation to set aside the perspective of justice and to use the power for selfish ends. The state has then failed in its function. Everything depends on whether the state upholds an order of justice which serves the law of God and its purposes. If this is not the case, that power which was meant to serve God by capturing and destroying the demonic powers enters the service of these powers.

If the question is now asked which divine law is connected with the state and its order or justice, we refer to the discussion in § 21 concerning the law of creation. We stated in that connection, among other things, that the law of God is always the same, and always in its inner essence a law of love. The question whether the law of love can be related to the state has occasioned much confusion. The reason for this has been that in the interpretation of the law of love the starting point has been the Sermon on the Mount. When we here read that we are not to oppose an injustice, we evidently encounter a statement which cannot be applied within the area of justice, since the function of the order of justice is to oppose evil. One may then be tempted to draw the conclusion that the law of God cannot be related to the state. The alternative seems to be: either a desperate effort to apply the propositions of the Sermon on the Mount to the order of justice, or a radical refusal to apply the law of God to it at all. In the latter case the result is a purely secularized conception which maintains that the state has its own laws, and that these have nothing to do with the divine law.

But this whole approach must be definitely rejected. Such a statement in the Sermon on the Mount that evil is not to be resisted does not belong to the sphere of "the secular government." Neither does it belong to the realm of law. As we have already noted (§ 47.1), it belongs to the sphere of the Gospel, and its presupposition and possibility lie in that Kingdom of God which is established and exists where the Gospel rules. If such a proposition were applied to the sphere of the state, it would mean a confusion of law and gospel, against which Luther so earnestly warned. But one must not draw the conclusion that the law of God with its demand of love is not concerned with the order of justice of the state. If the state is an expression of God's will, it must be animated by that purpose which inheres in God's law. This purpose is a positive caring for the neighbor. The intention is not that the ordinances of justice which belong to the government shall be taken directly from God's law. When the New Testament states that the law is fulfilled in "one word," the commandment of love to the neighbor, it expresses a fundamental principle which in the active life and in the order of justice may be applied in a great variety of ways. The important element is that this fundamental principle is allowed to determine the order of justice in a positive manner. If this is not the case, the positive fellowship, which is the prerequisite for human life even in the sphere of the state, cannot function. Without a positive concern for the neighbor no fellowship can be established and maintained.

2. The Functions of Church and State Must Not be Confused.

According to the previous paragraph, the state has an entirely different function than the church. The primary function of the state is to maintain order in contrast to chaos within human society. The function of the church is to establish that fellowship in which Christ is the Lord and to edify the Body of

Christ. The differentiation between the two functions already meets us in the New Testament. This has been further developed with energy and clarity by Luther, who maintains that the two governments, the spiritual and the secular, must not be confused. Both have been established by God, and each has its own function. In the secular government God is active through the law to preserve the order of justice and to put down violence and unrighteousness. In order to achieve this purpose the secular government uses "the power of the sword" as means. The means which the spiritual government uses are exclusively the Word and the sacraments. The function of the secular government is, therefore, of a "political" nature and consists primarily in maintaining the order of justice. It exercises its authority by force and compulsion, and it takes to the sword if necessary. The spiritual government is concerned only with the salvation of man. It rules only by means of the Word. It uses no secular powers. But when Luther thus maintains the mutual independence of these governments in terms of their independent functions, this does not mean that there is no relation between them. That they have something in common is clear from the fact that both have received their function from God, and that both, as Luther says, are to serve the glory of God.

During the course of time various connections have been established between church and state. These have also taken such forms that the church has become a so-called state church. This term does not belong to the constitutive factors of the church, it is simply a question of an external organization. "State church" is a relative concept. There are many degrees of relationship between church and state, and it is at times difficult to say when the relation has become sufficiently intimate to justify the term "state church." When the relation is of such a character as to be called state church, it implies that the state acknowledges the significance of the work of the church. It can exist only on the presupposition that the state leaves the church free to accomplish its work in accordance with the commission given to it by the Lord of the church. There is nothing about which the church is more sensitive than the attempt of the state to give directives for and establish limits to the preaching of God's Word. "The Word of God is not bound" (II Tim. 2:9).

A conflict between church and state must arise, both when the church exceeds its function and encroaches upon the function of the state, and when the state takes over churchly functions and seeks to appear more or less as a church. A conflict of the latter kind arises when the state enlarges its "sovereignty" to include all areas of life, and when it thus advocates a conception of life which is foreign and hostile to Christianity. History bears witness to many such conflicts from the earliest time down to our own day. During later centuries men have attempted to avoid a conflict between church and state by the theory that the state should be neutral in religious matters. History, however, gives no confirmation of the possibility of such an attitude. It confirms rather the words which Harold Hjärne wrote in his book, *State and Church:* "The government must always in one way or another assume a friendly or a hostile attitude to the church, either Christian or anti-Christian." [1]

3. The Church and the Order of Justice.

The functions of both the church and the state are given by God. The primary function of the state is to be the bearer of God's law as the preserver of an order of justice. It may fail in this respect. Ordinances may be established in the name of justice which grossly violate the elemental requirements of God's law. Power may become the master of justice instead of its servant. This self-contained and egotistical power appears then as a demonic power which is hostile to that order which the will of God intends and demands. Under such circumstances the church must function as the conscience of the state. It cannot avoid this obligation, because it is its duty to watch over the sanctity of God's law.

---

[1] H. Hjärne, *State and Church*, p. 209.

The opposition which the church maintains in this kind of conflict must be characterized by its own function. The struggle must be carried on entirely by the church's own spiritual weapons. The work of the church, as Luther said, is primarily to "admonish conscience." It must seek to awaken a consciousness of what an order of justice really requires and the responsibility imposed by the demand of the service of love to the neighbor which cannot be violated without releasing the powers of destruction. The testimony of the church must be just as clear whether it is a question of an open violation of the law of God, or whether the opposition is hidden behind a disguise of Christian phrases used as a cloak for selfish usurpation of power. Everything depends on the fact that this testimony to the sanctity of God's law does not fail even if the trials be ever so difficult and the testimony results in persecution and martyrdom.

When the church through its witnessing to the law of God thus functions as the conscience of the state, it does not exceed the responsibility given to it, nor does it claim superiority in relation to the state. The church does not regard its function as superior to that of the state. According to the Christian viewpoint it is a question of functions which God has given. Since both originate in the will of God, the obligation of the state in reference to the order of justice is just as essential as the function of the church is in its sphere. When the church finds it necessary to oppose violations of God's law, this means simply that the church performs that service which has been imposed upon it, and which consists in this—that it reminds the state of its own high function and the obligations which this entails. The church does this in the conviction that no more essential directive can be given for the order of justice than that this is developed and maintained in accordance with that principle which is indicated in the law of God.

49. Christian Unity

1. Unity, not uniformity, is the Christian watchword. In principle, Christian unity is a "unity in the Spirit." Variety is an expression of the rich content of Christianity, but this variety becomes an evil when it is connected with inner suspicion and rivalry. It is an inescapable obligation of Christendom continually to realize its inner, spiritual unity.

2. If this inner unity shall be permitted to express itself in the future in terms of more practical co-operation and closer ecclesiastical relationships than have obtained in the past, the starting point for such *rapprochement* must be both a careful assessment of common heritages and a preservation of those insights which the Spirit has given to the separate denominations. In both cases the course of action must be in the direction of a deepened apprehension of the *kerygma* of Christianity. However, such a *rapprochement* cannot be accomplished by the simple expedient of returning to a former position, or by attempting to achieve a common minimum viewpoint, or by means of compromising formulas.

3. As far as it is able, theology serves to realize Christian unity in the measure that, eschewing simply formal confessionalism, it removes false disagreements, clarifies actual differences and is finally ruled by the desire to penetrate more deeply into the essential significance of Christian faith.

1. Unity as an Obligation.

At present the question of Christian unity is being given renewed and revitalized attention. The inner impotence which is associated with the formidable divisions within Christianity has become all too apparent. The conviction is growing that the present condition is abnormal and that to make the Gospel prayer, "that they all might be one," a living reality is an inescapable obligation of Christendom.

There are many signs which seem to indicate that, with reference to unity of Christian denominations, a new period is about to dawn. In the past two periods may be distinguished: first, that of open conflict; and later, that of moderate toleration. The most recent decades of church history manifest tendencies which seem to promise that a new turning point has been reached and that more positive ideals than mere toleration are being advanced. In the face of the strong, though somewhat confused, endeavors to achieve unity which are characteristic of today, it is of special importance for Christian faith to clarify both the evil elements in present-day divisions and those ideals of unity which Christendom must increasingly endeavor to realize.

That with which Christianity has to contend, it must be borne clearly in mind, is not variety and differences. From the viewpoint of faith, variety and differences are not in themselves evil. The inexhaustible riches of Christianity are manifested in that creative power which permits the divine light to illumine both various human hearts and separated denominations. But that which is evil and abnormal is to be found in the suspicion and rivalry existing among Christian brethren, which has been associated with the differences and varieties. The realization of Christian unity must therefore involve first of all the removal of such suspicions. From this viewpoint, the inner dissensions and divisions appear as sin. Unity is a fellowship given in and through the Spirit, a "unity of the Spirit in the bond of peace" (Eph. 4:3). Sin is that power which rends and destroys this fellowship. Just as the individual Christian is at once both righteous and sinful, so also the church, while it exists in the world, is *simul iustus et peccator*. The Christian fellowship as a unity of the Spirit is rooted in the fact that the church is not of this world. The divisiveness, the inner dissensions and conflicts, are due to the fact that the church exists in the world and participates in its sin. The endeavors to realize in ever larger measure the unity which belongs to the Christian church are therefore a phase of that continuous conflict against sin which is a part of Christian life.

In a previous section (38.2) it was asserted that Christian unity appears as something given, as an inescapable reality in and with the Word and sacraments, but that this unity, however, cannot be realized in the form of uniformity in doctrine, life, or organization. From the very beginning the Christian message has been proclaimed in different types of doctrine. Christian life cannot be cast in any set patterns of uniformity. If it were possible to achieve unity in terms of uniformity, it would not enrich and strengthen, but would impoverish and narrow Christianity. In fact, those endeavors which look toward absolute uniformity do not serve the ideals of Christian unity. Christian unity cannot be realized by any attempts to coerce all Christians to accept some particular form of fellowship as being sacrosanct. Unity cannot be achieved by coercion. And in general, whenever a certain denominational form is regarded as the only one which enjoys divine sanction, whether it be the Roman type of ecclesiastical organization or that order which without sufficient reason has been called the biblical principle of congregational life, the result is simply to deny to other forms of congregational life Christian legitimacy. In view of the actual circumstances it must be conceded that Christianity can be found even outside the boundaries of one's own form and order. But such a more or less reluctant tolerance is nothing but a caricature of Christian unity. The ideal of Christian unity is something entirely different from mere toleration. Tolerance is simply a negative concept. It implies that we endure one another. In view of existing circumstances, even such a modest ideal may seem desirable. But it is not a positive expression of Christian unity. Christian unity does not consist simply in the fact that Christians endure one another, but in a positive and dynamic fellowship, in "the unity of the Spirit." It is also significant that the idea of tolerance tends to find currency in periods of religious lassitude, as for example, the age of the Enlightenment. In contrast thereto, the idea of unity is expressive of religious strength and is rooted in the assurance of a unity which is so substantial that no differences can dissolve it.

It is not the task of Christianity to create, but to realize, this unity. It does not need to be created, for it already exists and is based upon the fact that Christ is Lord in the spiritual life of the Christian. Wherever the Spirit of Christ actually reigns, there, both within the various denominations and in their relationships to one another, mutual suspicion is dissipated, and a free and indestructible unity is realized. All unity which does not rest upon and is not empowered by this foundation is merely fictitious. If this inner unity of the Spirit is missing there can be no other substitute. That unity which is based only upon external forms is fundamentally illusory and does not eventuate in real fellowship. Only in the measure that the dominion of divine love is realized in Christ can there be "one shepherd and one flock." But this unity is so strong that it perdures in the midst of differences and variations.

When the question of unity involves the problem of the different denominations and their relationship to one another, it must be asserted that the Christian church and its unity are primary in relation to the different denominations. The denominations are the heterogeneous forms of the one ecumenical church, which has its origin in Christ and his apostles and which builds on the Word and sacraments, the church of Easter and Pentecost. It is at this point that the problem is clarified with reference to the possibility of mutual recognition on the part of the different denominations. When the various denominations build on the Word and sacraments, such mutual recognition must unconditionally be given. When this condition obtains, no criticism which one denomination may wish to direct at another will be permitted to stand as a hindrance to Christian brotherhood. Luther spoke with clear Christian insight when he, in spite of his bitter attacks upon Rome, frankly acknowledged the Roman church as "holy." Fellowship among the different denominations involves this twofold rule: no insight into Christian truth can be obscured or surrendered, but, at the same time, all religious self-righteousness and arrogance must be renounced. In our evangelical fellowship we are deeply grateful for our spiritual heritage, for that sharp discernment with which Luther clarified the message of the New Testament. But this gratitude does not imply that we should therefore become guilty of self-righteous judgment, in the manner of the Jews who declared, "We are Abraham's children." We have very little reason to boast about the "sound doctrine" of the Reformation, inasmuch as we must acknowledge that the insight into the message of the New Testament which was given by the Reformation has by no means thoroughly characterized the life of the evangelical church. With reference to these matters we have very little to boast about, either in the past or the present. The evangelical church possesses no unified, stable, and trustworthy doctrinal front. This is evident in the fact that not even the unity within a single denomination rests upon the foundation of fixed doctrine. Here, as elsewhere, the foundation for unity is nothing but the Word and the sacraments. It is upon the Word and the sacraments, in spite of reinterpretations and misinterpretations, that the perduration of the church depends and that its unity, despite all, is not destroyed.

2. *The External Manifestations of Christian Unity.*

In regard to the mutual relations among the denominations, Christian unity can manifest itself externally in two principal forms: in part as practical co-operation in matters affecting the moral well-being of society, and in part by some form of church organization. In the first case the principal idea is that such practical co-operation may be established in spite of the differences which exist between the various denominations in regard to confession and organization. This possibility can be denied only by those denominations which deify their own organization to such an extent that, denying the ecumenicity of the church, they place the interests of their own denomination above the interests of Christendom. The presupposition of such co-operation is the "unity of the Spirit" which establishes the bounds of Christian fellowship, or, in other words, the fellowship of *faith* in the central, religious sense of this word.[1] The other type of endeavor toward Christian unity is designed to further this unity by a growing fellowship in regard to confession and organization.[2]

Both of these ecumenical endeavors undoubtedly possess rich possibilities in promoting the interest of Christian unity and in strengthening the consciousness in the various denominations of membership in the one ecumenical church. At the same time both contain certain dangers which must be clearly kept in mind.

The endeavor to bring about action by the church in the realm of social and ethical matters has its basis largely in the distressing and fearful situation in the world. The danger lies in the tendency of seeking to produce a full and definite Christian ethical program for the solution of the complicated, contemporary social and international problems. It is clear that, if this is the intention, we attempt something which lies beyond the possibilities of Christianity and at the same time confuses the functions of church and state (cf. § 48). The legitimacy of action by the church lies on a different plane, that of the law. The purpose must be that the Christian church, in accordance with its duty, guards the sanctity of God's law and its all-inclusive demand for the care of the neighbor, and thus serves as the conscience of the state.

Difficulties and dangers are also connected with those endeavors which are designed to strengthen the fellowship in regard to confession and organization. At this point Christian faith must maintain two fundamental principles. On the one

---

[1] Unity movements of this type have found their most conspicuous expression in two ecumenical conferences on "Life and Work" in Stockholm (1925) and Oxford (1937).

[2] Ecumenical conferences for this purpose, on "Faith and Order," were held in Lausanne (1927) and Edinburgh (1937).

hand, faith must be actively interested in everything that expresses Christian unity, and consequently cannot regard the present division as something permanent and desirable. On the other hand, faith can never countenance the demand for uniformity and the suppression of those differences which express the inner wealth of Christianity. It cannot surrender any spiritual gain in the interest of an external unity. When the endeavors to establish organizational unity are viewed from this angle, three possibilities appear for the manifestation of Christian unity: first, that the various denominations enter into more or less intimate relation one with the other, through which their unity appears; second, that various independent denominations enter into a federal union; and third, that various denominations unite in a complete and formal union. All three types of *rapprochement* have taken place within evangelical Christianity in recent times. In this regard it seems evident that the great separation within this branch of Christendom has reached its climax, that "evangelical catholicity" is growing, and that evangelical Christendom has begun to give expression to its inherent idea of fellowship. If these endeavors toward a closer fellowship among the churches shall be regarded as legitimate, it must be under the twofold supposition that we note carefully that which we actually have in common, and that we note just as carefully those insights which the Spirit has taught the different denominations. Neither of these can be ignored. Any intimate fellowship between the churches presupposes that the common possession is clearly recognized, not only with reference to the primary unity of the Spirit but also in regard to confession, cult, and organization; furthermore, and not least, that the differences are not neglected or obscured, but rather that the peculiar ethos of each denomination is clearly and frankly acknowledged. If the ecumenical fellowship is to be based on a firm foundation, it must be demonstrated that those differences which in the past caused schism no longer exist, that the elements in common have grown to such an extent that the differences need not cause separation, and that what has been gained by separation now can be appropriated by all.

If these fundamental principles are correct, it follows that those endeavors toward church unity are doomed to failure which ignore what the Spirit has taught the separate denominations and which endeavor to establish Christian unity by going back to a past period in the history of the church, whether this be to primitive Christianity or to the undivided church of the first centuries. Christianity is never a retrogression, a reproduction, but a living and active spiritual power. The idea of the primitive church as a foundation of unity is in a certain sense legitimate, since the testimony of the New Testament is fundamental for all forms of Christianity and consequently in eminent degree a unifying power. There is *only one* Christian message, and *every advance toward Christian unity must rest on a deeper insight into this message, this* kerygma *of Christianity*. But this is something entirely different from attempting a reproduction of primitive Christianity. Even the Pietistic forms which attempted to imitate primitive Christianity and its congregational life have not achieved a complete reproduction. On the one hand, primitive Christianity lacked the unity which is here assumed. On the other hand, such an imitation could not be defended as desirable unless it is assumed that the activity of the Spirit of God ceased at the end of that period. Neither can church unity be achieved simply by a return to the undivided church of the first centuries in accordance with those ideas which were expressed already by the "syncretism" of the seventeenth century. It is, of course, very important that Christianity appropriates this common and important heritage from the undivided church, but none of its doctrinal formulations can be regarded as having said the last word. To do so would be to disregard and despise that spiritual heritage which has accrued to Christianity since that time. It is certainly true that the Christological formulas of the ancient church represent a common interest and gain (cf. § 25), but this does not mean that the deepened interpretation of Christianity by the Reformation should be regarded as something relatively inferior (cf. § 8.3). In general it may be said that the unity which can be purchased by squandering one's own precious heritage is a betrayal not only of one's own but also of the ideal of unity of Christendom.

Nor can the cause of Christian fellowship be advanced on the basis of a reduction through formulas which weaken the central Christian content or through formulas of compromise (cf. § 3).

3. Theology and Church Unity.

Theology is one of the powers within Christianity which promote unity. The deepest factor, on which everything ultimately depends, is of a *purely religious* nature and consists in the fact that the Spirit of Christ by its very nature creates unity. The Christian ecumenical ideas which are emerging in the present are primarily due to this religious motive. The renewed interest is connected with a number of contributing factors, among which we may especially note the critical political situation, the work of Christian *missions,* and theological research. At first sight one might be inclined to doubt that theology promotes church unity. It is evident that theology has caused many bitter struggles both within and between the various denominations, and that theology is constantly causing strife and division within Christianity. The work of theology has in the past been connected with a confessional polemic which has not proved very edifying. But this does not nullify the fact that theology by its very nature is conducive toward unity, and that this character of theology appears more clearly in the measure that it really accomplishes its function. This is true both of systematic and historical theology, and is based on the fact that theology has no other function than to understand Christianity and to apprehend the significance and meaning of Christian faith.

If theology is characterized by an exclusive confessionalism which proceeds on the assumption that its own content represents that which is genuinely Christian and consequently seeks by all means to defend it, theology would be unable to perform any service for Christian unity. It would then be characterized by an exclusiveness which not only leads to an inflated self-sufficiency, but in reality it would also mean that the spiritual treasures which it possesses are kept within its own sphere and are not made available for Christendom as a whole. But theology, as we have seen (§ 1.1), has an entirely different function, viz., to clarify the meaning and significance of Christian faith. In that case it can be confessional only in so far as the confessional element can be shown to represent something genuinely Christian. When theology is completely guided by this purpose, it becomes by inner necessity a promoter of unity. This appears both in the fact that theology removes fictitious antitheses and clarifies real differences. Both of these are ultimately conducive to unity. The history of Christianity abounds in examples of sharp and bitter conflicts which have arisen because the antagonists were not able to understand one another's language; but it also manifests the fact that the causes of the struggle have been removed when the theologians have passed beyond mere formulas to the deeper religious ideas which in a more or less defective way have been expressed in them. Christian history also furnishes abundant examples of very bitter conflicts which have arisen because some particular aspect of the life of faith, which has been ignored or suppressed, has been proclaimed with a one-sided emphasis by neglecting other equally legitimate aspects. In these cases theology can serve the purposes of unity by a more comprehensive and complete viewpoint of the life of faith. But even though some antitheses can be removed in this way, it is not true of all disagreements. The positive and deep antitheses which are found within Christianity will appear much more clearly as theology penetrates deeper into the significance of Christian faith. But in the final analysis this, too, will serve the purpose of unity. Schleiermacher once said that no real unity will be achieved until all the various oppositions are allowed to come to maturity. But if that is to occur it is necessary that they be brought clearly into focus. When that happens, this much at least has been accomplished, that the opposite camps understand one another.

If in this way theology serves the cause of unity, it is not implied that it should be "irenical," and much less that it should endeavor to create smooth formulas whereby the differences are hidden. Such a procedure is not useful, it only apparently serves the purposes of Christian unity. Such adeptness at creating formulas may be left to the politicians. Theology does not endeavor to be irenic; it is interested only in understanding and clarifying the significance and meaning of Christian faith. But it *becomes* a promoter of unity in the measure that it accomplishes this purely scientific task.

DIVISION D

THE CHURCH FROM THE VIEWPOINT OF ESCHATOLOGY

50. The Living and the Dead

1. The church is an eschatological magnitude. Its goal lies beyond the boundaries of earthly life. Fellowship with God includes an indestructible relationship with those who have been subdued by divine love. Christian faith knows of no relation to the dead except in and through God. This viewpoint is decisive for all affirmations of faith relative to the relationship between the living and the dead.

2. Therefore all those conceptions which are characteristic of the Roman church and which are based upon the idea of merits are invalidated. Likewise, the spiritualistic attempts to effect an external connection with the dead are foreign to Christian faith.

3. The attitude of Reformation Christianity involves a wholesome concentration upon the decisive importance of the present period of grace through its emphasis upon the seriousness of death. This has resulted in a cleansing of the life of faith by

the removal of foreign speculations. But there has sometimes been a tendency to associate this attitude with a weakening of the idea of life after death, which has obscured that communion of saints which transcends the boundaries of life on earth. As far as faith is concerned, however, the character of this communion is given in and with the sovereignty of divine love.

1. Death and the Christian Communion of Saints.

The church lives in this world, but is not *of* this world. It is the child of the new age. Therefore the life of the church in its totality has an eschatological character. Everything which has previously been said about the church must be understood from the viewpoint of eschatology. Two principal ideas of faith are finally decisive; the one has reference to the relation between Christians now living and those who have died, and the other concerns the perfecting of the church (§ 51).

The Christian relationship between God and man does not isolate the individual Christian, but establishes him in that living spiritual community in which the divine and loving will realizes itself in conflict with inimical forces. Because faith is a living fellowship with God, it likewise expresses itself in fellowship with the brethren. This fellowship cannot be confined within the limits of life on earth. Just as faith, because it is fellowship with the *living* God, cannot be circumscribed by life on earth (§ 36.2), so the fellowship of Christians which is based upon and is characterized by the relationship between God and man, cannot be restricted to time. Those who are united with God are united with one another, and this union is indestructible because it is rooted and perdures in the Eternal God.

A variety of ideas about the Christian fellowship which transcends the limits of life on earth has emerged within Christendom during the ages. All of these have not been organically connected with Christian faith. In treating the subject of the relation between the quick and the dead, the task of theology is to establish the premises by which faith can enter this area of inquiry and thereby to guard against those postulates which are so foreign to faith that they either imply an actual dislocation of faith's perspective or simply have nothing whatsoever to do with faith. The basic and regulative principle governing this problem must be this: that the relation between the living and the dead, of which faith ventures to speak, must be established in and through God. If "immortality" is not simply a rational idea for faith, that is to say, does not have its basis in idealistic theories about the indestructible nature of man (cf. §§ 18, 34, and 36), and if, instead, "eternal life" is based entirely upon the relationship between God and man, in the creative and life-giving work of divine love, then faith can make no assertions about the relation between the quick and the dead which are not entirely determined by the Christian concept of the relationship between God and man.

2. The Limitations of Faith.

From the basic principle which maintains that the relation between the quick and the dead must be rooted in and through the relationship between God and man, it follows that faith must be critical of those ideas within the Roman church which are based upon the strange and foreign concept of merit. The Roman church speaks of a very far-reaching connection between the living and the dead. On the one hand, the dead who exist in an "intermediate state" are said to be subject to the influence of the church of the living; and on the other hand, the dead intervene very extensively in the affairs of the living church. The chief character of this mutual influence in both cases is its dependence upon the strange doctrine of merits (§ 35.2). In the first place, the living church acquires merit by the saying of masses, etc., which are of benefit to the dead; in the second place, the merits earned by the departed saints are of great benefit to the living (cf. § 41.2). In the measure that such ideas of merit are projected, the relation between the quick and the dead is established by the side of and apart from the relationship between God and man. And when this occurs the way is open for a lively and unrestrained vegetation in this sphere, because there is no longer any regulating and guarding principle to curb and restrain the imagination.

Since Christian faith must oppose all such Roman conceptions which are based upon the impure idea of merits and are therefore foreign to the Christian relationship between God and man, it must also unequivocally oppose all spiritualistic attempts to establish a direct connection between the living and the dead. Faith has, of course, no reason for expressing itself on the possibility or impossibility of actualizing such connections. Faith does not generally express itself with reference to the scientific investigations of those phenomena with which spiritualism is concerned. To undertake an examination of this field is not the responsibility of theology, but of psychology. Theology must only maintain that these spiritualistic endeavors do not belong to faith. Christian faith finds no religious interest in the attempt of spiritualism to materialize the departed spirits, and the like. The approach of faith to the living and the dead is fundamentally different from that of spiritualism because faith can conceive of no relation except that which is included in the fellowship between God and man. Any connection between the quick and the dead which is not conditioned by the divine fellowship, but seeks to establish itself apart from this fellowship with God, lies entirely outside the sphere of Christian faith. Therefore, when spiritualism attempts to become the representative spokesman for religion, Christian faith is compelled to repudiate it, for spiritualism leads away from that which is absolutely decisive for faith, namely, the relationship between God and man.

3. *The Premise of Faith.*

The religious awakening of the Reformation was characterized by a struggle against the intermingling of human merits with the relationship of God and man. It was natural, therefore, that evangelical Christianity opposed the development of the idea of a relationship between the quick and the dead based upon merit, which had occurred in the Roman church, and also turned against the dominant position which these ideas enjoyed in popular piety. Evangelical Christianity instituted a war of extermination upon all ideas which were not legitimately Christian, and thereby achieved a purification of the church which was desperately needed. A chaste temperance followed the former multifarious preoccupation with these matters. Men began at least to perceive that, relative to this aspect of eschatology, it was a matter which eye has not seen and ear has not heard. But most important was the fact that in contrast to the prevailing laxity in thought and conduct, the decisive gravity and obligation of the present period of grace and the unconditional seriousness of death were energetically inculcated.

It may be questioned, however, whether this process of purification, while it accomplished much that was good and inalienable, was not at the same time foreshortening the perspective of faith and restricting the hope and presentiment of Christian faith. It is not without reason that E. Rodhe has written, "It cannot be denied that this process of purification has cost something. It is indubitable that for many the eternal world has become distant and unreal. The memory of the departed has paled, reverence for death and the dead has declined. It is not easy to suggest how these lost values shall be recovered and new ones obtained, for under all circumstances care must be taken that the austere soundness and honest temperance which is our heritage from the Reformation is not lost."[1] The question is, therefore, if the soundness and temperance of evangelical Christianity can be united with the more meaningful, less negative approach to the relationship between the quick and the dead; that is to say, can we find room for those hopes and presentiments which are actually in harmony with the Christian relationship between God and man? In fact, the restriction of the perspective of Christian fellowship seems to imply a curtail-

---

[1] E. Rodhe, *Lifvet efter döden*, p. 35.

ment of those possibilities which are available to the sovereign love of God. In the measure that this sovereignty emerges in all the majesty which it has for Christian faith, the Christian fellowship also emerges inescapably and dynamically as transcending all circumstances of life on earth. Those who have been claimed by divine love are not severed from fellowship with the church militant. Indeed, faith cannot, without being presumptuous, maintain that physical death marks the boundary line of the possibilities of divine love (cf. § 19 excursus). To be sure, faith cannot employ this conception as a quietus for the purpose of abridging the decisive importance of the present period of grace, but it is entirely free to use it as a motive for that love which "hopeth all things."

If these viewpoints are in harmony with the Christian relationship between God and man, then a twofold perspective is given to the presentiment of faith, viz., a twofold prayer of intercession. When the eye of faith is raised to those who have been lifted beyond this life with its sin, tribulation, and need, it perceives them as a praying host and surmises that even intercession has its place in their prayers, along with thanksgiving, praise, and worship. Furthermore, when faith recalls the departed ones and thinks of the inexhaustible resources of divine love, such thoughts easily pass over into intercessory prayer.[2] Love is not halted by death. No speculations about the scope of such prayers are able to diminish their outreach. They have their Christian legitimacy because the communion here in question is entirely dependent upon the relationship between God and man, and all impure and foreign ideas about merits are therefore excluded. In other words, such prayer is genuinely

---

[2] It is noteworthy that the present Swedish Prayer Book has again made a place for such prayers (cf. prayer for Easter Day and prayer for the occasion "when someone has departed in death"). The Prayer Book has in fact made connection at this point with the tradition of evangelical Christianity of earliest times. Prayers of this nature are found in the writings of both Luther and Olaus Petri. See further, Rodhe, *op cit.*, pp. 35 f.

Christian simply because its matrix is love, and everything motivated by love is legitimately Christian because God is love.[3]

51. Regnum Gloriae

1. Christian faith looks forward in hope to that consummation in which the will of God is no longer obliged to realize its purposes through conflict with inimical forces as has been the case in the circumstances of life on earth. "The Kingdom of Glory" appears, on the one hand, as the result of the continuing and creative activity of the Holy Spirit in the present. On the other hand, it appears at the same time as a radical and revitalizing transformation of the existential conditions and circumstances of the church. The hope of a final consummation which is characteristic of Christian faith opposes, therefore, both that pessimism which curtails the task of the militant church and the optimism which in one way or another apotheosizes the earthly.

2. When the consummation appears to Christian hope as a spiritual kingdom in which the divine and loving will is at once realized and continues to actualize itself in ever greater degree, blessedness receives an inexhaustible and ineffable content which is completely in contrast to all egocentric ideals of bliss.

1. The Church and Regnum Gloriae.

The Christian hope is altogether a corporate hope. Since it is essential for Christianity that it exist as a fellowship and that the Christianity of the individual be given its character through participation in this fellowship, therefore the corporate character

---

[3] Cf. Rodhe, *op cit.*, pp. 36 ff. "Nothing can be more natural to the Christian than to connect his thoughts of the dead with his religious thought-world. Memories of the departed linger on even when one comes into the presence of God. It is assumed that this is legitimate as long as it is a question simply of religious meditation. But when this meditation is transformed into prayer, then the memories of the departed should be banished, for prayer for the dead must not be made. The result would be that just when the Christian begins to live most profoundly and seriously, he must banish from his mind the thought of the ones with whom he has been united in love."

of this hope is not a matter of secondary importance. On the contrary, hope is really Christian only in the measure that faith looks forward to the perfected spiritual communion, the Kingdom of Glory, which is a complete expression of the divine and loving will. This corporate hope of Christianity, like Christian hope in general (cf. § 36.2), emerges therefore out of the contrast between the richness of the present and its incompleteness. The background of hope, on the one hand, is the actual self-realization of the divine and loving will within the spiritual fellowship which continues to actualize itself in the present. On the other hand, this spiritual fellowship is actualized in the present only in bitter struggle against inimical forces, and therefore the actualization is only partial. The clearer the divine fellowship is seen as a living reality, the more inescapably do the difficult existential conditions and the defects and imperfections of the church's circumstances appear. But it is against precisely this background that the hope which is firmly rooted in the encounter of faith with sovereign divine love is delineated. Since divine love is a sovereign love, the spiritual fellowship of faith cannot be circumscribed by the narrow and cramped boundaries of earthly life. The horizons of this life are lifted, and the eye of faith perceives in expectant hope the spiritual fellowship wherein the loving will of God reigns unchallenged and in which all that is partial has passed away.

The emergence of *regnum gloriae* is apprehended by faith from two viewpoints (cf. § 18.2). From one point of view the Kingdom of Glory is based upon the militant church. The struggling church is transformed into the finished dominion of God. This is the result of the creative activity of the Holy Spirit in the circumstances of life on earth. But on the other hand, the relationship between these two magnitudes is not one in which the church is gradually developed and purified until it is finally transformed into the heavenly glory; nor does the opposition to the creative activity of the Holy Spirit steadily diminish until at last it ceases entirely and thus the church reaches the level of perfection. On the contrary, the opposition of inimical forces is indissolubly connected with the circumstances of earthly life. Therefore faith is compelled to look forward to the accomplishment of God's perfect dominion as being effected by an act of God's eternal power which involves a radical transformation and re-creation of things as they are. The consummation implies not only a continuation, a development of that which now is, but also a thorough, total transformation of the existential conditions and circumstances of the church. This transformation is connected with Christ's second coming, the judgment and final realization of the Kingdom of God. The twofold viewpoint with which faith apprehends the relation between the militant church and *regnum gloriae* confronts faith with a twofold antithesis. On the one hand, faith opposes that pessimism which regards the idea of transformation in such a way that the context disappears. On the other hand, it opposes that optimism which asserts the idea of continuity and development at the expense of the concept of transformation. The false pessimism curtails the task of the militant church and obscures the significance of history as being the laboratory of a universally purposeful divine will. The false optimism labors under the illusion that the divine will can be completely realized in the circumstances of life on earth, with the result that it ends by apotheosizing the earthly. Pessimism underestimates the power of God which lives and works in the militant church; optimism underestimates the opposition which in the circumstances of life on earth constantly renews its hostility to the struggling will of God, and ends therefore in Utopian dreams. Christian faith is much too aware of the actual situation to fall into such a naive and unrealistic optimism. But it is also much too conscious of the actual resources of power available to the church to embrace a pessimistic asceticism. Faith perceives that the divine and loving will realizes its dominion by bitter conflict with inimical forces; therefore it knows of no unrealistic optimism. But at the same

time it perceives that it is *God* who wages the warfare; therefore it knows of no pessimism.

2. *The Content of Christian Hope.*

The great consummation appears to Christian hope as a
spiritual kingdom in which the divine and loving will is at once
realized and continues to actualize itself in ever greater degree.
The content of that blessedness to which Christian faith looks
forward is determined by the unbroken fellowship with God
and by the fact that this fellowship is realized in the form of a
spiritual kingdom. Fundamentally, however, this does not imply
two complementary viewpoints; there is no fellowship with God
which does not thereby involve participation in the kingdom
where he reigns. Just as the character of Christian faith is theocentric, so also Christian hope is theocentrically determined. All
egocentric ideas of personal bliss are excluded from that spiritual
kingdom where the divine and loving will reigns. The fellowship of love determined by God is diametrically opposed to all
egocentricity.

Two viewpoints are indissolubly connected with faith's conception of *regnum gloriae,* viz., that on the one hand the domain
of the divine and loving will is here unopposed and perfect, and
on the other that this will continues to actualize itself in ever
greater measure. The latter viewpoint has often been excluded
from faith's consideration of eternal life. But when this has occurred and faith has been inclined to interpret eternal life in
terms of mere rest and blessed peace, then in the final analysis
eternal life has ceased to be eternal *life.* The state of blessedness
has taken on the character of an inert immutability which is
completely foreign to dynamic life. But such an interpretation
of blessedness has actually no vital connection with faith's conception of God. It is by an inner necessity, therefore, that the
two viewpoints of Christian faith are thrust into the foreground,
viz., that, in the first place, eternal life is a final goal, the character of which is rest with God, eternal peace; but, in the second

place, that the divine and loving will is continually active and that eternal life is therefore characterized by a divinely motivated activity. The inexhaustible content of blessedness is given in and with the indissoluble union of these two viewpoints. But at the same time, the content of life eternal is so ineffable that faith is unable to speak of it in any other terms than groping figures. Meanwhile, every attempt to define the content of eternal life in rigid concepts eventuates either in passive stagnation or in unfulfilled becoming. This circumstance does not imply, however, any abridgment of the assurance or richness of Christian hope. For Christian hope receives both its assurance and its richness in the encounter of faith with the sovereign, creative love of God.

INDEX

Absolution, 420
Act of God in Christ, 80, 87-89, 93
  117, 162, 207, 329
Activism, 320
Agape, 79, 117, 128-31, 135, 156,
  294-97, 301, 306-8, 311f., 321, 417
Allah, 196
Althaus, Paul, 404
Anglican theology, 220
Anglo-Catholic, 86
Annihilation, 179f.
Anselm, 227, 238
Anthropocentric, 123f.
Anthropological, 50
Anthropomorphism, 97f., 171, 297,
  300
Apokatastasis, 178f.
Apologetics, 20, 108, 111
Apologists, 216
Apostasy, 66-68, 71, 94
Apostles, 58f., 67, 336, 346, 410-12
Apostolic Creed, 246, 254
Aquinas, Thomas, 39, 104
Arianism, 63, 156, 216
Articuli mixti, 13f., 96, 147
Articuli puri, 13, 96
Assensus, 74f.
Assent, 26f., 315
Atonement, 64, 89, 104, 127, 141,
  156, 220f., 223, 227, 230f., 237-40,
  244, 297, 390, 411, 413
Augsburg Confession, 87
Augustine, 24, 131, 211, 274, 294,
  349

Baptism, 338, 345, 350, 352, 355,
  359, 371-85; emergency, 384; in-
  fant, 352, 379-85
Barth, Karl, 361
Bernard of Clairvaux, 52
Bible, 58, 81-84, 355, 364f., 369; can-

on of, 367; *see also* New Testament,
  Old Testament
Biblicism, 81-83
Biedermann, A. F., 159
Billing, Einar, 307, 310, 361, 408
Blessedness, 274, 291, 301-14, 324,
  347, 397f., 446f.
Brotherhood, 55, 344
Brunner, Emil, 361

Call, 350-53, 417f.
Calvin, John, 396
Chalcedon, 211, 217f.
Christ, *passim; see also* Jesus; ascension of, 246f.; crucifixion of, 219,
  246f.; *see also* Cross; divinity of, 62,
  214; exaltation of, 241, 245, 331,
  336; faith in, 59-66; incarnation of,
  34, 49f., 54, 60, 64, 131, 209-23,
  224, 227, 239, 359, 366; kingdom
  of, *see Regnum Christi;* passion of,
  52, 246; person of, 222; resurrection
  of, 180, 241, 246-49, 333; second
  coming of, 445; session of, 246f.;
  vicarious work of, 235f.; victory of,
  34, 44, 208f., 223-28, 237, 245,
  318; work of, 207-9
Christian life, 21, 347-53
Christian unity, 86, 399, 427-37; *see*
  also Church, unity of
Christianity, 65-73, *et passim*
Christocentricity, 59-65, 72, 364
Christology, 50, 54f., 60-64, 89, 131,
  156, 210-19, 434
Christus Crucifixus, 223-41
Christus in nobis, 244
Christus pro nobis, 244
Christus Victor, 223-41
Church, 8, 17, 31, 72, 86, 117f., 122,
  162, 243-47, 250, 329-56, 367, 372f.,
  377, 379, 399, 401, 408-20; ecu-

451

Type used in this book
Body, 11 on 14 and 9 on 11 Caledonia
Display, Caledonia bold